# PC LEARNING LABS TEACHES MICROSOFT EXCEL FOR WINDOWS 95

# PC LEARNING LABS TEACHES MICROSOFT EXCEL FOR WINDOWS 95

**By Laurie A. Perry for**

**Ziff-Davis Press**
Emeryville, California

| | |
|---|---|
| Copy Editor | Stephanie Raney |
| Technical Reviewer | Lorrie Hendron |
| Project Coordinators | Barbara Dahl and Madhu Prasher |
| Proofreader | Jeff Barash |
| Cover Illustration | Regan Honda |
| Cover Design | Regan Honda |
| Book Design | Laura Lamar/MAX, San Francisco |
| Technical Illustration | Steph Bradshaw |
| Word Processing | Howard Blechman |
| Page Layout | Tony Jonick |
| Indexer | Ted Laux |

Ziff-Davis Press, ZD Press, and the Ziff-Davis Press logo are licensed to Macmillan Computer Publishing USA by Ziff-Davis Publishing Company, New York, New York.

Ziff-Davis Press imprint books are produced on a Macintosh computer system with the following applications: FrameMaker®, Microsoft® Word, QuarkXPress®, Adobe Illustrator®, Adobe Photoshop®, Adobe Streamline™, MacLink®*Plus*, Aldus® FreeHand™, Collage Plus™.

If you have comments or questions or would like to receive a free catalog, call or write:
Macmillan Computer Publishing USA
Ziff-Davis Press Line of Books
5903 Christie Avenue
Emeryville, CA 94608
1-800-688-0448

ISBN 1-56276-318-0

Manufactured in the United States of America
10 9 8 7 6 5 4 3 2 1

# CONTENTS AT A GLANCE

# TABLE OF CONTENTS

# INTRODUCTION

Welcome to *PC Learning Labs Teaches Microsoft Excel for Windows 95*, a hands-on instruction book that will help you attain a high level of Excel fluency in the shortest time possible. And congratulations on choosing Excel for Windows 95, a powerful, elegant program that will greatly simplify your tasks of accounting, charting, and database management.

We at PC Learning Labs believe this book to be a unique and welcome addition to the ranks of "how to" computer publications. Our instructional approach stems directly from over a decade of successful teaching in a hands-on classroom environment. Throughout the book, we mix theory with practice by presenting new techniques and then applying them in hands-on activities. These activities use specially prepared sample Excel files, which are stored on the enclosed Data Disk.

Unlike a class, this book allows you to proceed at your own pace. And we'll be right there to guide you along every step of the way, providing landmarks to help you chart your progress and hold to a steady course.

When you're done working your way through this book, you'll have a solid foundation of skills in

- *Electronic accounting:* The organization and calculation of numeric data in spreadsheet form.

- *Database management:* The systematic arrangement of data that allows for easy searching, extracting, and rearranging.

- *Charting:* The visual display of numeric data in graph form.

We strongly recommend that you read through the rest of this Introduction before beginning Chapter 1.

## WHO THIS BOOK IS FOR

This book was written with the beginner in mind. Although experience with spreadsheets and personal computers is certainly helpful, little or none is required. You should know how to turn on your computer and use your keyboard. We explain everything beyond that.

## HOW TO USE THIS BOOK

You can use this book as a learning guide, a review tool, and a quick reference.

 ## AS A LEARNING GUIDE

Each chapter covers one broad topic or set of related topics. Chapters are arranged in order of increasing proficiency; skills you acquire in one chapter are used and elaborated on in later chapters. For this reason, you should work through the chapters in sequence.

Each chapter is organized into explanatory topics and step-by-step activities. Topics provide the theory you need to master Excel; activities allow you to apply this theory to practical, hands-on examples.

You get to try out each new skill on a specially prepared sample Excel file stored on the enclosed Data Disk. This saves you typing time and allows you to concentrate on the technique at hand. Through the use of sample files, hands-on activities, illustrations that give you feedback at crucial steps, and supporting background information, this book provides you with the foundation and structure to learn Excel for Windows 95 quickly and easily.

## AS A REVIEW TOOL

Any method of instruction is only as effective as the time and effort you are willing to invest in it. For this reason, we strongly encourage you to spend some time reviewing the book's more challenging topics and activities.

## AS A QUICK REFERENCE

General procedures such as opening a workbook file or changing a chart's color scheme are presented as a series of bulleted steps; you can find these bullets (•) easily by skimming through the book. These procedures can serve as a handy reference.

At the end of every chapter, you'll find a quick reference that lists the mouse/keyboard actions needed to perform the techniques introduced in that chapter.

## THE DATA DISK

One of the most important learning features of this book is the *Data Disk*, the 3½-inch floppy disk that accompanies the book. This disk contains the sample Excel files you'll retrieve and work on throughout the book.

To perform the activities in this book, you will first need to create a work directory on your hard disk (as explained in the Chapter 1 section "Creating Your Work Folder"). You'll then copy the sample files from the Data Disk to your work directory. This directory will also hold all the Excel files that you will be creating, editing, and saving during the course of this book.

## WHAT YOU NEED TO USE THIS BOOK

To run Excel for Windows 95 and complete this book, you need a computer with a hard disk and at least one floppy-disk drive, a monitor, a keyboard, and a mouse (or compatible tracking device). Although you don't absolutely need a printer, we strongly recommend that you have one. Windows 95 must be installed on your computer; if it is not, see your Windows reference manual for instructions. Excel for Windows 95 must also be installed; for help, see Appendix A.

 COMPUTER AND MONITOR

You need an IBM or IBM-compatible personal computer and monitor that are capable of running Microsoft Windows 95. A 386-based system is technically sufficient, but both Windows and Excel will run slowly on it; we recommend that you use a 486 or higher computer with 6 megabytes (MB) of random-access memory (RAM).

You need a hard disk with a minimum of 18 MB (18 million bytes) of free storage space if Excel for Windows 95 is not yet installed, or 5 MB of free space if Excel for Windows 95 is installed.

Finally, you need a VGA or higher (SVGA and so on) graphics card and monitor to display Windows and Excel at their intended screen resolution. (**Note:** The Excel screens shown in this book are taken from a VGA monitor; depending on your monitor type, your screens may look slightly different.)

 KEYBOARD

IBM-compatible computers come with various styles of keyboards; these keyboards function identically but have different layouts. Figures I.1, I.2, and I.3 show the three main keyboard styles and their key arrangements.

Excel uses all main areas of the keyboard:

- The *function keys*, which enable you to access Excel's special features. On the PC-, XT-, and AT-style keyboards, there are 10 function keys at the left end of the keyboard; on the 101-key Enhanced Keyboard there are 12 at the top of the keyboard.

**Figure I.1**   **IBM PC–style keyboard**

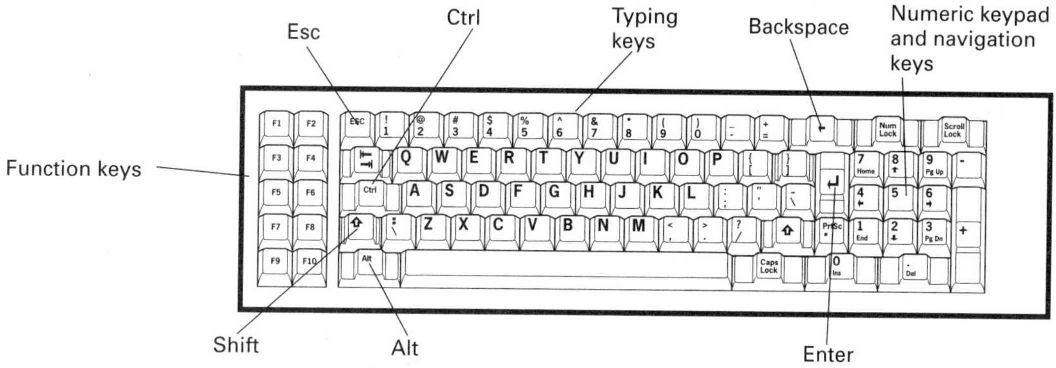

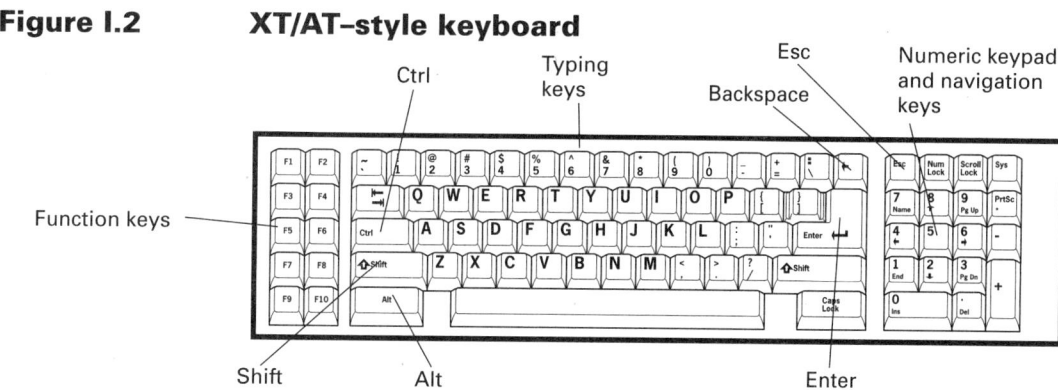

**Figure I.2**   **XT/AT–style keyboard**

**Figure I.3**   **The 101-key Enhanced Keyboard**

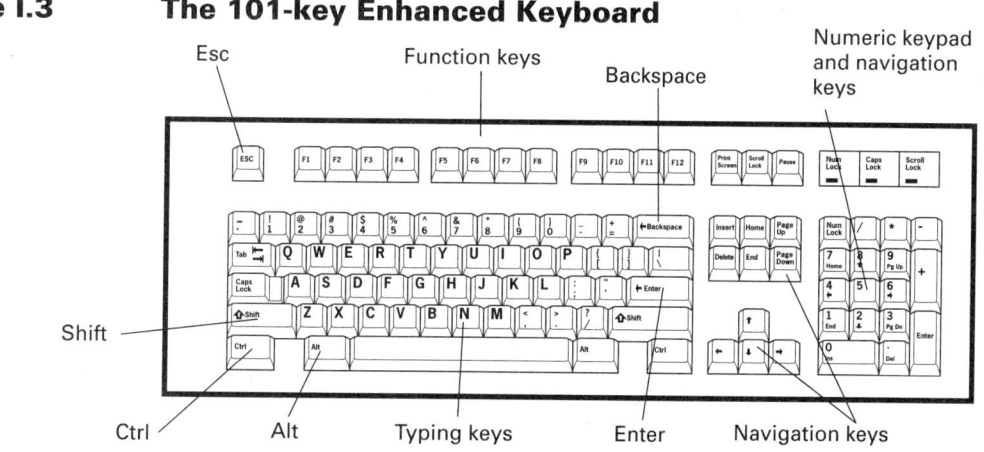

- The *typing keys*, which enable you to enter letters, numbers, and punctuation marks. These keys include the Shift, Ctrl, and Alt keys, which you need to access several of Excel's special features. The typing keys are located in the main body of all the keyboards.

- The *numeric keypad*, which enables you either to enter numeric data or to navigate through a document. When *Num Lock* is turned on, you use the numeric keypad to enter numeric data, just as you would on a standard calculator keypad. When Num Lock is turned off, you use the numeric keypad to navigate through a document by using the navigation keys: Up, down, left, and right arrows; Home, End, PgUp (Page Up), and PgDn (Page Down). To turn Num Lock on/off, simply press the Num Lock key. To enter numeric data when Num Lock is off, use the number keys in the top row of the typing area.

- The *navigation keypad*, which is available only on the Enhanced Keyboard, enables you to navigate through a document by using the Home, End, Page Up, Page Down, and arrow keys. The navigation keypad works the same when Num Lock is turned on or off. This enables you to use the numeric keypad for numeric data entry (that is, to keep Num Lock on) and still have access to navigation keys.

 MOUSE OR OTHER TYPE OF TRACKING DEVICE

You need a mouse or other type of tracking device to work through the activities in this book. Any standard PC mouse or tracking device (a trackball, for example) will do.

**Note:** Throughout this book, we direct you to use a mouse. If you have a different tracking device, simply use your device to perform all the mousing tasks: pointing, clicking, dragging, and so on.

## CONVENTIONS USED IN THIS BOOK

The following conventions used in this book will help you learn Excel for Windows 95 easily and efficiently.

- Each chapter begins with a short introduction and ends with a summary that includes a quick-reference guide to the techniques introduced in the chapter.

- Main chapter topics (large, capitalized headings) and subtopics (headings preceded by a cube) explain Excel features.

- Hands-on activities allow you to practice using these features. In these activities, keystrokes, menu choices, and anything you are asked to type are printed in boldface. Here's an example from Chapter 2:

  **4.** Type **=b1*b2** and click on the **Enter box** to calculate the product of the numbers in B1 and B2 (125000).

- A plus sign (+) is used with the Shift, Ctrl, and Alt keys to indicate a multi-key keystroke. For example, press Ctrl+F10 means "Press and hold down the Ctrl key, then press the F10 key, and then release them both."

- To help you distinguish between steps presented for reference purposes (general procedures) and steps you should carry out at your computer as you read (specific procedures), we use the following system:

- A bulleted step, like this, is provided for your information and reference only.

  **1.** A numbered step, like this, indicates one in a series of steps that you should carry out in sequence at your computer.

# CHAPTER 1:
# GETTING STARTED

**W**elcome to Excel for Windows 95 and the wonderful world of electronic accounting! Excel provides you with sophisticated tools for calculating, projecting, and analyzing your numeric data and presenting the results in professional-quality documents and charts. This first chapter gets you up and running in Excel, introduces you to the electronic spreadsheet working environment, and reviews your mouse skills.

When you're done working through the chapter, you will know

- How to start Excel
- How to navigate the Excel working environment
- How to use the mouse with Excel
- How to exit Excel

## THE EXCEL PROGRAM

Anyone who's ever managed a complex budget using paper, pencil, and calculator knows all too well the inherent difficulties: filling out and editing the ledger sheets; calculating totals, averages, maximums, and minimums; recalculating these values if one or more numeric entries change; redesigning entire sheets to add or delete rows or columns; preparing the finished sheets for presentation; and so on. The beauty of Excel lies in its ability to simplify—and, in some cases, entirely eliminate—these paper-world tasks.

**Figure 1.1**     **A sample paper spreadsheet**

```
               PERSONAL BUDGET for the First Quarter
              (excluding food and miscellaneous expenses)


                                                        QUARTER
                        JANUARY      FEBURARY     MARCH   TOTALS


    1. Rent              500.00       500.00     500.00  1,500.00
    2. Telephone          48.35        24.98      35.57    108.90
    3. Utilities          67.27        75.92      62.89    206.08
    4. Charge Cards      135.75        59.89      89.55    285.19
    5. Heating Oil       125.52       150.57      50.32    326.41
    6. Auto Insurance    113.50                            113.50
    7. Cable TV           30.25        30.25      30.25     90.75



    MONTHLY TOTALS    $1,020.64     $841.61    $768.58

    GRAND TOTAL (QUARTER)                              $2,630.83

    AVERAGE MONTHLY EXPENSE                              $876.94
```

- Information is arranged in columns (vertical) and rows (horizontal).

- Text identifies the numbers (Rent, JANUARY, and so on).

- Totals and averages have been calculated.

- Some numbers have ($) and (,) to make them easier to read.

- The first column (1. Rent, 2.Telephone, and so on) is wider than the others.

- The data are neatly arranged: titles are centered, headings are properly positioned, and numbers are decimal-aligned.

Figure 1.1 is an example of a spread sheet that was created using a calculator and a piece of paper. Observe the data of Figure 1.1 and consider these questions:

- How would you determine that the calculations are correct?

- How would you change a number?

- How would you then update the calculations?

- How would you add columns for the second, third, and fourth quarters?

- How would you add more expenses?

All of the above tasks are relatively involved and time-consuming. You would have to erase and reenter numbers, redo calculations, add rows and columns, and possibly revamp the entire page layout.

## CREATING YOUR WORK FOLDER

Throughout this book, you will be creating, editing, and saving several files. In order to keep these files together, you need to create a work folder for them on your hard disk. Your work folder will also hold the sample files contained on the enclosed Data Disk. Follow these steps to create your work folder. (**Note:** If Excel is not currently installed on your computer, please install it now, before you create your work folder. See Appendix A for instructions.)

1. Turn on your computer. After a brief internal self-check, Windows 95 will load and prompt you for a password. Type your password and press **Enter**.

**2.** From the Windows 95 desktop, click on the Start button. Point to Programs and select Windows Explorer. The Windows Explorer can be used to manage the folders and files on your computer.

**3.** In the Tree pane, click on the plus sign to the left of the My Computer branch to expand it so that you can view the floppy-disk drive and the hard drive. (The branch might already be expanded.) This branch may also contain folders, such as the Control Panel and Printers folders.

**4.** Click on the hard-disk icon **(C:)** in the Tree pane. From the menu bar, choose **File, New, Folder** to create a new folder. You will copy the contents of the Data Disk into this folder. The new folder is displayed in the Contents pane and is highlighted so that you can rename it now. Type **Excel Work** and press **Enter** to assign a new name to the folder.

**5.** Select the hard-disk icon **(C:)** and choose **File, Properties** to view the amount of available hard-disk space. On the General tab, the number of free bytes is displayed. If you have fewer than 5,000,000 (5MB) free bytes, you will not be able to create your work folder and perform the hands-on activities in this book (while still maintaining an adequate amount of free hard-disk space for your other computer activities). Click on Cancel to close the Properties dialog box. Before going any further, you must delete enough files from your hard disk to increase the free-byte total to at least 5,000,000. For help doing this, refer to your Windows 95 reference manual, or better yet, enlist the aid of an experienced Windows 95 user. (**Note:** Make sure you back up all your important files before deleting them!)

**6.** Remove the Data Disk from its envelope at the back of this book. Insert the Data Disk (label up) into the appropriately sized disk drive. Determine whether this is drive A or drive B. (On a single floppy-disk system, the drive is generally designated as A. On a double floppy-disk system, the upper or leftmost drive is generally designated as A and the lower or rightmost as B.)

**7.** The easiest way to copy the files from the floppy disk to your Excel Work folder is by dragging them. Display the contents of the 3½ Floppy (A:) branch. (Use the same technique that you used in step 3.) Then, select all of the files (Ctrl+A is a keystroke shortcut) in the Contents pane.

**8.** Drag the selected files to the Excel Work folder in the Tree pane. Release the mouse button to copy the files into the Excel Work folder. The folder name should be highlighted before you release the mouse button. As the files are copied, you will see a graphical display of the files flying from one folder to another.

Now, all the files that you need for this book are stored in the Excel Work folder. You might want to create a shortcut to this folder on the desktop. A shortcut will enable you to conveniently access the files in this folder. Creating a shortcut is strictly optional. You don't need the shortcut to work through the chapters in the book. However, if you would like to create a shortcut, you can use the following drag-and-drop technique.

• If the Windows Explorer window is maximized, click on the Restore button (in the upper-right corner of the window) so that you can see part of the desktop.

• Select the Excel Work folder icon. Press and hold the right mouse button and drag the icon to the desktop. Release the mouse button and choose Create Shortcut(s) Here from the shortcut's object menu.

**Important Note:** The hands-on activities in this book assume that your work folder is on the hard drive and is named Excel Work. If you specified a different location for the folder or a different name, remember to substitute this location and/or name whenever we mention the Excel Work folder.

## STARTING EXCEL

Before you start Excel, it must be installed on your hard disk. If it is not installed, please install it now. For help installing Excel, see Appendix A of this book.

You also need to have created a work folder on your hard disk and copied the files from the enclosed Data Disk to this directory. If you have not done this, please do so now; for instructions, see the previous section "Creating Your Work Folder."

**Note**: In this book, we present two types of procedures: bulleted and numbered. A *bulleted procedure*—one whose steps are preceded by bullets (•)—serves as a general reference; you should read its steps without actually performing them. A numbered procedure—one whose steps are preceded by numbers (1., 2., and so on)—is a specific hands-on activity; you should perform its steps as instructed.

To start Excel,

• Turn on your computer.

• Enter your Windows 95 password.

• From the Start menu, highlight *Programs* and select *Microsoft Excel*. If you have installed Microsoft Office, you might need to move through additional layers of the Start menu to locate Excel.

Let's follow this procedure to start Excel

1. Turn on your computer. After a brief internal self-check, your operating environment will automatically load and prompt you for the password.

2. In the Welcome to Windows dialog box, type your Windows 95 password and press **Enter**. After a few moments of furious hard-disk activity (indicated by the blinking hard-disk drive pilot light and the flashing arrows on the screen), the desktop (as shown in Figure 1.2) appears on your screen.

3. Now that Windows 95 is running, you can start Excel. In order to do this, you must locate the program Microsoft Excel in the Start menu. Because Windows 95 is a customizable program, we cannot know the details of your Windows 95 setup. So please bear with us as we search for your Microsoft Excel program. We'll begin by clicking on the Start button in the Taskbar.

4. Point to Programs to display the available programs. Depending on your Windows 95 setup, you might need to search through a few layers of menus to find Microsoft Excel or you might have created a shortcut to Microsoft Excel. (If Excel was installed as part of Microsoft Office, then you will probably find Excel in the Microsoft Office menu as shown in Figure 1.3.)

**Figure 1.2**      **The Windows 95 desktop**

**Figure 1.3**      **The Start menu with cascading menus**

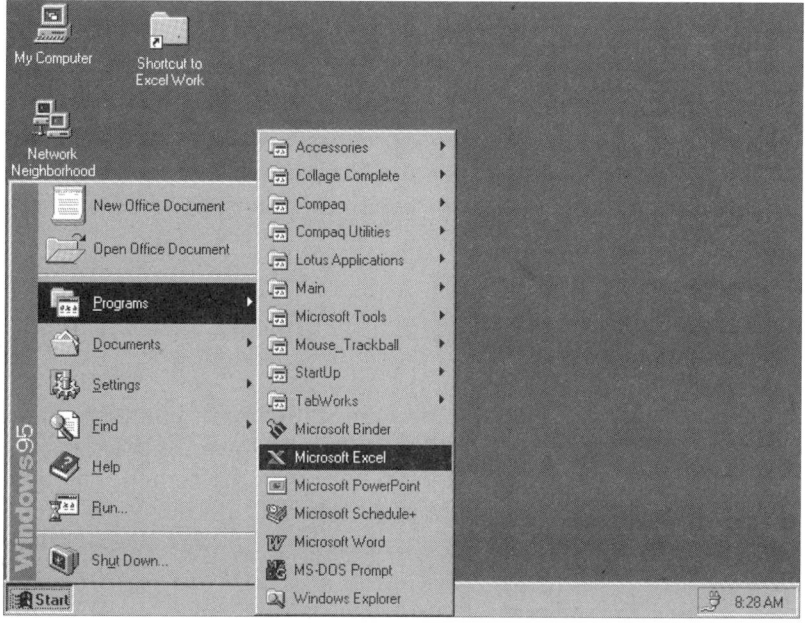

5. When Microsoft Excel is visible, click on it to begin the Excel program. Your screen should match—or closely resemble—that shown in Figure 1.4.

**Figure 1.4**          **Excel after start-up**

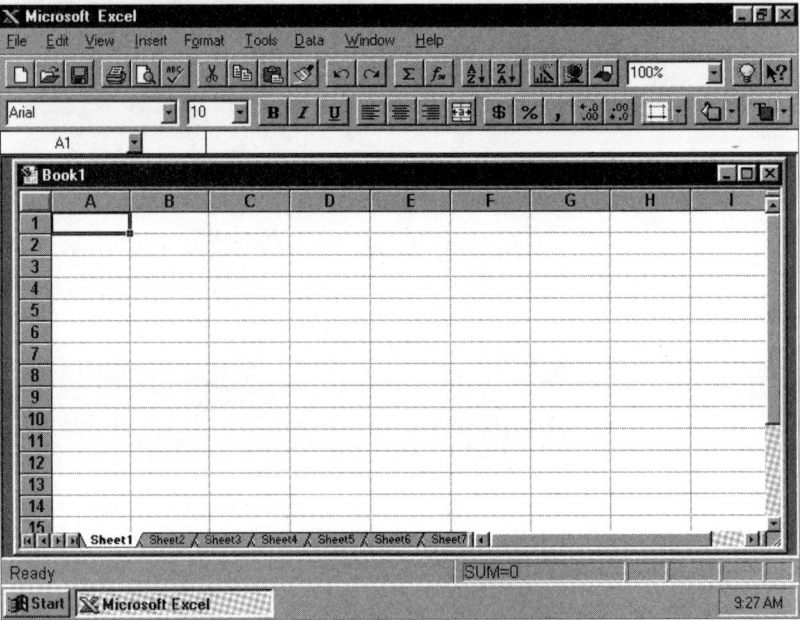

6. If your Microsoft Excel window does not fill the entire screen, click on the Maximize button in the upper-right corner of the screen. The Excel window should now fill the screen.

7. If the title bar at the top of your screen reads Microsoft Excel - Book1, click on the lower of the two Restore buttons in the upper-right corner of the screen. The title bar should now read Microsoft Excel.

**8.** If the window entitled Book1 in the middle of your screen is much smaller than our Book1 window (as shown in Figure 1.4), resize your Book1 window to match ours. To do this, place your mouse pointer on a Book1 window border (the pointer changes to a double-sided arrow), press and hold down the **left mouse button**, drag (slide) your mouse to resize the windows, then release the mouse button.

## PLEASE READ THIS—IT'S IMPORTANT

Like Windows 95, Excel can be customized. And depending on how you (or perhaps a colleague) have set up your Excel program, it may look very different from another user's Excel setup, or from the Excel setup used in this book. When faced with the daunting task of writing for an "invisible" audience—with hundreds, if not thousands, of different Excel setups—we decided to make the following assumption:

- We assume you are running Excel with the same *default* (standard) settings that were automatically chosen when you first installed Excel.

Of course, this assumption may not be true. You or a colleague may have customized your Excel program to show additional toolbars, run in full-screen view, display on-screen text as 20-point Antique English, hide the formula and status bars, and so on.

Here's our recommendation. First of all, relax. Chances are your program settings are fine. But if you should run into a snag while working through this book—for example, if your screen displays differ markedly from ours, or if tools we ask you to use are missing from your screen—simply use your increasing Excel expertise to make the changes necessary to match your Excel setup with ours.

## THE EXCEL WORKING ENVIRONMENT

Excel is built around a set of *interactive windows*—rectangular, on-screen boxes through which you communicate with the Excel program and create your worksheets and charts. When you start

Excel, two windows appear on the screen, one nestled snugly within the other. The larger of these, called the *application window*, frames the entire screen; you use it to communicate with the Excel program. (The terms *program* and *application* are synonymous.) The smaller window, called the *document window*, fits seamlessly within the application window; you use it to create and edit your Excel worksheets and charts.

## THE APPLICATION WINDOW

The Excel application window is like a program manager: It provides you with tools, commands, and status messages to use with your worksheets. Observe these elements, as shown in Table 1.1 and Figure 1.5.

**Figure 1.5**      **The Excel application window**

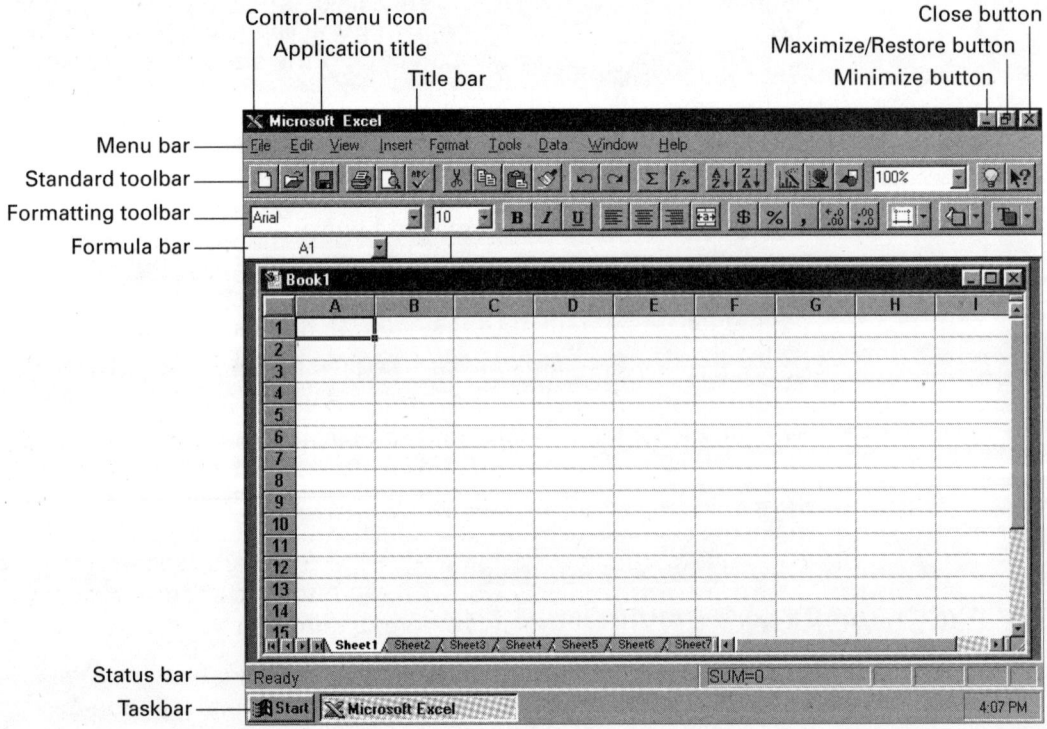

**Table 1.1**     **Excel Application-Window Elements**

| Element | Description |
|---|---|
| Title bar | The bar at the top of the application window. It displays the name of the application (Microsoft Excel). |
| Control-menu icon | The small Excel icon in the upper-left corner. It provides a list of commands you use to move, resize, and close the application window. |
| Minimize button | The leftmost of the three buttons at the right end of the title bar. It resembles a minus sign. You use it to minimize the application window to the taskbar. The application is still running, but it is not active. |
| Maximize/Restore button | The middle of the three buttons at the right end of the title bar. It resembles an outline of a small window. You use it to maximize or restore (shrink) the size of the application window. |
| Close button | The rightmost of the three buttons at the right end of the title bar. You use this button to close the application window. The Close button has the same function as that of the Close command in the Control menu. |
| Menu bar | The bar below the title bar. You use it to choose commands from Excel's drop-down menu system. |
| Standard toolbar | The bar below the menu bar. You click on its tool buttons to choose frequently used commands and utilities. |
| Formatting toolbar | The bar below the Standard toolbar. You click on its tool buttons to choose frequently used formatting commands. |
| Formula bar | The bar below the Formatting toolbar. It displays the contents of the currently active worksheet cell. |

**Table 1.1**     **Excel Application-Window Elements (Continued)**

| Element | Description |
|---|---|
| Status bar | The bar at the bottom of the application window. It displays information about the currently selected command and the current status of the workspace. |
| Taskbar | The bar at the bottom of the Windows 95 screen. It displays a Start button, a button for each application that is running, and a clock. The Start button is used to run applications (such as Excel), open documents, find information, or change computer settings. |

## THE DOCUMENT WINDOW

The Excel document window displays the currently active worksheet and the workbook in which it is contained. (A *workbook* is a group of related worksheets.) Familiarize yourself with the elements shown in Table 1.2 and Figure 1.6

**Figure 1.6**     **The Excel document window**

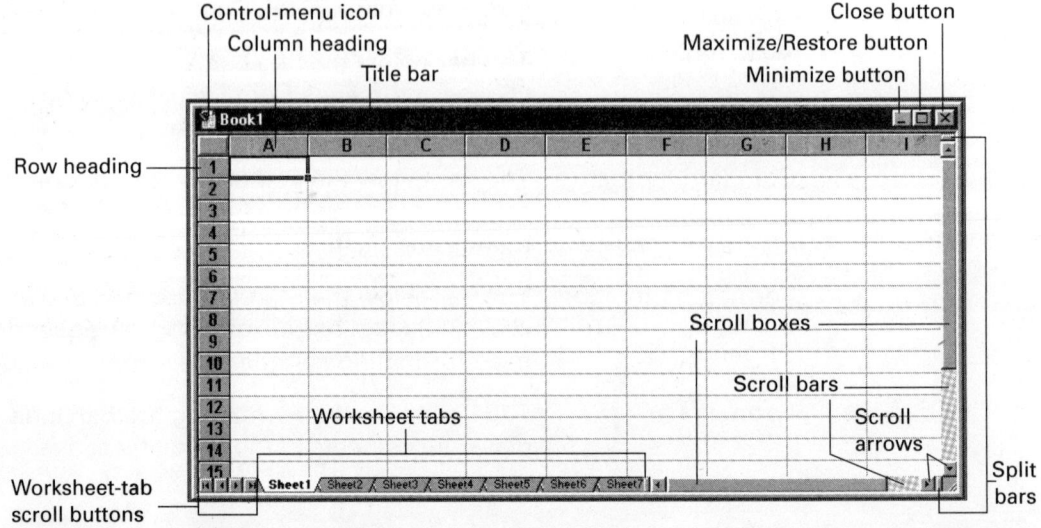

**Table 1.2**     **Excel Document-Window Elements**

| Element | Description |
| --- | --- |
| Title bar | The bar at the top of the document window. It displays the name of the workbook (Book1). |
| Control-menu icon | The small Excel icon in the upper-left corner. It provides a list of commands you use to move, resize, and close the document window. |
| Minimize button | The leftmost of the three buttons at the right end of the document title bar. It resembles a minus sign. You use it to minimize the document window so that only the title bar is visible. |
| Maximize/ Restore button | The middle of the three buttons at the right end of the document title bar. It resembles an outline of a small window. You use it to maximize or restore (shrink) the size of the document window. |
| Close button | The rightmost of the three buttons at the right end of the document title bar. You use this button to close the document window. The Close button has the same function as that of the Close command in the Control menu. |
| Worksheet tabs | The tabs at the bottom of the document window. You use these to select a different worksheet within the current workbook. |
| Worksheet-tab scroll buttons | The set of four boxes to the left of the worksheet tabs. You use them to scroll through the worksheet tabs. |
| Scroll bars | The vertical and horizontal bars framing the right and lower borders of the document window. You use the scroll bars, along with the *scroll boxes* and *scroll arrows* they contain, to change which portion of the worksheet is displayed in the document window. |

**Table 1.2**   **Excel Document-Window Elements (Continued)**

| Element | Description |
| --- | --- |
| Split bars | The gray sections located above the vertical scroll bar and to the right of the horizontal scroll bar. You use these to split the document window into *panes* that can be scrolled separately, enabling you to view several areas of the worksheet at once. |
| Column headings | The letters at the top of each worksheet column. |
| Row headings | The numbers at the left of each worksheet row. |

## THE WORKSHEET

An Excel worksheet is an electronic version of a paper spreadsheet, which is a tool you use to document and analyze numerical data (see Figure 1.7). You arrange your data in rows and columns just as on a standard paper spreadsheet or ledger sheet. As you add or change data, Excel automatically recalculates the relationships among the data.

A worksheet consists of a grid of 256 columns by 16,834 rows. Columns are designated by letters running across the top of the worksheet, and rows by numbers running down the left border. Column *headings* begin with the letter A and continue through the letter Z (columns 1 to 26). After the 26th column, headings become double letters, from AA to IV (columns 27 through 256).

The intersection of a column and a row is called a *cell*. A single worksheet contains over four million cells (256 multiplied by 16,834). You enter data (text or numbers) directly into the currently *active* cell. This cell is outlined with a dark border.

The *formula bar* is the bar below the Formatting (lower) toolbar. It displays the contents and name of the active cell. When you enter data into a cell or select a cell containing data, the data appears in both the cell and the formula bar. The name of the active cell appears in the cell-reference area on the far left of the formula bar. For example, the formula bar might display the cell reference A1 on the far left and 500 (the value in cell A1) on the right.

**Figure 1.7**    **The Excel worksheet**

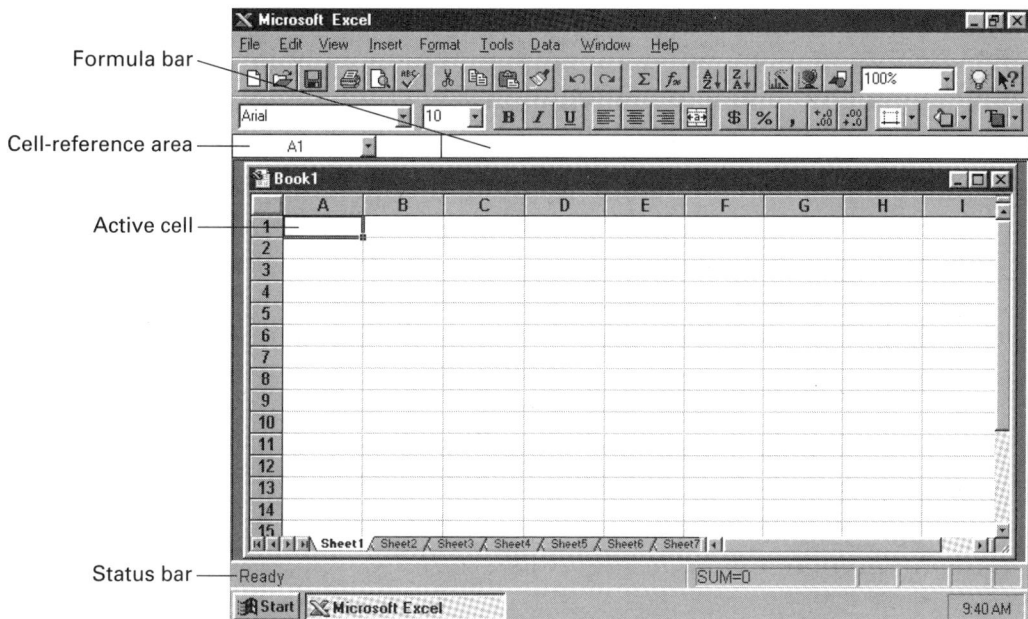

When you are typing data into a cell, a boxed check mark (the *Enter* box) and a boxed X (the *Cancel* box) appear in the formula bar. When you enter the data into the cell, these boxes are removed.

A *status bar* frames the bottom of the application window. It displays information about the currently selected command and about the current status of the worksheet.

Let's take a look at some of these basic worksheet features:

1. Observe the new, blank worksheet on your computer screen (Sheet1, as indicated by the highlighted tab at the bottom of the worksheet). Note that it resembles an accountant's ledger paper. What you see represents only a tiny portion of your available worksheet space. As mentioned, Excel allows you to create a worksheet up to 256 columns wide and 16,834 rows long!

2. Observe the column and row headings. Depending on the size of your screen, you can see approximately nine columns (A through I) and 16 rows. The 144 cells that are visible represent only a small portion of the entire worksheet.

3. Observe the active cell. Note that the borders of the active cell are darker than the other worksheet cells.

4. Observe the cell reference that is displayed in the formula bar. Examine the cell reference to verify the location of the active cell. Whenever you open a new worksheet, Excel selects A1 as the active cell.

5. Press the **right arrow key** to select **B1** as the active cell. Note that B1 is now outlined, and that the cell-reference area reads B1.

### PRACTICE YOUR SKILLS

- Use the directional arrow keys (left, up, and down) to select other cells in the worksheet.

- Verify that the cell-reference area displays the active cell.

## A QUICK REVIEW OF MOUSING SKILLS

The mouse is a hand-operated device that enables you to communicate with Excel by manipulating (selecting, deselecting, moving, deleting, and so on) graphical and text objects that are displayed on your computer screen. When you move the mouse across the surface of your mouse pad, a symbol called the *mouse pointer* moves across the screen. You use this mouse pointer to point to the on-screen object that you want to manipulate. On top of the mouse are two or more buttons. You use these buttons to communicate with Excel in various ways, as detailed in Table 1.3.

**Note:** Read through the following table to familiarize yourself with standard Excel mousing techniques. Do not, however, try to memorize these techniques. Instead, use this table as a quick-reference guide, referring back to it whenever you need to refresh your mousing memory.

**Note:** You can issue each of Excel's commands by using either the mouse or the keyboard. In general, this book will teach you to use the mouse; only the most convenient keyboard commands are mentioned. If you would like to learn more about keyboard commands, see Appendix B, "Keystroke Reference," or the Excel reference manuals.

**Table 1.3**     **Mousing Techniques**

| Technique | How to Do It |
| --- | --- |
| Point | Move the mouse until the tip of the mouse pointer is over the desired object. "Point to the word *File*" means "move the mouse until the tip of the mouse pointer is over the word *File*." |
| Click | Press and release the left or right mouse button. When we want you to click the left mouse button, we'll simply say "click." For example, "click on the word *File*" means "point to the word *File* and then press and release the left mouse button." When we want you to click the right mouse button, we'll explicitly say so. For example, "point to the Standard toolbar and click the right mouse button." |
| Double-click | Press and release the left mouse button twice in rapid succession. "Double-click on the file name CHAP14" means "point to the file name CHAP14 and then press and release the left mouse button twice in rapid succession." |
| Choose | Click on a menu command or a dialog-box button. "Choose File, Open" means "click on the word *File* (in the menu bar), and then click on the word *Open* (in the File menu)." |
| Drag | Press and hold the left mouse button while moving the mouse. "Drag the scroll box upward" means "point to the scroll box, press and hold the left mouse button, move the mouse upward, and then release the mouse button." |
| Scroll | Click on a scroll arrow or within a scroll bar, or drag a scroll box. |
| Select | Click on an object (to select the entire object), or drag over part of a text object (to select part of the text). "Select the file CHAP14" means "click on the file name CHAP14." "Select the first letter of *Sales Totals*" means "drag over the letter S." |

**Table 1.3**     **Mousing Techniques (Continued)**

| Technique | How to Do It |
| --- | --- |
| Check | Click on a check box to check (turn on) that option. "Check the Match Case option" means "click on the Match Case check box to check it." |
| Uncheck | Click on a check box to uncheck (turn off) that option. "Uncheck the Match Case option" means "click on the Match Case check box to uncheck it." |

Perform the following steps to acquaint yourself with the mouse.

1. Move the mouse. Note the direction and speed of the mouse pointer in relation to the movements of your hand. Also, note the changing shape of the mouse pointer as it moves across different areas of the screen.

2. Point to cell **D1** (that is, move the mouse pointer until its tip is over the middle of cell D1). Note that the pointer changes to a cross.

3. Click (the left mouse button) on cell **D1** to *select* it. Note the outline around the cell, indicating that it is selected.

4. Point to cell **D1** and click the **right mouse button** to display the shortcut menu. (You'll learn more about shortcut menus in Chapter 4.) Remember, when we want you to click the right mouse button, we'll say so explicitly (as we did in this step); when we want you to click the left mouse button, we'll simply say "click" (as in the previous step). Press the **Esc** key to remove the shortcut menu.

5. Point to cell **B2**. Press and hold down the **left mouse button**, and then drag the mouse pointer to cell **E5**. Release the mouse button. Note that all 16 cells bounded by B2 and E5 are selected, as shown in Figure 1.8. To select a range of cells, you drag the mouse pointer over them. Note that the active cell (B2) is white and the rest are black.

**Figure 1.8**    **Selecting a range of cells**

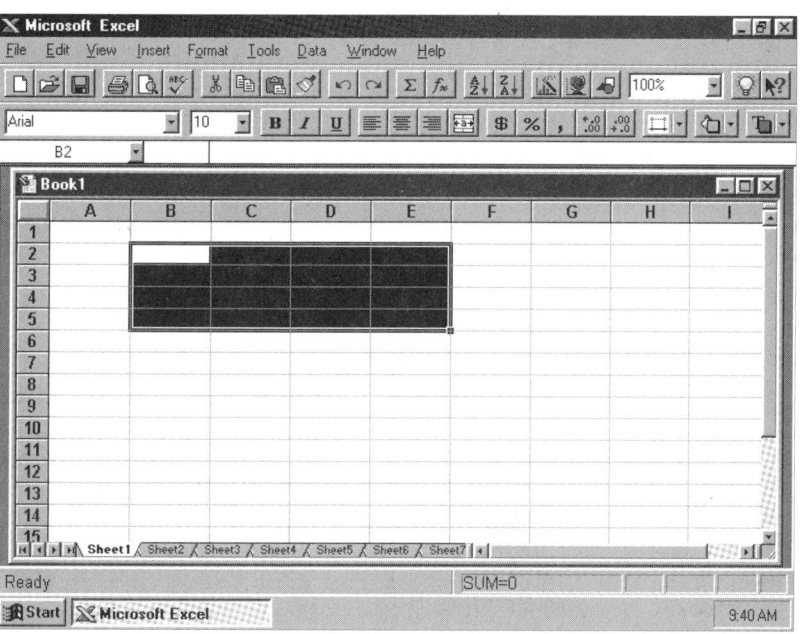

PRACTICE YOUR SKILLS

1. Select cell **F5**. (Note that when you select a cell, the previously active cells are *deselected*.)

2. Select cell **G13**.

3. Select cell **A1**.

4. Select cells **A4** through **G12**.

## EXITING EXCEL

When you finish an Excel work session and want to turn off your computer, you must exit Excel. Use either of the following two methods to do this:

- Click on *File* (in the menu bar) to display the drop-down File menu. In this menu, click on *Exit*.

- Or, double-click on the Control-menu icon of the Excel application window.

Let's use the second of these techniques to exit from Excel:

1. Double-click on the application-window **Control-menu icon** (the small Excel icon in the upper-left corner of the screen) to exit from Excel.

2. If you are prompted Save changes in 'Book1'? click on **No**. (You'll learn more about this prompt in Chapter 3.) The Windows 95 environment reappears. You can now use another program, exit to DOS, or turn off your computer. For more information, see your Windows 95 reference manuals.

## SUMMARY

In this first chapter, you've learned some important Excel fundamentals. You now know how to start Excel 7.0, how to navigate in the Excel working environment, how to use the mouse with Excel, and how to exit Excel. Congratulations: You're well on your way to Excel mastery!

Here's a quick reference guide for the Excel features introduced in this chapter:

| Desired Result | How to Do It |
|---|---|
| Start Excel | Turn on computer; enter Windows 95 password; display the **Start** menu; point to Programs, and click on **Microsoft Excel**. Your path to find Excel might be different, depending on your Windows 95 setup. |
| Exit Excel | Click on *File* and click on *Exit*; or double-click on the application-window **Control-menu icon**. |

In Chapter 2, you'll explore basic worksheet mechanics. You'll learn how to enter and revise text, numbers, and formulas; how to save and close a workbook; how to create a new worksheet (and workbook); and how to use the mouse and the keyboard to enter menu commands.

## A NOTE ON HOW TO PROCEED

If you want to take a break here, please feel free to do so now. If you feel energetic and want to press onward, please proceed directly to the next chapter. Remember to allot enough time to work through an entire chapter in one sitting.

# CHAPTER 2:
# BASIC WORKSHEET
# MECHANICS

Entering Data

Saving and
Closing a Workbook

Creating a New
Worksheet

In Chapter 1, you learned some fundamental Excel survival skills: How to start and exit the Excel program, and how to navigate the Excel application and document windows. In this chapter, you'll build on these skills by learning basic worksheet mechanics: How to enter and revise data in Excel, and how to save a workbook to a file on your hard disk.

When you're done working through this chapter, you will know

- How to enter and revise data (text, numbers, and formulas)

- How to save and close a workbook

- How to use the mouse and the keyboard to choose menu commands

- How to create a new worksheet

## ENTERING DATA

Worksheet cells can contain two types of data: *constant values* and *formulas*. Constant values are text or numbers that, once entered, do not normally change (for example, an employee's name or a fixed sales commission rate). Formulas are instructions designed to perform specific calculations (determine totals, averages, projected profits, and so on).

To enter data in a cell,

- Select the desired cell.

- Type the data.

- Click on the Enter box (the boxed check mark in the formula bar), or press the Enter key.

If you are not already running Excel on your computer, please start it now (for help, see "Starting Excel" in Chapter 1). Your document window should contain a new, blank workbook, and the Sheet1 worksheet tab (at the bottom of the workbook) should be selected.

Let's begin this chapter's activities by entering text into a cell in our blank Sheet1 worksheet:

1. Select cell **A1**.

2. Type **cases**. Note that the text appears in both the cell and the formula bar, as shown in Figure 2.1.

3. Observe the *insertion point* (the flashing vertical line at the end of the text in the cell). This line marks where your next character will be inserted as you type.

4. Observe the Cancel box and the Enter box (the boxed letter *X* and the check mark to the left of the text in the formula bar). These boxes appear in the formula bar as you type

**Figure 2.1**     **Entering text into a cell**

Function Wizard

Enter box

Cancel box

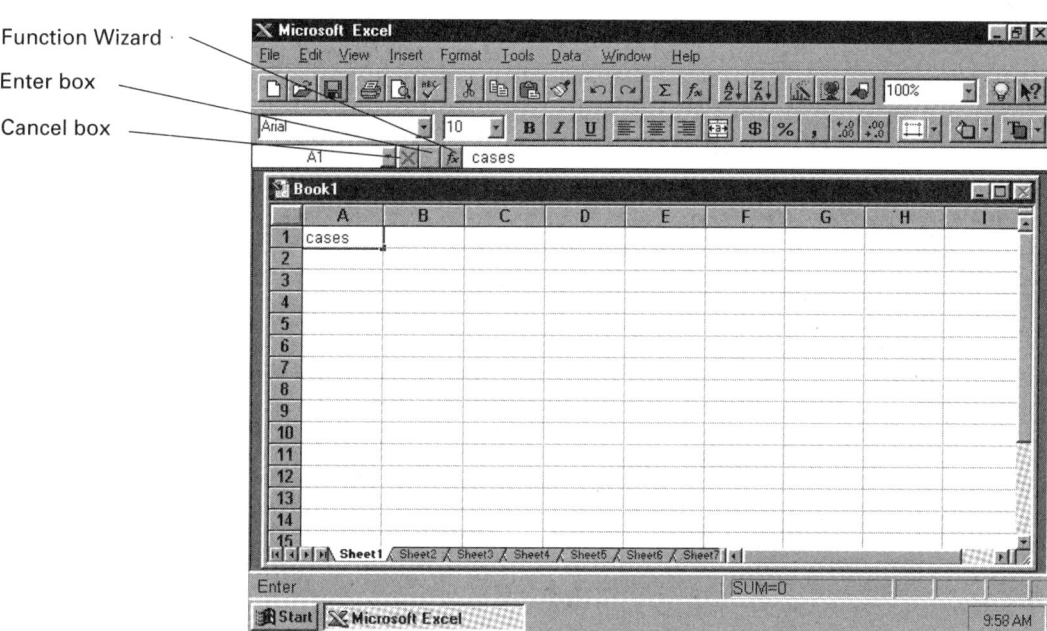

your data; you use them to enter or cancel what you've typed. (The box to the right of the Enter box runs the Function Wizard tool; you'll learn more about this in Chapter 4.)

5. Click on the **Enter box** to enter your data (in this case, the word *cases*) into the active cell, A1.

6. Observe the results. The Cancel box, Enter box, Function Wizard tool, and insertion point disappear. The text is entered into the cell and aligned to the left.

## CORRECTING DATA

You can easily correct any mistakes in your worksheet data. To correct a mistake *while* you are typing data into a cell (that is, *before* you've actually entered the data into the cell),

• Use the Backspace key to erase one or more of the characters to the left of the insertion point, and then retype the desired characters.

- Or, click on the Cancel box or press the Esc key to erase everything you've typed, and then retype it from scratch.

To correct data *after* you've entered it into a cell,

- Select the cell.

- Retype the data, and then reenter it. The new data replaces the old.

Let's try out these data-correction techniques:

1. Select cell **A2**.

2. Type **boxs** (a misspelling of *boxes*).

3. Press the **Backspace key** to delete the *s* (the character to the left of the insertion point). Your text should now read *box*.

4. Type **e** and then press and hold down the **s** key for a few seconds. Note that several *s*'s appear in a row. You can use this *autorepeat* feature to repeat desired keystrokes. For example, press and hold down **Backspace key** to delete all the *s*'s you just typed.

5. Click on the **Cancel box** (the boxed *X* in the formula bar) to clear your entire entry.

6. Reselect cell **A2**, if necessary, and type **boxes**.

7. Click on the **Enter box** to enter your correctly spelled data into cell A2.

## CREATING FORMULAS

A formula is a set of mathematical instructions that you enter in a worksheet cell. Each formula carries out its instructions to perform a specific calculation (for example, to multiply 5 by 100, or to add 300 to 700). Formulas can be very short and simple or very long and complex. However, each formula—no matter how simple or complex—calculates a single result (in the above example, 500 or 1,000).

To enter a formula into a worksheet cell,

- Select the desired cell.

- Type an equal sign (=).

- Type your desired formula. Use + for addition, – for subtraction, * for multiplication, and / for division.

- Enter the formula (by pressing Enter or clicking on the Enter box).

You can create formulas containing fixed numbers (for example, =300+700, which generates the value 1000). However, you'll find it far more efficient to enter the numbers into individual worksheet cells and then to create formulas that refer to these cells. That way, Excel automatically updates (recalculates) your formula whenever you change the contents of any of the cells to which it refers.

For example, if you entered 300 in cell B1, 700 in cell B2, and =B1+B2 in cell B3, the value 1000 (300 + 700) would appear in cell B3. If you then changed the contents of cell B2 to 800, Excel would automatically recalculate your formula and display the value 1100 in cell B3.

Let's enter a few numbers into our Sheet1 worksheet:

1. Select cell **B1**.

2. Type **500**.

3. Press **Enter** to enter 500 into cell B1. Note that pressing the Enter key enters the data and selects the next cell down (B2). The number is aligned to the right side of the cell. In Excel, numbers are automatically right-aligned and text is left-aligned (for example, *cases* and *boxes*).

4. Verify that cell B2 is the active cell.

5. Type **100**.

6. Press **Enter** to enter 100 into cell B2.

Now let's create two formulas. In the first formula, we'll use fixed numbers; in the second, we'll use cell references:

1. Select cell **B4**.

2. Type **500+100** (don't type any spaces between the numbers and the +).

3. Click on the **Enter box** to enter what you've typed. Observe the results. Instead of displaying 600 (the result of the calculation 500+100), Excel displays 500+100. Why? Because Excel treats your entry as text, rather than as a formula. Why? Because you didn't begin the entry with an = sign! (As you'll remember from the bulleted procedure for entering a

formula in a cell, which we presented at the beginning of this section, you must begin each and every formula you create by typing =.)

4. Reselect cell **B4**, if necessary.

5. Type **=500+100** and click on the **Enter box** to enter the formula =500+100 into cell B4. This time, Excel treats your entry as a formula (because it begins with =), and displays the correct result (600), as shown in Figure 2.2.

**Figure 2.2**      **Creating a fixed-number formula**

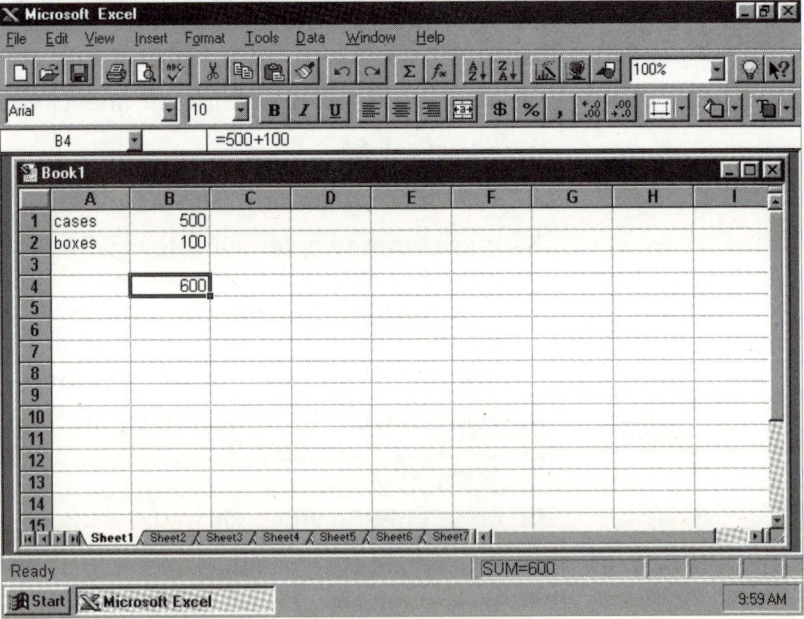

6. Select cell **B6**.

7. Type **=b1+b2**. You're telling Excel to add the contents of cells B1 and B2 and to display the result in cell B6. (You needn't worry about capitalization when typing cell references; Excel considers =b1+b2 to be exactly the same as =B1+B2.)

8. Click on the **Enter box** to enter your formula. As shown in Figure 2.3, cell B6 displays 600, the result of adding 500 (in B1) and 100 (in B2).

**Figure 2.3** **Creating a formula with cell references**

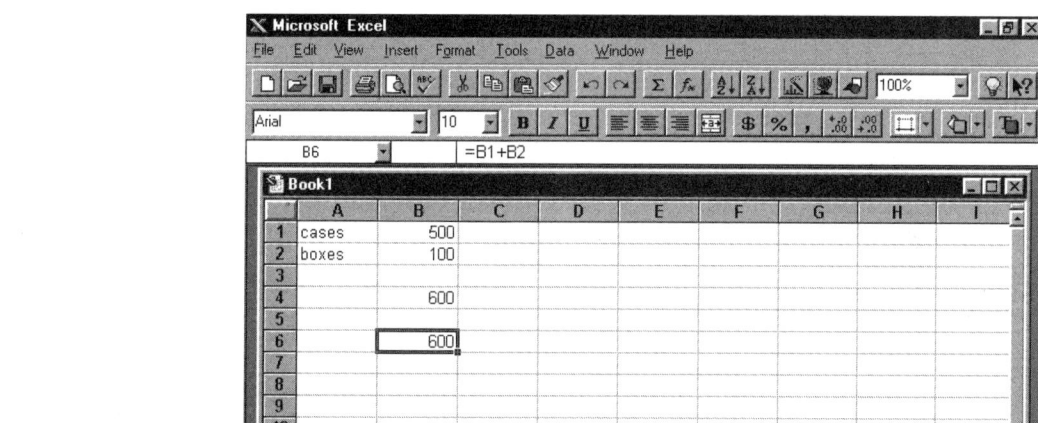

Let's take a look at an important difference between how Excel displays a cell's contents in the cell itself and in the formula bar:

1. Observe the worksheet cells (not the formula bar). Fixed numbers (in cells B1 and B2) cannot be distinguished from formula results (in cells B4 and B6).

2. Select cell **B2**. Both the formula bar and cell B2 display a fixed number (100).

3. Select cell **B6**. In this case, the formula bar displays the formula contained in cell B6 (=B1+B2), while cell B6 itself displays the result of this formula (600).

## AUTOMATIC RECALCULATION

For many users, the chief advantage of Excel over a paper ledger sheet is its *automatic recalculation* feature: Whenever you change a number in a worksheet, Excel automatically recalculates the result of every formula that references this number.

Let's see the automatic recalculation feature in action:

1. Observe the contents of cells B2, B4, and B6. B2 contains the number 100. Cells B4 and B6 contain the calculated result, 600.

2. Select cell **B2**.

3. Type **400** and press **Enter** to replace the old cell contents (100) with your new entry (400).

4. Observe the contents of cells B4 and B6. Cell B4 still contains 600. Cell B6, however, now displays 900.

5. Select cell **B6**. The formula bar displays the formula =B1+B2, while the worksheet displays the result (900). When you changed the number in cell B2, Excel automatically recalculated all the formulas in your worksheet that referred to the contents of that cell. In this case, only one formula referred to cell B2, your =B1+B2 formula in cell B6.

6. Select cell **B4**. The value in this cell is still 600, because its formula, =500+100, simply adds the values 500 and 100.

7. Select cell **B2**.

8. Type **250** and press **Enter** to replace the old cell contents (400) with 250. Cell B4 still displays 600 (500+100). Cell B6, however, which adds the numbers in cells B1 and B2, has been updated to 750 to reflect the new number in cell B2, as shown in Figure 2.4.

In general, you should use cell references (B1, B2, and so on) in your formulas rather than fixed numbers (100, 200, and so on). By doing this, you'll create *dynamic worksheets:* worksheets whose calculated results automatically change to reflect the changes you make to your numeric data.

Let's end this section by creating three more dynamic formulas. We'll use the enter key to enter the data and move the cell pointer. You can decide which method of entering data works best for you.

**Figure 2.4**     **Cell B6 (750), automatically recalculated**

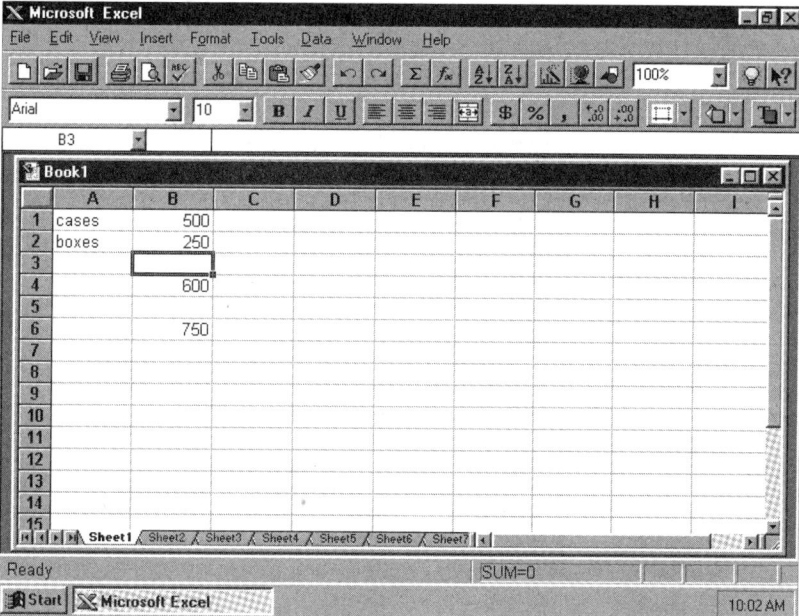

1. Select cell **B7**.

2. Type **=b1-b2** and press **Enter** to enter a formula that calculates the difference between the numbers in cells B1 and B2
   (250).

3. In cell B8, type **=b1*b2** and press **Enter** to calculate the product of the numbers in B1 and B2 (125000).

4. In cell B9, type **=b1/b2** and press **Enter** to divide the number
   in B1 by the number in B2 (2).

5. Select cell **B2**.

6. Type **750** and press **Enter** to change B2's value to 750. Your
   screen should match that shown in Figure 2.5. Note that all
   the cells that contain formulas referencing cell B2 have been
   automatically recalculated (cells B6, B7, B8, and B9). Note
   also that the formula in cell B4, which contains fixed numbers rather than cell references, remains unchanged.

**Figure 2.5**     **The completed worksheet**

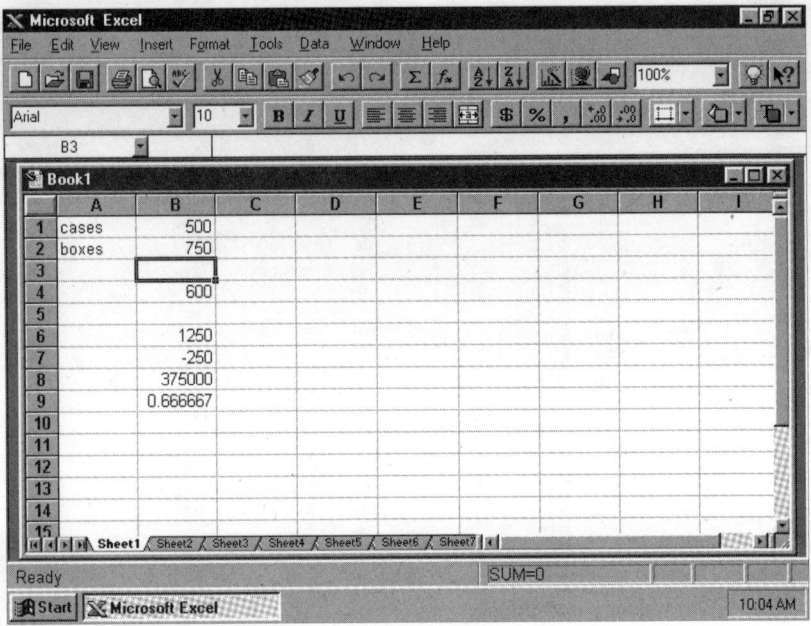

## NUMERIC DISPLAY

By default, Excel displays numbers in worksheet cells as follows:

- Numbers greater than 999 do not contain commas as separators (for instance, 1250 and 375000).

- Negative numbers are preceded by a minus sign (–250).

- As many decimals as will fit in the cell are displayed (.666667).

As you'll learn in Chapter 5, you can change these *default* (standard) settings to suit your specific needs (for example, you can choose to have Excel display 1,250, $375,000.00, ($250), .67, and so on, instead of the values displayed above).

## SAVING AND CLOSING A WORKBOOK

After you complete a workbook, you must *save* it in a file on a disk for permanent storage. After saving the workbook, you must *close* it to remove it from the screen and free up the computer memory it occupied. In order to perform these tasks, you need to learn some Excel menu basics.

## USING THE MOUSE TO CHOOSE MENU COMMANDS

The Excel menu system allows you to perform tasks by choosing them from the menu bar. When you click on a menu-bar item (File, for example), Excel displays a *drop-down menu* of related commands (New, Close, Save, and so on). To perform a command in this drop-down menu, you click on it (for example, to close the active workbook, you would click on Close).

Use the following procedure to choose a menu command:

- Click on the desired option in the menu bar to open its drop-down menu of related commands. The menu is displayed until you select a command.

- Click on the desired command in this drop-down menu.

When we want you to choose a menu command in this book, we'll say "choose *option, command,*" where *option* is the option on the menu bar and *command* is the command in the drop-down menu. For example, when we say *"choose File, Save,"* we want you to click on the File option (in the menu bar) and then click on the Save command (in the drop-down File menu).

## SAVING A WORKBOOK

Until you save a workbook, it exists only in computer memory (RAM). This is a *temporary* storage place. If you should happen to shut off your computer (accidentally, perhaps), its memory would empty and your unsaved workbook would be lost. For permanent storage, you must save your workbook to a file on a disk.

As a responsible computer user, you should save your active workbooks frequently, say every 10 to 15 minutes. That way, if your computer ever shuts off (due, for example, to a blackout or a colleague tripping over your power cord), the most recent version of your workbook will have been saved to disk, and you'll only lose 10 to 15 minutes (instead of possibly hours!) of work.

### The File, Save As Command

You use the *File, Save As* command to save a newly created workbook for the first time. You also use File, Save As to save a revised workbook under a different file name or to a different disk location.

To use File, Save As to save a workbook file,

- Choose *File, Save As* from the menu to open the Save As dialog box.

- In the File Name text box, type the desired file name.

- If necessary, change the current folder (in the Save In text box) to the folder in which you want to save the file.

- Click on Save.

- If the Summary tab of the Properties dialog box appears, fill in the desired information, and then click on OK.

Before you save a file, you must name it. Windows 95 supports long file names, so your file names can contain up to 255 characters and can include spaces and other selected punctuation. Name your files descriptively to help you remember their contents (September 93, My Accounts, and so on). Excel automatically appends the extension .xls to all workbook file names.

Let's save the active workbook as a file on your hard disk:

1. Click on **File** (in the menu bar) to open the drop-down File menu, as shown in Figure 2.6. This menu contains commands that allow you to open, close, save, or print a document.

2. Observe the Save As... option. When you choose a menu command that is followed by an ellipsis (...), Excel opens a *dialog box*, in which it prompts you for further information before performing your command (for example, the name of the file you are about to save). When you choose a menu command without an ellipsis (such as Close), Excel performs the command immediately, with no intervening dialog box.

3. Click on **Save As...** to open the Save As dialog box, as shown in Figure 2.7. Move the mouse pointer outside the borders of this dialog box and click; nothing happens. When you open a dialog box, you must specify the necessary information in the dialog box and then close it before returning to your worksheet. (**Note:** To simplify this book's layout, from now on we won't display command ellipses. For example, we'll tell you to choose File, Save As rather than File, Save As...)

**Figure 2.6**     **Opening the drop-down File menu**

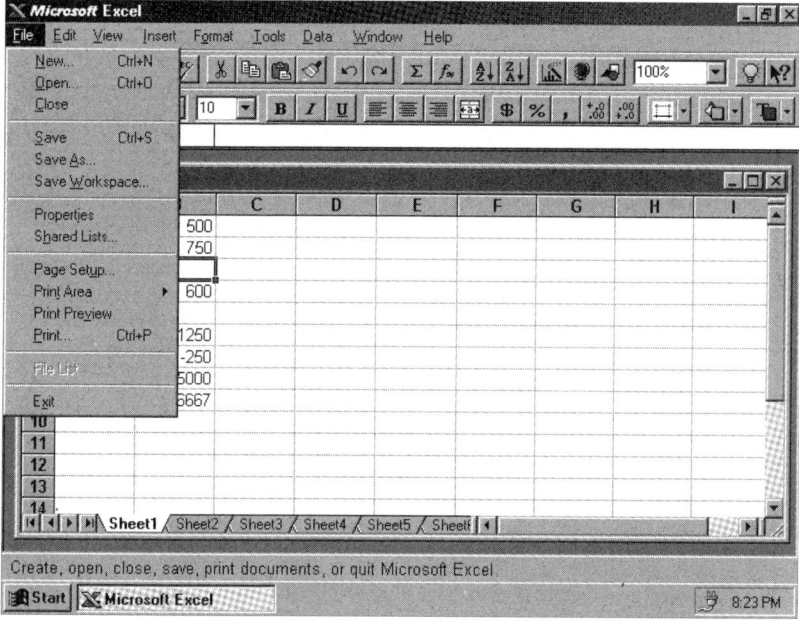

**Figure 2.7**     **The Save As dialog box**

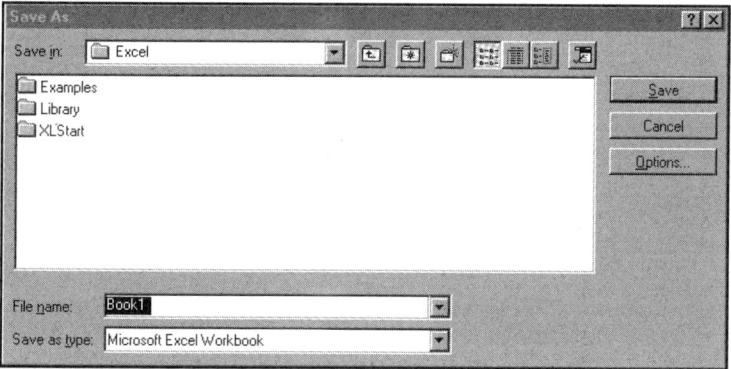

**4.** Note the highlighted file name, Book1, in the File name text box at the bottom of the dialog box. This is Excel's standard name for a new workbook file. Let's overwrite this with a more descriptive name.

5. Type **mybook**. Note that your new file name replaces the old name (Book1). You needn't worry about capitalization when typing your file name; Excel considers *mybook* to be exactly the same as *MyBook* or *MYBOOK*.

6. Observe the current folder, which is displayed in the Save In text box at the top of the dialog box. You must change this to your work folder, Excel Work, because—as mentioned in Chapter 1—that's where you'll save all the files you create in this book. Follow these steps to do so:

- The folder is located on the hard drive, so you need to display its contents. To display the contents of C:, click on the **Up One Level** button twice.

- Locate the Excel Work folder and double-click on it.

- The Excel Work folder should be displayed in the Save In text box and its contents are displayed in the window. If not, repeat the first two steps.

7. Now that you've named your workbook file and specified the correct folder, click on **Save** to save the file. Excel saves a copy of the active workbook in the Excel Work folder on your hard disk. The workbook remains on screen, allowing you to continue working on it. Note that the document-window title bar displays the workbook's new name, mybook. As mentioned earlier, Excel automatically appends the extension .xls to your workbook files.

**Note:** Depending on your Excel setup, the Properties dialog box may or may not be displayed. The Summary tab of this dialog box is used to enter general information about the workbook you're saving (title, subject, author, any comments you may have, and so on). By default, the Prompt for File Properties option is turned off.

### The File, Save Command

You choose File, Save As to save a workbook for the first time. You choose *File, Save* to save this same workbook on all subsequent occasions (unless you want to rename the file or save it to a new location). When you choose File, Save, Excel *updates* the active workbook by saving it under the same file name and to the same disk location to which you assigned it previously. No dialog box is displayed, since Excel needs no additional information to save the file.

Let's do some more work on the active worksheet (Sheet1) and then use File, Save to save the revised workbook file:

1. Select cell **A6**.

2. Type **total** to add identifying text to the worksheet.

3. Press **Enter** to enter the text into the cell. As mentioned earlier in this chapter, you can either click on the Enter box or press the Enter key to enter data into a cell.

4. Choose the **File, Save** command (that is, click on **File** in the menu bar, and then click on **Save** in the drop-down File menu) to update the revised workbook file; that is, to save it under the same name (mybook) and in the same location (Excel Work, your work folder).

**A Word of Caution:** Be aware that when you choose File, Save to save the active workbook, the current version of the workbook replaces—and, in doing so, permanently deletes—the previously saved version of the same workbook. For example, in the activity you just performed, you erased the previous version of mybook (the one without *total* in cell A6) when you chose File, Save to save the revised version (the one with *total*). If you'd wanted to preserve both versions, you could have chosen File, Save As to save the revised workbook under a different name (such as mybook2), leaving the original version (mybook) intact.

## USING AUTOSAVE TO SAVE WORKBOOKS AUTOMATICALLY

As mentioned earlier, you should save your active workbooks every ten to fifteen minutes to prevent catastrophic data loss in case of accidental power shutoff or system meltdown. If you're the forgetful type, you might want to consider using the *AutoSave* add-in to automate this procedure. An *add-in* is a special file that, once installed, adds commands and functionality to Excel.

To use the AutoSave add-in to save your workbooks automatically,

- Click on *Tools* to open the drop-down Tool menu.
- If the AutoSave command is listed in this menu, click on it to open the AutoSave dialog box. If the AutoSave command is not listed,

  - Click on *Add-Ins* to open the Add-ins dialog box.
  - Check the *AutoSave* check box.
  - Click on OK to install the AutoSave add-in.
  - Choose *Tools, AutoSave* to open the AutoSave dialog box.

- Change the AutoSave options, if desired.
- Click on OK.

We will *not* activate the AutoSave feature. Instead, we'll "force" you to save your files manually and, in doing so, to learn good, reliable file-saving habits! If AutoSave appeals to you, feel free to use the above procedure to activate it when you're done working through this book.

 A SPECIAL NOTE FOR EXCEL 5.0 FILE USERS

Excel for Windows 95 and Excel 5.0 for Windows 3.1 use the same file format with one exception (see the important note below). You can share files between these two versions of Excel with no conversion hassles. You can also open files from earlier versions of Excel (4.0, 3.0, or 2.1) and save them as Excel for Windows 95 files by verifying that the selected Save as Type option is Microsoft Excel Workbook. This is the default file type, so you do not need to change anything if you want to save the files as Excel for Windows 95.

If you intend to use an Excel 4.0 (or 3.0 or 2.1) file on a computer equipped with Excel version 4.0 or earlier, but not Excel for Windows 95, do not save the file as an Excel for Windows 95 file. The Excel 4.0, and earlier, program cannot open Excel for Windows 95 files! Likewise, if you create a workbook file in Excel for Windows 95 and need to use it on a computer equipped only with Excel 4.0 (or 3.0 or 2.1), save the workbook as an Excel 4.0 (or 3.0 or 2.1) file. To do so, use the following procedure:

- Choose *File, Save As.*

- In the Save as Type list box, select the applicable version of Excel (4.0, 3.0, or 2.1).

- Specify the necessary Save As dialog box information.

- Click on *Save.*

**Important note:** While Excel for Windows 95 supports long file names, Excel 5.0 does not. So, if you plan to use the same file in both programs, you will need to comply with the eight character maximum when naming files.

## CLOSING A WORKBOOK

When you close a workbook, Excel removes the workbook (and all the worksheets it contains) from computer memory and removes the document window from the screen. If only one workbook is open, closing it leaves the Excel application window alone on the screen. Any workbooks that you do not close remain in memory until you exit Excel.

To close the active workbook,

- Choose *File, Close* or double-click on the document-window Control-menu icon.

- If you changed the workbook since you last saved it, Excel asks you whether you wish to save your changes before closing the workbook. To save the changes, click on *Yes;* to close the workbook without saving the changes, click on *No.*

Let's close our mybook workbook:

1. Choose **File, Close** to close the workbook and its document window. Note that File and Help are the only options available in the menu bar. This stripped-down set of menu options is referred to as the *Null menu bar,* as shown in Figure 2.8.

**Figure 2.8**     **The Null menu bar**

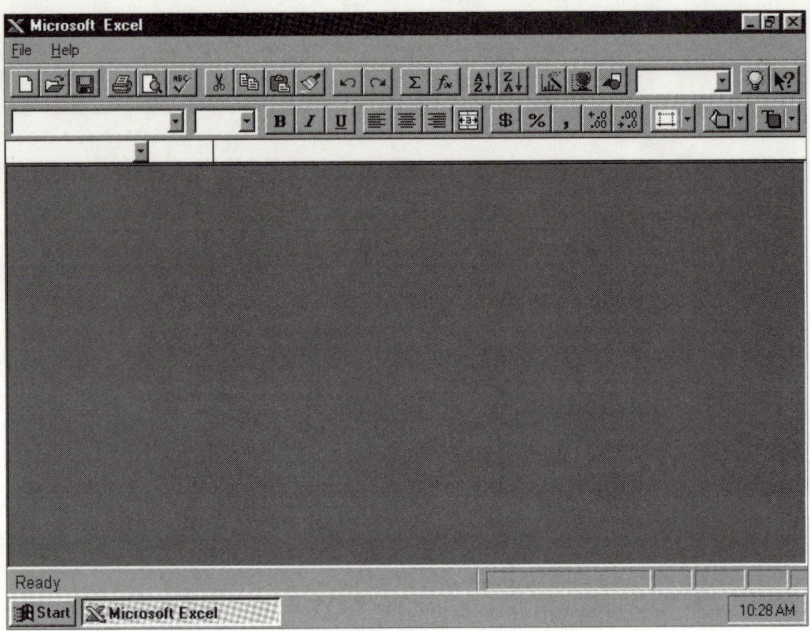

## CREATING A NEW WORKSHEET

Before creating a new worksheet, you must ask yourself two questions:

- Do I want to store my new worksheet together with other worksheets in an *existing* workbook?

- Or, do I want to store my new worksheet all by itself in a *new* workbook?

You would answer yes to the first question if your new worksheet were closely related to the worksheets in an existing workbook. For example, let's say that you had a workbook named abcwork, which contained several worksheets filled with ABC Company data. If you created a new ABC Company worksheet, you would probably want to store it in abcwork together with its siblings.

You would answer yes to the second question if your new worksheet were not closely related to any existing worksheets. For example, in the next activity, you'll create a *Garlic Club* worksheet that is not related to any other worksheets. To do so, you'll open a new workbook and then create your worksheet in it.

To create a new worksheet in an existing workbook,

- Open the workbook.
- Select a blank worksheet by clicking on its tab (at the bottom of the document window).
- Fill in the blank worksheet as desired.

To create a new worksheet in a new workbook,

- Choose *File, New*.
- Click on the General tab. (If other Microsoft Office applications are installed, you will need to select the Excel tab.)
- Double-click on the Workbook icon. The new workbook is named BookN, where N is the number of new workbooks you opened during the current work session (Book1, Book2, and so on).

Or

- Click on the New Workbook button in the Standard toolbar.

To rename a worksheet,

- Double-click on the worksheet tab.
- Type the desired worksheet name (up to 31 characters long).
- Click on *OK*.

Let's create a new worksheet that keeps track of the Garlic Club breakfast fund. Since this worksheet is not related to any existing worksheets, we'll create it in a new workbook:

1. Choose **File, New**. Select the General tab and double-click on the Workbook icon. As shown in Figure 2.9, the new work-book is named Book2, because it's the second new workbook you opened during this work session. (Book1 was opened automatically when you started Excel.)

**Figure 2.9**     **Opening a new, blank workbook**

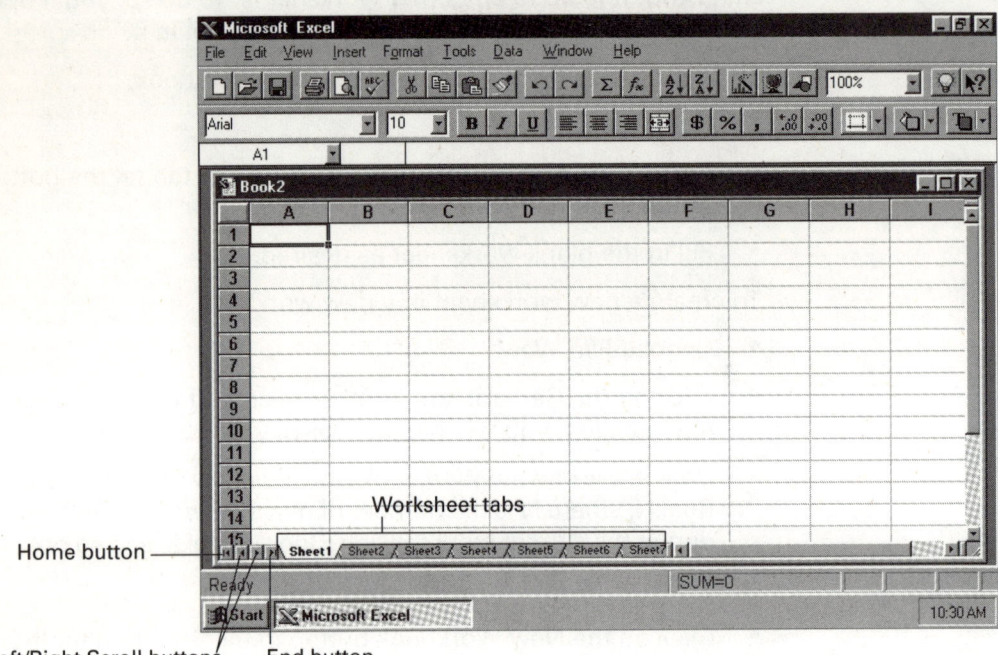

2. Observe the worksheet tabs at the bottom of the document window. Note that the active worksheet is named Sheet1.

3. Click repeatedly on the **worksheet-tab right scroll button** (as shown in Figure 2.9) to scroll through the 16 worksheet tabs. When you've reached Sheet16, click once on the **worksheet-tab home button** to scroll back to Sheet1.

4. Double-click on the **Sheet1 tab** to open the Rename Sheet dialog box. Type **Garlic Club** and then click on **OK**. Note that this name now appears on the worksheet tab, replacing the previous name (Sheet1).

5. Select cell **B2**.

6. Type **Vlad** and enter it (by clicking on the **Enter box** or pressing **Enter**).

7. In cell **B3**, type **Mina** and enter it.

PRACTICE YOUR SKILLS

1. Using Figure 2.10 as a guide, enter the data (numbers and text) in cells B2 through C5.

2. In cell C7, enter a formula to calculate the total breakfast money paid by all four Garlic Club members. (**Hint:** Use cell references, not fixed numbers!)

**Figure 2.10**  **The completed Garlic Club worksheet**

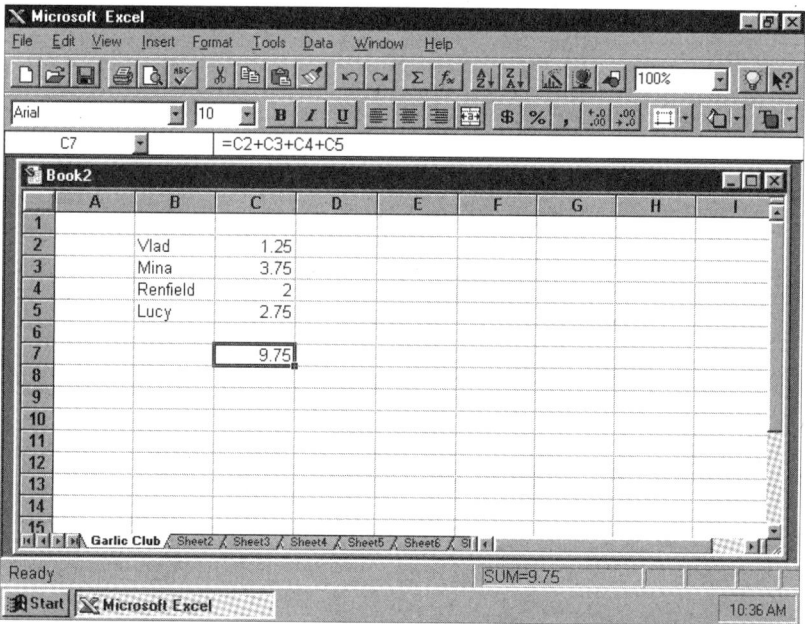

 SAVING THE NEW WORKSHEET

Now let's save our Garlic Club worksheet. To do this, we'll have to save the entire workbook in which this worksheet is contained:

1. Choose **File, Save As**. Remember, you use the Save As command to save a workbook for the first time. If you mistakenly choose the Save command, Excel recognizes the default file name (Book2) and displays the Save As dialog box anyway.

2.  Type **mygarlic** to specify a file name.

3.  Verify that the current folder is set to your work folder, Excel Work. Click on **Save** to copy the active workbook to a file named mygarlic.

## USING THE KEYBOARD TO CHOOSE MENU COMMANDS

Up to now, you've always used the mouse to choose Excel menu commands. You can also use the keyboard to choose commands, a very nice feature for those who prefer the keyboard to the mouse. To do this,

*   Press the *Alt key*.

*   Type the letter that is underlined in the desired menu-bar option (for example, to choose the File option, you would type *f* or *F*).

*   Type the letter that is underlined in the desired drop-down menu command (for example, to choose Save, you would type *s* or *S*).

Let's close mygarlic by using the keyboard to choose the File, Close command:

1.  Press **Alt**.

2.  Type **f** to choose the File menu option and open the drop-down File menu.

3.  Type **c** to choose the Close command.

## SUMMARY

In this chapter, you learned some basic procedures that you'll use throughout this book, as well as in your day-to-day work with Excel. You now know how to enter and revise text, numbers, and formulas in a worksheet cell; how to save and close a workbook file; how to use the mouse and the keyboard to choose menu commands; and how to create a new worksheet (and workbook).

Here's a quick reference guide to the Excel features introduced in this chapter:

| Desired Result | How to Do It |
| --- | --- |
| Select cell | Click on cell or use arrow keys |
| Enter text in cell | Select cell; type text; click on **Enter box** or press **Enter** |
| Enter formula in cell | Type =; type formula; click on **Enter box** or press **Enter** |
| Erase character while typing | Press **Backspace** |
| Repeat character while typing | Hold down key |
| Erase everything you've typed | Click on **Cancel box** or press **Esc** |
| Choose menu command using the mouse | Click on menu-bar option, and click on command in drop-down menu |
| Choose menu command using keyboard | Press **Alt**; press underlined letter of menu option; press underlined letter of command |
| Save workbook | Choose **File, Save As** for new or renamed/relocated workbooks; or choose **File, Save** to update current file |
| Activate AutoSave feature | Click on **Tools**; if AutoSave command is listed, click on it and skip to last step; if not, click on **Add-Ins**; check **AutoSave** check box; click on **OK**; choose **Tools, AutoSave**; change desired AutoSave options; click on **OK** |
| Close file | Choose **File, Close** or double-click on the document-window **Control-menu icon** |

| Desired Result | How to Do It |
|---|---|
| Create new worksheet | Choose **File, New,** select General tab and double-click on Workbase icon; fill in active worksheet; or open existing worksheet, select blank worksheet, and fill in |
| Rename worksheet | Double-click on worksheet tab; type name; click on **OK** |

The next chapter delves deeper into the practical applications of Excel. You'll examine worksheets for design and formula construction ideas, learn about "what if" analysis, and explore such topics as disk-file retrieval, new movement techniques, cell ranges, on-line help, and the further joys of automatic recalculation.

## IF YOU'RE STOPPING HERE

If you want to break off here, please exit Excel (for help, see "Exiting Excel" in Chapter 1). If you want to proceed directly to the next chapter, please do so now.

# CHAPTER 3:
# "WHAT IF" ANALYSIS

In the last chapter, you learned the mechanics of creating, modifying, and saving workbooks and worksheets. In this chapter, you'll improve your Excel skills while learning the basics of "what if" analysis, a powerful tool for data analysis and financial projection. Traditionally a difficult and time-consuming task, "what if" analysis is delightfully easy to perform in the Excel environment.

When you're done working through this chapter, you will know

- How to open a workbook file stored on disk

- How to perform "what if" analysis on worksheet data

- How to move around quickly within a worksheet

- How to construct more complex formulas

- How to work with cell ranges

- How to clear (erase) cells

- How to undo and redo actions

- How to use the online Help feature

## OPENING A WORKBOOK FILE

When you save a workbook, it is stored as a file on a disk. When you open a workbook file, a *copy* of that file is loaded from the disk into the memory of your computer (RAM). The original file remains intact on disk.

To open a workbook file,

- Choose *File, Open* to open the Open dialog box.

- If necessary, change the current folder (in the Look In text box) to the folder containing the file you wish to open.

- Click once on the desired file (in the File Name list box) to select it, then click on OK; or double-click on the file.

If you are not already running Excel, please start it now; for help, see Chapter 1. If there is a workbook on your screen (other than the standard startup workbook, Book1), please close it (use File, Close).

Let's open a workbook file stored in your Excel Work folder:

1. Choose **File, Open** to display the Open dialog box.

2. Observe the current folder, displayed in the Look In text box at the top of the dialog box. You must change this to your work folder, Excel Work, because that's where the desired workbook file is stored. Follow these steps to do so. (**Note:** This is the same procedure you used in Chapter 2 to change

to the Excel Work folder when you used the File, Save As command to save a workbook file.)

- The folder is located on the hard drive, so you need to display its contents. To display the contents of the C drive, click on the **Up One Level** button twice.

- Locate the Excel Work folder and double-click on it.

- The Excel Work folder should be displayed in the Look In text box and its contents are displayed in the window, as shown in Figure 3.1. If not, repeat the above two steps.

**Figure 3.1**     **An example of the Open dialog box, set to the Excel Work folder**

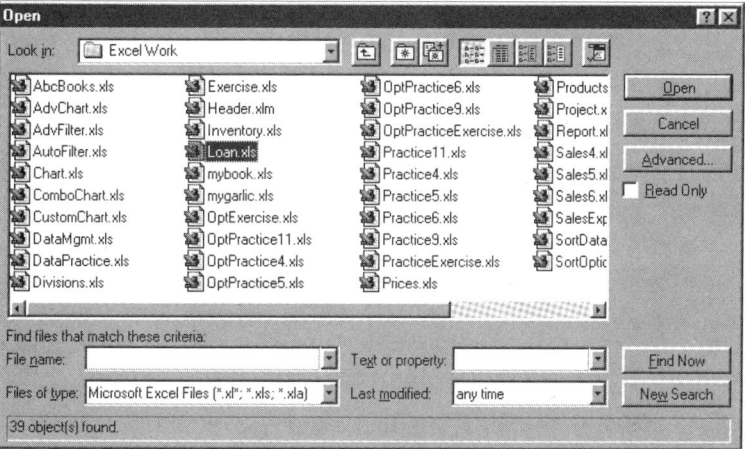

3. Observe the Files of Type text box. The text "Microsoft Excel Files" causes all the Excel files in the current folder (Excel Work) to be listed.

4. In the list of files, locate *loan*.

5. Double-click on **Loan** to open this workbook file. (You could also have opened Loan by clicking on it once to select it, then clicking on **Open**. However, most users find double-clicking easier.)

Before proceeding, let's maximize both the application and document windows:

1. If your application window is not already maximized—that is, if it does not fill the entire screen—click on its **Maximize/Restore button** to maximize the window.

2. If your document window is not already maximized—that is, if there is a window entitled *Loan* beneath the formula bar—click on its **Maximize/Restore button** to maximize the window.

3. Observe your screen; it should match the screen shown in Figure 3.2. Note that when the document window is maximized, its title bar disappears, and the title of the active workbook is displayed in the application-window title bar (*Microsoft Excel - Loan*).

4. Note that both the application- and document-windows contain a Maximize/Restore button. Clicking on these buttons would restore (shrink) the windows to their nonmaximized sizes. Please do not do this now.

## "WHAT IF" ANALYSIS

As you saw in Chapter 2, whenever you add or modify a numeric value in a worksheet, Excel immediately recalculates every formula in the worksheet that references this value. You can use Excel's automatic recalculation feature to perform *"what if" analysis*, in which you modify numeric values and observe the overall impact on the worksheet. Here are two typical "what if" analysis situations:

• What if I increased my retail markup rate by 10, 20, 35, or 50 percent? How would each of these increases affect my projected yearly profit?

• What if I increased or decreased the down payment on my 30-year fixed mortgage? How would these changes affect my monthly payments?

**Figure 3.2**    **Maximizing the application and document windows**

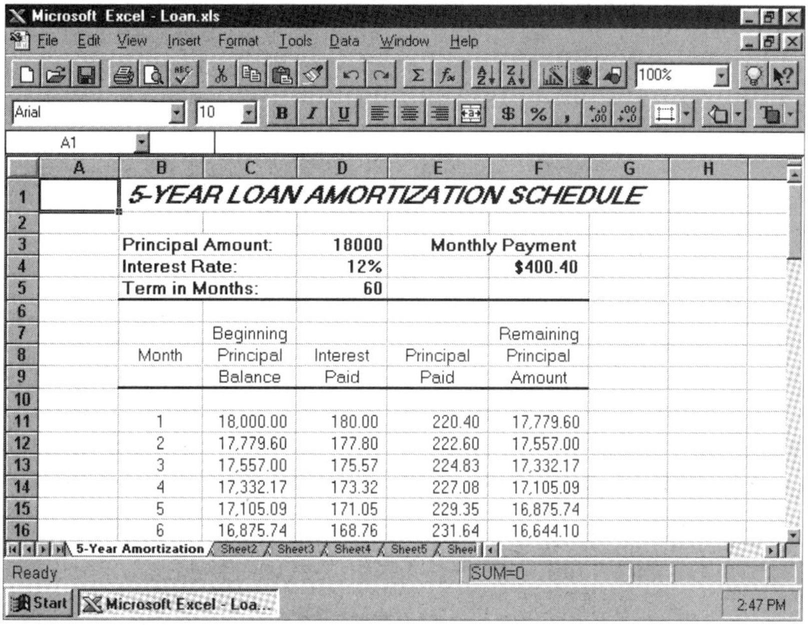

When it comes to such "what if" analysis, Excel is clearly superior to paper spreadsheets, in which each new numeric value (that is, each new "what if") requires you to perform time-consuming manual recalculation and data reentry.

Let's perform some simple "what if" analyses on our 5-Year Amortization worksheet:

1. Observe the active worksheet. It shows a five-year loan-amortization schedule that calculates the monthly payment for a given principal, interest rate, and term, as well as the breakdown into interest and principal payments.

2. Select cell **D3**. The current loan (principal) amount in cell D3 is $18,000 (displayed as 18000). Note the monthly payment of $400.40 in cell F4.

3. In cell D3, type **30000** (do not type $ or ,). Enter this value to change the loan amount to $30,000.

4. Observe the results. Note that the monthly payment has grown from $400.40 to $667.33. Many cells in this worksheet contain formulas that depend upon the principal amount in

cell D3. When you change this value, the results of all the dependent formulas change accordingly.

**5.** In cell D4, change the value to 9 percent by entering **9** (you do not need to type the % sign) to change the interest rate for the loan.

**6.** Observe the results. The new interest rate affects the monthly payment amount ($622.75), along with any other formulas that reference cell D4.

## MOVING AROUND A WORKSHEET

Given the potential size of an Excel worksheet (over four million cells), you need to know how to move quickly and easily from cell to cell. Excel offers several convenient movement techniques, listed below in two groups: the first for those who prefer to use the mouse, and the second for those who prefer the keyboard.

### USING THE MOUSE TO MOVE AROUND

All the mouse techniques presented in Table 3.1 and Figure 3.3—with the exception of the final table entry (Formula, Go To)—change the area of the worksheet displayed on screen but do not select a new cell. To select a new cell, click on it.

**Table 3.1**      **Mouse-Scrolling Terminology**

| Technique | Action |
| --- | --- |
| Click on the up or down scroll arrow | Moves the screen up or down one row per click |
| Click on the left or right scroll arrow | Moves the screen left or right one column per click |
| Click and hold on the up or down scroll arrow | Continuously moves the screen up or down one row |
| Click and hold on the left or right scroll arrow | Continuously moves the screen left or right one column |

**Table 3.1**     **Mouse-Scrolling Terminology (Continued)**

| | |
|---|---|
| Click within the vertical scroll bar between the vertical scroll box and the up or down scroll arrow | Moves up or down one screen per click |
| Click within the horizontal scroll bar between the horizontal scroll box and the right or left scroll arrow | Moves right or left one screen per click |
| Drag the scroll boxes | Moves the screen a long distance, vertically or horizontally, through the active worksheet area |
| Hold the Shift key and drag the scroll box to either end of the scroll bars | Moves rapidly, vertically or horizontally, to the end or beginning of the worksheet |
| Choose Edit, Go To | Moves to and selects any cell in the worksheet |

Let's practice using these mousing techniques to scroll through the worksheet:

1. Observe your active cell and make a mental note of its address.

2. Click on the **down scroll arrow** several times to move the worksheet down one row per click.

3. Drag the **vertical scroll box** halfway down the scroll bar (press and hold the left mouse button as you move the mouse) to move rapidly to the middle of the worksheet. As you drag the scroll box, the row number that will be at the top of the screen is displayed next to the scroll bar (see Figure 3.3).

4. Drag the **vertical scroll box** back to the top of the scroll bar to move rapidly to the top of the worksheet.

5. Click several times within the **vertical scroll bar** below the scroll box to move down one screen per click.

6. Click several times within the **vertical scroll bar** above the scroll box to move up one screen per click.

**Figure 3.3**         **Mouse-scrolling terminology**

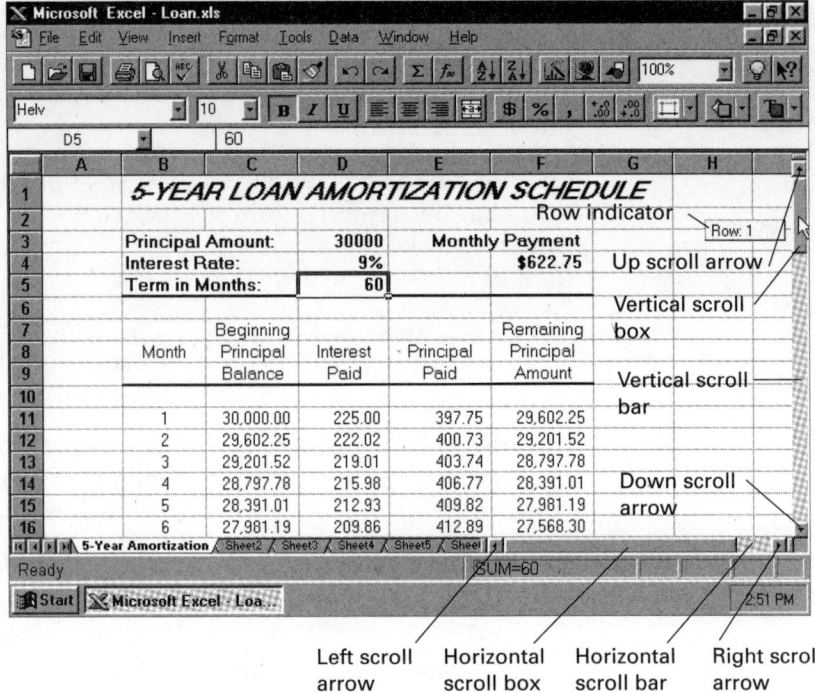

Left scroll      Horizontal      Horizontal      Right scroll
arrow            scroll box      scroll bar      arrow

7. Drag the **vertical scroll box** down as far as it will go to move rapidly to the bottom of the active worksheet area. Short distances on the scroll bar represent long distances in the worksheet.

8. Drag the **vertical scroll box** to the top of the scroll bar to return to the top of the active worksheet area.

9. Note that your active cell did not change throughout this entire activity. As mentioned, these mousing movement techniques change the worksheet display, not the active cell.

## USING THE KEYBOARD TO MOVE AROUND

All the keyboard techniques presented in Table 3.2 change the worksheet display *and* select a new cell.

**Table 3.2**      **Keyboard Movement Techniques**

| Technique | Action |
|---|---|
| Press the left, right, up, or down arrow key | Moves one cell to the left, right, up, or down |
| Press Home | Moves to the first column (A) of the current row |
| Press Ctrl+Home | Moves to cell A1 |
| Press Ctrl+End | Moves to the intersection of the last active row and the last active column of the worksheet |
| Press the Page Up key | Moves up one screen |
| Press the Page Down key | Moves down one screen |
| Press F5 (Go To key ) | Moves to any cell address in the worksheet |

Now let's practice using the keyboard to navigate through the Loan worksheet:

1. Press **Ctrl+End** (press and hold down the **Ctrl key**, press the **End key**, then release both keys) to move to cell F72 (as shown in the cell-reference area of the formula bar), the intersection of the last active row and column of the worksheet.

2. Press **Ctrl+Home** to move to the *home cell*, A1.

3. Choose **Edit, Go To** to open the Go To dialog box.

4. Type **d3** and click on **OK** to move to cell D3.

5. Press **F5** and type **iv16384**. Take a moment to observe the Go To dialog box. Note that the OK button is outlined (its border is dark). Whenever a dialog box contains an outlined button, you can choose this button either by clicking on it or by simply pressing Enter.

6. Press **Enter** to choose the OK button and move to the last available cell of the worksheet, the intersection of the last available column (IV) and row (16384), as shown in Figure 3.4.

**Figure 3.4**     **Cell IV16384: The end of the world**

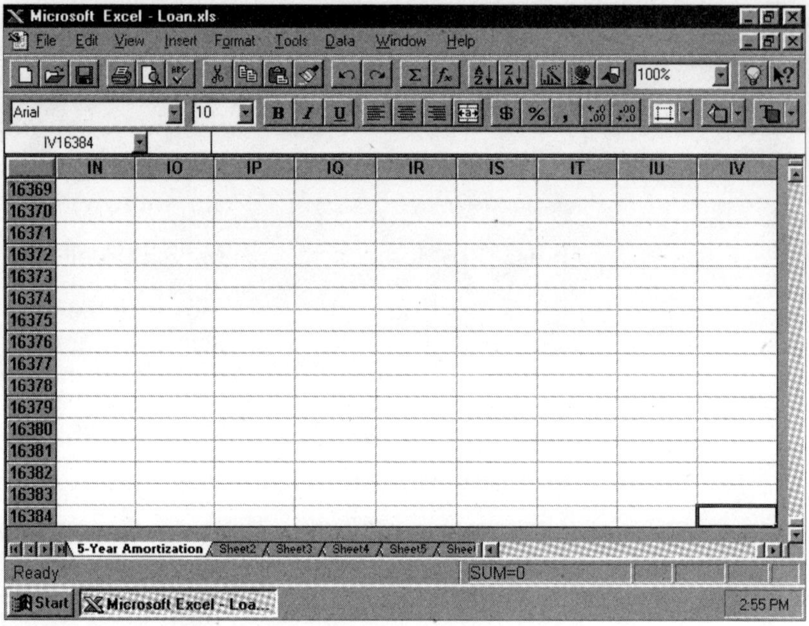

7. Press the **down arrow key**, and then press the **right arrow key**. Note that you cannot move past cell IV16384; it's the end of the world.

8. Select cell **A1** (press **Ctrl+Home**).

## PRACTICE YOUR SKILLS

Practice using both the mouse and the keyboard to navigate through the worksheet until you feel relatively comfortable getting around. Are you a mouser or a keyboardist (or perhaps a mouser/keyboardist)?

## CLOSING A MODIFIED, UNSAVED WORKBOOK

As mentioned in "Closing a Workbook" in Chapter 2, if you modify a workbook and then attempt to close it without having saved the modified version, Excel interrupts the file-closing procedure and asks you whether you wish to save your changes. This safe-guard prevents you from accidentally losing the changes you made to the workbook. If you want to save your changes, click on Yes; if you want to close the workbook without saving the changes, click on No.

**Note:** This same safeguard appears when you attempt to exit Excel without having saved an open, modified workbook file.

Let's observe this safeguard feature in action:

1.  Press **Alt+F** to open the menu-bar File option, and then type **C** to choose the Close command. A dialog box appears with the prompt

    ```
    Save changes in 'LOAN'?
    ```

2.  Observe the option buttons at the bottom of this dialog box (Yes, No, and Cancel). Note that the *N* is underlined in the No button. You can choose a dialog-box button (like a menu command) by typing its underlined letter.

3.  Type **N** to choose No. Excel closes the workbook file without saving the changes you made to its principal amount and in-terest rate. Had you wanted to save these changes, you could have typed *y* (for Yes) and Excel would have updated (saved) the file before closing it.

## EXAMINING FORMULAS: ORDER OF OPERATIONS

The following formula involves more than one mathematical operation:

```
=B1+B2*B4-B5/B8
```

When creating or examining such a formula, you must know Excel's *order of operations*. Operations are not simply performed left to right through the length of a formula. Certain operations are performed before others. Table 3.3 lists Excel's order of opera-tions (from first to last).

**Table 3.3**     **Excel's Order of Operations**

| Operation | Description |
|---|---|
| Parentheses | Calculations enclosed in parentheses are performed first. Calculations in *nested* parentheses (parentheses within parentheses) are performed in order of nesting, deepest first. For example, in the formula =(B1*(B2+B4)), B2 and B4 are added first (deepest nesting), then this sum is multiplied by B1. |
| Exponents | Calculations involving exponential numbers are performed second. |
| Multiplication and Division | These operations are performed third. Because they are considered equal in importance, they are performed in the order in which they appear (from left to right). |
| Addition and Subtraction | These operations are performed last. They also are performed in the order in which they appear (from left to right). |

Here's a mnemonic to help you remember the order of operations. **P**lease **E**xcuse **M**y **D**ear **A**unt **S**ally: **P**arentheses, **E**xponents, **M**ultiplication, **D**ivision, **A**ddition, **S**ubtraction (**PEMDAS**).

Let's take a look at a formula involving several operations:

    =B1*C5/100-(D6+J8)*J9

The order of calculation for this formula is

- Add D6 and J8, and hold the result.

- Multiply B1 by C5, and hold the result.

- Divide the product of step 2 by 100.

- Multiply J9 by the sum of step 1.

- Subtract the product of step 4 from the quotient (division result) of step 3.

## PRACTICE YOUR SKILLS

List the order of calculation for the following formula:

=(B1*C5)/((100-D6)+(J8*J9))

**Hint:** Note the use of nested parentheses to the right of the division sign (/). Remember that calculations within the deepest nested parentheses are performed first.

## EXAMINING SOME TYPICAL FORMULAS

Now let's examine some typical worksheet formulas:

1.  Open the workbook file **Prices**. (Choose **File, Open**; verify that Excel Work is the current folder and double-click on **Prices**.) This worksheet is used by International Express, Ltd., to determine if their retail selling prices will yield the desired profit margin.

2.  If the document window is not maximized, maximize it now (by clicking on its **Maximize/Restore button**). Your screen should match that shown in Figure 3.5.

3.  Select cell **C6**. This cell contains the cost of the bonnets.

4.  Select cell **D6**. This cell contains the number of bonnets currently in inventory.

5.  Select cell **E6**. This cell contains a formula that calculates the total item cost by multiplying the bonnet cost in cell C6 by the number of bonnets on hand in cell D6. To see this formula, observe the formula bar.

6.  Select cell **F6**. This cell contains the retail selling price to be charged for each bonnet.

7.  Select cell **G6**. This cell contains a formula that calculates the net profit on bonnets by multiplying the number of bonnets on hand in cell D6 by their selling price in cell F6, and then subtracting the total bonnet cost in cell E6.

**Figure 3.5**     **The Prices workbook**

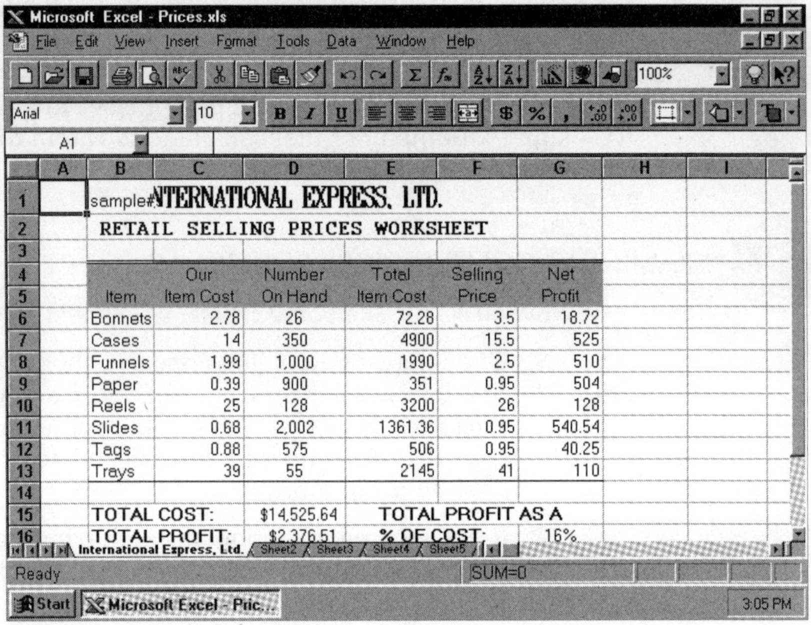

| | A | B | C | D | E | F | G | H | I |
|---|---|---|---|---|---|---|---|---|---|
| 1 | | sample# | INTERNATIONAL EXPRESS, LTD. | | | | | | |
| 2 | | RETAIL SELLING PRICES WORKSHEET | | | | | | | |
| 3 | | | | | | | | | |
| 4 | | | Our | Number | Total | Selling | Net | | |
| 5 | | Item | Item Cost | On Hand | Item Cost | Price | Profit | | |
| 6 | | Bonnets | 2.78 | 26 | 72.28 | 3.5 | 18.72 | | |
| 7 | | Cases | 14 | 350 | 4900 | 15.5 | 525 | | |
| 8 | | Funnels | 1.99 | 1,000 | 1990 | 2.5 | 510 | | |
| 9 | | Paper | 0.39 | 900 | 351 | 0.95 | 504 | | |
| 10 | | Reels | 25 | 128 | 3200 | 26 | 128 | | |
| 11 | | Slides | 0.68 | 2,002 | 1361.36 | 0.95 | 540.54 | | |
| 12 | | Tags | 0.88 | 575 | 506 | 0.95 | 40.25 | | |
| 13 | | Trays | 39 | 55 | 2145 | 41 | 110 | | |
| 14 | | | | | | | | | |
| 15 | | TOTAL COST: | | $14,525.64 | TOTAL PROFIT AS A | | | | |
| 16 | | TOTAL PROFIT: | | $2,376.51 | % OF COST: | | 16% | | |

# WORKING WITH CELL RANGES

In many situations, you'll find it far more convenient to work with a group of cells than with a single cell. For example, if you wanted to clear (erase) the contents of 20 cells, you'd find it much easier to select all these cells at once and clear them as a group (by issuing one Clear command) than to clear each cell one at a time (by issuing 20 Clear commands).

A group of two or more contiguous (adjacent) cells (for example, cells A1, A2, B1, and B2) is called a *cell range* or simply a *range*. Excel uses the format *UL:LR* to define a range, where *UL* stands for the upper-left corner cell and *LR* stands for the lower-right corner cell. For example, the range comprising cells A1, A2, B1, and B2 is defined as A1:B2.

Let's examine some formulas that use ranges:

1. Select cell **D15**. This cell contains a special formula called a *function,* which calculates the total cost of all the retail items by summing the values in the range E6 through E13 (E6:E13). You'll learn more about functions in Chapter 4.

2. Select cell **D16**. This cell contains a function that calculates the total net profit of all the items by summing the values in the range G6 through G13 (G6:G13).

3. Select cell **G16**. This cell contains a simple formula that calculates the total profit (cell D16) as a percentage of the total cost (cell D15).

Now suppose you wanted to explore the relationship between retail selling price and profit for International Express, Ltd. Follow these steps to perform a "what if" analysis:

1. Note that the total profit (cell D16) is $2,376.51, and the total profit as a percent of cost (cell G16) is 16 percent.

2. In cell F6, enter **4.95** to change the retail price of bonnets from $3.50 to $4.95. The formulas in cells D16 and G16 automatically recalculate: cell D16 is now $2,414.21 and cell G16 is 17%.

 ## SELECTING A RANGE OF CELLS

Use either of these methods to select a range of cells:

- Drag over the desired cells with the mouse.

- Or, click on one of the range's corner cells, press and hold the Shift key, and then click on the range's diagonally opposite corner cell.

### PRACTICE YOUR SKILLS

1. Use the dragging method to select the range **A1:A7**. You can drag down or up to select the range.
   (**Hint:** Click on any cell to deselect the range between these two steps.)

2. Use the click-Shift-click method to select the range **A1:D7**. You can click on any of the corner cells, but you must Shift-click on the corner cell that is diagonally opposite.

## CLEARING CELLS

In Excel, *clearing* a cell is very different from *deleting* a cell. Clearing a cell erases its contents (data and formulas), but leaves the cell in the worksheet. Deleting a cell erases its contents and re-moves the cell from the worksheet, thus changing the work-sheet's overall structure. Here, you'll learn how to clear cells; in Chapter 5, you'll learn how to delete them.

To clear the contents (data and formulas) of one or more cells,

- Select the cell or range of cells.

- Choose *Edit, Clear, Contents* or press the *Del* key.

Let's clear a single cell in the active workbook. (**Note:** If you intend to use the Del key on your numeric keypad to do this—rather than the Del key on the cursor keypad to the left of the numeric key-pad—make sure that Num Lock is off. To toggle Num Lock on/off, press the Num Lock key.)

1. Select cell **B1**. Note that the contents of this cell (*sample#s*) obscure the first few letters of the heading *INTERNATIONAL EXPRESS, LTD.*

2. Press the **Del key** to erase cell B1's contents. Note that the en-tire heading is now visible. (You can see this more clearly by selecting cell A2.)

Now let's clear a range of cells:

1. Drag to select cells **F6:F13**.

2. Choose **Edit, Clear, Contents** to clear the contents of your se-lected cells. As the numbers are cleared, the formulas that refer to these cells are automatically recalculated. Note the resulting negative values (losses) in the Net Profit column, as shown in Figure 3.6.

3. Please don't touch your keyboard or mouse until we ask you to do so in the next activity. You'll see why in a moment.

## UNDOING AND REDOING ACTIONS

If you make a mistake when entering or editing data, clicking on a button or tool, pressing a key, or choosing a menu command, you can use the Undo feature to *undo* (reverse) your last action. For example, if you cleared a cell's formula, then realized you'd made a mistake and desperately needed that formula back, you could choose *Edit, Undo* to undo your Clear command, thus restoring the cell's original contents.

**Figure 3.6**     **Prices, after clearing F6:F13**

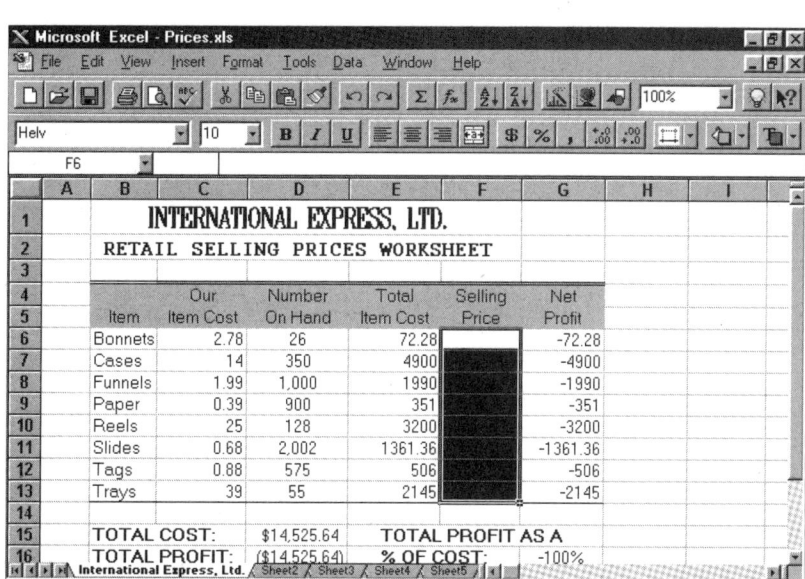

You can undo any entry or edit you make to a cell (such as entering a new value to replace the old one) or any command you choose from the Edit menu (such as Edit, Clear). You may or may not be able to undo other actions, however; for example, once you've saved a file, you cannot "unsave" it. If you attempt to choose Edit, Undo to undo a "non-undoable" action, Excel displays the message *Can't Undo*.

Use any of these three methods to undo your last action:

• Choose *Edit, Undo*.

• Click on the *Undo tool* in the Standard toolbar.

• Press *Ctrl+Z*.

Excel also provides a Redo feature you can use to *redo* (re-perform) an action that you just "undid." Redo, in effect, "undoes" an Undo command. Staying with the earlier example, if you cleared a cell, then changed your mind and used Undo to restore the cell's contents, then changed your mind *again* and decided to (once and for all!) get rid of that darn cell's contents, you could choose *Edit, Redo* to re-perform the Clear command that you just undid, thus clearing the cell.

Use any of these three methods to redo your last Undo action:

- Choose *Edit, Redo.*

- Click on the *Redo tool* in the Standard toolbar.

- Press *Ctrl+Z.*

**Important Note:** You can only undo/redo the *last* Excel action that you performed. For this reason, if you decide to undo/redo, be sure to do it immediately, before you perform any other action!

Let's undo your last action, the clearing of cells F6:F13. Now you understand why we asked you not to touch your keyboard or mouse at the end of the previous activity—we wanted to make sure that the last action you performed was to clear cells F6:F13, so that you could successfully undo this action now.

1. Click on **Edit** to open the drop-down Edit menu. Observe the uppermost command in this menu, Undo Clear. Undo is telling you which action you can undo (the Clear command). Had Excel been unable to undo your most recent action, the command would have read *Can't Undo.*

2. Click on **Undo Clear** to undo the Clear command. The cleared data is restored to cells F6:F13.

3. Choose **Edit, Redo [u] Clear** to re-perform the Clear command you just used Undo to reverse. The selected cells are cleared once again. The underlined *[u]* in this command indicates that you must type a *u*—after pressing Alt+E to open the Edit menu—to choose the command from the keyboard.

4. Click on the **Undo tool** to repeat the Undo Clear command you issued in step 3 (in other words, to undo your Redo command). The cell contents reappear.

PRACTICE YOUR SKILLS

1. Select and clear the range **D6:G13**.

2. Undo the above Clear command. (Use the menu or toolbar.)

3. Use **File, Save As** to save the modified workbook as **myprices**.

4. Close the workbook.

## GETTING HELP

Now that we've introduced several new concepts to you, it might be a good idea to tell you how to use the help system. Excel provides an extensive online help system that you can use any time you need to get help with Excel. To access Help, you can choose *Help, Microsoft Excel Help Topics* to display the Help Topics window. This window contains four tabs: Contents, Index, Find, and Answer Wizard, as shown in Figure 3.7. You will find each of the tabs fairly self-explanatory. Here's a quick overview of each tab.

**Figure 3.7**     **The Help Topics window**

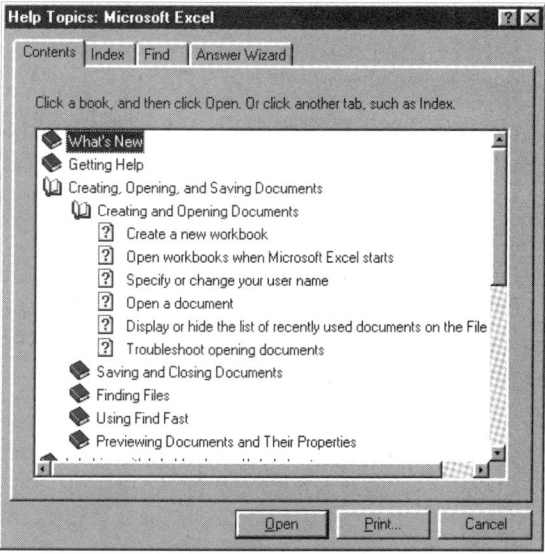

- The *Contents* tab resembles a table of contents. Each main help topic has a book icon to the left of the topic. You can double-click on the book icon to view the contents of each topic, as shown in Figure 3.7. Select a topic and click on Display (or double-click on the topic) to display the Help screen.

- The *Index* tab enables you to electronically search through the Help index. Follow the steps by first entering the word or first letter. Then, you can select the desired index entry and click on Display.

- The *Find* tab enables you to search for topics by word. While this is similar to the Index tab, you are not limited to the index entries. The Find tab creates a listing of all words in the Excel help file. Follow the steps to enter a word, narrow the search, and select a topic. If desired, you can access additional options by clicking on the Options button. When the desired topic is found, click on Display to view the Help screen.

- The *Answer Wizard* tab enables you to search for information by entering a request, or phrase, such as *clearing a cell*. Then from the resulting list of topics, you can select one and click on Display.

To access help on Excel commands and dialog box options as questions arise, you can use any of these methods:

- Press *F1* to open a Help window containing information relevant to your current working situation. This is called *context-sensitive* help.

- Or, click on the *Help tool* in the Standard toolbar, and then click on a command, button, tool, or other window element to open a Help window containing information on whatever you selected.

- Or, click on the question mark button in the dialog box title bar and click on an item to display a ScreenTip. *ScreenTips* are displayed as pop-up boxes which contain definitions for the dialog box components and options.

- Or, click on the *Help button* in a dialog box to open a Help window containing information on the options in that dialog box.

Once you've opened a Help window, its contents and appearance will vary depending on the selected topic. You can use any of the following techniques in the Help window.

- Point to the items in the Help screen. When the mouse pointer changes to a hand, click on the word or phrase to display yet another Help screen.

- To display the Help screen for any solid-underlined topic, click on that topic.

- To display the *pop-up definition* of any dotted-underlined term, click on that term. To remove the definition, click again.

- To display the main Help screen, click on the *Help Topics button*.

- To redisplay Help screens you viewed during the current Help session, click on the *Back button*.

- To minimize Help, click on the *Minimize button* in the Help window title bar.

- To exit Help and return to your Excel worksheet exactly where you left off, click on the Help window Control-menu icon and choose Close. You can also double-click on the Help window Control-menu icon or click on the Close button in the Help window title bar.

Don't be afraid to explore! You might want to take a moment to browse through the Help system at this time. If not, you can access Help at any time during an Excel session.

## SUMMARY

In this chapter, you learned the basics of "what if" analysis, a powerful projection and analysis tool. You also learned how to open a workbook file stored on disk, how to move quickly within a worksheet, how to use cell ranges in formulas, how to clear cells, how to undo and redo actions, and how to get help.

Here's a quick reference guide to the Excel features introduced in this chapter:

| Desired Result | How to Do It |
| --- | --- |
| Open workbook file | Choose **File, Open**; specify the necessary information; click on **OK** |
| Maximize/restore window | Click on its **Maximize/Restore button** |
| Move screen up or down | Click on **up** or **down scroll arrow** or **vertical scroll bar**, or drag **vertical scroll box**, or press **Page Up** or **Page Down key** |
| Move screen left or right | Click on **left** or **right scroll arrow** or **horizontal scroll bar**, or drag **horizontal scroll box** |
| Select higher or lower cell | Press **up** or **down arrow key** |
| Select left or right cell | Press **left** or **right arrow key** |
| Move to specific cell | Choose **Edit, Go To** or press **F5**; type cell address; press **Enter** |
| Move to home cell (A1) | Press **Ctrl+Home** |
| Move to last active cell | Press **Ctrl+End** |
| Move to first column of current row | Press **Home** |
| Select range | Drag over range; or click on corner cell, press and hold **Shift**, click on diagonally opposite corner cell (click-Shift-click) |
| Clear cell(s) | Select cell(s) and choose **Edit, Clear, Contents** or press **Del** |
| Undo or redo last action | Choose **Edit, Undo** or **Edit, Redo**; or click on **Undo tool** or **Redo tool**; or press **Ctrl+Z** |

| Desired Result | How to Do It |
|---|---|
| Access help | Choose **Help, Microsoft Excel Help Topics**; select either the Contents, Index, Find, or Answer Wizard tab; select the desired help topic; click on **Display** |
| Get context-sensitive help | Press **F1**; or click on **Help tool** and click on desired command, button, tool, or window element; or click on **question mark button** and click on desired dialog box element; or click on **Help button** in a dialog box |

In the next chapter, we'll explore the basics of creating a larger, more involved worksheet. You'll learn how to enter data into a range of cells, how to use functions in your formulas, how to copy cell contents, and how to choose commands from shortcut menus.

## IF YOU'RE STOPPING HERE

If you want to break off here, please exit Excel. If you want to proceed directly to the next chapter, please do so now.

# CHAPTER 4:
# BASIC WORKSHEET
# DEVELOPMENT

**Entering Data into a Range of Cells**

**Using Functions in Your Formulas**

**Copying Cell Contents**

In Chapters 1 through 3, you learned how to create and modify simple worksheets and how to perform elementary "what if" analysis on your numeric data. In this chapter, you'll build on those skills by learning how to develop a larger, more sophisticated worksheet containing powerful formulas and real-world applications.

When you're done working through this chapter, you will know

- How to enter data into a range of cells

- How to use functions in your formulas

- How to copy cell contents from one area of the worksheet to another

- How to choose commands from shortcut menus

## ENTERING DATA INTO A RANGE OF CELLS

In your day-to-day work with Excel, you'll often need to enter data into a range of worksheet cells, rather than just a single cell. For example, you might need to enter a long list of names or several columns of numbers. Doing this cell by cell—by selecting a cell, entering its data, using the mouse or arrow keys to select the next cell, entering its data, and so on for all the cells in your range—is tedious and time-consuming. Fortunately, Excel provides a short-cut to make multiple-cell data entry much more convenient.

To enter data into a range of cells,

- Select the range of cells.

- Enter data into the active cell.

- To activate the next cell down in the range, press Enter or click on the Enter box in the formula bar. If the active cell is at the bottom of a multicolumn range, pressing Enter activates the top cell of the next column to the right.

- To activate the next cell to the right in the range, press Tab. If the active cell is at the right end of a multirow range, pressing Tab activates the leftmost cell of the next row down.

- If the active cell is in the lower-right corner of the range, pressing Enter or Tab activates the cell in the upper-left corner.

- To move backward within the range, hold down the Shift key, then press Enter (to move up) or Tab (to move to the left).

**Note:** Do not use the arrow keys or mouse to select a cell, as this will deselect the entire range.

If you are not running Excel, please start it now. If there is a workbook on your screen (other than the startup workbook, Book1), please close it.

Let's open a workbook file and then practice entering data into a range of cells. But first, let's take a minute to explore a handy new Excel feature:

1. Point to—but don't click on—the leftmost tool in the Standard (upper) toolbar.

2. Observe the mouse pointer. After a moment, it displays *New Workbook*. This is the name of the tool to which you're pointing. You use the New Workbook tool to open a new workbook.

3. Now point to the next tool to the right. Excel displays the word *Open*. You use the Open tool to open a workbook file stored on disk.

4. Spend some time pointing to various Standard and Formatting toolbar tools and reading their names. You can use this *ToolTips* feature to help remember what the various tools do.

Now let's go ahead and open Sales4, a workbook file stored in your Excel Work folder:

1. Click on the **Open tool** to display open the Open dialog box. Clicking on the Open tool is equivalent to choosing File, Open from the menu.

2. Open the file **Sales4** from your Excel Work folder. (Change the current folder to Excel Work, and double-click on **Sales4**.) This simple worksheet lists two salespeople and their quarterly sales figures. You will add two new salespeople to the list.

3. If the application window is not already maximized, maximize it (by clicking on its **Maximize/Restore button**).

4. If the document window is not already maximized, maximize it. Both the application and document windows should now be maximized.

5. Press **Ctrl+F10** (press and hold **Ctrl**, press **F10**, and then release both) to restore the document window to its nonmaximized

size, as shown in Figure 4.1. Ctrl+F10 is the *keyboard shortcut* for clicking on the document window's Maximize/Restore button. You'll learn several keyboard shortcuts in this book. For a complete list, see Appendix B, "Keystroke Reference."

6. Press **Ctrl+F10** again to maximize the document window.

**Figure 4.1**      **Sales4 with restored document window**

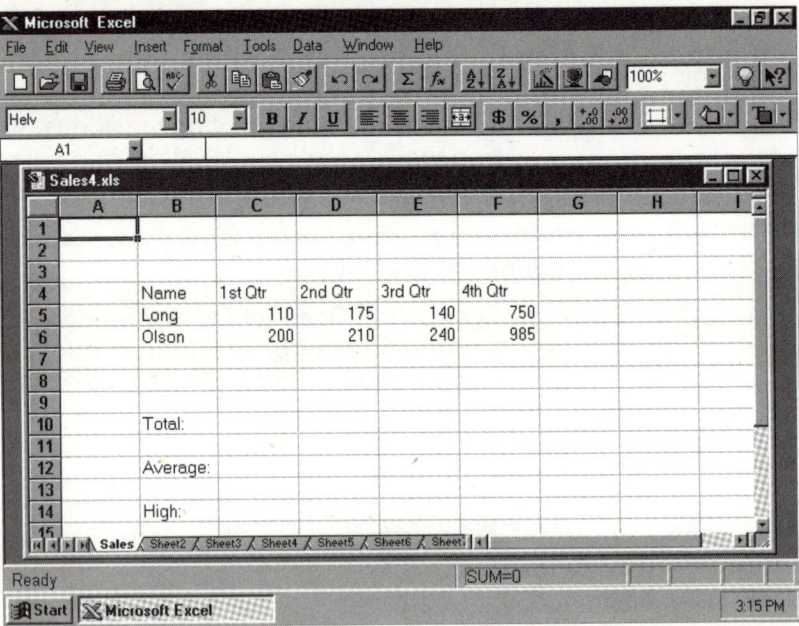

Now let's select a range and practice moving around within it:

1. Select cell **B7**.

2. Press and hold the **Shift key**, click on cell **F8**, then release Shift to select the range B7:F8. As you learned in Chapter 3, the click-Shift-click method selects the range bound by the two cells you click on (in this case, B7 and F8).

3. Press **Enter** to activate cell B8, the next cell down in the range. Press **Enter** again to activate cell C7. As mentioned, if the active cell is at the bottom of a multicolumn range (B8), pressing Enter activates the top cell of the next column (C7).

**4.** Press **Enter** seven more times to activate cell F8. Press **Enter** again to activate cell B7. If the active cell is in the lower-right corner of the range (F8), pressing Enter or Tab activates the cell in the upper-left corner (B7).

**5.** Press **Tab** to activate cell C7, the next cell to the right in the range. Press **Tab** four more times to activate cell B8. If the active cell is at the right end of a multirow range (F7), pressing Tab activates the leftmost cell of the next row (B8).

**6.** Press **Tab** five more times to return to cell B7. Now press and hold **Shift**, press **Tab** ten times, then release **Shift** to complete the circuit backwards and land back on cell B7. Holding down Shift while pressing Enter or Tab activates cells in reverse.

**7.** Press the **right arrow key** to activate cell C7. Oops! You've deselected the entire range. Do not use the arrow keys to activate cells in a range, as this deselects the range.

### PRACTICE YOUR SKILLS

**1.** Reselect the range **B7:F8**. (**Hint:** Drag or click-Shift-click.)

**2.** Use the cell-activation techniques you just learned to enter the following new data in the selected range:

|   | B | C | D | E | F |
|---|---|---|---|---|---|
| 7 | **Stark** | **300** | **180** | **295** | **1100** |
| 8 | **Unger** | **220** | **195** | **185** | **1025** |

**3.** Press **Ctrl+Home** to select cell A1. Your screen should match that shown in Figure 4.2.

## USING FUNCTIONS IN YOUR FORMULAS

*Functions* are calculation tools that help you create powerful formulas. The SUM function, for example, sums the numeric values in a specified range of cells; the AVERAGE function averages the values in a cell range; and so on. Excel provides a large selection of functions, organized into several categories (financial, statistical, logical, text, database, and so on). You can use a function by itself within a formula or in combination with other functions.

**Figure 4.2**  **Sales4, after initial data entry**

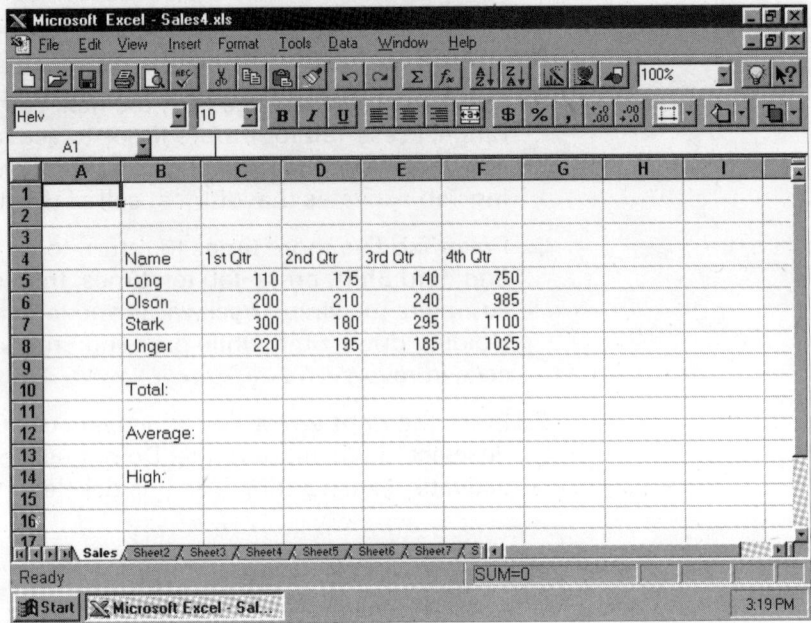

## FUNCTION STRUCTURE

Functions generally have two components:

- The function *name* or an abbreviation of it
- The *argument*, which consists of required data enclosed in parentheses

Here are some examples of typical Excel functions:

| Function | Description |
| --- | --- |
| SUM(A4:A10) | SUM is the function name; the range A4:A10 is the argument. This function adds all values in cells A4 through A10. |
| AVERAGE(A4:A10) | AVERAGE is the function name; the range A4:A10 is the argument. This function averages all values in cells A4 through A10. |

| Function | Description |
|----------|-------------|
| MAX(A4:A10) | MAX is the function name; the range A4:A10 is the argument. This function finds the largest value in cells A4 through A10. |

## ENTERING FUNCTIONS MANUALLY

You enter a function into a cell just as you would enter a formula,

- Select the cell.
- Type = and then type the function.
- Press *Enter* or click on the Enter box.

As with a formula, entering a function in a cell causes the numeric result of that function to be displayed. This result is automatically recalculated when the contents of a cell referenced in the function change.

Let's enter some functions in our Sales worksheet:

1. Select cell **C10**.

2. Enter **=SUM(C5:C8)** to enter a function that adds the values in the specified range (cells C5 through C8, the first-quarter sales figures). Cell C10 displays the sum (830).

3. You can enter both functions and formulas in upper- or lowercase letters, whichever you prefer. We recommend using lowercase letters; that way, you won't have to bother with the Shift or Caps Lock keys. Also, Excel converts correctly entered functions to uppercase letters.

4. Select cell **C12**.

5. Enter **=average(c5:c8)** or **=AVERAGE(C5:C8)**. The cell displays the average of the specified range (207.5).

## PRACTICE YOUR SKILLS

In cell **C14**, enter a function to find the highest value within the range **C5:C8** (300). (**Hint:** Use the **MAX** function.) Your screen should match that shown in Figure 4.3.

**Figure 4.3**    **Entering functions**

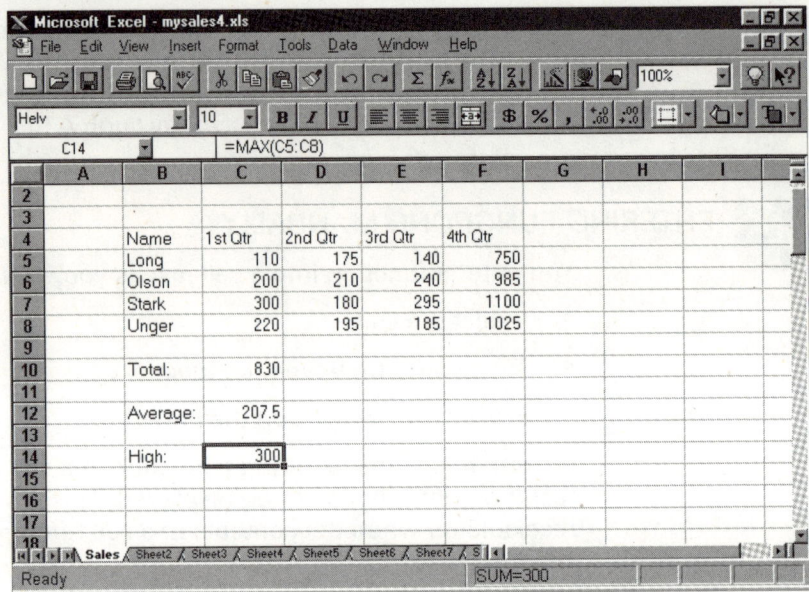

## USING THE ANSWER WIZARD TO EXPLORE FUNCTIONS

As you learned in the last chapter, you can get help any time you need it. Let's use the Answer Wizard to explore Excel functions:

1. Choose **Help, Answer Wizard**.

2. Type **Using Average** and click on Search (or press Enter). Note the topics that are displayed. Depending on the specific topic that you select, the Answer Wizard might guide you through the steps to perform a task or it might simply provide a Help screen.

3. In the Tell Me About list, select AVERAGE Worksheet Function and click on Display to view the Help screen for this topic. (You can also double-click on a topic to select and display its Help screen.)

4. Maximize the Help window, as shown in Figure 4.4. Skim through the information on the AVERAGE function. Note the text See Also at the top of the Help window. If you click on this text, a list of related topics is displayed in a Topics Found dialog box. Help screens often cross-reference other

Help screens. You can easily display the Help screens for these related topics. Please do not do this now. (Click on Cancel, if necessary, to return to the Average window.)

**Figure 4.4**     **The AVERAGE Help screen, maximized**

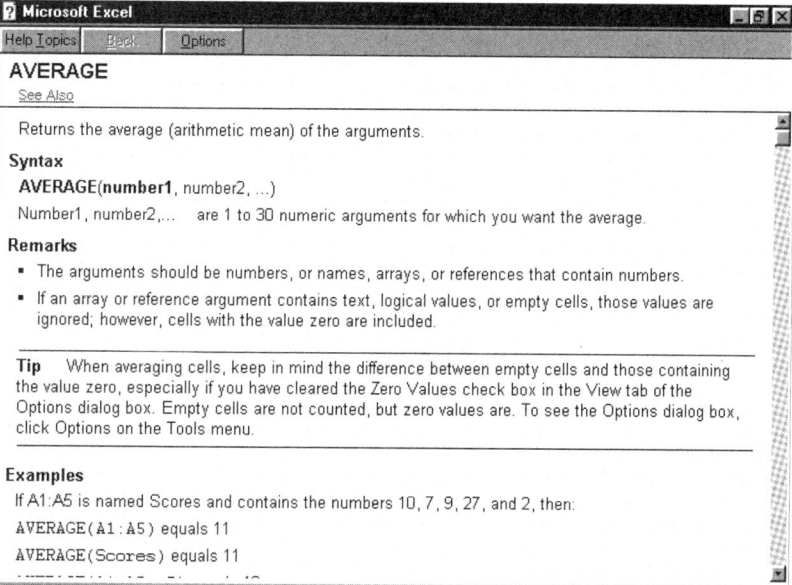

5. Restore the Help window to its nonmaximized size.

6. Press **Ctrl+F10** to attempt to maximize the Help window. Alas, it doesn't work! Pressing Ctrl+F10 maximizes/restores document windows only.

## PRACTICE YOUR SKILLS

1. Display and skim the Help screen for the MAX function. (**Hint:** Click on the Help Topics button and enter Using MAX on the Answer Wizard tab.)

2. Display and skim the Help screen for the SUM function.

3. From the SUM screen, display the Help screen for the cross-referenced **PRODUCT** function. (**Hint:** The cross-reference is at the top of the SUM screen.)

4. Exit Help.

## USING THE MOUSE TO SELECT FUNCTION ARGUMENTS

Earlier in this chapter, you learned how to enter a function into a cell manually by typing out the entire function and argument (cell range). You can streamline this procedure by using the mouse to select the argument. In general, dragging with the mouse to select a cell range is quicker and more accurate than typing the range.

Let's enter some new functions and use the mouse to select their arguments:

1. In cell D10, begin entering the SUM function by typing **=sum(** (don't skip a space after the open parenthesis).

2. Select the range **D5:D8** by dragging over it with the mouse (or click-Shift-clicking). Note the flashing *marquee* around the selected range. Now look at the formula bar. Excel has inserted the marqueed range into the function after the open parenthesis you typed in step 1.

3. Type **)** (a close parenthesis) to complete the function. Note that the marquee disappears.

4. Press **Enter** to enter your SUM function. Cell D10 displays the second-quarter sales total (760).

5. In cell D12, type **=average(** (again, don't type a space).

6. Drag to select the range **D5:D8**.

7. Without typing a close parenthesis, enter the function. Note that the correct second-quarter average is displayed (190).

8. Reselect cell D12, if necessary, and observe the formula bar. Excel was smart enough to add the close parenthesis that you left out.

### PRACTICE YOUR SKILLS

In cell D14, enter a function to find the highest value within the range **D5:D8** (210). (**Hint:** Use the **MAX** function, and drag to select the argument range.)

## USING THE FUNCTION WIZARD TO ENTER FUNCTIONS

Excel provides several *wizards*, special tools that walk you through complex procedures. There's a Tip Wizard to help you perform your daily Excel chores more efficiently, a Chart Wizard to help you create charts, and—as you'll see here—a Function Wizard to help you create functions. Think of a wizard as an imaginary tutor, sitting right there next to you, guiding you step by step through the current procedure. (You might not want to tell your colleagues about this.)

To use the Function Wizard to enter a function,

- Select the desired cell.

- Choose *Insert, Function* or click on the *Function Wizard button* to open the Function Wizard dialog box.

- Follow the dialog-box prompts to enter the desired function.

Let's meet the Function Wizard:

1. Select cell **E10**.

2. Click on the **Function Wizard button** to open the Function Wizard dialog box, as shown in Figure 4.5. Note that the title bar reads *Step 1 of 2*. The Function Wizard leads you through a two-step process to create and enter your function. This first dialog box represents step 1.

**Figure 4.5**     **The Function Wizard—Step 1 of 2 dialog box**

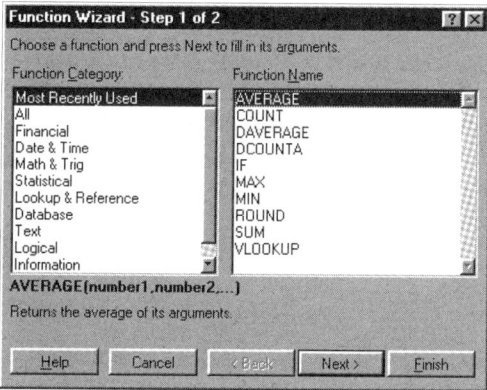

3. Note the prompt at the top of the dialog box,

   ```
   Choose a function and press Next to fill in
   its arguments.
   ```

   We want to calculate the third-quarter sales total. To do this, we'll choose the SUM function.

4. Observe the Function Category list box. This lists all the various categories in which Excel's functions are grouped. Note the currently selected category, *Most Recently Used*. (If this category is not selected, please select it now.) This category contains the functions that you used most recently in your worksheets.

5. Observe the Function Name list box. This lists all the functions contained in the currently selected category; in our case, it lists your most recently used functions. SUM, the function we're looking for, should be in this list.

6. In the Function Name list box, click on **SUM** to select it. Now that you've chosen a function, all that remains is to fill in its arguments.

7. Click on **Next >** (as directed by the prompt you observed in step 3) to display the Step 2 of 2 Function Wizard dialog box.

8. Observe the number1 text box. The insertion point is there, waiting for you to enter the first (number1)—and in our case, the only—argument of the SUM function. Remember, the SUM argument is a cell range. Let's use the mouse to select this range. But first, you'll have to move the Function Wizard dialog box out of the way, so that you can drag over the desired range in the worksheet (E5:E8).

9. Point to the **title bar** of the Function Wizard dialog box, press and hold the **left mouse button**, drag the mouse (and attached dialog box, which is now a dotted frame) downward until cells E5 through E8 are uncovered, and then release the mouse button. Your Function Wizard dialog box should no longer be covering cells E5:E8, yet the bottom row of buttons (Help, Cancel, < Back, and so on) should be visible, as shown in Figure 4.6. If necessary, move the dialog box again. You might need to scroll the worksheet up to make room for the dialog box at the bottom.

**Figure 4.6**     **Moving the Function Wizard dialog box out of the way**

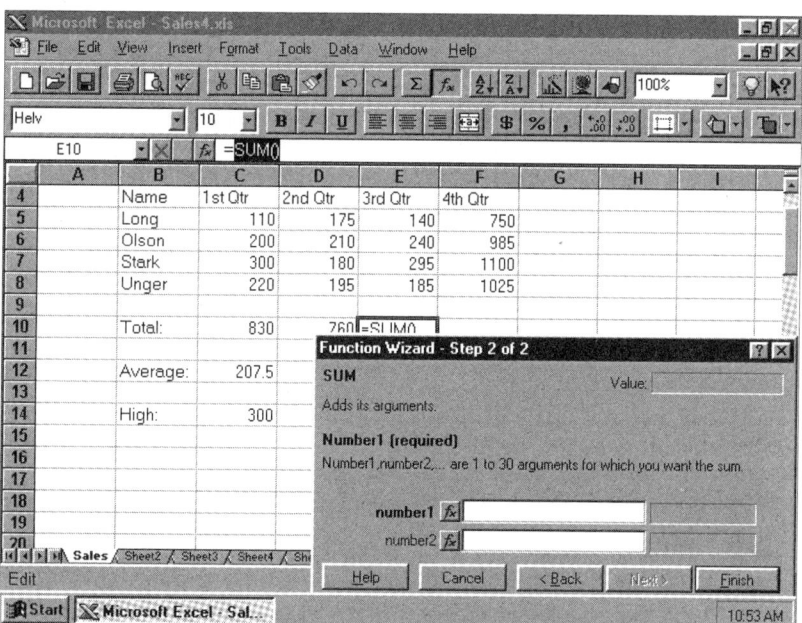

**10.** Drag over cells **E5:E8** to select them. Note that this range is displayed both in the Function Wizard dialog box and in the formula bar. You've specified your function (SUM) and its argument (E5:E8). All done!

**11.** Click on **Finish** to enter your completed SUM function into the active cell (E10). Note the correct result (860).

## PRACTICE YOUR SKILLS

**1.** Use the Function Wizard to enter a function in cell **E12** to calculate the third-quarter average sales. (Choose **Insert, Function** this time to open the Function Wizard dialog box.)

**2.** Use the Function Wizard to enter a function in cell **E14** to calculate the third-quarter maximum sales figure. (Use **Insert, Function** or the **Function Wizard button**, whichever you prefer.) Your screen should now match that shown in Figure 4.7.

**Figure 4.7**      **Using the Function Wizard to enter third-quarter functions**

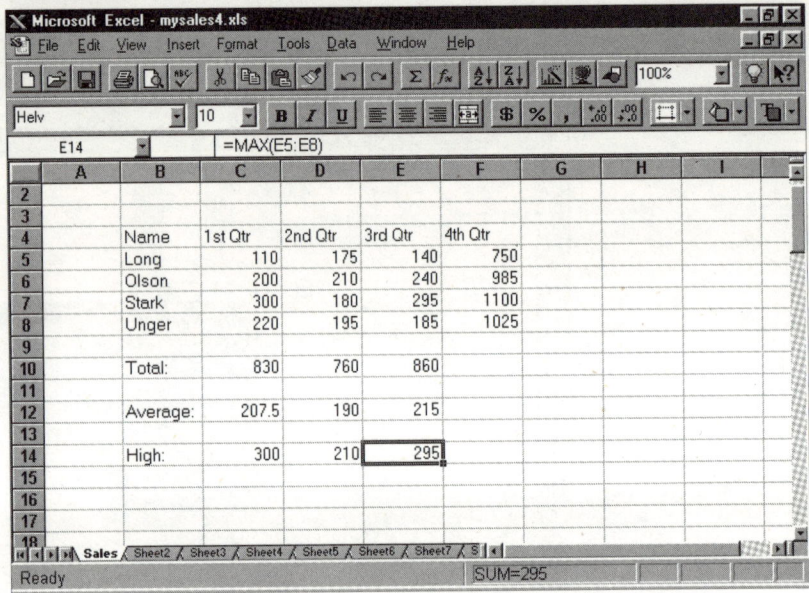

3. Use **File, Save As** to save the file to your Excel Work folder directory as **mysales4**.

## COPYING CELL CONTENTS

Copying cell contents from one worksheet location to another is very easy in Excel. Compare this to the noncomputerized, paper world, where copying involves tedious data reentry and possibly traumatic restructuring of the entire spreadsheet! You can use any of these three methods to copy cell contents:

• The *Fill* command

• The *Copy* and *Paste* commands

• Drag-and-drop

You use Fill to copy cell contents within a selected range. For example, in your current worksheet, you could copy your third-quarter total, average, and high formulas to the corresponding fourth-quarter cells by selecting the range E10:F14 and then issuing a Fill Right command.

You use Copy and Paste or drag-and-drop to copy cell contents to any location (adjacent or nonadjacent) in the worksheet. Staying with our example, you could copy your first- through fourth-quarter total, average, and high formulas all the way over to columns H through K by selecting the range C10:F14 and then copying and pasting or dragging-and-dropping these cells to columns H through K.

As a rule of thumb:

- Use Fill to copy to an adjacent worksheet location.

- Use Copy and Paste (if you're a keyboardist) or drag-and-drop (if you're a mouser) to copy to a nonadjacent worksheet location.

 THE FILL COMMAND

The Fill command includes four related commands:

| Command | What It Does |
| --- | --- |
| Fill Left | Copies cell contents from the rightmost column of the selected range into all columns to the left within that range |
| Fill Right | Copies from the leftmost column of the range into all columns to the right within that range |
| Fill Up | Copies from the bottom row of the range into all upper rows within that range |
| Fill Down | Copies from the top row of the range into all lower rows within that range |

To use Fill to copy cell contents,

- Select a range that contains both the cells you want to copy *from* and the cells you want to copy *to*.

- Choose *Edit, Fill* to open the Fill drop-down submenu.

- Click on the appropriate Fill command (as described above): *Left*, *Right*, *Up*, or *Down*.

Let's use Fill to copy our third-quarter total formula (in cell E10) to the adjacent fourth-quarter cell (F10):

1. Select the range **E10:F10**. This range includes the cell you want to copy *from* (E10) and the cell you want to copy *to* (F10).

2. Choose **Edit, Fill, Right** to copy the contents of the leftmost column of the selected range (the formula in cell E10) into all the remaining columns to the right within this range (cell F10). The sales total in F10 should read 3860.

## ADJUSTMENT OF CELL REFERENCES DURING COPYING

When you copy a formula to a new location, Excel automatically adjusts the cell references in the formula relative to that new location. Cell references that change when copied are called *relative references*. Constant values—both numbers and text—do not change when copied to another location.

Let's look at how Excel adjusted the cell references in the Fill Right command you just issued:

1. Select cell **E10**. Observe its formula, =SUM(E5:E8), in the formula bar. The cell references in the argument range E5:E8 are relative references; they will change when copied.

2. Select cell **F10** and observe its formula, =SUM(F5:F8). Note that Excel changed the argument references from E5:E8 (in cell E10) to F5:F8 (in cell F10). You copied the original formula, =SUM(E5:E8), one column to the right and Excel adjusted its references by adding one to the original column (column E plus one equals column F).

Now let's copy the third-quarter average and high formulas (cells E12 and E14) to the fourth quarter:

1. Select the range **E12:F14**.

2. Choose **Edit, Fill, Right** to copy the formulas from the leftmost column in the range (column E) to all the remaining columns to the right (column F). Your worksheet should match that shown in Figure 4.8.

Now let's practice using the Fill Down command. First, we'll create a new column to hold our salespeople's yearly sales totals:

1. In cell **G4**, enter the column heading **Yr. Total**.

**Figure 4.8**　　**Using Fill Right to copy formulas**

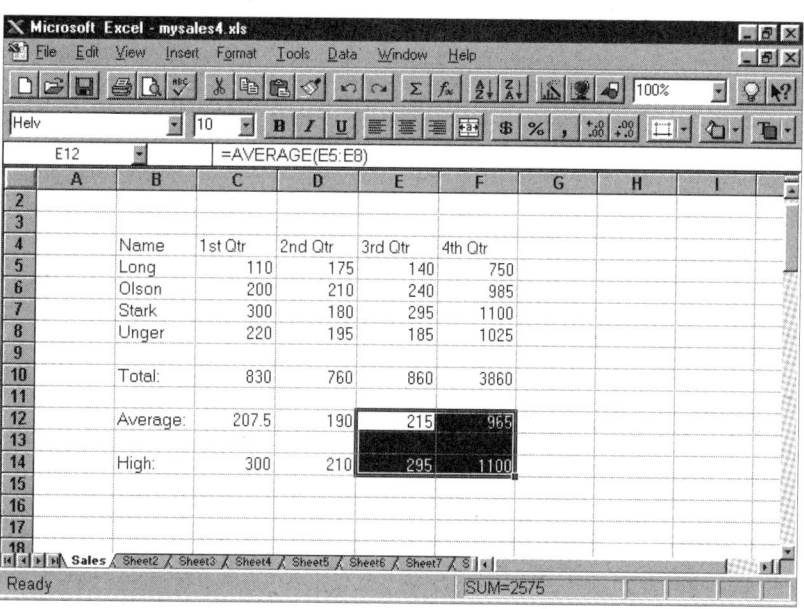

2. Select cell **G5** and type **=sum(** to begin entering a SUM function.

3. Drag over the range **C5:F5** to select it. Note that this range is automatically inserted within the parentheses of the SUM function.

4. Type **)** to complete the function, and then press **Enter** to enter it into cell G5 (Long's yearly total).

5. Select the range **G5:G8**.

6. Choose **Edit, Fill, Down** to copy the yearly total formula from cell G5 down through the remainder of the range. Your worksheet should match that shown in Figure 4.9.

## LONG TEXT ENTRIES

A standard worksheet cell is approximately eight characters wide, as displayed on the screen. This same cell, however, can contain up to 255 characters of data (text, numbers, functions, and so on). This presents a display dilemma. If a cell contains more characters

**Figure 4.9**     **Using Fill Down to copy formulas**

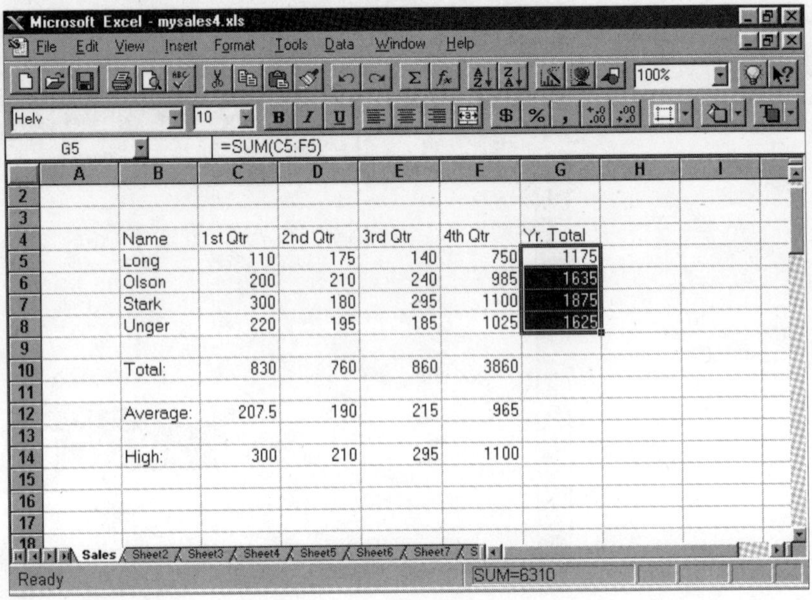

| | A | B | C | D | E | F | G | H | I |
|---|---|---|---|---|---|---|---|---|---|
| 4 | | Name | 1st Qtr | 2nd Qtr | 3rd Qtr | 4th Qtr | Yr. Total | | |
| 5 | | Long | 110 | 175 | 140 | 750 | 1175 | | |
| 6 | | Olson | 200 | 210 | 240 | 985 | 1635 | | |
| 7 | | Stark | 300 | 180 | 295 | 1100 | 1875 | | |
| 8 | | Unger | 220 | 195 | 185 | 1025 | 1625 | | |
| 10 | | Total: | 830 | 760 | 860 | 3860 | | | |
| 12 | | Average: | 207.5 | 190 | 215 | 965 | | | |
| 14 | | High: | 300 | 210 | 295 | 1100 | | | |

G5 =SUM(C5:F5)

SUM=6310

than can be accommodated by its onscreen width, one of two things can happen:

- The extra characters will be displayed in the adjacent cell(s) to the right, if these cell(s) are empty.

Or

- The extra characters will not be displayed, if the adjacent cell(s) to the right are not empty.

Let's enter a title that has more than eight characters and see what happens:

1. In cell **C2**, enter **European Division**. Note that the text display spills over into the adjacent cell, D2.

2. Select cell **D2**. Note that the formula bar is empty. Though, from a quick glance at the worksheet, it appears as if cell D2 contains text, it doesn't; what you're seeing is the spillover from cell C2.

3. Enter **5**. Note that the text display is truncated (only *European* is displayed). As mentioned, text can spill over to an adjacent cell only if that cell is empty.

4. Select cell **C2**. Note that the full text entry appears in the formula bar (*European Division*). When Excel truncates text due to lack of empty adjacent cell(s), it truncates the text *display*, not the actual text *entry*.

5. Clear cell **D2**. (Select it and press **Del**.) Note that C2's full text entry is once again displayed.

## THE *COPY* AND *PASTE* COMMANDS

You can use the Copy and Paste commands to copy the contents of one or more cells to another (adjacent or nonadjacent) worksheet location. There are numerous ways to select the Copy and Paste commands. For example, you can use the Edit menu, the keyboard shortcuts, or the tools on the Standard toolbar (see Figure 4.10).

**Figure 4.10**  **The Copy and Paste tools**

Copy tool ———  ——— Paste tool

To copy and paste data:

• Select the cell(s) that you want to copy *from*.

• Choose *Edit, Copy*. A marquee encloses the selected cell(s).

• Select the cell(s) that you want to copy *to*. If you're copying a range of cells, you need only select the upper-left cell of the range you're copying to.

• Choose *Edit, Paste*, or simply press *Enter* to paste (copy) the marqueed cell contents. You can continue to paste the selected data into additional worksheet locations as long as the marquee is visible. However, if you paste the data by pressing the Enter key, the marquee is removed. For this reason, press Enter only when you're performing a one-time copy.

• When you're finished pasting, press *Esc* to remove the marquee.

**A word of caution:** When you paste data into a range of cells, it replaces (erases) the current data in these cells. So make sure to paste (copy) your data into an empty cell range or into a range containing data you can afford to lose.

Let's practice copying with the Copy and Paste commands:

1.  In cell **C18**, enter **Australian Division**.

2.  Select the range **B4:G4**. These are the cells you want to copy *from*.

3.  Choose **Edit, Copy**. Note the marquee enclosing the selected cells.

4.  Select cell **B20** (you may need to scroll the worksheet) to tell Excel where you want to copy *to*. As mentioned, if you're copying a range of cells, you need only select the upper-left cell of the range you're copying to.

5.  Choose **Edit, Paste** to paste (copy) the marqueed range to the specified destination range (B20:G20).

6.  Note that cells B4:G4 are still enclosed by the marquee. As long as this marquee remains on screen, you can paste the enclosed range to additional worksheet locations. We won't do this now.

7.  Press **Esc** to clear the marquee. Your worksheet should match that shown in Figure 4.11.

## DRAG-AND-DROP

If you're a mouser, you may want to use drag-and-drop to copy the contents of one or more cells to another (adjacent or nonadjacent) worksheet location. To do this,

*   Select the cell(s) that you want to copy *from*.

*   Point to the outline of the selected cell(s).

*   Press and hold the right mouse button, then drag the selected cell(s) to the desired new location.

*   Release the right mouse button. A shortcut menu appears.

*   In this shortcut menu, click on *Copy*.

**Figure 4.11**    **Using Copy and Paste to copy a range**

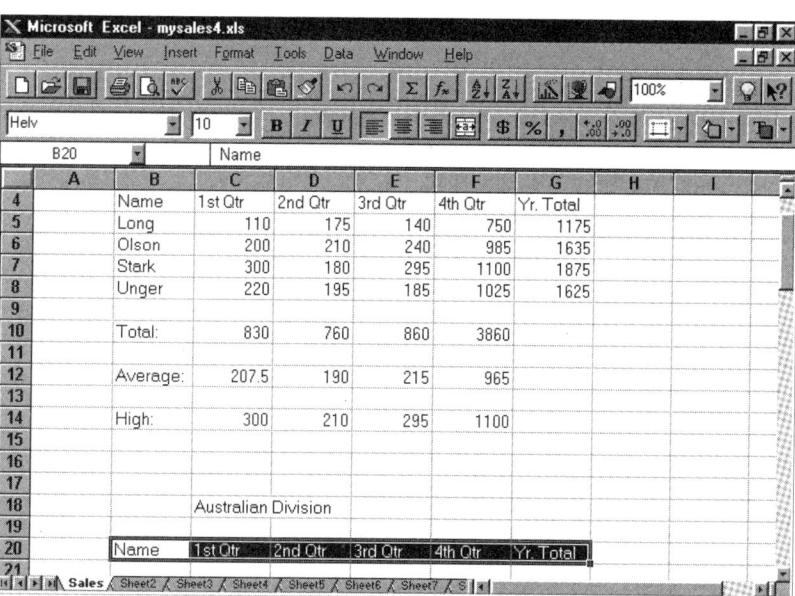

Let's use drag-and-drop to reperform the copying task from the last activity. That way, you can see which method you find easier to use:

1. Clear the contents of cells **B20:G20**.

2. Select the range **B4:G4**.

3. Point to the outline of the selected cell range. Note that the mouse pointer changes to an arrow.

4. Press and hold the **right mouse button**, and then drag the selected cell range to cells **B20:G20**.

5. Release the mouse button. A shortcut menu appears. Click the **left mouse button** on **Copy** in this menu to perform the copying.

6. Choose **File, Save** to *update* your modified workbook; that is, to save it under the same name (mysales4) and in the same location (Excel Work, your work folder).

7. Close the file.

 CHOOSING COMMANDS FROM SHORTCUT MENUS

Shortcut menus are wonderful time-saving tools, particularly for you devoted mousers out there. (Come on, admit it!) You can use shortcut menus to move and copy cells (as you saw in the last activity); to insert, clear, delete, and format cells and entire worksheet columns and rows; to show, hide, or customize toolbars; and to save, print, spell-check, and change the page setup of your workbooks.

To choose a command from a shortcut menu,

- Point to (or select) the desired screen element. For example, to clear a cell, you'd point to (or select) it.

- Click the right mouse button (or press *Shift+F10*) to open the shortcut menu.

- Click on the desired shortcut command. Or, use the arrow keys to select the command and then press Enter.

**Note:** You can open some, but not all of the available shortcut menus by using the keyboard (Shift+F10). Only mousers can take full advantage of Excel's shortcut menus!

Rather than present an activity here exploring shortcut menus, we'll use shortcut menus on an ad hoc basis throughout the rest of this book, whenever we feel they'd be most useful.

# PRACTICE YOUR SKILLS

You've learned a great deal in the first four chapters of this book: how to create, modify, save, open, and close Excel workbooks; how to navigate through a worksheet; how to select, clear, and copy a range of cells; how to create formulas and functions; how to perform "what if" analysis; and how to use Help and shortcut menus. The following activity will increase your fluency with these techniques.

Other "Practice Your Skills" activities appear at key points throughout the course of this book. Please don't think of these activities as tests, but rather as opportunities to hone your Excel skills. Only through repetition will you internalize the techniques you've learned. In case you need help, you'll find the relevant chapter numbers in parentheses after each activity step.

In the following activity, you will edit the workbook file Practice4 to match Figure 4.12.

**Figure 4.12**  **The completed ExMac Corporation worksheet**

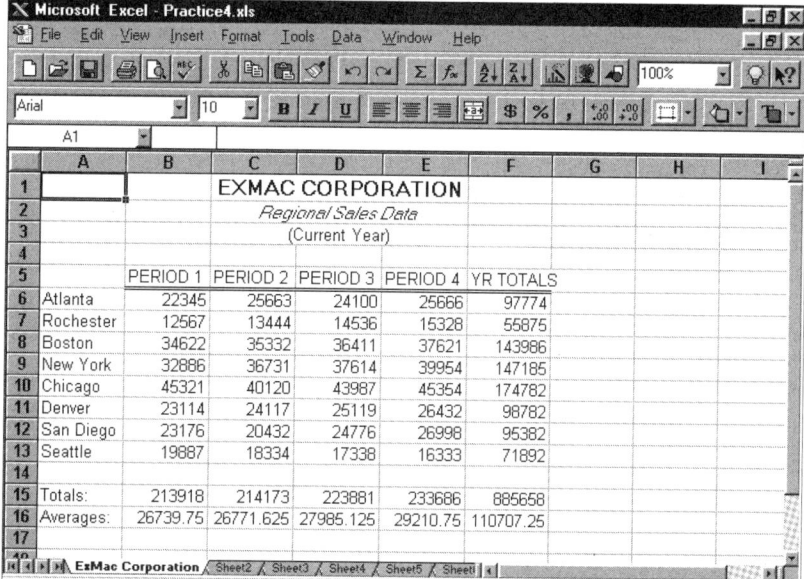

1. Open the workbook file **Practice4** from your Excel Work folder (Chapter 3).

2. Maximize the document window, if it is not already maximized (Chapter 3).

3. In cell **F6**, enter a function to sum the range **B6:E6** (Chapter 4).

4. Copy (fill) the formula in cell F6 into the range **F7:F13** (Chapter 4).

5. In cell **B15**, enter a function to sum the range **B6:B13** (Chapter 4).

6. Copy (fill) the formula in cell B15 into the range **C15:F15** (Chapter 4).

7. In cell **B16**, use the Function Wizard to create a function to average all city sales for Period 1 (Chapter 4).

8. Copy (fill) the formula in cell B16 into the range **C16:F16** (Chapter 4).

9. Select cell **A1**. Your worksheet should now match that shown in Figure 4.12.

10. Save your file as **mypractice4** in your Excel Work folder (Chapter 2).

11. Close the file (Chapter 2).

## SUMMARY

In this chapter, you learned the basics of creating a larger, more involved worksheet. You now know how to enter data into a range of cells, how to use functions in your formulas, how to copy cell contents, and how to choose commands from shortcut menus.

Here's a quick reference guide to the Excel features introduced in this chapter:

| Desired Result | How to Do It |
|---|---|
| Activate right or left cell within selected range | Press **Tab** (right) or press **Shift+Tab** (left) |
| Activate lower or upper cell within selected range | Press **Enter** (down) or press **Shift+Enter** (up) |
| Maximize/restore document window | Click on **Maximize/Restore buttons** or press **Ctrl+F10** |
| Enter function | Type **=** type entire function; or type **=** type function name, type **(**, select argument range, then type **)**; or click on **Function Wizard button** or choose **Insert, Function** and follow prompts |
| Enter function argument range | Type range or use mouse to select range |
| Sum range | Use **SUM** function |
| Average range | Use **AVERAGE** function |

| Desired Result | How to Do It |
|---|---|
| Find maximum within range | Use **MAX** function |
| Fill selected columns to right, left, up, or down | Choose **Edit, Fill** and click on **Right, Left, Up,** or **Down** |
| Copy cell(s) | Select cell(s) to copy from; choose **Edit, Copy,** or press **Ctrl+c,** or click on **Copy tool**; select cell(s) to copy to; choose **Edit, Paste,** or press **Ctrl+v,** or click on **Paste tool,** or press **Enter.** Or select cell(s) to copy from; point to outline of selected range; press and hold **right mouse button**; drag selected cell(s) to desired location; release mouse button; in shortcut menu, click on **Copy** |
| Choose shortcut command | Point to (or select) desired screen element; click **right mouse button** or press **Shift+F10**; click on desired shortcut command, or use arrow keys to select command and press **Enter** |

In the next chapter, we'll show you the fundamentals of worksheet editing and formatting. You'll learn how to edit the contents of a cell, how to enter absolute cell references in formulas, how to insert and delete cells, columns, and rows, how to move cell data, how to change the format of worksheet numbers and text, and how to copy specific attributes of cells.

## IF YOU'RE STOPPING HERE

If you want to break off here, please exit Excel. If you want to proceed directly to the next chapter, please do so now.

# CHAPTER 5:
# EDITING AND
# FORMATTING YOUR
# WORKSHEETS

Editing Cells

Absolute
References

Inserting and
Deleting Cells,
Columns, and
Rows

Moving a Range of
Cells

Formatting

Copying Specific
Cell Attributes

**A** properly formatted, well laid-out worksheet is not only attractive to the eye, but vital for an accurate portrayal of your data. In this chapter, you'll learn how to *format* a worksheet; that is, how to tailor its data display and page layout to your specifications. You'll also learn how to *edit* the contents of a cell and how to create more sophisticated formulas.

When you're done working through this chapter, you will know

- How to edit the contents of a cell

- How to enter absolute (rather than relative) cell references in formulas

- How to insert and delete cells, columns, and rows

- How to move (rather than copy) cell data

- How to change the format of worksheet numbers and text

- How to change column width and row height

- How to copy specific attributes of cells (formulas, values, formats, and so on)

**A special note for this chapter:** We recommend that you allot enough time to work through each chapter without interruption. However, because this chapter is so long, you may want to divide it into two work sessions. About halfway through (right before the section entitled "Formatting"), we've added a note telling you how to do this.

## EDITING CELLS

Excel's *editing* feature allows you to change the contents of a cell without retyping the entire entry. Editing is particularly useful for longer entries. For example, if you wanted to change a single cell reference in the middle of a long, complex formula, you could simply edit this reference rather than retyping the entire formula from scratch. As explained in the next two sections, you can switch to Edit mode either by pressing F2 (the Edit key) or by double-clicking on the cell. Once in Edit mode, you can use the arrow keys, the mouse, or a combination of the two to move the insertion point and edit the data.

 ## USING F2 (THE EDIT KEY) TO EDIT A CELL

To edit a cell using F2 and the arrow keys,

- Select the desired cell.

- Press F2.

- Use the left or right arrow keys to move the insertion point to the desired location in the cell contents.

- Use Backspace or Del to delete any undesired text.

- Type any corrections or insertions.

- Enter the revised cell contents.

If you are not running Excel, please start it now. If there is a workbook on your screen (other than Book1), please close it. Let's begin this chapter's activities by opening a workbook file and using F2 to edit some of its text:

1. Open the file **Sales5** from your Excel Work folder.

2. Maximize the application and document windows, if necessary. Your screen should match that shown in Figure 5.1.

**Figure 5.1**      **Sales5, newly opened and maximized**

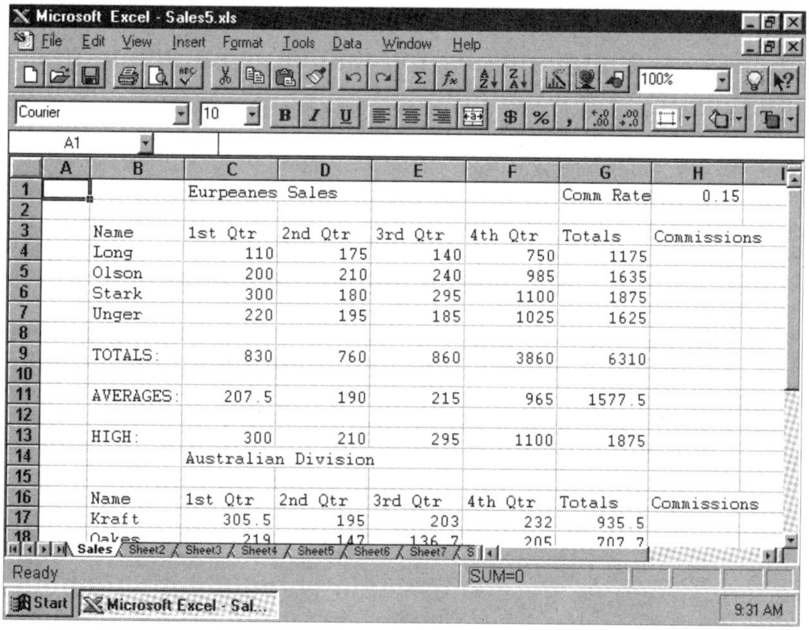

3. Select cell **C1**. This is the cell whose contents you'll edit.

4. Press **F2**. Note that the Cancel and Enter boxes appear in the formula bar, and that the insertion point appears at the end of the contents in the cell. The word *Eurpeanes* is misspelled; it should be *European*.

5. Use the **left arrow key** to move the insertion point between the *r* and the *p* of *Eurpeanes*.

6. Type **o** to insert an *o* between the *r* and *p*.

7. Enter the partially corrected text in cell C1. The cell now reads *Europeanes Sales*.

## USING THE MOUSE TO EDIT A CELL

To edit a cell using the mouse,

- Double-click on the desired cell. You can edit the data in the cell or in the formula bar.

- To insert data, point to the desired location. Click to place the insertion point, and type the new data.

- To overwrite data, drag to select the desired data, and type the new data.

- To delete data, drag to select the desired data, and press **Del**.

- Enter the revised cell contents.

Let's use the mouse to finish editing cell C1:

1. Double-click on cell **C1**.

2. In the formula bar, point anywhere in the word *Sales*. Note that the mouse pointer changes to an I-beam.

3. Double-click on *Sales* to select the entire word. Note that the highlight extends to the end of the formula bar.

4. Type **Division** to replace the selected text (*Sales*).

5. In the cell, drag the I-beam across the final **es** of *Europeanes*.

6. Press **Del** to delete these two letters. Note that you can edit a cell's contents in the formula bar or in the cell itself.

7. Enter the revised text. Note that cell C1 now reads *European Division*, as shown in Figure 5.2.

**Figure 5.2**    **Editing cell C1**

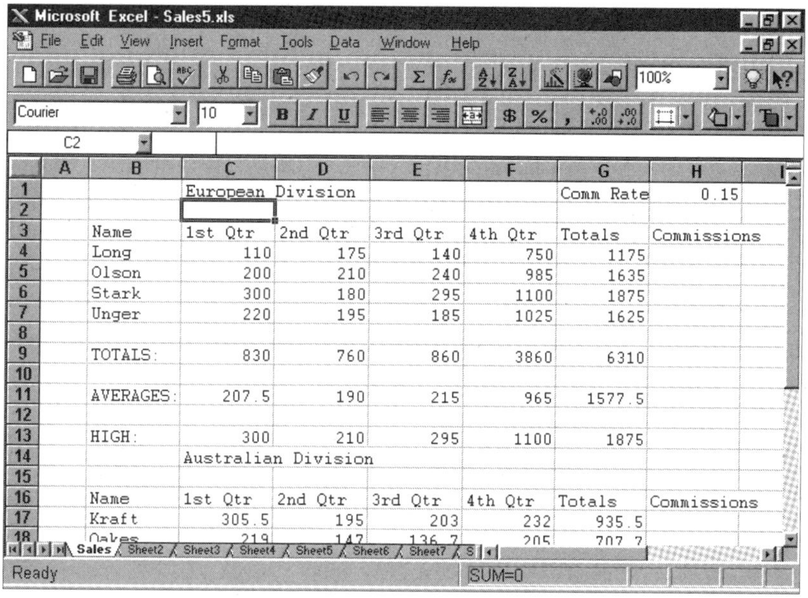

# ABSOLUTE REFERENCES

As you learned in Chapter 4, when you copy a cell containing a formula, Excel automatically adjusts the formula's cell references relative to the new location. For example, copying the formula =A1+A2 one column to the right automatically changes the formula to =B1+B2. There are times, however, when you'll want to copy a formula *without* having all its references adjusted. Let's look at such a situation:

1. In cell **H4**, enter the formula =**g4\*h1** to calculate Long's sales commission (Long's total sales multiplied by the commission rate). The result is 176.25.

2. Select the range **H4:H7**.

3. Choose **Edit, Fill, Down** to copy the sales-commission formula in cell H4 to cells H5, H6, and H7.

4. Observe the bizarre results: Olson's sales commission (in cell H5) reads 0; Stark's reads *#VALUE!*; and Unger's reads

286406.3 (an unusually generous commission, considering that Unger's total sales are 1625). Let's see why.

When you copied the original formula in cell H4, Excel automatically changed its cell references relative to the copied locations. The reference H1 in the original formula was changed to H2 in cell H5, H3 in cell H6, and H4 in cell H7. (Verify this by selecting each of these cells and observing its formula.) The problem is that the commission rate—which is a fixed value that we want all the copied formulas to reference—resides *only* in cell H1 (not in H2, H3, or H4). In this case, you need Excel *not* to adjust the H1 references when you copy the formula.

To do this, you must create an *absolute*, rather than a relative, reference. To create an absolute cell reference, simply insert a dollar sign ($) before both the column and row of the reference; for example, F22 is relative and $F$22 is absolute. In Edit mode, you can also press the F4 key to quickly create an absolute reference. To prevent either the column or the row (but not both) of a cell reference from being adjusted, you must create a *mixed reference* ($F22 or F$22). Study the following examples to understand what happens when relative, absolute, and mixed references are copied:

| Type | Reference | When Copied One Row Down and One Column Right |
| --- | --- | --- |
| Relative | A1 | B2 |
| Absolute | $A$1 | $A$1 |
| Mixed | A$1 | B$1 |
| Mixed | $A1 | $A2 |

## USING FILL TO COPY ABSOLUTE REFERENCES

Let's redo our failed copy operation, using absolute referencing:

1. Select cell **H4**. You must modify the formula in this cell to prevent errors from occurring when you copy it.

2. Press **F2** to begin editing.

3. Press **F4** to create an absolute reference. You can manually insert a $ character before the H and the 1, but isn't pressing F4 easier?

4. Observe the formula. The cell reference should now read $H$1. This is an absolute reference.

5. Enter the revised formula. Note that the result is the same (176.25). Cell references H1 (in the original formula) and $H$1 (in the revised formula) refer to the same cell. The difference is that the absolute reference ($H$1) will not change when you copy it.

6. Select the range **H4:H7**.

7. Choose **Edit, Fill, Down**. Note the correct results, as shown in Figure 5.3. Each of these four formulas now correctly refers to the sales-commission rate in cell H1. Let's verify this.

**Figure 5.3**  **Copying a formula with an absolute reference**

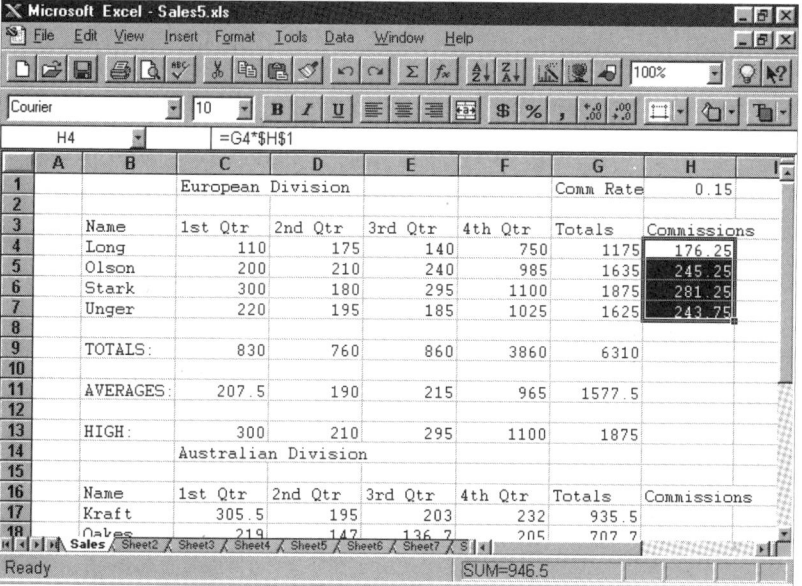

8. Select cell **H4**. The formula reads =G4*$H$1.

9. Select cell **H5**. The formula reads =G5*$H$1. When you copied the formula from cell H4, the relative reference G4 was automatically updated to G5. However, the absolute reference $H$1 remained the same.

10. Examine cells H6 and H7. Note the changes analogous to those in cell H5.

## USING COPY AND PASTE TO COPY ABSOLUTE REFERENCES

Now let's copy an absolute reference using Copy and Paste, instead of Fill. Remember, you use Fill to copy within a range of adjacent cells, and you use Copy (or drag-and-drop) to copy anywhere on the worksheet.

1. Select cell **H4**.

2. Press **Ctrl+C**. This is the keyboard shortcut for the Edit, Copy command. Note the copy marquee.

3. Select the range **H17:H21**.

4. Press **Ctrl+V**—the keyboard shortcut for the Edit, Paste command—to paste (copy) the formula from cell H4 into all the cells in the selected range, H17:H21.

5. Press **Esc** to remove the copy marquee from cell H4.

6. Examine the contents of cells H17:H21. The formulas all correctly refer to the commission rate in cell H1 ($H$1).

Finally, let's save our revised Sales5 workbook under a new file name:

1. Choose **File, Save As** to open the Save As dialog box.

2. Verify that your Excel Work folder is selected; if not, please select it now. Excel "remembers" the last folder you selected in the current work session. Because you selected Excel Work when you opened Sales5 at the beginning of this chapter, Excel automatically selects Excel Work now when you use File, Save As to save a file. Likewise, if you changed the folder now (please don't do this), Excel would automatically select it when you next chose File, Open or File, Save As.

3. Type **mysales4** in the File Name text box and press **Enter** (which is the same as clicking on Save, since the Save button is outlined). The dialog box shown in Figure 5.4 appears,

informing you that a file named mysales4 already exists. (You created it in Chapter 4.) What does this mean?

**Figure 5.4**      **Attempting to replace an existing file**

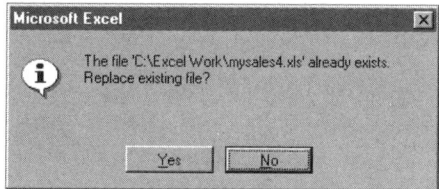

4. If you save the workbook currently on screen as mysales4, it will replace (permanently erase!) the previous version of mysales4. In this case, it's perfectly okay to do this, since you don't need to keep the old mysales4.

5. Click on **Yes** to replace the old mysales4 with your new (on-screen) version.

**A word of caution**: Always remember that replacing a file (as you just did) *permanently* erases it from your disk. Do not, therefore, replace a file if you want to keep a disk copy (rather than just a paper copy) of it. To preserve different versions of the same worksheet, use File, Save As to save them under different names (Mysales1, Mysales2, and so on).

## INSERTING AND DELETING CELLS, COLUMNS, AND ROWS

Inserting or deleting cells, columns, or rows in a paper spreadsheet can be a formidable task. You may have to erase and reenter large chunks of data, manually recalculate formulas, and possibly even redo the entire page layout. Once again, Excel excels by making insertions and deletions delightfully easy to perform.

To insert cells in a worksheet,

• Select the desired cell range. Make sure it is of the same size and in the same place as the range you want to insert.

• Choose *Insert, Cells* to open the Insert dialog box.

- Select *Shift Cells Right* or *Shift Cells Down*. Shift Cells Right causes Excel to move the selected cells to the right when it inserts the new cells; Shift Cells Down causes Excel to move the selected cells down when it inserts the new cells.

- Click on OK to insert a blank cell range of the same size and in the same place as the range you selected in step 1.

To insert columns or rows in a worksheet,

- Select the desired adjacent columns or rows. Select as many columns or rows as you want to insert, in the place where you want to insert.

- Choose *Insert, Columns* or *Insert, Rows* to insert the same number of columns or rows that you selected. Columns are inserted to the left of the selection; rows are inserted above the selection.

To delete cells from a worksheet,

- Select the desired cells.

- Choose *Edit, Delete* to open the Delete dialog box.

- Select *Shift Cells Left* or *Shift Cells Up*. When you delete cells, Excel erases their contents and removes the cells from the worksheet. Excel then fills in the gap created by removing these cells with the contents of adjacent cells. Shift Cells Left shifts the contents of those cells to the right of the selected cells leftward into the gap. Shift Cells Up shifts the contents of those cells below the selected cells upward into the gap.

- Click on OK to delete the selected cells.

To delete columns or rows from a worksheet,

- Select the desired adjacent columns or rows.

- Choose *Edit, Delete*. If you delete columns, the columns to the right of the deleted columns are shifted leftward into the gap. If you delete rows, the rows below the deleted rows are shifted upward into the gap.

**Note:** You can also choose Insert or Delete from the shortcut menu to quickly insert columns or rows. Remember how to use the right mouse button to display the shortcut menu?

Take care to distinguish between deleting and clearing. *Deleting* erases the contents of the selected cells, columns, or rows; removes the selected area from the worksheet; and then fills in the gap with the contents of adjacent cells, columns, or rows. *Clearing* (using Edit, Clear or the Delete key) erases the contents of the selected area without removing the selection from the worksheet.

Let's insert some rows in our Sales worksheet:

1. Select rows **1**, **2**, and **3**. To do this, point to the row heading 1 (on the left side of the screen), press and hold down the **mouse button**, drag the pointer down to row heading 3, then release the mouse button. To select a single column or row, click on its heading; to select two or more adjacent columns or rows, drag across their headings.

2. Without deselecting the rows, click once in the horizontal scroll bar to scroll the worksheet to the right. Note that rows 1, 2, and 3 remain selected no matter how far you scroll. When you select a row or column, the selection extends across or down the entire worksheet.

3. Scroll back to the beginning of the worksheet. Rows 1, 2, and 3 should still be selected.

4. Choose **Insert, Rows** to insert three blank rows above your selected three rows. As mentioned, Excel inserts the same number of rows or columns you selected. Rows are always inserted above the selected rows; columns are always inserted to the left of the selected columns.

5. Examine the formulas in cells H7:H10. Note that all the absolute references to the commission-rate cell now read $H$4 instead of $H$1 (as they did previously). By inserting three rows at the top of the worksheet, you moved the commission-rate cell from H1 down to H4. Excel automatically adjusted all formulas that referred to this cell.

Now let's add a new sales rep to the European Division list, between Stark and Unger. To do this, we'll insert an entire new row above row 10:

1. Scroll to display the Sales Inventory data in columns J to N. Note that from row 8 down, no blank rows appear in the inventory list; in a moment, you'll see why this is important.

2. Press **Ctrl+Home** to select cell A1.

3. Select row **10** (by clicking on the row heading 10).

4. Choose **Insert, Rows** to insert a new row across the entire worksheet. Note that the desired gap opens up between Stark and Unger in the European Division list. That's the good news. Here's the bad:

5. Redisplay the Sales Inventory data (columns J to N). Note that your new row left an undesired gap in the inventory list, as shown in Figure 5.5. Why? Because a newly inserted row spans the entire length of the worksheet.

**Figure 5.5**    **Creating an undesired gap by inserting a row**

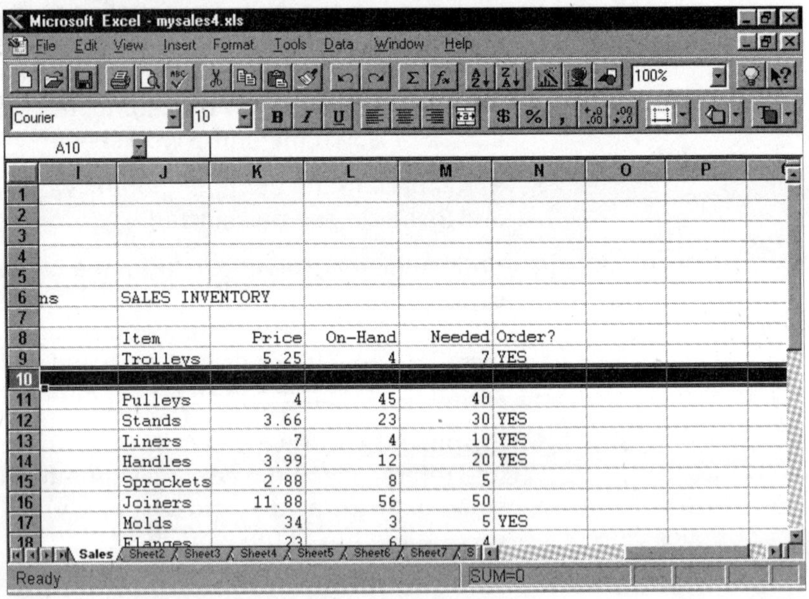

6. Choose **Edit, Undo Insert Rows** to undo your row insertion. Once again, Undo comes to the rescue!

Let's try again. This time, we'll insert a range of cells between Stark and Unger, rather than an entire row:

1. Observe the formula in cell C12, the first-quarter sales totals, =SUM(C7:C10). We'll revisit this formula in a moment.

2. Select the range **B10:H10**. These are the cells above which you want to insert new, blank cells to hold the data for your new sales rep.

3. Choose **Insert, Cells** to open the Insert dialog box.

4. If necessary, select **Shift Cells Down**.

5. Click on **OK**. The selected cells (Unger's sales totals) are shifted down and an equal-sized range of new, blank cells are inserted above them.

6. Observe the formula in cell C13, the first-quarter sales totals, =SUM(C7:C11). (This is the same cell you observed in step 1; it was shifted down one row when you inserted your new cells.) Excel automatically adjusted the formula's cell references by one row when you inserted the new cells (C7:C11 instead of C7:C10).

7. Redisplay the Sales Inventory data in columns J to N. Note that there is no undesired gap. By inserting a range of cells, rather than an entire row, you limited the gap (new, blank cells) to the width of your selected range, rather than the width of the entire worksheet.

## PRACTICE YOUR SKILLS

Now that we've successfully inserted a blank row of cells between Stark and Unger without creating an undesired gap in the sales inventory list, let's enter the data for Todd, a new sales rep:

1. Enter the following data:

|    | B    | C   | D   | E   | F   |
|----|------|-----|-----|-----|-----|
| 10 | Todd | 150 | 200 | 125 | 185 |

2. Use the appropriate Fill command to copy the totals and commissions formulas from cells G9:H9 to cells G10:H10. Your worksheet should match that shown in Figure 5.6.

3. Choose **File, Save** to update the file.

# MOVING A RANGE OF CELLS

In Chapter 4, you learned how to copy a range of cells from one location to another. Here, you'll learn how to *move* a selected range. Copying preserves both the original and the copied range. Moving preserves only the moved range.

**Figure 5.6**     **Inserting Todd's data in the worksheet**

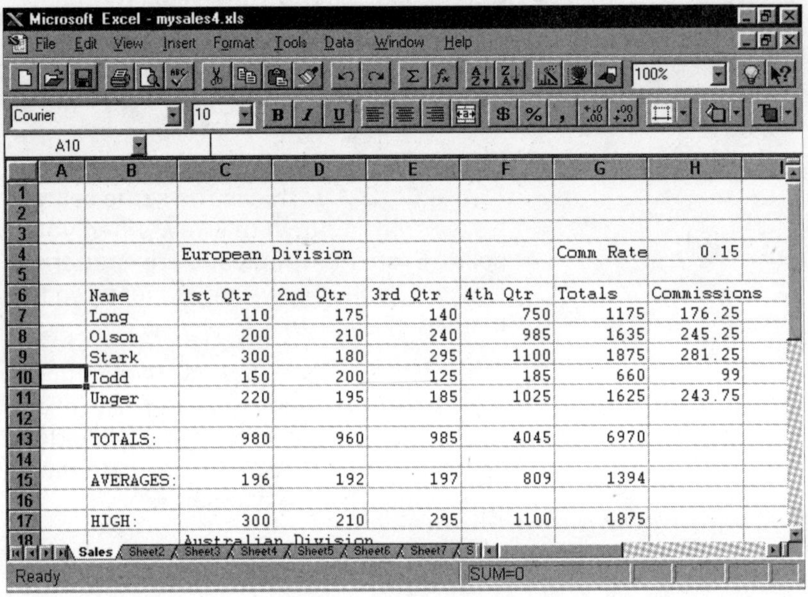

To move a range of cells by using the Cut and Paste commands,

- Select the cells you want to move.

- Choose *Edit, Cut*, press *Ctrl+X*, or click on the *Cut tool* (in the Standard toolbar), or choose *Cut* from the shortcut menu. A marquee encloses the selected cells.

- Select the range where you want to move the marqueed cells. As with copying, you need only select the upper-left cell of this range.

- Choose *Edit, Paste*, or press *Ctrl+V*, or click on the *Paste tool* (in the Standard toolbar), or choose *Paste* from the shortcut menu, or press *Enter* to paste the marqueed cell contents.

To move a range of cells using drag-and-drop,

- Select the cells you want to move.

- Point to the outline of the selected cell(s).

- Press and hold the left mouse button, and drag the selected cells to the desired new location.

**A word of caution:** As we mentioned in Chapter 4, when you paste data into a range of cells, it replaces (erases) the current data in these cells. So make sure to paste your data into an empty cell range or into a range containing data you can afford to lose.

Let's use the Cut and Paste commands to move a single cell:

1. Select cell **C4**, which contains the text *European Division*. Remember, even though this text spills into cell D4 on screen, it is really contained only in cell C4.

2. Choose **Edit, Cut**. Note the marquee surrounding cell C4.

3. Select cell **C2**.

4. Press **Enter** to move the contents of cell C4 to C2. The marquee disappears.

Now let's move a range of cells. While doing this, we'll explore the reason for the "word of caution" presented above:

1. Enter your initials in cell B33. (You'll see why in a moment.)

2. Select **B18:H31**. This is the range you want to move.

3. Press **Ctrl+X** to cut the selected cell range.

4. Select cell **B20** to tell Excel where you want to copy these cells. Remember, you need only select the upper-left corner of the range where you want to move the selected cells.

5. Press **Enter** to paste the cut cell data into the new range, B20:H33.

6. Select cell **B33**. Your initials are no longer here. Why not? Because pasting the cut cell data into the range B20:H33 replaced (erased) B33's previous data (your initials). The moral is this: Paste data into empty cells only, or into cells whose contents you can afford to lose.

## FOR THOSE WHO WANT TO STOP HERE

As mentioned earlier, you may want to work through this chapter in two sessions. To do this,

1. Choose **File, Save** to save the current version of mysales4.

2. Close the file and exit from Excel.

**3.** When you are ready to continue, start Excel, open **mysales4** from your Excel Work folder, and begin with the following section ("Formatting").

If you don't want to stop, please proceed directly to "Formatting."

# FORMATTING

The *format* of a cell determines how that cell's contents are displayed. For example: the number 10 could be formatted (displayed) as 10, 10.00, $10, or $10.00; the word "Totals" could be formatted as <u>Totals</u>, **Totals**, or *Totals*; and so on. You must format your cells properly to produce an effective and accurate representation of your worksheet data.

Bear in mind that when you change a cell's format, you change its appearance (how it looks on screen or on paper), not its contents. No matter how you formatted the first cell in the above example, the cell would still contain the number 10. The formula bar will always display the true contents of a cell.

 ## NUMBER FORMATS

Unless you specify otherwise, all numeric cells use Excel's *general* number format: no commas (1250), a minus sign to denote a negative number (–250), and as many decimals as will fit in the cell (.666667). You can change this format either by using the Formatting toolbar, or the Format Cells dialog box.

### Using the Formatting Toolbar

The Formatting toolbar provides a quick and easy way to apply common number formats to selected cells. To use the Formatting toolbar,

- Select the cells whose numeric display you want to reformat.

- Click on the desired number format tool in the Formatting toolbar (as shown in Figure 5.7).

Let's have some fun with these tools and apply a new number format to the entire worksheet:

**1.** Select cell **A1** to reorient your screen.

**Figure 5.7**    **The number format tools**

Currency Style tool

Percent Style tool

Comma Style tool

Increase Decimal tool

Decrease Decimal tool

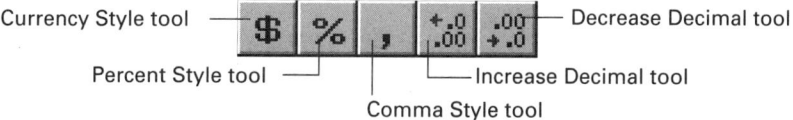

2.  Point to the empty box above the *1* of row 1 and to the left of the *A* of column A.

3.  Click on this box to select the entire worksheet (every cell).

4.  Click on the **Percent Style** tool to change the number format to the percent style. The results are, of course, ridiculous; you'd never want to display fixed dollar figures as percentages.

5.  Click on the **Undo** tool to undo your last action and restore the previous number format.

6.  The entire worksheet should still be selected; if not, select it. Click on the **Currency Style** tool to apply the currency style to your worksheet numbers. Note the overflow markers (######) in columns F and G. (Depending on your Windows setup, these markers may not appear.) These indicate that the cell contains more characters than can be displayed in the allotted onscreen cell width. You'll learn more about overflow markers in the next section.

7.  Click on the **Decrease Decimal** tool to remove one decimal place.

8.  Click on the **Decrease Decimal** tool again to remove another decimal place. Note that your numbers now have no decimal places.

9.  Click on the **Increase Decimal** tool to add a decimal place to your numeric cell display.

10. Select cell **A1** to deselect the worksheet. Observe the results, as shown in Figure 5.8. (Again, depending on your Windows setup, your screen display may not match ours exactly.) The numbers are displayed with a $ sign and one decimal place.

11. In cell F1, enter **20**. Note that it is displayed as $20.0. All four million-plus cells in the worksheet are now formatted to display numbers as currency with one decimal place.

**Figure 5.8**     **Applying the currency style by using the Formatting tools**

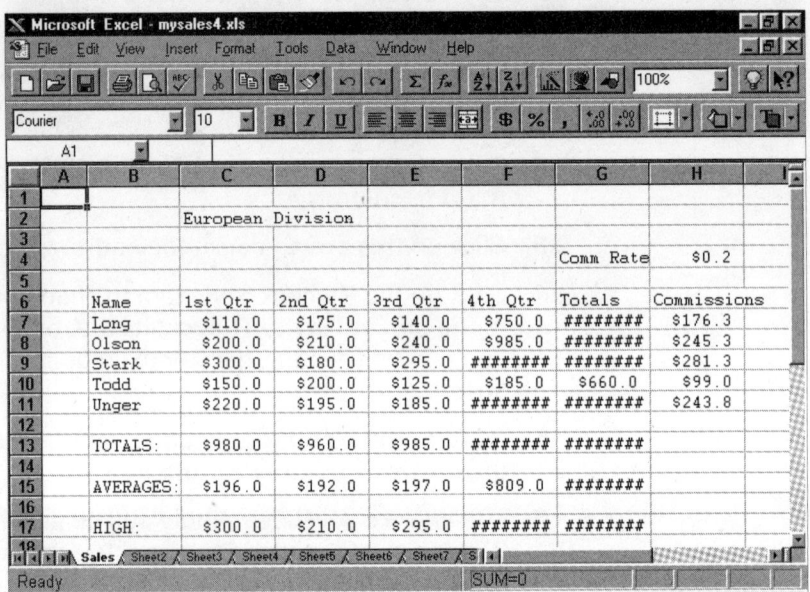

The Currency Style, Percent Style, and Comma Style tools are very convenient and are probably the most common number formats that you will use in your worksheets. There might be occasions when you want to use other formats though. Excel provides a multitude of formatting options that can be found in the Format Cells dialog box.

## Using the Format Cells Dialog Box

To change the number format by using the Format Cells dialog box,

- Select the cells whose numeric display you want to reformat.

- Choose *Format, Cells*, or press *Ctrl+1*, or open the shortcut menu and choose *Format Cells*. All these actions open the Format Cells dialog box.

- Click on the *Number tab*, if necessary, to display the number format options.

- Select the desired format category in the Category list box. In addition to the General number format, Excel provides 11 format categories that contain built-in number formats.

- Specify additional format options, such as decimal places or the use of a dollar sign.
- Click on OK.

**Note:** If you wanted to change, or "personalize," the built-in number formats, you would use the Custom category. Doing so, however, is beyond the scope of this book; if you are interested in this topic, refer to your Excel documentation.

Let's use the Format Cells dialog box to reformat some of the worksheet cells:

1. Select the range **C7:C11**.

2. Choose **Format, Cells** to open the Format Cells dialog box. Click on the **Number tab**, if necessary.

3. In the Category list box, observe the available categories. (You might want to take a moment and scroll through the list. In the middle of the dialog box, the additional formatting options will change to reflect the selected category.)

4. Select the **Accounting** category. Observe the description of the Accounting number format at the bottom of the dialog box. Also, a Sample of the format is displayed at the top of the dialog box.

5. Verify that Decimal Places is set at 1 and the Use $ check box is checked.

6. Click on **OK** to format the selected range with the Accounting number format.

7. Compare the newly formatted range to the rest of the worksheet cells. The difference between the Currency and Accounting formats is the alignment of the dollar sign. For our purposes, let's use the Currency format.

## PRACTICE YOUR SKILLS

Now you know how to change number formats by using the Formatting toolbar and the Format Cells dialog box. Use either method to practice your formatting skills.

1. Reformat the entire worksheet to Currency with two decimal places.

2. Select cell **H4**. Note the discrepancy between its actual value in the formula bar (0.15) and the screen display ($0.15). Change the format of cell H4 to reflect the correct commission rate of 15%.

3. Clear the contents of cell **F1**. (**Hint:** *Clear*, do not *delete*.) Your screen should match that shown in Figure 5.9.

**Figure 5.9**     **Formatting worksheet numbers**

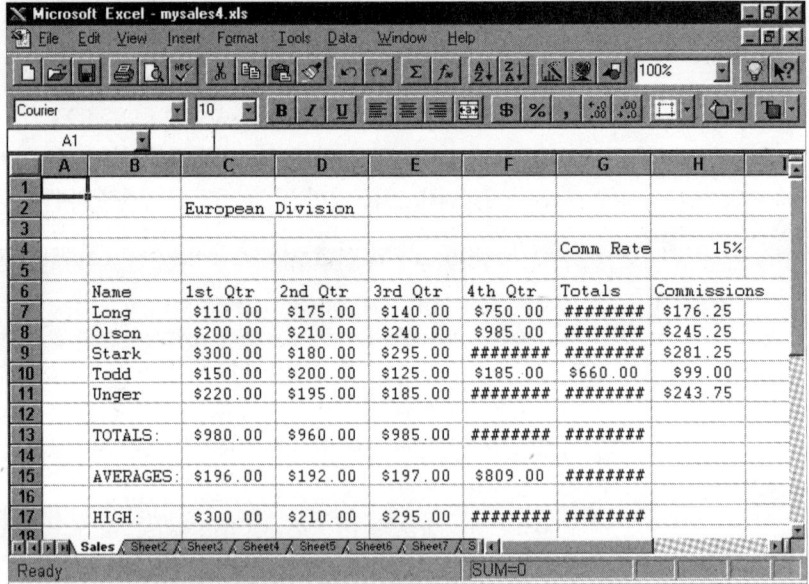

OVERFLOW MARKERS

Applying a number format to a cell may cause additional characters to be displayed in this cell. For example, as you saw in the last section, clicking on the Currency Style tool adds a $, commas, a decimal point, and two decimal places to a numeric cell display. When the number of characters contained in a numeric cell is greater than the cell's onscreen width, Excel displays overflow markers (######) to indicate that it could not display the entire data. Excel does not truncate numeric displays (as it does with text displays), because of the possible dire consequences. Imagine the confusion that might result if $14,971,000.00 were displayed as $14,971!

Let's take a closer look at overflow markers:

1. Select cell **F9**. (This cell should display overflow markers; it may not, however, depending upon your Windows setup.) Note from the formula bar that it contains the number 1100, despite the fact that the display reads ########. Overflow markers refer to the cell display only, not its actual numeric contents. A cell with overflow markers will still deliver its correct numeric value to any formula in which it is referenced.

2. Select cell **G7**. (This cell also should display overflow markers.) Note that it contains the formula =SUM(C7:F7), despite its overflow-marker display.

To remove a cell's overflow markers, you simply widen the cell's column until all its numeric data is displayed.

## CHANGING COLUMN WIDTH AND ROW HEIGHT

To change the width of a worksheet column, use any of the following methods:

- Point to the right border line of the column heading, and drag this line to the right (to widen the column) or to the left (to narrow the column).

- Select any cell in the desired column and choose *Format, Column, Width*. Or, select the entire column, open the shortcut menu, and choose *Column Width*. Type the new width (in characters) and click on OK.

- Select the entire column, and choose *Format, Column, Auto-Fit Selection*. Or, double-click on the right border line of the column heading. Both of these actions automatically set the column to the minimum width necessary to display the full contents (text and numeric) of all its cells.

To change the height of a worksheet row, use any of the following methods:

- Drag the lower border line of the row heading down (to lengthen) or up (to shorten).

- Select any cell in the row. Choose *Format, Row, Height* or choose *Row Height* from the shortcut menu. Type the new height and click on OK.

- Select the entire row and choose *Format, Row, AutoFit*. Or, double-click on the lower border line of the row heading.

Let's change column G's width by using the Format, Column, Width command:

1.  Select cell **G1**. You can select any cell in a column you want to widen; you need not select the entire column.

2.  Choose **Format, Column, Width** to open the Column Width dialog box.

3.  Type **12** and press **Enter** to change the width of column G to 12 characters. The missing numbers are displayed.

Now let's change column width by using the mouse:

1.  Point to the **border line** between the F and G column headings. Note that the mouse pointer changes to a cross with right and left arrows.

2.  Double-click on the **border line**, or drag it to the right, to widen column F and display the missing numbers in the overflow-marker cells.

3.  Widen any columns on your screen that still display overflow markers. (**Hint**: If you need to widen column C, don't use the double-click method, as this would widen the column to display all the text in cell C2, *European Division*.)

4.  Update the file.

## ALIGNING CELL CONTENTS

Excel lets you change the *alignment* (positioning) of the data displayed in a cell. You can *left-align*, *right-align*, *center*, *general-align* (left-align text, right-align numbers), or *fill* (fill the entire cell by repeating its data) a cell's contents. Figure 5.10 shows each of these alignments as applied to text (hello!), numbers (1,246,780), and symbols (!@#$%).

To change the alignment of cell contents,

- Select the desired cells.

- Choose Format, Cells (or press Ctrl+1, or open the shortcut menu and choose Format Cells) to open the Format Cells dialog box. Click on the *Alignment tab*, if necessary, to display

**Figure 5.10**     **Applying different alignments to cells**

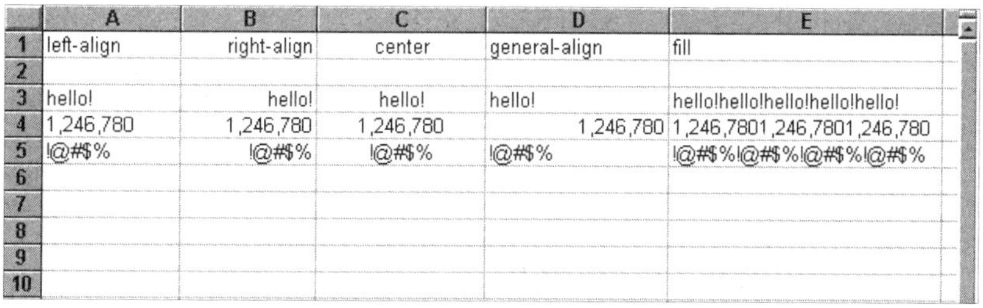

| | A | B | C | D | E |
|---|---|---|---|---|---|
| 1 | left-align | right-align | center | general-align | fill |
| 2 | | | | | |
| 3 | hello! | hello! | hello! | hello! | hello!hello!hello!hello!hello! |
| 4 | 1,246,780 | 1,246,780 | 1,246,780 | 1,246,780 | 1,246,7801,246,7801,246,780 |
| 5 | !@#$% | !@#$% | !@#$% | !@#$% | !@#$%!@#$%!@#$%!@#$% |
| 6 | | | | | |
| 7 | | | | | |
| 8 | | | | | |
| 9 | | | | | |
| 10 | | | | | |

the alignment options and under Horizontal, select the desired alignment. Click on OK.

- Or, use the alignment tools in the Formatting toolbar (as
  shown in Figure 5.11). To left-align the selected cells, click on
  the *Align Left tool*; to center the cells, click on the *Center tool*;
  or to right-align the cells, click on the *Align Right tool*.

**Figure 5.11**     **The alignment tools**

Align Left tool 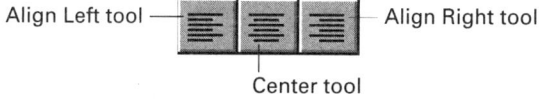 Align Right tool

Center tool

Let's use the Format, Cells command to right-align a range's
contents:

1. Select the range **C6:G6**.

2. Choose **Format, Cells** to open the Format Cells dialog box. If
   necessary, click on the **Alignment tab** to display the alignment options.

3. Under Horizontal, select **Right**. Click on **OK** to right-align the
   selected text.

Now let's use the Center tool to center a cell's contents:

1. Select cell **C2**.

2. Click on the **Center tool** (as shown in Figure 5.11) to center the contents of C2. Note that the text spills over into cells B2 and D2. When you center a long text entry, the middle of the text is displayed in the cell-of-origin, while the remaining text spills out to either side (provided, of course, that the cells to the side are empty).

3. Examine cells B2, C2, and D2 to verify that *European Division* is contained wholly in cell C2.

### PRACTICE YOUR SKILLS

Center the contents of the cells in the range G4:H4.

### CHANGING THE FONT FORMAT

Excel allows you to change the font (typeface), size, style, and color of the data displayed in a cell. To do this,

• Select the desired cells.

• Choose Format, Cells (or press Ctrl+1, or open the shortcut menu and choose Format Cells) to open the Format Cells dialog box. Click on the *Font tab*, if necessary, to display the font options and change the desired options (change the font in the Font list box, change the font size in the Size list box, change the style in the Font Style box, change the effects under Effects, change the underline in the Underline list box, or change the color in the Color list box). Click on OK.

• Or, use the font tools in the Formatting toolbar (as shown in Figure 5.12). To change the font, use the Font list box; to change the font size, use the Font Size list box; to bold, italicize, or underline the text, click on the *Bold*, *Italic*, or *Underline tool*; or to change the font color, use the Font Color list box.

**Figure 5.12**     **The font tools**

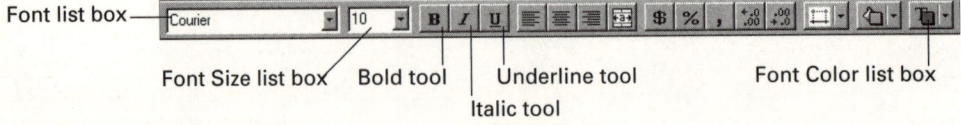

Font list box

Font Size list box    Bold tool    Underline tool    Font Color list box

Italic tool

Let's use the Format Cells dialog box to change the font of the data displayed in cell C2:

1. Select cell **C2**, which contains *European Division*.

2. Press **Ctrl+1** to open the Format Cells dialog box.

3. Click on the **Font tab**, if necessary, to display the font options. Observe the Preview box; it shows you a sample of the selected font (Courier).

4. In the Font list box, select **Times New Roman**. (If this font is not available on your system, select the closest alternative: Times Roman, or so on.) Observe the change in the Preview box.

5. In the Size list box, select **14**. This stands for 14 points; a 72-point font is 1 inch in height. Observe the Preview box.

6. In the Font Style list box, select **Bold Italic**. Observe the Preview box.

7. Click on **OK** to apply your font changes to the text displayed in cell C2. Note that the first four tools in the Formatting toolbar—the Font and Size list boxes and the Bold and Italic tools—reflect these changes. Note also that Excel automatically increased the height of row 2 to accommodate the larger font size.

## PRACTICE YOUR SKILLS

1. Use the font tools in the Formatting toolbar to format the data in cells B6:H6 to **Times New Roman** (or the closest alternative), **10 points, Italic**.

2. Widen columns F and G to remove the overflow markers.

3. Press **Ctrl+Home** to deselect the selected range. Your worksheet should match that shown in Figure 5.13.

4. Update the file.

 ## ADDING BORDERS AND PATTERNS TO CELLS

You can make important cells stand out in your worksheet by changing their background color and adding borders to them. In

**Figure 5.13**     **Changing the font format**

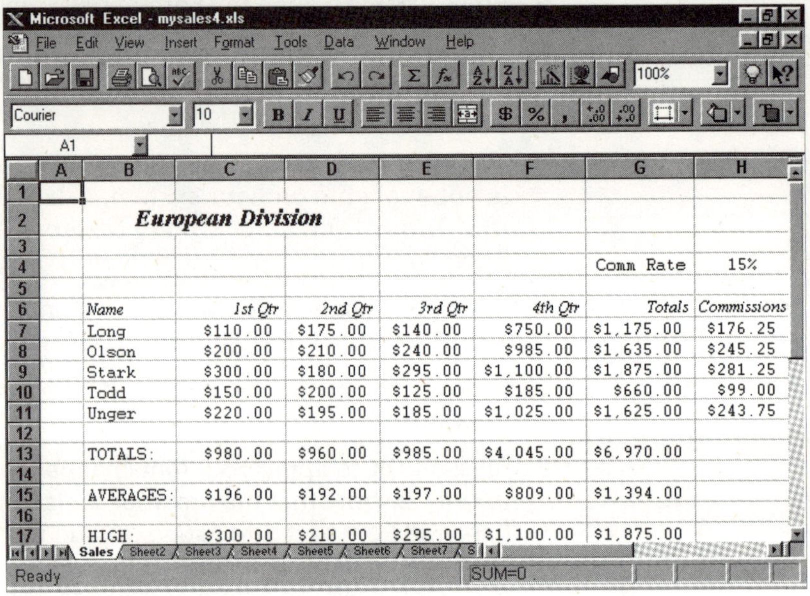

the next activity, for example, you'll use this technique to accentuate the totals, averages, and high data of the current worksheet.

To change cells' background color,

- Select the desired cells.

- Choose Format, Cells (or press Ctrl+1, or open the shortcut menu and choose Format Cells) to open the Format Cells dialog box. Click on the *Patterns tab*, if necessary, to display the patterns options and select the desired background color under Color. Click on OK.

- Or, use the Font Color list box in the Formatting toolbar.

To add borders to cells,

- Select the desired cells.

- Choose Format, Cells (or press Ctrl+1, or open the shortcut menu and choose Format Cells) to open the Format Cells dialog box. Click on the *Border tab*, if necessary, to display the border options and change the desired options (change the border location under Border; change the border style under Style or change the color under Color). Click on OK.

- Or, use the Borders list box in the Formatting toolbar.

Let's emphasize the totals, averages, and high data in our worksheet by changing the background color and adding a border to the cells in which this data is displayed. We'll use the Format Cells dialog box to change the background color and the Borders list box (in the Formatting toolbar) to add a border:

1. Select the range **B13:G17**.

2. Point anywhere within this range and click the **right mouse button** to open the shortcut menu. Choose **Format Cells** to open the Format Cells dialog box, and click on the **Patterns tab** to display the pattern options.

3. Under Color, select (click on) the light gray color at the intersection of the second row and seventh column of displayed colors.

4. Click on **OK** to apply a light gray color to the background of your selected cells. You won't be able to see this color very clearly until you deselect the selected range. Please don't do this now.

5. Click on the **down arrow** to the right of the Borders list box to open its *option palette*, which displays a set of border options.

6. Click on the option in the lower-right corner (as shown in Figure 5.14) to place a border around the entire outer edge of the selected range.

**Figure 5.14**     **The Borders palette**

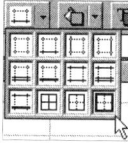

7. Press **Ctrl+Home** to deselect the selected cells. The background color and border are now clearly visible, as shown in Figure 5.15.

**Figure 5.15**     **Coloring and bordering cells**

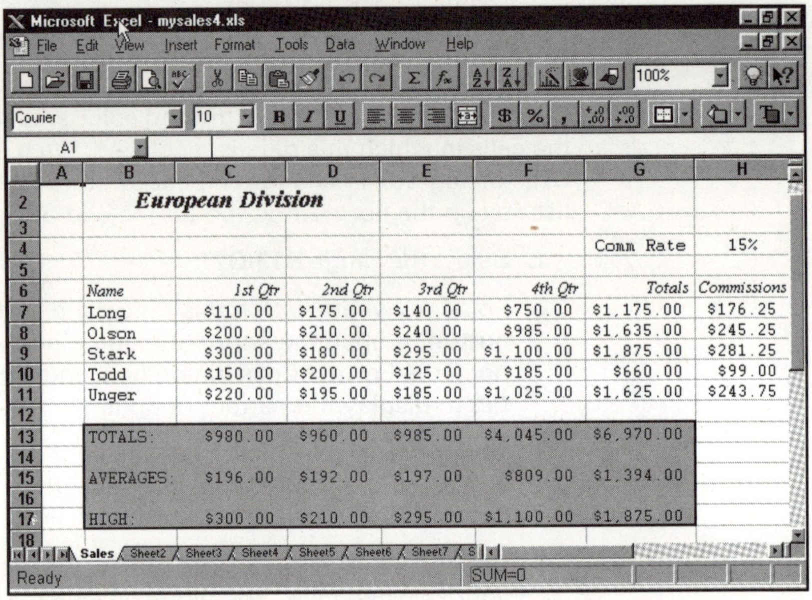

## COPYING SPECIFIC CELL ATTRIBUTES

When you use the Paste command to copy the contents of a cell to a new location, Excel copies every *attribute* (characteristic) of the cell: its text, formulas, numeric values, and formats. At times, however, you may want to copy just one of these attributes; for example, you may want to copy a cell's format—but not its contents—to another cell. You can use the *Paste Special* command to do this.

To copy specific cell attributes,

- Select the cells whose attributes you want to copy.

- Choose Edit, Copy (or press Ctrl+C, or click on the *Copy tool,* or choose Copy from the shortcut menu). As you've no doubt realized, Excel provides two or more methods for performing most common tasks.

- Select the upper-left cell of the range of cells to which you want to copy the attributes.

- Choose *Edit, Paste Special* (or choose *Paste Special* from the shortcut menu) to open the Paste Special dialog box.

- Under Paste, select the desired Paste option (*All, Formulas, Values, Formats,* or *Notes*).

- Click on OK.

Let's use the Paste Special command to copy the formatting, but not the contents, of a single cell:

1. Select cell **C2**, the cell containing *European Division*.

2. Click on the **Copy tool**.

3. Select cell **C20**, the cell containing *Australian Division*. It's here that you'll copy the format from cell C2.

4. Point to cell **C20** and click the **right mouse button** to open the shortcut menu. Click on **Paste Special** in this menu to open the Paste Special dialog box.

5. Under Paste, select **Formats**.

6. Click on **OK** to copy the formatting (alignment, font, and so on)—but not the contents—of cell C2 to cell C20. Note that *Australian Division* now looks just like *European Division*.

7. Note that cell C2 is still marqueed, indicating that you could copy the selected cell's attributes to another cell. Please don't.

8. Press **Esc** to remove the marquee.

## USING THE FORMAT PAINTER TOOL TO COPY CELL FORMATTING

Excel provides a *Format Painter tool* that you can use to quickly and easily copy cell formatting. To do this,

- Select the cells whose formatting you want to copy.

- Click on the *Format Painter tool*. Or, if you intend to copy the selected formatting to more than one location, double-click on the Format Painter tool.

- Click on the upper-left cell of the range of cells to which you want to copy the selected formatting. Excel copies the formats as soon as you perform this step.

- If you double-clicked on the Format Painter tool to enable further copying, repeat the previous step as many times as necessary. When you're done copying, click once again on the Format Painter tool.

Let's use the Format Painter tool to copy the formatting of a range of cells:

1. Select the range **B6:H17**. This is the range whose format you'll copy.

2. Click on the **Format Painter tool**. Note that the mouse pointer now shows a paintbrush next to its standard cross.

3. Click on cell **B22** (you may need to scroll), the upper-left cell of the range where you want to copy the formatting.

4. Observe the results. Excel copied the formatting from cells B6:H17 (European Division data) to cells B22:H33 (Australian Division data).

5. Scroll down until the entire Australian Division data is visible. If necessary, widen column C to display the full contents of cell C29.

6. Select cell **A20** to deselect the range. Your screen should match that shown in Figure 5.16.

7. Update and then close the workbook file.

## PRACTICE YOUR SKILLS

This activity will sharpen the Excel formatting skills you acquired in this chapter. Perform these steps to edit the Sheet1 worksheet in the workbook Practice5 to match Figure 5.17:

1. Open **Practice5** from your Excel Work folder (Chapter 3).

2. Maximize the document window, if necessary (Chapter 3).

3. Insert a new, blank row between rows 2 and 3 (Chapter 5).

**Figure 5.16** **The completed Australian Division**

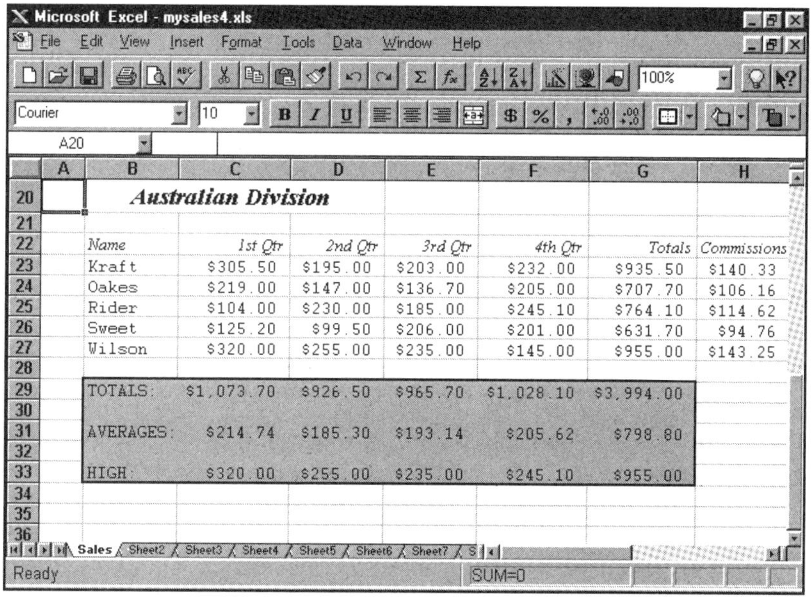

| | A | B | C | D | E | F | G | H |
|---|---|---|---|---|---|---|---|---|
| 20 | | *Australian Division* | | | | | | |
| 21 | | | | | | | | |
| 22 | | *Name* | *1st Qtr* | *2nd Qtr* | *3rd Qtr* | *4th Qtr* | *Totals* | *Commissions* |
| 23 | | Kraft | $305.50 | $195.00 | $203.00 | $232.00 | $935.50 | $140.33 |
| 24 | | Oakes | $219.00 | $147.00 | $136.70 | $205.00 | $707.70 | $106.16 |
| 25 | | Rider | $104.00 | $230.00 | $185.00 | $245.10 | $764.10 | $114.62 |
| 26 | | Sweet | $125.20 | $99.50 | $206.00 | $201.00 | $631.70 | $94.76 |
| 27 | | Wilson | $320.00 | $255.00 | $235.00 | $145.00 | $955.00 | $143.25 |
| 28 | | | | | | | | |
| 29 | | TOTALS: | $1,073.70 | $926.50 | $965.70 | $1,028.10 | $3,994.00 | |
| 30 | | | | | | | | |
| 31 | | AVERAGES: | $214.74 | $185.30 | $193.14 | $205.62 | $798.80 | |
| 32 | | | | | | | | |
| 33 | | HIGH: | $320.00 | $255.00 | $235.00 | $245.10 | $955.00 | |

**Figure 5.17** **The completed ExMac Corporation worksheet**

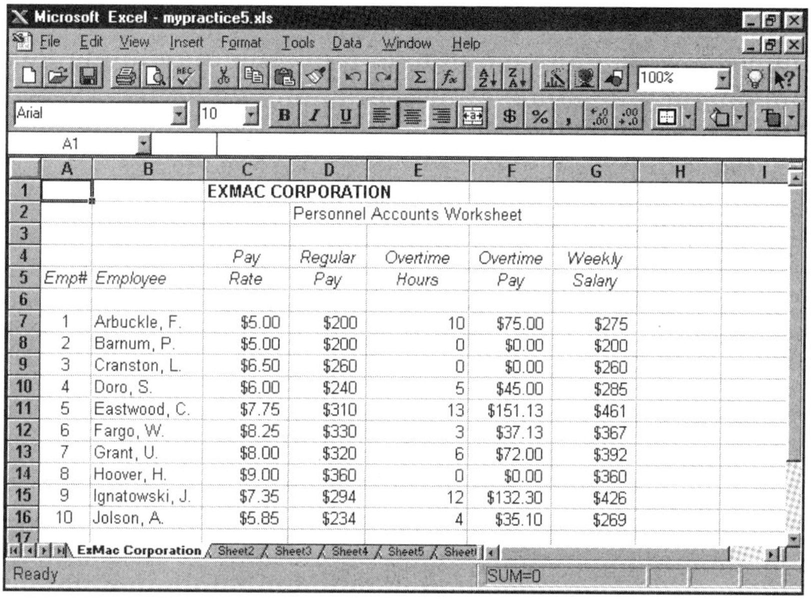

| | A | B | C | D | E | F | G |
|---|---|---|---|---|---|---|---|
| 1 | | | EXMAC CORPORATION | | | | |
| 2 | | | | Personnel Accounts Worksheet | | | |
| 3 | | | | | | | |
| 4 | | | *Pay* | *Regular* | *Overtime* | *Overtime* | *Weekly* |
| 5 | *Emp#* | *Employee* | *Rate* | *Pay* | *Hours* | *Pay* | *Salary* |
| 6 | | | | | | | |
| 7 | 1 | Arbuckle, F. | $5.00 | $200 | 10 | $75.00 | $275 |
| 8 | 2 | Barnum, P. | $5.00 | $200 | 0 | $0.00 | $200 |
| 9 | 3 | Cranston, L. | $6.50 | $260 | 0 | $0.00 | $260 |
| 10 | 4 | Doro, S. | $6.00 | $240 | 5 | $45.00 | $285 |
| 11 | 5 | Eastwood, C. | $7.75 | $310 | 13 | $151.13 | $461 |
| 12 | 6 | Fargo, W. | $8.25 | $330 | 3 | $37.13 | $367 |
| 13 | 7 | Grant, U. | $8.00 | $320 | 6 | $72.00 | $392 |
| 14 | 8 | Hoover, H. | $9.00 | $360 | 0 | $0.00 | $360 |
| 15 | 9 | Ignatowski, J. | $7.35 | $294 | 12 | $132.30 | $426 |
| 16 | 10 | Jolson, A. | $5.85 | $234 | 4 | $35.10 | $269 |

4. Insert new, blank cells in the range **A4:A17**, shifting the old cell contents to the right (Chapter 5).

5. In cell **A5**, enter the text **Emp#** (Chapter 2).

6. In column **A**, number the employees **1** through **10** (Chapter 4).

7. Delete row **6** (Chapter 5). (Hint: Delete the row, don't just clear it.)

8. Bold the contents of cell **A1** (Chapter 5).

9. Italicize the contents of cells **A4:G5** (Chapter 5).

10. Format the range **C7:C16** to currency with two decimal places (Chapter 5).

11. Format the range **D7:D16** to currency with no decimal places (Chapter 5).

12. Copy the formatting of cells **C7:D16** to cells **F7:G16** (Chapter 5).

13. Move the range **A1:B2** to the range **C1:D2** (Chapter 5). (**Hint:** Use drag-and-drop.)

14. Reduce the width of column **A** to slightly wider than the text in cell A5 (Chapter 5).

15. Center the contents of column **A** (Chapter 5).

16. Widen column **B** to exactly 12 characters (Chapter 5).

17. Center the contents of the range **C4:G5** (Chapter 5).

18. Rename the current worksheet **ExMac Corporation** (Chapter 2).

19. Save the modified workbook file as **mypractice5** (Chapter 2).

20. Your worksheet should match that shown in Figure 5.17.

21. Close the file (Chapter 2).

## SUMMARY

In this chapter, you learned the fundamentals of worksheet editing and formatting. You now know how to edit the contents of a cell; how to enter absolute cell references in formulas; how to insert and delete cells, columns, and rows; how to move cell data; how to change the format of worksheet numbers and text; and how to copy specific attributes of cells.

Here's a quick reference guide to the Excel features introduced in this chapter:

| Desired Result | How to Do It |
|---|---|
| Edit a cell | Select cell; use **F2** and arrow keys or mouse to place insertion point; insert/replace data; enter revised data |
| Create absolute reference | Type **$** before row and column in reference |
| Create mixed reference | Type **$** before row or column in reference |
| Insert columns/rows | Select columns/rows and choose **Edit, Insert** (or choose **Insert** from shortcut menu) |
| Select columns/rows | Click on (or drag over) adjacent column/row headings |
| Insert cells | Select range where you want to insert; choose **Insert, Cells** (or choose **Insert Cells** from shortcut menu); select **Shift Cells Down** or **Shift Cells Right**; click on **OK** |
| Move cells | Select cells to move; choose **Edit, Cut** (or press **Ctrl+C**, or click on the **Cut tool**, or choose **Cut** from shortcut menu); select upper-left corner of destination range; choose **Edit, Paste** (or press **Ctrl+V**, or click on **Paste tool**, or choose **Paste** from shortcut menu, or press **Enter**). Or, use drag-and-drop |
| Change number format | Select cells; choose **Format, Cells** (or press **Ctrl+1**, or choose **Format Cells** from shortcut menu); click on **Number tab**; select desired category and format; click on **OK**. Or, use number format tools in Formatting toolbar |

| Desired Result | How to Do It |
|---|---|
| Change column width | Drag column border line. Or select cell in column and choose **Format, Column, Width** (or select entire column and choose **Column Width** from shortcut menu); type new width; click on **OK**. Or choose **Format, Column, AutoFit Selection** or double-click on column right border line to use AutoFit |
| Change row height | Drag row border line. Or select cell in row; choose **Format, Row, Height** (or choose **Row Height** from shortcut menu); type new height; click on **OK**. Or choose **Format, Row, AutoFit** or double-click on row's lower border line to use AutoFit |
| Change alignment | Select cells; choose **Format, Cells** (or press **Ctrl+1**, or choose **Format Cells** from shortcut menu); click on **Alignment tab**; select desired alignment; click on **OK**. Or use alignment tools in Formatting toolbar |
| Change font | Select cells; choose **Format, Cells** (or press **Ctrl+1**, or choose **Format Cells** from shortcut menu); click on **Font tab**; select desired font options; click on **OK**. Or use font tools in Formatting toolbar |
| Add border to cell | Select cells; choose **Format, Cells** (or press **Ctrl+1**, or choose **Format Cells** from shortcut menu); click on **Border tab**; select desired border; click on **OK**. Or use Borders list box in Formatting toolbar |

| Desired Result | How to Do It |
|---|---|
| Color cell background | Select cells; choose **Format, Cells** (or press **Ctrl+1**, or choose **Format Cells** from shortcut menu); click on **Patterns tab**; select desired color; click on **OK**. Or use Color list box in Formatting toolbar |
| Copy specific cell attributes | Select cells to copy from; choose **Edit, Copy** (or press **Ctrl+C**, or click on the **Copy tool**, or choose **Copy** from shortcut menu); select upper-left cell of range to copy to; choose **Edit, Paste Special** (or choose **Paste Special** from shortcut menu); select attributes to copy; click on **OK** |
| Copy cell formatting | Select cells to copy from, click on **Format Painter tool**; select upper-left cell of range to copy to |

In the next chapter, you'll learn how to center data across columns; sum a range automatically; and spell-check, print, print-preview a worksheet, and enhance your printouts.

## IF YOU'RE STOPPING HERE

If you want to break off here, please exit Excel. If you have the energy to proceed directly to the next chapter, please do so now.

# CHAPTER 6:
# ENHANCING AND
# PRINTING YOUR
# WORKSHEET

Centering Data
across Columns

Summing a Range
Automatically

Spell-Checking a
Worksheet

Printing a
Worksheet

Print-Previewing a
Worksheet

N ow that you've mastered basic worksheet mechanics, you can move on to the final steps of the worksheet-creation process, spell-checking and printing. First, we'll introduce a couple of handy Excel techniques: how to center data across several worksheet columns, and how to use the AutoSum tool and AutoCalculate feature to sum a range of cells automatically. Then, we'll show you how to spell-check the text in a worksheet and create professional-looking printouts.

When you're done working through this chapter, you will know

- How to center data across columns

- How to sum a range automatically

- How to spell-check a worksheet

- How to print a worksheet

- How to print-preview a worksheet on your screen

- How to control page setup options

## CENTERING DATA ACROSS COLUMNS

In the last chapter, you learned how to center data within a cell. Here you'll learn a related technique: how to center data within two or more adjacent cells (or, as Excel puts it, across two or more columns). As you'll see in the following activity, this feature allows you to center headings over groups of irregularly spaced worksheet columns.

To center data across columns,

- Select the cell containing the data you want to center.

- Extend the selection to include the blank adjacent cells to the right across which you want to center the data.

- Click on the *Center Across Columns tool* (in the Formatting toolbar).

If you are not running Excel, please start it now. If there is a workbook on your screen (other than Book1), please close it. Let's open a file and center a text heading across a group of irregularly spaced columns:

1. Open the workbook file **Sales Express** from your Excel Work folder, and maximize the document window, if necessary.

2. Observe the active worksheet, Sales Inventory. It keeps track of International Express, Ltd.'s retail items (trolleys, pulleys, and so on). Note the irregular spacing of columns A through E; B through E are equally spaced, but A is wider.

3. Select cell **A1**. Note that the Bold, Italic, and Align Left tools are selected in the Formatting toolbar, indicating that the text in A1 (*International Express, Ltd.*) is bolded, italicized, and left-aligned.

**4.** Extend the selection to the range **A1:E1**. You're telling Excel that you want to center the contents of the leftmost cell of this range (A1) across the entire range (A1:E1).

**5.** Click on the **Center Across Columns tool**. The heading *International Express, Ltd.* is centered across columns A through E, as shown in Figure 6.1.

**Figure 6.1**     **Centering data across columns**

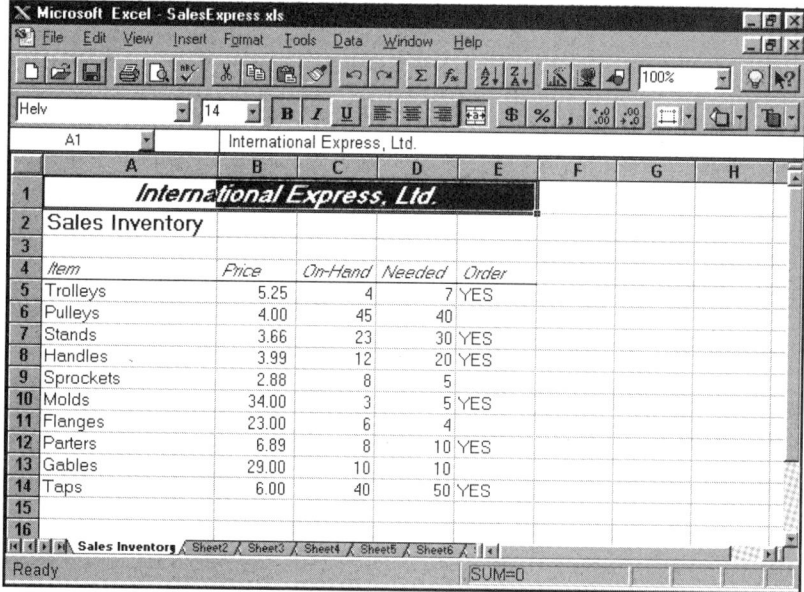

PRACTICE YOUR SKILLS

**1.** Center the heading **Sales Inventory** (in cell A2) across columns A through E (cells A2:E2).

2. Center the contents of cells A4:E4 within their respective cells. (Hint: Use the **Center tool**, not the Center Across Columns tool.)

3. Center the contents of cells C5:E14 within their respective cells.

4. Save the file to your Excel Work folder as **myexpress**. Your screen should match that shown in Figure 6.2.

**Figure 6.2**      **Centering data within their respective cells**

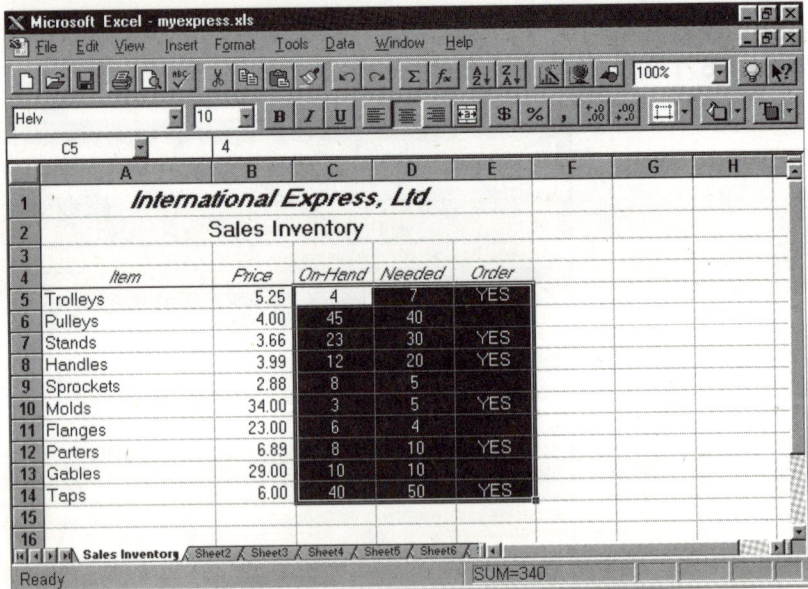

## SUMMING A RANGE AUTOMATICALLY

In Chapter 4, you had plenty of practice entering SUM functions to sum ranges of numbers. Here, you'll learn how to use the *AutoSum tool* and *AutoCalculate feature* to help automate this process.

## USING THE AUTOSUM TOOL

To use the AutoSum feature to automatically sum a range,

- Select the cell where you want the sum to appear. This cell must be directly beneath a column of contiguous numbers to be summed or directly to the right of a row of contiguous numbers to be summed.

- Click on the *AutoSum tool*. Excel automatically enters a SUM function in the selected cell, specifying as its SUM argument the contiguous range of cells in the column above or the row to the left of the selected cell.

- Enter the SUM function into the cell.

Let's use the AutoSum tool to sum a range automatically:

1. Select cell **C15**.

2. Click on the **AutoSum tool**.

3. Observe the results. Excel automatically created a SUM function that sums the contents of the contiguous range of cells above C15, =SUM(C5:C14).

4. Enter this function (by pressing **Enter** or clicking on the **Enter box**). The result is 159, the sum of the contents of cells C5:C14.

Now let's see what happens if you try to use AutoSum to sum a column of cells containing text, rather than numbers:

1. Select cell **A15**.

2. Click on the **AutoSum tool**. Note that the formula bar contains the argumentless formula =SUM(), as shown in Figure 6.3. Excel did not specify a SUM argument, because the cells you asked it to autosum contain text rather than numbers (*Trolleys*, *Pulleys*, and so on), and you can't sum text.

3. Press **Esc** (or click on the **Cancel box**) to cancel the AutoSum procedure.

**Figure 6.3**       **Attempting to use Σ to sum text**

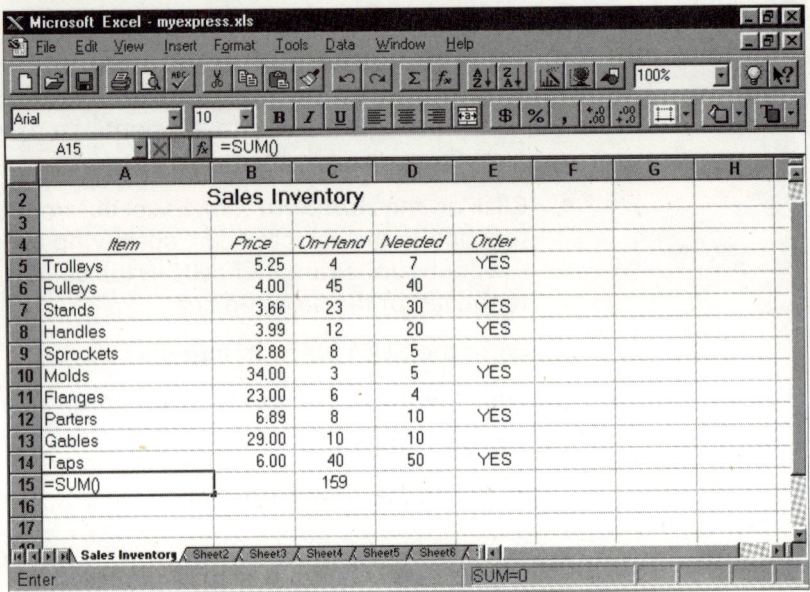

USING THE AUTOCALCULATE FEATURE

As you've worked with Excel, you might have noticed the SUM= indicator in the status bar. The *AutoCalculate area* displays the sum of the selected cell(s). The selected cells must contain numerical data; if the cells contain text, then the Auto-Calculate area will display SUM=0. AutoCalculate enables you to view the sum of a range without having to use a calculator or enter a temporary formula.

Let's experiment with the AutoCalculate feature:

1. Select cell **D5**.

2. Observe the AutoCalculate area in the status bar. It displays SUM=7.

3. Select the range **D5:D14**. The AutoCalculate area in the status bar displays SUM=181.

4. Select cell **E5**. Note that the AutoCalculate area displays SUM=0. Excel cannot display a total when cells contain text.

**5.** Update and close the file.

## SPELL-CHECKING A WORKSHEET

No matter how dazzling its data and layout, if your worksheet is laced with misspellings, it just won't be very effective. Misspellers rejoice! Excel provides a Spelling command that allows you to quickly and easily spell-check the text contained in your worksheet cells. To do this,

- To spell-check the entire worksheet, select any single cell. To spell-check part of the worksheet, select the desired cell range (at least two cells).

- Choose *Tools, Spelling*, or press F7, or click on the *Spelling tool* to open the Spelling dialog box and begin the spell check. If Excel finds a word that is not in its internal dictionary, it displays this word in the Not In Dictionary line at the top of the dialog box, along with a group of alternative spellings in the Change To and Suggestions boxes. (For example, in the Spelling dialog box in Figure 6.4, Excel found the misspelled word *Interntional* and offered the suggestions *Intentional, Intentionally*, and so on.) At this point, you can choose any of the following options:

  - To change the Not In Dictionary word to the word in the Change To box, click on *Change* (to change the current instance of the Not In Dictionary word) or on *Change All* (to change all instances of the word).

**Figure 6.4**     **The Spelling dialog box**

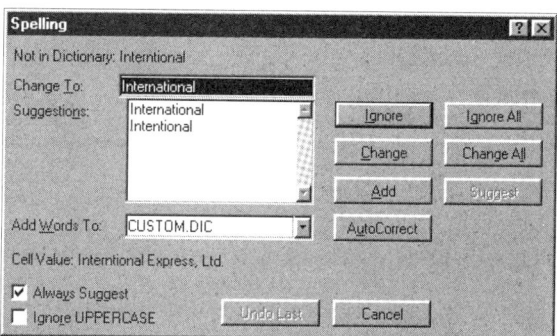

- To change the Not 1n Dictionary word to a word in the Suggestions box, click on the Suggestions word to move it to the Change To box, and then click on Change (to change the current instance) or on Change All (to change all instances).

- To leave the Not In Dictionary word as is, click on *Ignore* (to leave the current instance as is) or on *Ignore All* (to leave all instances as is).

- To add the Not In Dictionary word to the custom dictionary currently selected in the Add Words To list box, click on *Add*.

- To enter a spelling not displayed in the Change To or Suggestions boxes, select the current Change To box contents, type your desired spelling, then click on Change or Change All.

- A dialog box informs you when the spell check has been completed. Click on OK to remove this dialog box and return to your workbook.

Let's spell-check a selected range of cells from a new worksheet:

1. Open the file **Spell** from your Excel Work folder.

2. Maximize the document window, if necessary.

3. Observe the worksheet; press **PgDn** to view the bottom half. Note that there are several misspellings.

4. Select cells **B1:B2**. These cells contain two misspelled words, *Interntional* and *Amercan*. Note that the Center Across Columns tool is selected. The headings are centered across columns B through G.

5. Choose **Tools, Spelling** to open the Spelling dialog box and begin the spell check. Excel displays the misspelled word *Interntional* in the Not in Dictionary line as shown in Figure 6.4. Note that the correctly spelled word, *International*, is displayed in the Change To box.

6. Click on **Change** to change the misspelled word (*Interntional*) to the correctly spelled word in the Change To box (*International*).

7. The spell check continues. Excel displays the misspelled word *Amercan* in the Not in Dictionary line. Note that the correctly

spelled word, *American*, is once again displayed in the Change To box.

**8.** Click on **Change** to correct the spelling. A dialog box informs you that your selected cells have been spell-checked.

**9.** Click on **OK** to remove this dialog box and return to your worksheet. Note that Excel corrected the spellings of *International* and *American*.

Now let's spell-check the entire worksheet:

**1.** Press **Ctrl+Home** to select cell A1. You could have selected any single cell in preparation for spell-checking the entire worksheet; we had you select A1 because pressing Ctrl+Home is so convenient.

**2.** Click on the **Spelling tool**.

**3.** Excel displays *Quartr* in the Not in Dictionary line. *Quartr* is a misspelling of *Quarter*. Alas, our erroneous *Quartr* appears several times throughout the worksheet! Let's correct all these misspellings at once.

**4.** Verify that **Quarter** is in the Change To box, and then click on **Change All** to change every instance of *Quartr* to *Quarter*. There; that was easy!

**5.** Excel displays *Mott* in the Not in Dictionary line. Mott is the correct spelling of a sales rep's surname, so we'll tell Excel to leave it as is.

**6.** Click on **Ignore** to do this.

**7.** Excel displays *Totl* in the Not in Dictionary line, a misspelling of *Total*.

**8.** In the Suggestions box, click on **Total** to move this correct spelling to the Change To box. Click on **Change** to change *Totl* to *Total*.

9. Excel displays *Kane* in the Not in Dictionary line. Kane—like Mott—is a correctly spelled rep's surname, so we want to leave it as is. Moreover, since Kane is such an important rep (he's been with the company for twenty-nine years!), and since his name appears in so many of our worksheets, we want to add it to our custom dictionary.

10. Click on **Add** to do this. From now on, whenever Excel encounters Kane while spell-checking, it will consider it to be correctly spelled.

11. Excel displays *Sbrtshr* in the Not in Dictionary line. *Sbrtshr* is a bizarre misspelling caused by typing the word *Average* one key too far to the right on the keyboard. Note that the correctly spelled word (Average) does not appear in the Suggestions box. We'll have to enter the proper spelling manually.

12. Select **Sbrtshr** in the Change To box, if necessary, and type **Average**. Click on **Change** to change *Sbrtshr* to *Average*.

13. Excel displays *Hiigh* in the Not in Dictionary line. Verify that the correctly spelled word, *High*, is displayed in the Change To box and click on **Change**.

14. A dialog box informs you that Excel has finished spell-checking the entire worksheet.

15. Click on **OK** to remove this box and return to your worksheet. Scroll through and observe the spelling changes.

16. Save the worksheet as **myspell** to your Excel Work folder.

17. Close the file.

## PRINTING A WORKSHEET

Screen displays are nice, but you can't slap them on your boss's desk or pass them around in a meeting. Welcome to the world of printouts! Printing can be as simple as clicking on a single tool. Excel also gives you the power, however, to exercise control over the way in which a worksheet prints. You can change the orientation of the paper, add headers or footers, insert page breaks, change margins, and so on.

To discuss printing, we'll need a worksheet that presents us with some printing difficulties. Let's open and examine a worksheet that's been created for this purpose.

1. Open **Report** (in your Excel Work folder). This large worksheet contains the three-year sales data for each sales representative.

2. Scroll to view the length of the worksheet. The worksheet extends to row 107.

3. Press **Ctrl+Home** to return to cell A1, and then click once in the horizontal scroll bar to view the portion of the worksheet one screen to the right. The sales report data extends through column S.

4. Return to cell A1.

## EXPLORING PRINT OPTIONS

Printing a worksheet can be very simple. To print a worksheet using its current print settings,

- Choose *File, Print* or press *Ctrl+P* to open the Print dialog box.

  - Use the Print What section of the dialog box to specify whether you want to print a selection, selected sheet(s), or the entire workbook. The current, or selected, sheet is the default setting.

  - If you want to print only certain pages, use the Page Range section to specify a starting and ending page. By default, all pages will be printed.

  - Use the Copies section to specify how many copies you wish to print and whether they need to be collated or not.

- Click on OK to print using the current settings or click on Cancel to close the dialog box without printing.

Let's take a look at the Print dialog box:

1. Choose **File, Print** to display the Print dialog box (see Figure 6.5—your dialog box may look slightly different, depending upon the printer you are using).

2. Note the print options and their default settings.

**Figure 6.5**     **The Print dialog box**

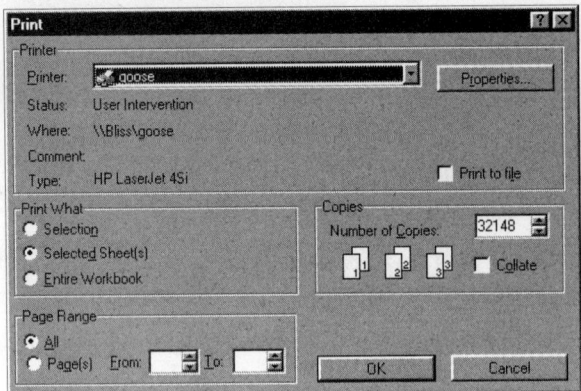

3. Click on **Cancel** to close the dialog box.

## EXPLORING THE PRINT PREVIEW

It is useful to know what your printed worksheet will look like *before* you actually print it. You can display a preview of how a worksheet will look when printed, in several ways.

• Choose *File, Print Preview* to display the print preview.

• Click on the *Print Preview tool* in the Standard toolbar.

• In the Page Setup dialog box, click on the *Print Preview* button.

When you are in print preview, you can control the preview by using the buttons at the top of the window. These buttons can be used to move to the next or previous page, enlarge or reduce the current page, open the Print dialog box, open the Page Setup dialog box to change page settings, change the current margins, close print preview, and access online Help.

Let's preview the workbook Report:

1. Choose **File, Print Preview** to display the print preview.

2. Point to the previewed page. Note that the mouse pointer changes to a magnifying glass. Click the mouse button to enlarge the preview.

**3.** Click on **Zoom** to reduce it. Clicking on Zoom is the same as using the magnifying glass tool to toggle between enlarging and reducing the print preview.

**4.** Click on **Next** to preview the next page of the printed worksheet.

**5.** Click on **Next** four more times to preview the remaining pages of the printed worksheet. Note that the last two pages are blank.

**6.** Click on **Close** to return to the worksheet.

If you were to print this worksheet right now, Excel would chop it into six pages in a way that would make the data hard to understand. We'll discuss how Excel determines the page order in the next section.

## CONTROLLING THE PAGE SETUP OPTIONS

You can control the way in which a worksheet prints by using the File, Page Setup command. As shown in Figure 6.6, the Page Setup dialog box contains four tabs: Page, Margins, Header/Footer, and Sheet. Each tab contains options that are used to control the page orientation, margins, headers and footers, and many other aspects of the printed worksheet.

**Figure 6.6**     **The Page Setup dialog box**

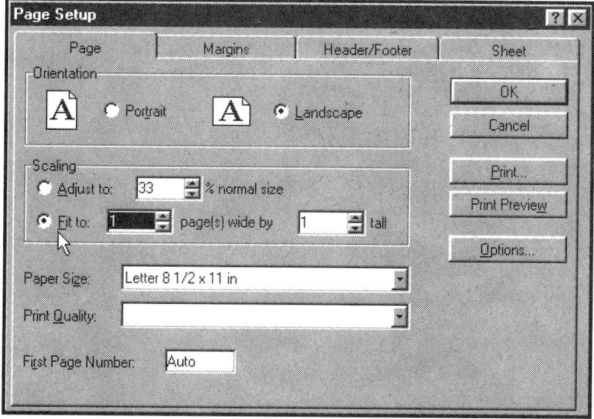

 **CHANGING THE SIZE AND ORIENTATION OF THE PRINTOUT**

In the Report worksheet, the columns of sales data do not fit on the same page. By using the options on the Page tab in the Page Setup dialog box, you can change the size and print orientation of the printout.

To reduce or enlarge a printout:

- Open the Page Setup dialog box. (Choose *File, Page Setup* or click on *Setup* in print preview.)

- Click on the *Page* tab.

- To reduce/enlarge the worksheet by a specific percentage, select the *Adjust To ___% Normal Size* option and type the desired percentage. Normal is 100 percent; you can reduce to 10 percent or enlarge to 400 percent.

- Or, to reduce or enlarge the worksheet to fit on a specific number of pages, select the *Fit To __ Page(s) Wide By __ Tall* option and type the desired number of pages wide and number of pages tall.

- Click on OK.

To change the print orientation of the active worksheet:

- Open the Page Setup dialog box.

- Click on the *Page* tab.

- Under Orientation, select *Portrait* or *Landscape*.

- Click on OK.

Let's use the Page Setup dialog box to change the size and orientation of the printout:

1. Choose **File, Page Setup** to open the Page Setup dialog box.

2. Verify that the Page tab is selected and observe the Scaling options.

3. In the Scaling section, select the **Fit To __ Page(s) Wide By __ Tall** option. Note that the default is one page wide by one page tall.

4. Click on **Print Preview** to display the print preview. Although the entire printout now fits on a single page, the text is some-

what cramped. This worksheet might look better if it were
printed using *Portrait* orientation.

5. Click on **Setup** to open the Page Setup dialog box.

6. In the Orientation section, click on **Portrait**.

7. In the Scaling section, click on the **Adjust To ___% Normal
   Size** option and type **100** to return the printout to normal size.

8. Click on **OK** to accept the page setup changes and return to
   print preview. The text is no longer cramped, but the worksheet has returned to a six-page printout.

## REMOVING GRIDLINES AND ROW/COLUMN HEADINGS

One way to fit more data on a printed page is to reduce the printout. Another way is to remove unnecessary elements from the
printout, such as gridlines and row/column headings.

Let's remove these from our printouts:

1. In the print preview, use the magnifying glass tool to note
   the bottom name in the leftmost column of the previewed
   page; on our screen, it's Wilhelm Konrad. Click anywhere on
   the previewed page to return to normal view.

2. Click on **Setup** and select the **Sheet** tab.

3. Uncheck **Gridlines** and **Row And Column Headings** to remove these from the printout.

4. Observe the Page Order options and the accompanying
   graphic at the bottom of the Page Setup dialog box. By default, Excel prints all of the cells going down the worksheet
   and then across. Remember when we first viewed the print
   preview? By default, Excel prints the entire active area of
   your worksheet even if parts of the active area are blank.

5. Click on **OK** to return to print preview. Your screen should resemble Figure 6.7.

6. Again, note the bottom name on the previewed page; on our
   screen, it's Helmut Krank, one row below the previous bottom name, Wilhelm Konrad. Removing these sheet options
   freed up enough vertical space for this extra row of data.

**Figure 6.7**     **Removing the gridlines and row/column headings**

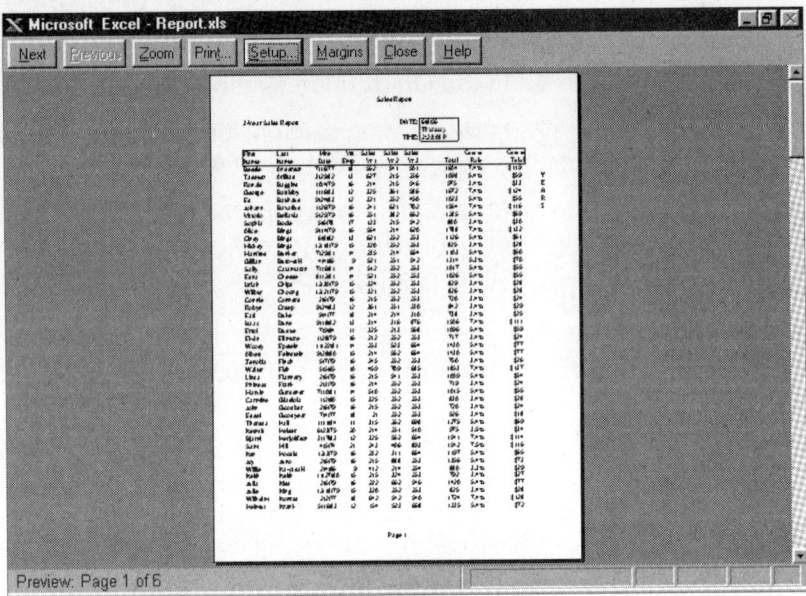

**7.** Click on **Close** to return to the worksheet.

## INSERTING A PAGE BREAK

When you print a multipage worksheet, Excel automatically paginates the worksheet; that is, divides it into separate pages according to your current print settings. You may, however, want to change a worksheet's pagination. For example, let's say that Excel inserted an automatic page break in the middle of a table, placing half the table on page 1 and half on page 2. You might decide to veto this arrangement by inserting a page break before the table, thus placing the entire table on the same page.

To insert a page break,

* Select the cell that you want to appear in the upper-left corner of a new page.

* Choose *Insert, Page Break*.

To remove a page break:

- Select the cell in the upper-left corner of the page to be changed.

- Choose *Insert, Remove Page Break.*

**Note:** You can't use Edit, Undo to remove a page break. You must use the above procedure instead.

Let's practice inserting page breaks:

1.  Observe the commission-rates table of the Sales Report worksheet (columns L through Ṡ). Note the dashed line between columns L and M. The automatic page break splits the table into two parts, an undesirable division.

2.  Select cell **K1**. Choose **Insert, Page Break** to insert a page break. Column K will now appear at the left edge of a new page, keeping the table intact.

3.  Scroll down to examine the area below the commission-rates table; it is empty. The table will appear on a page by itself.

4.  Click on the **Print Preview tool**.

Note that the commission-rates table no longer appears on page 1, as it did in Figure 6.7.

## DEFINING HEADERS AND FOOTERS

You can use the Page Setup dialog box to define headers and footers for your worksheets. A *header* is text that repeats on the top of every worksheet page; a *footer* is text that repeats on the bottom of every page. Unless you specify otherwise, Excel automatically adds a header and a footer to every worksheet that you print. The default header is the name of the active worksheet, centered at the top of the page; the default footer is the word *Page* followed by the page number, centered at the bottom of the page.

If you don't like the default header and footer, you can select a new one from the Header and Footer drop-down list boxes or create a custom header or footer. If you choose to create a custom header or footer, Excel provides you with seven header/footer tools, as shown in Figure 6.8 and explained in Table 6.1.

**Figure 6.8**        **The header/footer tools**

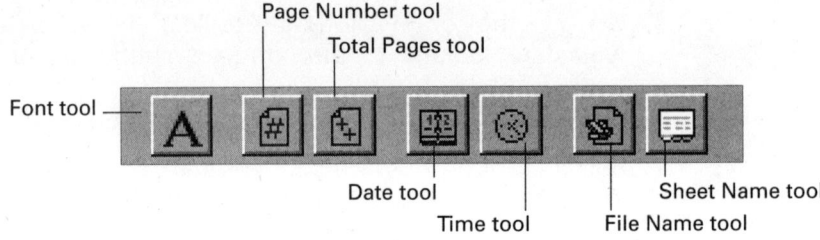

**Table 6.1**        **Header/Footer Tools**

| Tool | Code | Click on This Tool To |
|------|------|----------------------|
| Font | | Specify font, size, and style of selected header/footer text |
| Page Number | &[Page] | Insert active page number |
| Total Pages | &[Pages] | Insert total number of pages in worksheet |
| Date | &[Date] | Insert current date |
| Time | &[Time] | Insert current time |
| File Name | &[File] | Insert file name of active worksheet |
| Sheet Name | &[Tab] | Insert name of the active worksheet |

To create or modify a header or footer for the current worksheet,

• Choose File, Page Setup to open the Page Setup dialog box.

• Click on the *Header/Footer tab*, if necessary, to display the header/footer options.

- If desired, select a new header or footer from the Header or Footer drop-down list boxes.

- Or, to create a custom header or footer, click on the *Custom Header* or *Custom Footer* button to open the Header or Footer dialog box, enter your desired header or footer, and click on OK.

- In the Page Setup dialog box, click on OK.

Note that the last six tools each have a corresponding text code (&[Page], &[File], and so on). In the next activity, you'll see how these codes are used.

Let's create a custom header for the current worksheet:

1. Open the Page Setup dialog box. Click on the **Header/Footer tab**.

2. Click on the **down arrow** next to the Header list box to open the list of available headers. Scroll up to the top of the list. Note the large selection of standard headers that Excel provides. (**Note:** Commas are used to separate the left-aligned, centered, and right-aligned portions of Excel's standard headers and footers.) Since we're creating a custom header, we won't select any of the headers in this list. Click in the gray area of the dialog box to close the list.

3. Click on the **Custom Header button** to open the Header dialog box. Note the seven tools shown in Figure 6.8. Note also the three text boxes—Left Section, Center Section, and Right Section—allowing you to enter left-aligned, centered, and right-aligned text.

4. Double-click on the **&[Tab]** code (in the Center Section text box) to select it. As shown in Table 6.1, this code displays the name of the active worksheet (*Sales Report*) in the header.

5. Type *?????'s Report*, substituting your name for *?????* (for example, *Bill's Report* or *Virginia's Report*). This text will now appear, centered, in the worksheet header.

6. Press **Tab** to move the insertion point into the Right Section text box. Click on the **Date tool** (see Figure 6.8) to enter the date code, &[Date]. The current date will now appear, right-aligned, in the worksheet header.

**7.** Click on **OK** to accept your customized header and return to the Page Setup dialog box. Note that Excel displays the new header above the Header list box.

Now let's select a new footer from the Footer list box:

**1.** Click on the **down arrow** next to the Footer list box to open the list of available footers.

**2.** Select (click on) the footer **Page 1, Sales Report.** (You'll have to scroll.) Observe the new footer displayed below the Footer list box.

**3.** Click on **OK** to accept the new header and footer.

**4.** Print preview the worksheet. Use the magnifying glass tool to zoom in and view the new header and footer.

**5.** Click on **Close** to close the print preview and return to the worksheet.

**6.** Save the file as **myreport**. Excel saves your customized print settings along with the worksheet.

## PRINTING A SELECTED PART OF A WORKSHEET

By default, Excel defines the print area as the entire current worksheet. However, as we discovered earlier, the worksheet might contain empty areas that we really do not want to print. Excel allows you to print selected ranges in a worksheet so you can avoid printing empty cells or superfluous data. Printing a selected range is as easy as selecting the range and choosing the File, Print command. This approach is problematic if you need to print the same selected area many times, in that you must reselect the same cells every time you want to print, an act that soon grows tiresome.

 ### SETTING THE PRINT AREA

Fortunately, Excel provides a much better approach when you need to print the same area many times. You select the desired cells just once and define this range as the *print area*. From then on (until you change or remove the print area), whenever you tell Excel to print the worksheet, it will automatically print only your selected cells. As expected, Excel provides more than one way to set a print area. The following procedure is the most straightforward.

To set the print area for the current worksheet,

- Select the area you want to print.

- Choose *File, Print Area, Set Print Area*.

To clear the print area,

- Choose *File, Print Area, Clear Print Area*.

To print a worksheet's print area,

- Click on the *Print tool*.

- Or, choose *File, Print* and under Print What, select *Selected Sheet(s)*. If desired, specify the number of copies and/or page range. Click on OK.

Let's avoid printing the empty cells beneath the commission-rates table. To do this, we'll set a print area that consists solely of the sales data and commission-rates table.

1. Press **Ctrl+Home** to reorient the screen.

2. Select the range **A1:J107**. (**Hint:** Use the click-Shift-click method.)

3. Press and hold **Ctrl**, drag to select **L1:S14**, then release Ctrl. Your selection should now comprise the two noncontiguous ranges. Note that you have not selected the empty cells beneath the commission-rates table.

4. Choose **File, Print Area, Set Print Area**. Observe the dotted lines surrounding the newly defined print area.

5. Preview page 1 of the worksheet. Demagnify the view, if necessary. Click on **Next** to preview page 2.

6. Click on **Next** twice to preview pages 3 and 4, the commission-rates table.

7. Note that the Next button is dimmed. Next is unavailable because the worksheet now consists of only four pages. By excluding the empty cells beneath the commission-rates table from the print area, you avoided printing any blank pages.

8. Close the print preview.

9. Update the workbook file.

## PRINTING ROW AND COLUMN TITLES ON EVERY PAGE

It can be very difficult to interpret a page of unlabeled data as shown in Figure 6.9.

**Figure 6.9**     **Page 2 with no column titles**

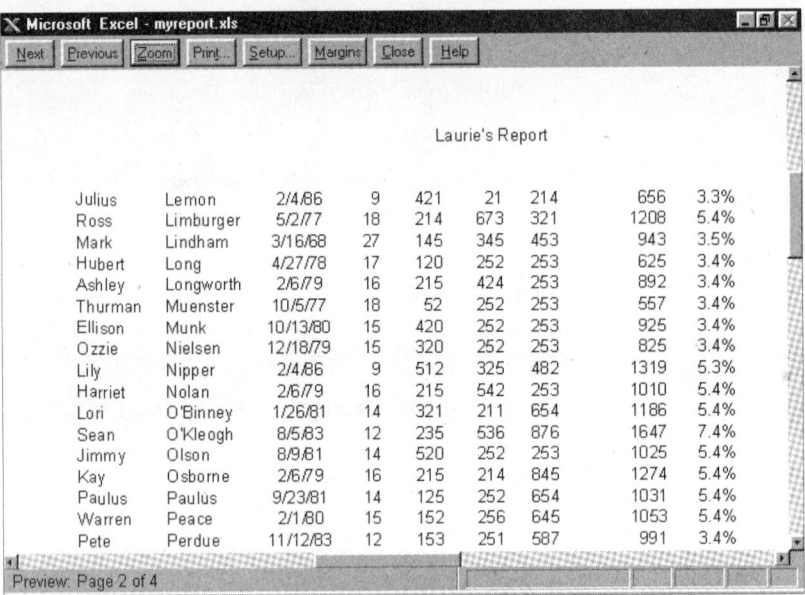

Fortunately, Excel provides an easy fix: You simply print row and/or column titles on every page, as follows:

- Open the Page Setup dialog box.

- Click on the *Sheet tab.*

- To print column titles, place the insertion point in the *Rows To Repeat At Top* text box (if the box is empty) or select its contents. Drag in the worksheet (or type) to select the entire rows whose contents you want to print on the top of every page.

- To print row titles, place the insertion point in the *Columns To Repeat At Left* text box (if the box is empty) or select its contents. Drag in the worksheet (or type) to select the entire columns whose contents you want to print on the left side of every page.

- Click on OK.

Let's add column titles to our worksheet printout:

1. Press **Ctrl+Home** to reorient the screen.

2. Choose **File, Page Setup** and display the sheet options. Observe that the print area remains A1:J107, L1:S14 even though the range is not selected in the worksheet.

3. Click in the **Rows To Repeat At Top text box** to place the insertion point there.

4. Type **1:6** to tell Excel to print the text from rows 1 through 6 at the top of every printout page. (You also could have dragged in the worksheet to select this range of rows.)

5. Click on the **Print Preview button** to apply your specified column titles and preview the results.

6. Observe the column titles at the top of each page.

7. Display page 2, as shown in Figure 6.10. (Magnify the view, if necessary.) Note how much easier it is to interpret the data with column titles than without (Figure 6.9).

## CENTERING DATA ON PRINTOUT PAGES

You can use the Center On Page feature to center data horizontally and/or vertically on your printout pages. To do this,

- Open the Page Setup dialog box.

- Click on the *Margins tab.*

- Under Center On Page, select *Horizontally* (to center the data between the left and right margins) and/or *Vertically* (to center the data between the top and bottom margins).

- Click on OK.

Let's use this simple procedure to center our data horizontally:

1. In the print preview window, demagnify the view, if necessary.

2. Display page 1, and click on **Margins** to display the margin markers and lines. Note that the data is not centered between the left and right margins.

**Figure 6.10**    **Page 2 with column titles**

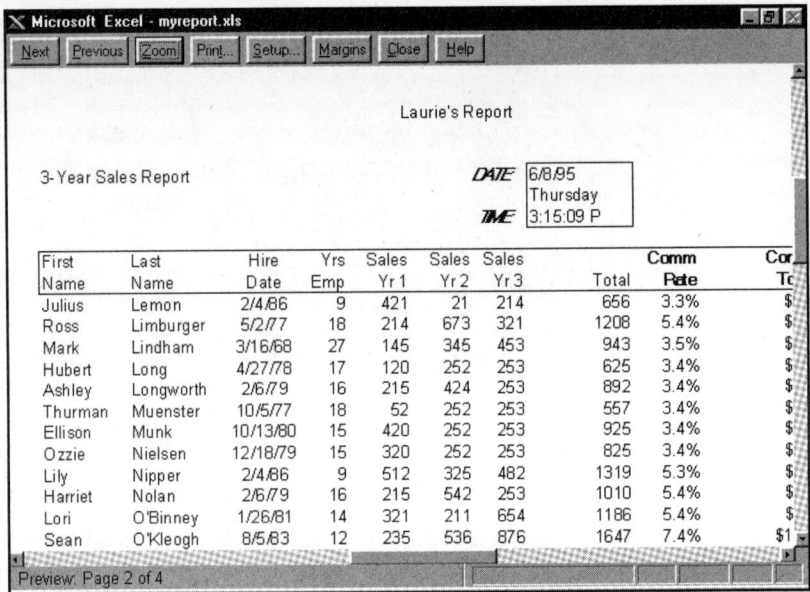

3. Click on **Setup**, and click on the **Margins tab.**

4. Under Center On Page, select **Horizontally** to center the data between the left and right margins.

5. Click on **OK** and observe the results, as shown in Figure 6.11. The data is centered horizontally, between the left and right margins.

   **Note:** You can drag the margin markers to change any of the printout's margins. You can also use the Margins tab in the Page Setup dialog box to change margin settings.

6. Click on **Margins** to turn off the margin display.

7. If you have a printer, use the **Print button** to print the worksheet.

8. Update the workbook file, and then close it.

## PRACTICE YOUR SKILLS

This activity reviews the major topics covered in the electronic accounting section of this book, Chapters 1 through 6. Perform these

**Figure 6.11**  **Centering the data horizontally**

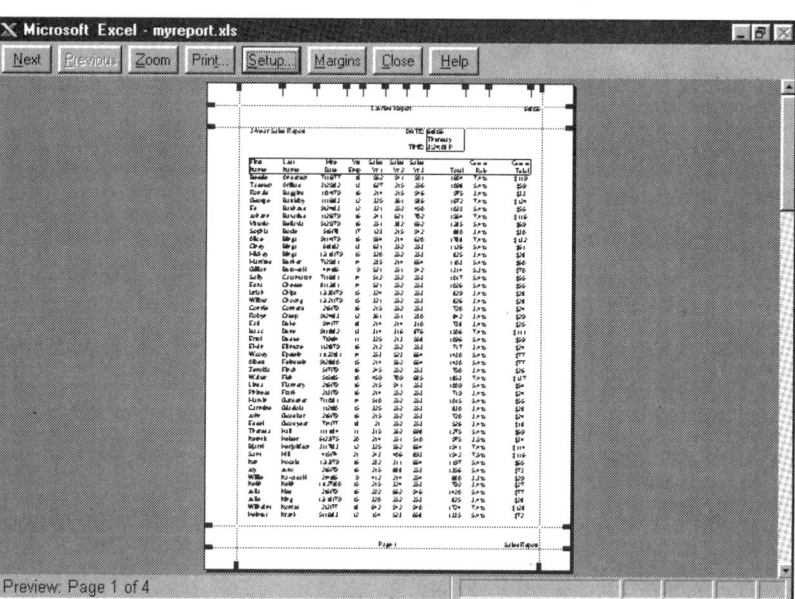

steps to edit and print the worksheet Northern and Southern Divisions in the workbook Practice Exercise to match Figure 6.12:

1. Open **Practice Exercise** from your Excel Work folder (Chapter 3).

2. Maximize the document window, if necessary (Chapter 3).

3. In cell D9, enter a formula to calculate the percentage increase in Mott's sales from the first year to the second year (Chapter 3). (**Hint:** Subtract Mott's first-year sales from his second-year sales, then divide the result by his second-year sales; you'll need to use parentheses. The final result should be 0.118603.)

4. In cell E9, enter a formula to calculate Mott's projected third-year sales (Chapter 3). (**Hint:** Multiply Mott's percentage increase by his second-year sales, then add the result to his second-year sales. The final result should be 1001.15.)

5. In cell F9, enter a formula to calculate Mott's projected third-year commissions (Chapter 5). (**Hint:** Use an absolute reference to the commission-rate cell C4, because you're going to copy the formula in the next step. The result should be 75.08625.)

**Figure 6.12** **Printout of the Northern and Southern Divisons worksheet**

### Northern Division
### 2 Year Sales Report and 3rd Year Projections

Commission Rate                 7.5000%

| Name | Sales 1st Year | Sales 2nd Year | Percentage Increase | Sales Projection 3rd Year | Projected Commissions 3rd Year |
|------|------|------|------|------|------|
| Mott | $788.85 | $895.00 | 11.8603% | $1,001.15 | $75.09 |
| Abel | $566.00 | $619.55 | 8.6434% | $673.10 | $50.48 |
| Cole | $300.95 | $429.45 | 29.9220% | $557.95 | $41.85 |
| King | $388.00 | $445.00 | 12.8090% | $502.00 | $37.65 |
| Wolf | $713.89 | $924.66 | 22.7943% | $1,135.43 | $85.16 |
| Hart | $995.95 | $1,367.00 | 27.1434% | $1,738.05 | $130.35 |
| Adams | $899.15 | $1,013.75 | 11.3046% | $1,128.35 | $84.63 |
| Kane | $582.65 | $661.00 | 11.8533% | $739.35 | $55.45 |
| TOTALS: | $5,235.44 | $6,355.41 | | $7,475.38 | $560.65 |

### Southern Division
### 2 Year Sales Report and 3 Year Projections

| Name | Sales 1st Year | Sales 2nd Year | Percentage Increase | Sales Projection 3rd Year | Projected Commissions 3rd Year |
|------|------|------|------|------|------|
| Binga, A. | $345.80 | $567.80 | 39.0983% | $789.80 | $59.24 |
| Califano | $1,010.76 | $1,212.56 | 16.6425% | $1,414.36 | $106.08 |
| Chen | $789.67 | $950.00 | 16.8768% | $1,110.33 | $83.27 |
| Pedro | $567.27 | $489.00 | -16.0061% | $410.73 | $30.80 |
| Roland | $874.90 | $998.89 | 12.4128% | $1,122.88 | $84.22 |
| Binga, S. | $560.00 | $760.89 | 26.4020% | $961.78 | $72.13 |
| Tranler | $990.00 | $1,100.56 | 10.0458% | $1,211.12 | $90.83 |
| Biron | $1,080.45 | $1,020.67 | -5.8569% | $960.89 | $72.07 |
| TOTALS: | $6,218.85 | $7,100.37 | | $7,981.89 | $598.64 |

**6.** Copy (fill) the range **D9:F9** to the range **D10:F16** (Chapter 4).

**7.** Copy the formulas in the range **D9:F16** to the range **D23:F30** (Chapter 5).

**8.** In cell D2, change 3 to **3rd** (Chapter 5).

**9.** Use drag-and-drop to move the range **D1:D2** to the range **A1:A2** (Chapter 5).

**10.** Center the range **A1:A2** over columns **A** through **F** (Chapter 6).

**11.** Bold the range **A1:A2** (Chapter 6).

**12.** Insert five blank rows above row 23 (Chapter 5). (**Hint:** Select rows **23:27**, then issue your **Insert** command.)

**13.** Copy the range **A6:F8** to the range **A25:F27** (Chapter 4).

**14.** Calculate totals by entering or copying SUM functions into the following cells (Chapter 4):

B18

C18

E18

F18

B37

C37

E37

F37

**15.** Right-align the contents of cells **B6:F8** (Chapter 6).

**16.** Italicize cells **A6:F8** (Chapter 6).

**17.** Format the ranges **B9:C18** and **E9:F18** to display currency to two decimal places (Chapter 5).

**18.** Format cell **C4** and the range **D9:D16** and format both to display percentages to four decimal places (Chapter 5).

**19.** Copy the formatting from the range **A6:F18** to the range **A25:F37** (Chapter 5). (**Hint:** Use the **Format Painter tool**.)

**20.** Autofit the widths of columns **A:F** to display their longest text (Chapter 5). (**Hint:** Select all the columns, then issue one **AutoFit** command.)

**21.** Set the range **A1:F37** as the print area (Chapter 6).

**22.** Save the workbook to your Excel Work folder as **my practice** (Chapter 2).

**23.** Preview the worksheet (Chapter 6).

**24.** From print preview, open the Page Setup dialog box and do the following (Chapter 6):

- Center the data horizontally and vertically on the page.

- Remove the gridlines.

- Remove the header and footer.

**25.** From print preview, print the worksheet, if you have a printer (Chapters 6).

**26.** Compare your printout to Figure 6.12.

**27.** Close the print preview, if necessary.

**28.** Update the workbook file, and then close it (Chapter 2).

## SUMMARY

In this chapter, you learned how to center data across columns, how to sum a range automatically, how to spell-check a worksheet, how to print and print preview a worksheet, and how to enhance the appearance of your worksheet.

Here's is a quick reference guide to the Excel features introduced in this chapter:

| Desired Result | How to Do It |
|---|---|
| Autosum column/row of numbers | Select cell below column or to right of row; click on **AutoSum tool**; enter function |

| Desired Result | How to Do It |
|---|---|
| Spell-check worksheet | Select any cell (to spell-check entire worksheet) or select desired range (to spell-check range only); choose **Tools, Spelling** (or click on **Spelling tool**, or press **F7**); follow Spelling dialog box prompts |
| Print worksheet | Select desired cells (if printing selected cells); choose **File, Print** (or press **Ctrl+P**); select desired options; click on **OK**. Or, click on **Print tool** |
| Print preview worksheet | Choose **File, Print Preview** or click on **Print Preview tool** |
| Enlarge/reduce print preview | Click on preview or click on **Zoom** |
| Close print-preview window | Click on **Close** |
| Set print area | Drag in worksheet to specify print area; choose **File, Print Area, Set Print Area** |
| Remove current print area | Choose **File, Print Area, Clear Print Area** |
| Define header or footer | Choose **File, Page Setup**; display Header/Footer options; specify desired options; click on **OK** |
| Set margins | Choose **File, Page Setup**; display Margins options; set margins. Or choose **File, Print Preview**; click on **Margins**; drag margins |
| Center data on page | Choose **File, Page Setup**; click on **Margins tab**; select desired Center on Page option; click on **OK** |
| Change print orientation | Choose **File, Page Setup**; click on **Page tab**; under Orientation, select Portrait or Landscape; click on **OK** |

| Desired Result | How to Do It |
|---|---|
| Reduce or enlarge printout | Choose **File, Page Setup**; enter percentage to adjust or number of pages to fit; click on **OK** |
| Insert/Remove page break | Select upper-left corner of new page (to insert) or current page (to remove); choose **Insert, Page Break** or **Insert, Remove Page Break** |
| Suppress gridline and row and column headings from printout | Choose **File, Page Setup**; display sheet options; uncheck **Gridlines**; uncheck **Row and Column Headings**; click on **OK** |
| Add print titles to printout | Choose **File, Page Setup**; display **Sheet options**; enter desired rows or columns to be repeated; click on **OK** |

In the next chapter, we'll introduce you to a number of advanced worksheet topics. You'll learn how to display additional toolbars, tear off a toolbar option palette, select a noncontiguous cell range, create a number format, work with names, work with multiple-worksheet workbooks, create 3-D formulas, and use macros to automate tasks.

## IF YOU'RE STOPPING HERE

If you want to break off here, please exit Excel. If you want to proceed directly to the next chapter, please do so now.

# CHAPTER 7:
# ADVANCED
# WORKSHEET TOPICS

Displaying
Additional
Toolbars

Selecting a
Noncontiguous
Range of Cells

Creating a
Number Format

Working with
Names

Working with
Multiple-
Worksheet
Workbooks

Using Macros to
Automate Tasks

In this chapter, we'll introduce a number of advanced Excel worksheet topics. You'll begin by learning how to display additional toolbars, and how to use new methods for selecting, formatting, and naming cell ranges. Then you'll find out how to work with multiple-worksheet workbooks, and how to use *3-D spearing* to share data and formulas among worksheets. Finally, you'll learn the basics of using *macros* to automate repetitive tasks.

When you're done working through this chapter, you will know

- How to display additional toolbars
- How to tear off a toolbar option palette
- How to select a noncontiguous cell range
- How to create a custom number format
- How to work with names
- How to work with multiple-worksheet workbooks
- How to create 3-D formulas
- How to use macros to automate tasks

## DISPLAYING ADDITIONAL TOOLBARS

The Standard and Formatting toolbars afford you quick and easy access to a wide assortment of commonly used tools. Many other tools, however, are not included in these toolbars. To resolve this shortcoming, Excel provides 11 additional toolbars, for a grand total of 13, as shown in Table 7.1.

**Table 7.1** **Excel's 13 Toolbars**

| Toolbar Name | You Use Its Tools To |
| --- | --- |
| Standard | Perform everyday Excel tasks |
| Formatting | Format worksheets |
| Chart | Create and modify charts |
| Drawing | Draw onscreen graphics |
| Full Screen | Toggle between full screen and normal display |
| Tip Wizard | Get tips on how to use Excel more efficiently |
| Stop Recording | Stop a running macro or the macro recorder |
| Visual Basic | Create, modify, and run visual basic modules and macros |

**Table 7.1**        **Excel's 13 Toolbars (Continued)**

| Toolbar Name | You Use Its Tools To |
|---|---|
| Auditing | Audit worksheets |
| Forms | Create custom forms |
| Query and Pivot | Analyze pivot-table data |
| WorkGroup | Share, locate, and update files |
| Microsoft | Switch from Excel to other Microsoft programs (Word, PowerPoint, Access, and so on), provided—of course—that these programs are installed on your computer |

You can display anywhere from none to all 13 of these toolbars at once; and you can move each of them to any desired screen position. Excel remembers the position and shape of all displayed toolbars when you exit and restores this setup when you restart.

Use either of these methods to display or hide a toolbar,

- Choose *View, Toolbars* (or choose *Toolbars* from the shortcut menu) to open the Toolbars dialog box. In the Toolbars list box, check (to display) or uncheck (to hide) the desired toolbar. Click on OK.

- Or, simply display the Toolbars shortcut menu (by clicking the right mouse button) and click on the toolbar you want to display or hide. This method allows you to display/hide only eight of Excel's 13 toolbars.

To hide a toolbar whose close box is visible,

- Click (once) on the *close* box.

To move a toolbar,

- Press and hold the left mouse button on a blank area of the desired toolbar or on its title bar (if visible) to select it.

- Drag the selected toolbar to the desired location. Depending upon where you are moving from or to, the shape of the toolbar may change.

If you are not running Excel, please start it now. If there is a workbook on your screen (other than the startup workbook, Book1), please close it. Let's explore the world of toolbars:

1. Open **Project** from your Excel Work folder, and maximize the document window, if necessary.

2. Choose **View, Toolbars** to open the Toolbars dialog box. Scroll through the Toolbars list box; note that Standard and Formatting are the only checked toolbars.

3. Check **Drawing**.

4. Check **Full Screen** and click on **OK** to display the Drawing and Full Screen toolbars, as shown in Figure 7.1. (Depending upon your Excel setup, your toolbars may appear in different places.) As stated in Table 7.1, you use the Full Screen toolbar to toggle between full and normal screen display.

**Figure 7.1**     **Displaying the Full Screen toolbar**

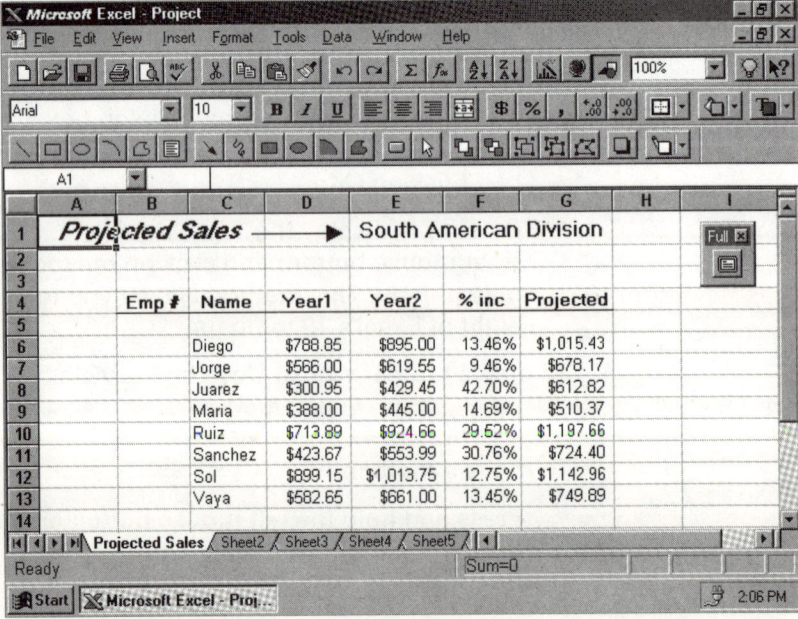

5. Click on the **Full Screen tool** to change to full-screen view. This view maximizes the worksheet area by hiding all toolbars

displayed at the top (above the formula bar) and bottom (below the worksheet tabs) of the screen.

6. Click on the **Full Screen tool** again to change back to normal view. The missing toolbars (Standard and Formatting) are redisplayed.

**Note:** You'll hide the Full Screen toolbar later in this chapter. For now, leave it onscreen.

Let's use the shortcut menu to display another toolbar:

1. Point to the gray area on any displayed toolbar and click the **right mouse button** to display the shortcut menu.

2. Check **Drawing**.

3. Let's move the Drawing toolbar to the bottom of the screen, where it will not block our view of the current worksheet or get confused with the other displayed toolbars.

4. Point to the title bar (if visible), or to any gray area, of the Drawing toolbar. Press and hold the **left mouse button** to select the toolbar (it should be surrounded by a dashed outline if you've done this correctly). Drag the toolbar slowly downward, until this outline changes to a long, narrow rectangle.

5. Release the mouse button. The Drawing toolbar reappears directly under the worksheet tabs, as shown in Figure 7.2. As mentioned, toolbars may take on different shapes, depending upon their locations.

## PRACTICE YOUR SKILLS

1. Move the Drawing toolbar to the middle of the screen.

2. Hide the Drawing toolbar by clicking on its **Close box**. You'll get a chance in Chapter 11 to work with this toolbar.

## TEARING OFF A TOOLBAR OPTION PALETTE

Several toolbars contain list boxes that use *option palettes*—drop-down lists or palettes—to display their available options. For example, the rightmost three list boxes on the Formatting toolbar (Borders, Color, and Font Color) all use option palettes to display

**Figure 7.2**    **Moving the Drawing toolbar to the bottom**

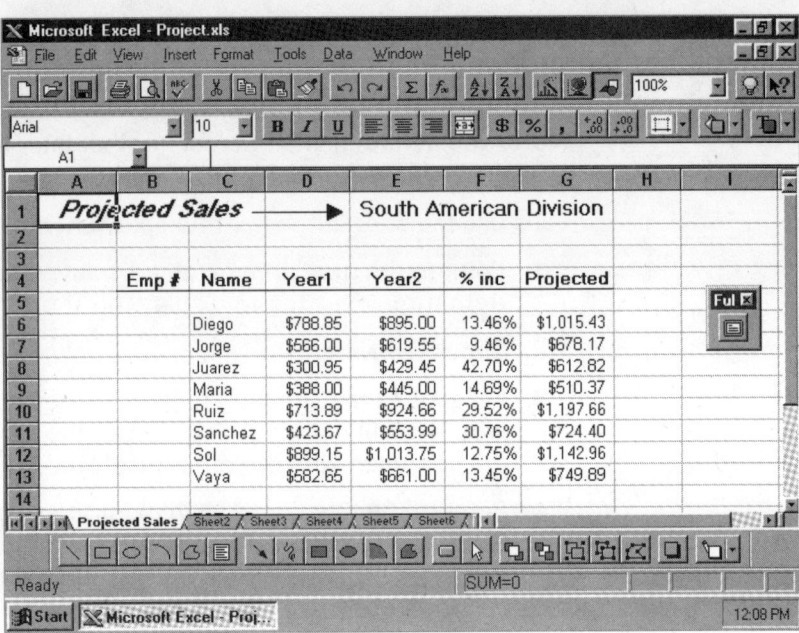

their respective options (border types, background colors, and font colors).

When you work with such a list box frequently, you may find it inconvenient to have to reopen the option palette every time you want to choose a new option. To ease your burden, Excel lets you *tear off* the option palette and move it to any desired screen location, much as you just did with the Drawing and Full Screen toolbars. When you need to choose an option from this palette, you need only click on that option (because the palette is already displayed), rather than reopening the palette and then clicking on the option.

To tear off a toolbar option palette,

- Point to the desired list box's down arrow.

- Press and hold the left mouse button to open the option palette.

- Drag the option palette to the desired worksheet location.

- Release the mouse button.

To remove a torn-off option palette,

- Click on the palette's *Close* box.

Let's tear off the Borders option palette in order to conveniently explore the available border options.

**1.** Point to the down arrow to the right of the Borders list box.

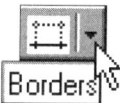

**2.** Press and hold the **left mouse button** to open the Border option palette, and then drag the palette to an empty spot to the right of the worksheet data, as shown in Figure 7.3.

**Figure 7.3**     **Tearing off the Border option palette**

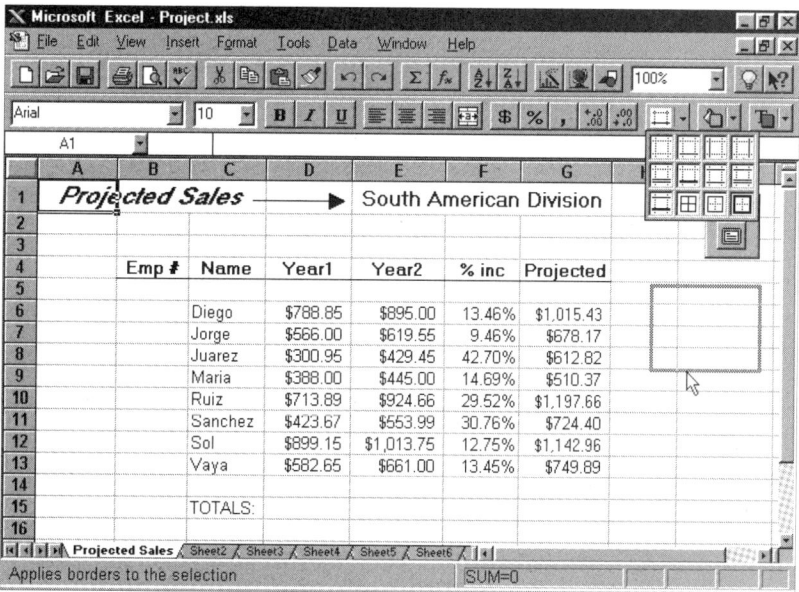

**3.** Select cells **C6:G13**. These are the cells to which we'll apply several different borders.

4. In the Border option palette, click on the second option in the top row to apply a single underline to each selected row.

5. Press **Ctrl+Home** (or click on any cell) to deselect the selected range. Note the single-underlined rows.

6. Reselect cells **C6:G13**. Let's try a different border option.

7. In the Border option palette, click on the first option in the top row to apply no border to the selected cells. Before you apply a new border, you must clear the old.

8. In the Border option palette, click on the first option in the middle row to apply a double underline to each selected row.

9. Deselect and observe the results.

10. Click on the **Undo tool** to undo your last action and reselect cells C6:G13. A nice shortcut for reselecting the desired range, yes?

## PRACTICE YOUR SKILLS

1. Clear the border (by choosing the first option in the first row), then apply the second border option in the bottom row of the palette. Deselect and observe the results; every cell is bordered.

2. Use the Undo trick to reselect cells **C6:G13**.

3. Clear the border, then apply the fourth border option in the bottom row of the palette. Deselect and observe the results; the entire range is bordered by a thick line. Your screen should match that shown in Figure 7.4.

4. Click on the Border option palette's **Close box** to remove the torn-off palette from the worksheet.

## SELECTING A NONCONTIGUOUS RANGE OF CELLS

Until now, you've always selected *contiguous* cell ranges, ranges containing adjacent cells (for example, cells G6:G12). Here, you'll learn how to select *noncontiguous* ranges, ranges containing nonadjacent cells (for example, cells G6, G10, and G12).

To select a noncontiguous range of cells,

**Figure 7.4**       **Using the Border option palette to apply a border**

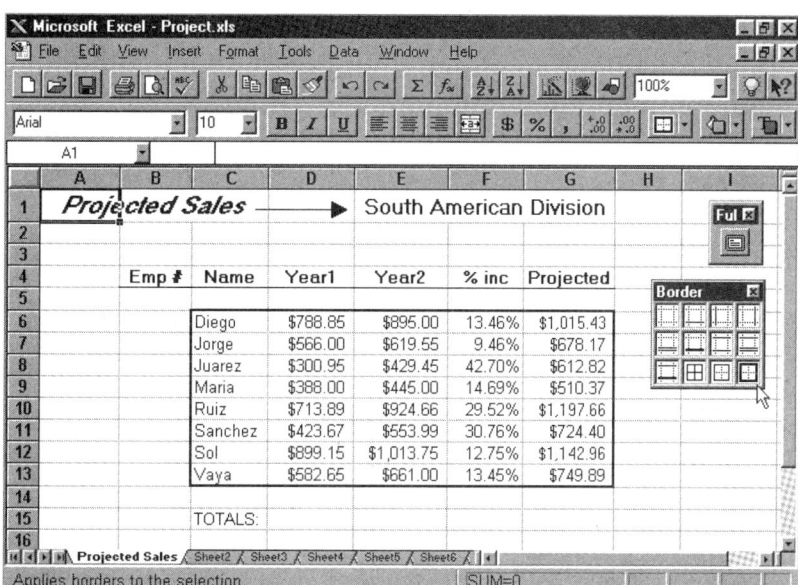

- Select one of the cells in the desired range.

- Press and hold the *Ctrl* key.

- Use the mouse to select the remaining cells.

- Release the Ctrl key.

Let's select a noncontiguous range:

1. Observe cells G6, G10, and G12. These values are the highest projected sales.

2. Select cell **G6**.

3. Press and hold down the **Ctrl key**.

4. Click on cell **G10** to select it.

5. Release the Ctrl key. Cell G10 is outlined to indicate that it is the active cell. Let's add a third cell to our noncontiguous range.

6. Press and hold **Ctrl**, click on cell **G12**, then release Ctrl to add cell G12 to the noncontiguous selection, as shown in Figure

7.5. Note that cell G12 is now the active cell, because you selected it last.

**Figure 7.5**     **Selecting a noncontiguous cell range**

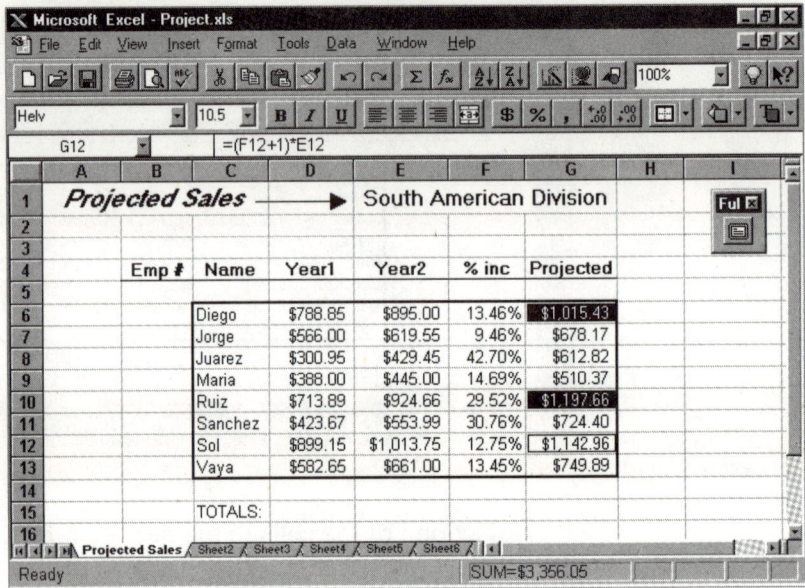

Now we'll draw attention to these values by applying a new background color to their cells:

1. Open the **Color option palette**.

2. Select the light gray color at the intersection of the seventh column and second row.

3. Deselect the range to get a better view of your color change.

4. Save the workbook to your Excel Work folder as **myproject**.

## CREATING A CUSTOM NUMBER FORMAT

As you learned in Chapter 5, Excel provides you with a large selection of standard number formats. At times, however, none of these formats may meet your exact needs. To create a new number format,

- Select the cells to which you want to apply the new format.

- Choose *Format, Cell* (or press *Ctrl+1,* or choose *Format Cells* from the shortcut menu) to open the Format Cells dialog box. Click on the *Number tab,* if necessary, to display the number options.

- Select *Custom in Category* list box.

- Change (edit or retype) the current number format in the Type text box to your desired new format. Or, to save time, if your new format is similar to an existing format, select this format and edit it as necessary in the Type text box.

- Click on OK. Excel adds your new number format to the list of available formats, allowing you to use it again at a later date.

When creating number formats, you can use *digit placeholders* (0 displays a nonzero digit or a zero, # cancels the display of unnecessary zeros), decimal points, commas, dollar signs, and text.

### ADDING TEXT TO A NUMBER FORMAT

You can include text in your number formats by enclosing the desired text in quotation marks. For example, if you formatted a cell as *"Department" 00* and entered 5 in it, Excel would display *Department 05.* (The quotation marks appear in the number format, but not in the cell.)

Let's create a number format that includes text:

1. Select the range **B6:B13**.

2. Point to the selected cells, open the shortcut menu, and choose **Format Cells** to open the Format Cells dialog box. Display the number options.

3. Select **Custom** in the Category list box.

4. Select the current entry in the Type text box (**General**). Type **"EN-"00** (no spaces). (The abbreviation *EN* stands for Em-

ployee Number.) Remember, to include text in a number format, you must enclose the text in quotation marks.

5. Press **Enter** to apply your new format to the selected cells. You can use this new custom format anywhere in this workbook. You can't, however, use it in any other workbook; to do so, you'd have to re-create it within the new workbook. Since you haven't entered anything yet in these cells, they remain blank.

6. In cell B6, enter **2**. Note that this entry is displayed as *EN-02*; the quotation marks around the text *EN-* do not appear. Your *"EN-"00* format causes the number you enter in the cell (2, in this case) to be preceded with *EN-* and forces this number to take at least two digits (02 instead of just 2).

7. In cell B7, enter **15**. *EN-15* is displayed.

8. In cell B8, enter **100**. *EN-100* is displayed. Note that Excel displays a three-digit number, 100, even though the number format includes only two zeros, *"EN-"00*. If the number you enter has more digits to the left of the decimal point than there are zeros to the left of the decimal point in the number format, Excel displays the extra digits.

## PRACTICE YOUR SKILLS

1. Enter the following numbers:

|    | B   |
|----|-----|
| 9  | 7   |
| 10 | 9   |
| 11 | **46** |
| 12 | **133** |
| 13 | **58** |

2. Left-align the contents of cells B6:B13.

3. Change to full-screen view. (**Hint:** That's what your Full Screen toolbar is for!)

4. Deselect and compare your worksheet with Figure 7.6.

**Figure 7.6**      **Creating a number format with text**

**5.** Change back to normal screen view.

## WORKING WITH NAMES

Excel allows you to name a single cell or a cell range. You use these names for clarity and convenience. For example, in a large worksheet, you might name several key cell ranges, then use the Go To command to move quickly to these ranges by name (*totals*, for example), instead of by range (D15:G15, for example). Or, you might clarify your formulas by replacing hard-to-read ranges, such as =SUM(D6:D13), with descriptive names, such as =SUM(year1).

To name a cell range,

- Select the range of cells you want to name.

- Choose *Insert, Name, Define* to open the Define Name dialog box. In the Names In Workbook text box, type the desired name (or, use the name Excel proposes in this text box). Click on OK.

- Or, click in the Name list box (in the formula bar) to select its contents, type the desired name, and click on OK.

Follow these guidelines when defining a name:

- The name can contain up to 255 characters. We recommend creating short, descriptive names (5-10 characters); that way, you can easily type these names into your formulas.

- The first character of the name must be a letter.

- After the first character, you can use letters, numbers, periods (.), and underlines (_).

- Spaces are not allowed in the name. (*August Totals* is invalid; *August_Totals* is valid.)

- The name cannot resemble a cell reference or range. (*A1*, *B12*, *D100*, *E14:E18* are all invalid names.)

- Capitalization is insignificant. (*TOTALS*, *Totals*, and *totals* are all interpreted as the same name.)

Let's practice naming cells. First, we'll look on as Excel names a range automatically:

1. Set the print area to cells C4:E15. (Hint: Choose **File, Print Area, Set Print Area**.)

2. After setting the print area, choose **Insert, Name, Define** to open the Define Name dialog box. Observe the name *'Projected Sales'!Print_Area* in the Names In Workbook list box. When you set the print area in step 1, Excel automatically defined this name for it. *'Projected Sales'* is the name of the worksheet in which the print area resides. If the worksheet had been named *Sheet17*, Excel would have named the print area *'Sheet17'!Print_Area*.

3. Click on **'Projected Sales'!Print_Area** to select it. Observe the Names In Workbook text box and the Refers To box. Note that the name *'Projected Sales'!Print_Area* refers to the absolute range $C$4:$E$15 in the Projected Sales worksheet, the range you selected in step 1.

4. Click on **Close** to return to the worksheet.

Now let's name a range of cells:

1. Select the range **D6:D13**.

**2.** Click anywhere within the **Name list box** (it currently displays D6) to choose its current contents.

**3.** Type **year1** and press **Enter** to name the selected range *year1*, an appropriate choice, as it mirrors the column heading (in cell D4).

**4.** Choose **Insert, Name, Define** to open the Define Names dialog box. Note that your *year1* name appears in the Names In Workbook list.

**5.** Press **Esc** to close the dialog box.

## USING NAMES IN FORMULAS

As mentioned, you can use names instead of hard-to-read cell references in formulas. The more ranges a formula contains, the more useful this technique is. Let's enter a formula and then replace its argument range with a name:

**1.** In cell D15, enter **=sum(D6:D13)** to sum the Year1 projected sales values for all sales reps. The result is $4,663.16.

**2.** Change the formula in cell D15 to **=sum(year1)** and reenter it. The result is the same as in step 1 ($4,663.16). By substituting the name *year1* for the SUM argument range D6:D13, you've created a tidier, more readable formula.

### PRACTICE YOUR SKILLS

**1.** Name the range E6:E13 **year2**.

**2.** In cell E15, enter a formula that uses the name *year2* to sum the values in cells E6:E13 ($5,542.40).

## SELECTING NAMED RANGES

One of the advantages of naming your ranges is the ease with which you can select these ranges, and thus move to the desired areas of your worksheet. To select a named range,

• Choose *Edit, Go To* or press F5 to open the Go To dialog box. Select or type the desired name and click on OK.

- Or, open the Name drop-down list (in the formula bar) and click on the desired name.

Let's use the Go To dialog box to select named ranges:

1. Press **F5** to open the Go To dialog box. Note that your *year1* and *year2* names appear in the Go To list box. Note also that the print-area name is called *Print_Area* here, not *'Projected Sales'!Print_Area,* as in the Define Names dialog box. How come? The Define Names dialog box lists all the names of all the worksheets in the current workbook; since each worksheet can have its own unique print area, the worksheet name must precede it. The Go To dialog box, on the other hand, lists only the names of the current worksheet; since each worksheet can have only one print area, the name *Print_Area* suffices.

2. Select **year1** in the Go To list box and click on **OK** to select the range named year1, D6:D13, as shown in Figure 7.7.

**Figure 7.7**     **Using Go To to select a named range**

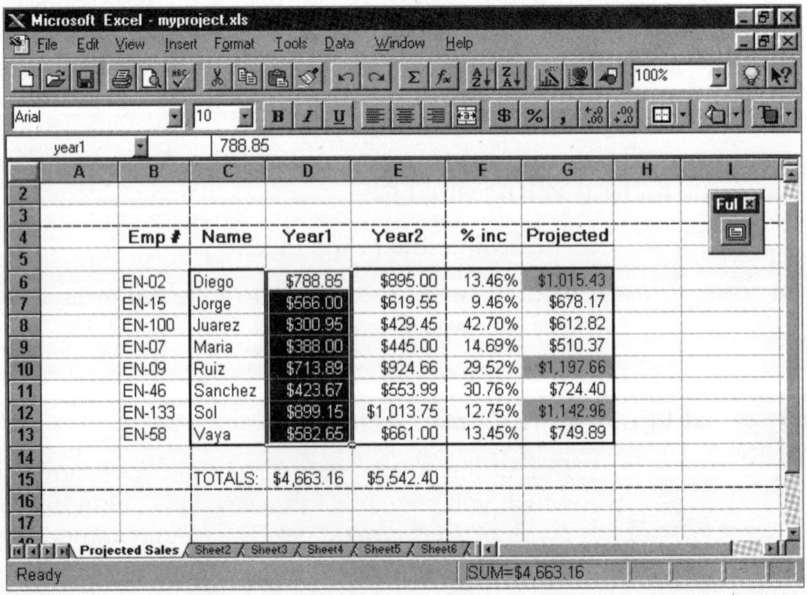

3. Use this same technique to select the range **Print_Area**. (Try this shortcut: Instead of selecting Print_Area in the Go To dialog box and then clicking on OK, simply double-click on Print_Area.)

Now let's use the Name list box to select a named range:

1. Open the Name box drop-down list (by clicking on its **down arrow**). Note your three named ranges: Print_Area, year1, and year2.

2. Click on **year2** to select this range, E6:E13.

3. Use this same technique to select the range **Print_Area**. Which selection method do you prefer, the Go To dialog box or the Name list box?

4. Choose **File, Save** to update the file.

5. Close the workbook by double-clicking on the document-window—not the application-window!—**Control-menu icon**. As mentioned in Chapter 2, you can close a workbook either by choosing File, Close, by double-clicking on its Control-menu icon, or clicking on its Close box.

6. Hide the Full Screen toolbar by clicking on its **Close box**. We'll revisit this very useful tool in the charting section of this book.

## WORKING WITH MULTIPLE-WORKSHEET WORKBOOKS

Until now, all the workbooks you've opened have contained one nonempty worksheet and 15 empty worksheets (Sheet2 through Sheet16). Here, you'll learn how to work with workbooks that contain multiple nonempty worksheets.

Let's open a workbook that contains five nonempty worksheets:

1. Click on the **Open tool** to open the Open dialog box. Verify that your Excel Work folder is selected.

**2.** Type **Divisions** in the File Name text box, then press **Enter** to open the workbook. You can select the file you want to open by clicking on it in the File Name list box or by typing its name in the File Name text box. Use whichever method you find easier.

## PRACTICE YOUR SKILLS

**1.** Observe the structure of the active worksheet, All Divisions.

**2.** Activate the **Australia worksheet**. (**Hint:** Click on its worksheet tab.) Note that its structure is the same as that of All Divisions.

**3.** Activate each of the remaining worksheets: **S. America**, **Europe**, and **N. America**. Note that all five worksheets are structured identically. You'll see why in a moment.

**4.** Activate the All Divisions worksheet.

 ## 3-D SPEARING

You can share data and formulas among different worksheets in the same workbook. For example, you can enter a formula in one worksheet that refers to numeric data in another worksheet. If you change the numeric data in the worksheet to which your formula refers, Excel automatically recalculates the formula result. This feature—called *3-D spearing*, since it lets you "spear" through two or more worksheets to connect their data and formulas— allows you to consolidate data from several worksheets into a single, "master" worksheet. This, in turn, allows you to divide large, complex worksheets into smaller worksheets that are easier to maintain.

Let's see how you can use 3-D spearing to connect worksheet data and formulas:

**1.** Observe the formula in cell B4 of the All Divisions worksheet,

```
=SUM('Australia:N.America'!B4)
```

This is a *3-D formula* that sums the numeric values in cells B4 (bonnet sales) of all the worksheets in the range Australia through N. America. In other words, the formula sums the value in cell B4 of the Australia worksheet, cell B4 of the S.

America worksheet, cell B4 of the Europe worksheet, and cell B4 of the N. America worksheet. Imagine a stack of four worksheets and a spear going through cell B4 of each: That's 3-D spearing!

2. Note that the value in cell B4 of the All Divisions worksheet is 900. Verify that this is, in fact, the sum of the four B4 cells in the worksheets Australia:N. America. (**Hint:** Activate each of these four worksheets and mentally add their cell B4 values.)

3. Select the Australia worksheet, and change its cell B4 value from 200 to **500**.

4. Observe cell B4 of the All Divisions worksheet. Note that its value has changed from 900 (in step 2) to 1200. The formula in this cell is "speared" to the value in cell B4 of the Australia worksheet (and the S. America, Europe, and N. America worksheets); changing the cell B4 value in the Australia worksheet caused Excel to automatically recalculate the value in the All Divisions worksheet.

5. Close the file without saving the changes.

**Note:** This section gave you a mere taste of Excel's 3-D spearing capabilities. Further discussion of 3-D spearing and 3-D formulas is beyond the scope of this book. If you are interested in this topic, we encourage you to refer to your Excel documentation.

## USING MACROS TO AUTOMATE TASKS

A macro is a set of actions that Excel automatically performs. For example, the macro you'll run in the next activity automatically inserts a four-row header in a worksheet, types and formats a heading, and alphabetically sorts the worksheet data. Macros are used to automate complex or repetitive tasks; instead of performing these tasks manually, you run the macro and let it do all the work for you.

To run a macro,

- Open the macro sheet that contains the desired macro program.

- Activate the worksheet in which you want to run the macro.

- Choose *Tools, Macro* to open the Macro dialog box, select the desired macro in the Macro Name/Reference list box, and click on *Run*. Or, if the macro has a shortcut key, press it. Capitalization is significant; if the assigned shortcut key were

Ctrl+h, pressing Ctrl+h would run the macro, but pressing Ctrl+H would not.

To find out if a macro has a shortcut key,

- Activate the macro sheet.

- Choose *Tools, Macro* to open the Macro dialog box.

- Select the desired macro in the Macro Name/Reference list box.

- Click on *Options* to open the Macro Options dialog box. Observe the Shortcut Key and Ctrl+ boxes; if there is a shortcut key assigned to the macro, it is shown here.

- Press **Esc** twice to close the Macro Options dialog box and the Macro dialog box.

Let's run a simple macro. But first, we'll take a moment to explore Excel's ability to have two or more files open at the same time:

1. Display the Open dialog box and the contents of the Excel Work folder.

2. Locate the file names *Header* and *Inventory*. Click once on **Header** to select it. Press and hold the **Ctrl key**, click once on **Inventory** to select it, then release the Ctrl key. You can use this Ctrl-click technique to select multiple files in a list box, just as you used it earlier in this chapter to select noncontiguous cells in a worksheet.

3. Click on **Open** to open both selected files. Note that Inventory is active (displayed on screen). Let's see what happened to Header.

4. Click on **Window** (in the menu bar) to open the drop-down Window menu. Observe the file names listed at the bottom, *1 Inventory* and *2 Header*. These are your currently open files. Inventory is active (hence the check mark preceding its name in the drop-down menu), while Header is inactive, hidden away behind Inventory.

5. Click on **2 Header** to activate (display) this file. Note that it consists of a single column of formulas; these are the macro commands. Let's see if the macro has a shortcut key.

6. Choose **Tools, Macro** to open the Macro dialog box.

7. Select **Header** (the name of the macro) in the Macro Name/Reference list box.

8. Click on **Options** to open the Macro Options dialog box. Note that the Shortcut Key check box is checked, meaning that the macro does have a shortcut key. The shortcut key itself is displayed in the Ctrl+ box. It is Ctrl+h. (All macro shortcut keys begin with Ctrl.)

9. Press **Esc** twice to close the Macro Options dialog box and the Macro dialog box.

10. Press **Ctrl+F6** to activate Inventory.

11. Press **Ctrl+F6** again to reactivate Header. You can use Ctrl+F6—instead of the Window drop-down menu, as in steps 5 and 6—to cycle through all your currently open files.

Now let's run the Header macro:

1. Press **Ctrl+H** to run the macro. After a moment, the macro stops and a Macro Error dialog box appears. Why? Because, as explained in the general procedure at the beginning of this section, before running the macro, you must activate the worksheet in which the macro will run.

2. Click on **Halt** to terminate the macro and close the Macro Error dialog box. Let's try again.

3. Press **Ctrl+F6** to activate the Sales Inventory worksheet of Inventory. Note that the worksheet contains no header, and that the inventory items are not alphabetically arranged.

4. Press **Ctrl+H** to run the macro. Voilà! This time, the macro runs properly. **(Note:** If the macro had had no shortcut key, you would have had to choose Tools, Macro to open the Macro dialog box, select the Macro in the Macro Name/Reference list box, and then click on Run.)

5. Observe the changes in the worksheet, shown in Figure 7.8. The Header macro automatically inserted four rows in the worksheet, typed and formatted a four-line heading, and sorted the inventory items alphabetically, saving you the time and tedium involved in doing this.

6. Hold down the **Shift key** and choose **File, Close All** to close all your open files (in this case, Header and Inventory). Don't save the changes. (If multiple files are open, holding down Shift while opening the File drop-down menu causes the Close All (rather than the Close) command to be displayed.)

**Figure 7.8**    **Running the Header macro**

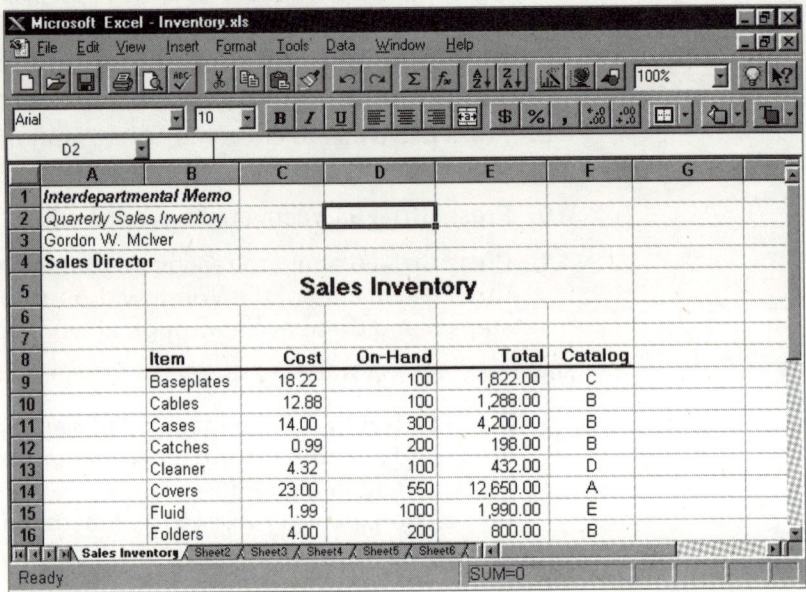

**Note:** Again, this section gave you the merest taste of Excel's extensive macro capabilities. Further discussion of macros—and their more powerful cousins, *visual basic modules*—is beyond the scope of this book. If you are interested in more information, please refer to your Excel documentation.

## SUMMARY

In this chapter, we introduced a hodgepodge of advanced worksheet topics. You learned how to display additional toolbars, tear off a toolbar option palette, select a noncontiguous cell range, create a custom number format, work with names, work with multiple-worksheet workbooks, create 3-D formulas, and use macros to automate tasks.

With this chapter, you've completed your foundation in Excel electronic accounting techniques. Congratulations! You now possess the wherewithal to create and print sophisticated, professional-looking worksheets.

Here's a quick reference guide to the Excel features introduced in this chapter:

| Desired Result | How to Do It |
| --- | --- |
| Display/hide toolbar | Choose **View, Toolbars** (or choose **Toolbars** from shortcut menu); check/uncheck desired toolbar; click on **OK**; or open Toolbars shortcut menu and click on desired toolbar |
| Move toolbar | Drag toolbar by title bar to new location |
| Select a noncontiguous range | Select one cell in range; hold **Ctrl**, select remaining cells, release Ctrl; repeat to add cells to range |
| Create number format | Select cells to format; choose **Format, Cell** (or press **Ctrl+1**, or choose **Format Cells** from shortcut menu); display number options; change current number format (in Type text box) to desired format; click on **OK** |
| Include text in number format | Enclose text in quotation marks |
| Name cell range | Select desired cells; choose **Insert, Name, Define**; in Names In Workbook text box, type the desired name (or use the name Excel proposes); click on **OK**; or select desired cells, click in Name list box, type desired name, press **Enter** |
| Use name in formula | Replace formula range with name |
| Select named range | Choose **Edit, Go To** (or press **F5**); select desired name; click on **OK** (or double-click on desired name); or open Name box drop-down list and click on desired name |

| Desired Result | How to Do It |
|---|---|
| Open multiple files | Choose **File, Open;** select the folder; use the Ctrl+click technique to select the files; click on **Open** to open all files at once |
| Activate open file | Click on **Window** and click on file name, or press **Ctrl+F6** |
| Close multiple windows | Hold **Shift** and choose **File, Close All** |
| Create 3-D formula argument | Type ', type name of first worksheet in argument range, type :, type name of last worksheet in range, type '; type !; type cell or cell range (for example, 'Australia:N. America'!B4) |
| Run a macro | Open macro sheet; activate worksheet in which you want to run macro; choose **Tools, Macro;** select desired macro from list; click on **Run;** or open macro sheet, activate worksheet, press shortcut key |
| Find out if macro has shortcut key | Activate macro sheet; choose **Tools, Macro;** select desired macro; click on **Options;** observe Shortcut Key and Ctrl+ boxes |

In the next chapter, you'll begin a three-chapter exploration of Excel's charting features. You'll learn how to create a column chart, how to add text to a chart, how to change the chart type and format, and how to create multiple charts from a single worksheet.

## IF YOU'RE STOPPING HERE

If you want to break off here, please exit Excel. If you want to proceed directly to the next chapter, please do so now.

# CHAPTER 8:
# CREATING A CHART

It's often much easier to understand trends and patterns in numeric data by viewing these data in graphic form, rather than as columns of numbers in a worksheet. Visually accessible data is particularly effective in business presentations and reports. In this chapter, you'll begin exploring the second major topic of this book, *charting:* the display of worksheet data in graphic (chart) form.

When you're done working through this chapter, you will know

- How to create a column chart

- How to add text to a chart

- How to change the chart type and format

- How to create multiple charts from a single worksheet

## CHART TERMINOLOGY

Before you begin creating Excel charts, you should be familiar with the following terms, as shown in Table 8.1 and Figure 8.1:

**Table 8.1**　　　**Chart Terminology**

| Element | Description |
|---------|-------------|
| Chart | A graphic representation of selected worksheet data. |
| Chart title | The title you specify for the chart. |
| Data marker | A symbol that marks a data value in a chart. The data marker varies with the chart type. Column and bar charts use rectangular-bar data markers (as shown in Figure 8.1), pie charts use wedge shapes, line charts use dots, and so on. |
| Gridlines | Lines that extend across the plot area to make it easier to view data values. |
| Chart text | Text that describes chart data or objects. *Attached text* is attached to a chart object; *unattached text* is not attached to any chart object. |
| Legend | A box that identifies the chart's data markers. |
| Axis | A reference line along which chart data is plotted. Categories (row headings) are plotted along a *category axis* or *x-axis* (1st, 2nd, 3rd, and 4th in Figure 8.1). Data (numeric) values are plotted along a *value axis* or *y-axis* ($0 through $70,000 in Figure 8.1). |

**Table 8.1**          **Chart Terminology (Continued)**

| Element | Description |
| --- | --- |
| Tick mark | A small line that intersects an axis and is used to delineate categories and data values. |
| Plot area | The area in which data are plotted, including all axes and data markers. |
| Data series | A series of related data values. (The chart in Figure 8.1 contains three data series: Gross Revenues, Expenses, and Profits. Each series contains four values, one for each of the four quarters.) A data series typically includes all the values in a single worksheet column. |

**Figure 8.1**          **Chart terminology**

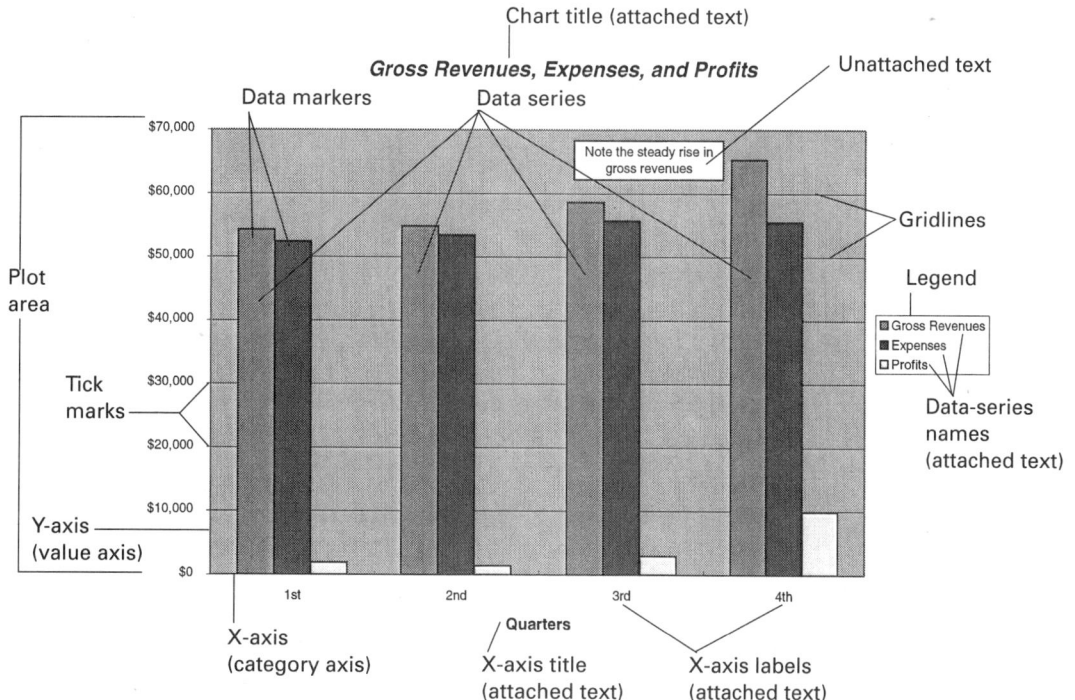

## CREATING A COLUMN CHART

To create a column chart,

- Activate (display) the worksheet containing the data you want to chart.

- Select the range of data to chart, including both the numeric data and the row/column headings that you want to appear as axis labels in the chart. (For help doing this, see the next section, "Selecting the Range to Chart.")

- Press *F11* or *Alt+F1* (if you don't have an F11 key on your keyboard). Or, choose *Insert, Chart, As New Sheet* to open the Chart Wizard dialog box, and click on the *Finish button*.

If you are not running Excel, please start it now. If there is a workbook on your screen (other than the startup workbook, Book1), please close it. Let's open a workbook and create a column chart depicting data in its Quarterly Report worksheet:

1. Open **Chart** from your Excel Work folder, and maximize the document window, if necessary.

2. Select cells **C4:E8**, the range comprising four quarters of gross revenues and expenses data (text and numbers).

3. Press **F11** (or **Alt+F1**, if you don't have an F11 key) to create a column chart depicting these selected data, as shown in Figure 8.2.

4. Observe the chart. The four quarters are plotted along the x-axis (1st, 2nd, 3rd, and 4th); the dollar amounts are plotted along the y-axis ($0 to $70,000). Two data series are plotted, gross revenues and expenses (as identified in the chart legend box). The gross revenues are represented by the left columns in each 2-column cluster; the expenses are represented by the right columns.

5. Observe the worksheet tabs at the bottom of the document window. Note that Excel placed your chart in a separate *chart sheet* named Chart1, and that it inserted this chart sheet before the Quarterly Report worksheet. Note also that the Chart toolbar is displayed. (See Figure 8.3 for a detail of the Chart toolbar.)

**Figure 8.2**     **Creating a column chart**

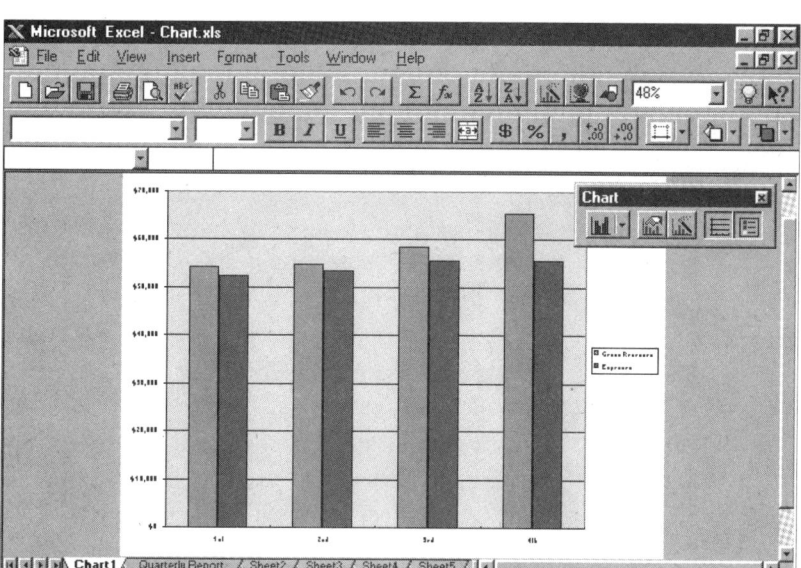

**Figure 8.3**     **The Chart toolbar**

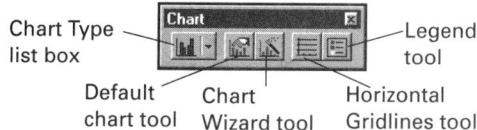

Chart Type list box

Legend tool

Default chart tool     Chart Wizard tool     Horizontal Gridlines tool

## SELECTING THE RANGE TO CHART

The shape and content of the range of cells you select in your worksheet determine the layout of the resultant chart. Follow these basic guidelines when selecting a range to chart:

* The leftmost column of your worksheet selection should contain text labels. These become the x-axis (category) labels in the chart (*1st, 2nd, 3rd,* and *4th* in Figure 8.2).

* The top row of your worksheet selection also should contain text labels. These become the data-series labels in the chart legend (*Gross Revenues* and *Expenses* in Figure 8.2).

- The rest of your worksheet selection should contain the numeric data you want to plot.

### PRACTICE YOUR SKILLS

1. Activate the **Quarterly Report** worksheet (by clicking on its tab).

2. Cells C4:E8 should still be selected; if not, please select them. These are the cells you used to create your Chart1 column chart.

3. Examine the selected range with regard to the guidelines presented above. Note that all three guidelines have been followed.

4. Activate the **Chart1** chart sheet.

## ADDING TEXT TO A CHART

Well-placed, succinct text labels and notes can significantly enhance a chart's clarity and effectiveness. You can add *attached text* and *unattached text* to your charts. Attached text is text that is attached to a chart object; for example, in your Chart1 chart, the text labels *1st*, *2nd*, *3rd*, and *4th* are all attached to the x-axis. Unattached text is text that is not attached to any chart object; for example, in Figure 8.1, the text *Note the steady rise in gross revenues* is unattached.

We'll cover attached text below and unattached text in the next chapter.

### ADDING ATTACHED TEXT

Attached text includes the following items (as shown in Figure 8.1): chart title, x- and y-axis titles, data-marker labels, legend, and x- and y-axis labels. To add attached text to a chart,

- Activate the chart sheet.

- To add a chart title, x-axis title, or y-axis title, choose *Insert, Titles*. Check *Chart Title, Value (Y) Axis* or *Category (X) Axis*. Click on OK. To change the title text, select the desired title, type your new text, and press Enter.

- To add data-marker labels, choose *Insert, Data Labels*. Check *Show Value* (to add value labels) or *Show Label* (to add text labels) and click on OK.

- To add a legend, choose *Insert, Legend* or click on the *Legend tool* (shown in Figure 8.3).

- To add x-axis labels and/or y-axis labels, choose *Insert, Axes*. Check *Category (X) Axis* and/or *Value (Y) Axis* and click on OK.

**Note:** To remove attached text from a chart, follow the above procedure but *uncheck* the specified options, instead of checking them.

Let's add a title to Chart1:

1. Click on **Insert** to open the drop-down Insert menu. Note that the chart-sheet Insert options differ from the worksheet Insert options (Cells, Rows, Columns, and so on). Click on **Titles** to open the Titles dialog box.

2. Check **Chart Title** and click on **OK**. *Title* appears at the top of the chart, surrounded by black selection squares.

3. Type the new chart title, **ABC Company Revenues and Expenses** (it will appear in the Formula bar), and press **Enter** to enter it in the chart title text box. Note that the title is bolded.

4. Click on the **Bold tool** to unbold the title. Click on the **Bold tool** again to rebold the title. You can use the formatting tools to modify chart text just as you would to modify worksheet text.

## PRACTICE YOUR SKILLS

1. Attach the title **Quarters** to the x-axis of Chart1. (**Hint:** Use the **Insert, Titles** command.)

2. Press **Esc** to deselect the x-axis title, and compare your chart with that shown in Figure 8.4.

3. Rename your chart sheet to **ABC Revenues and Expenses**.

4. Save the chart sheet. To do this, you must save the entire workbook in which the chart sheet resides. Use the **Save As** command to save the workbook file to your Excel Work folder as **mychart**. This saves both the chart sheet and the Quarterly Report worksheet.

**Figure 8.4**       **Adding a chart title and x-axis title**

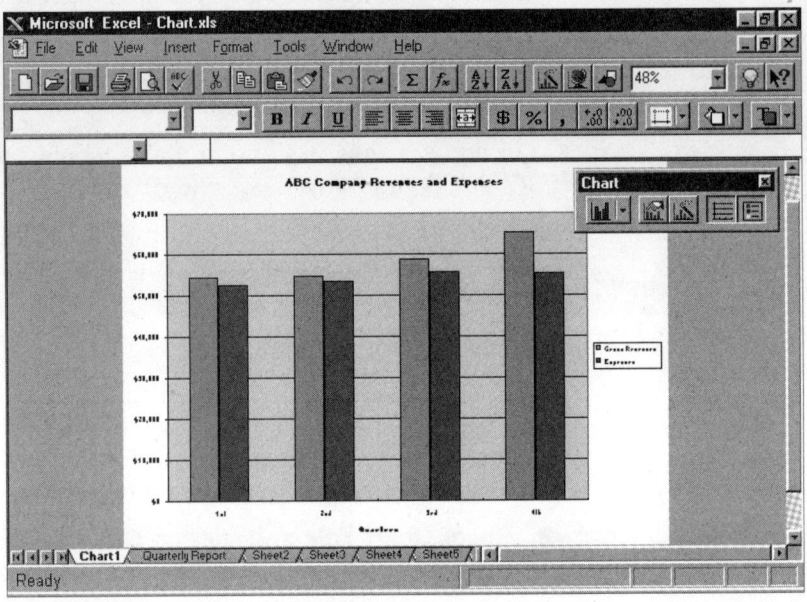

# CHART TYPES

Thus far, you've looked at one type of chart, a standard column chart. Excel offers a total of 15 chart types. Table 8.2 provides a complete list, along with brief descriptions of each chart's primary use:

**Table 8.2**       **Chart Types**

| Chart Type | You Use This Chart Type to Show: |
|---|---|
| Area | The relative importance of data values over a period of time |
| Bar | Individual data values |
| Column | Individual data values over a period of time |
| Line | Trends in data over a period of time |
| Pie | The relationship of parts to a whole within a single data series |

**Table 8.2**        **Chart Types (Continued)**

| Chart Type | You Use This Chart Type to Show: |
| --- | --- |
| Doughnut | The relationship of parts to a whole within one or more data series |
| Radar | Relative comparison between numeric data |
| XY (scatter) | Relationships among numeric values in different groups of data |
| Combination | Relationships among data by superimposing two types of charts |
| 3-D area | A three-dimensional view of an area chart |
| 3-D bar | A three-dimensional view of a bar chart |
| 3-D column | A three-dimensional view of a column chart |
| 3-D line | A three-dimensional view of a line chart |
| 3-D pie | A three-dimensional view of a pie chart |
| 3-D surface | A "topographic" variation of a 3-D column chart |

Excel offers several *formats* for each chart type; each format is a variation of its parent chart type. For example, the column chart type has a total of ten formats: five side-by-side column formats (Chart1 is a side-by-side column chart), four stacked-column formats, and one overlapped-column format. You choose the chart type and format best suited for depicting your selected data.

## CHANGING THE CHART TYPE AND FORMAT

To change the chart type and format by using the *AutoFormat* command,

- Activate the chart sheet.

- Choose *Format, AutoFormat* to open the AutoFormat dialog box.

- Under Formats Used, verify that *Built-In* is selected.

- In the Galleries list box, select the desired chart type.

- Under Formats, select the desired chart format.

- Click on OK.

To change the chart type by using the Chart Type list box in the Chart toolbar,

- Activate the chart sheet.

- If the Chart toolbar is hidden, display it.

- Open the Chart Type option palette. (You can tear off this option palette, like you did with the Borders option palette in Chapter 7.)

- Click on the desired chart type.

**Note:** You cannot use the Chart toolbar to change the chart format; you must use the AutoFormat command.

Let's use the AutoFormat command to explore different chart types and formats:

1. Choose **Format, AutoFormat** to open the AutoFormat dialog box.

2. Under Formats Used, verify that Built-In is selected. This option displays Excel's standard formats for the selected chart type. Observe these formats; they are the ten column-chart formats we mentioned earlier.

3. Under Galleries, click on **Bar** to change the chart type from column to bar. Observe the different bar-chart formats, each a variation of the standard bar chart. As reported in Table 8.2, you use bar charts to depict and compare individual data values. A bar chart is essentially a column chart flipped on its side, categories (in this case, quarters) are displayed on the vertical axis rather than on the horizontal axis.

4. Under Galleries, click on **Line** to change the chart type from bar to line. Observe the different formats; note that format 1 displays lines and square markers.

5. Double-click on format **1** to select it and apply it to your chart. (You also could have clicked on format 1 to select it, then clicked on OK to apply it to the chart. Double-clicking, though, is easier.) You use line charts to show trends in data over a period of time.

6. Choose **Format, AutoFormat** to redisplay the AutoFormat dialog box. Verify that Built-In is selected.

7. Under Galleries, click on **Area** to change the chart type from line to area.

8. Double-click on format **1** to apply it to your chart. You use area charts to show the relative importance of data values over a period of time.

9. Choose **Edit, Undo Area** to undo your area-chart formatting. The line chart reappears.

Now let's use the Chart toolbar to change chart types:

1. If the Chart toolbar is hidden, display it. (**Hint:** Select **Chart** from the Toolbars shortcut menu.) Observe the leftmost item in the toolbar; this is the Chart Types list box.

2. Open the Chart Types option palette (shown in Figure 8.5), and click on the **Area** option to change the chart type from line back to area.

**Figure 8.5**    **The Chart Type option palette**

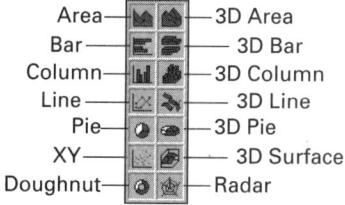

```
Area ——      —— 3D Area
Bar ——       —— 3D Bar
Column ——    —— 3D Column
Line ——      —— 3D Line
Pie ——       —— 3D Pie
XY ——        —— 3D Surface
Doughnut ——  —— Radar
```

3. Open the Chart Types option palette, and click on the **3-D Area** option to change the chart type from 2-D area to 3-D area. Observe the results, as shown in Figure 8.6; impressive, yes?

4. Choose **Format, AutoFormat**, and verify that Built-In and 3-D Area are selected. Note the seven different 3-D area chart formats. To change the chart type, you can use the Chart toolbar or the AutoFormat command; to change the chart format, you must use the AutoFormat command.

**Figure 8.6**     **Changing the type to 3-D area**

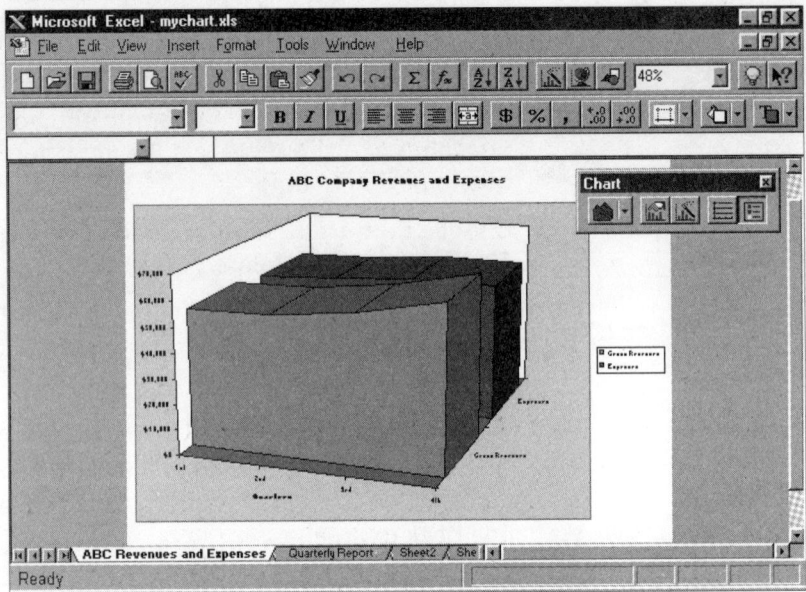

5. Double-click on format **1** to apply a new format to your 3-D area chart.


## PRACTICE YOUR SKILLS

1. Click repeatedly on the **Undo tool** to flip back and forth between your two 3-D area charts, the one you created with the Chart toolbar and the one you created with the AutoFormat command. Observe the way in which these two charts use different formats to depict identical data.

2. Use the AutoFormat command to return the chart type to **Column**, format **1**.

3. Update the chart sheet (by updating the entire workbook file).

4. If you have a printer, print the chart sheet (proceed as you would to print a worksheet). If not, preview the chart sheet and then close the print preview.

## CREATING MULTIPLE CHARTS FROM A SINGLE WORKSHEET

At times, you may want to create two or more charts from a single worksheet to depict different aspects of the worksheet data. For example, you might want to present a bar chart and a 3-D area chart for the same range of data, to present these data in different lights; or you might want to create five different charts for five different data ranges from the same worksheet. Excel allows you to create an unlimited number of charts from a single worksheet.

Let's create a second column chart using data from our Quarterly Report worksheet:

1. Activate the **Quarterly Report** worksheet. Observe the formula in cell F5. It calculates profit by subtracting expenses (E5) from revenues (D5).

2. Select the range **C4:C8**. This range contains the Quarter column heading and labels.

3. Without deselecting cells C4:C8, add the range **F4:F8** to your selection (by holding down the **Ctrl key** while dragging from F4 to F8). Cells F4:F8 contain the Profits column heading and numeric data.

4. Press **F11** (or **Alt+F1**) to create a column chart depicting the data in the two noncontiguous worksheet ranges you've selected, as shown in Figure 8.7.

5. Observe that Excel automatically entitled your new chart Profits. When you select only one numeric data column in your worksheet—column F, in this case (column C contains text labels, not numeric data)—Excel uses this column's heading for the chart title.

6. Select the title and bold it.

Now let's change the chart type:

1. Use the Chart Type list box to change the chart type from column to pie. You use pie charts to show the relationship of parts to a whole within a single data series (Profits, in this case).

2. Choose **Format, AutoFormat** and double-click on pie-chart format **6** to apply this format to the chart. Each slice of a pie chart represents a percentage of the whole; now you can see these percentages.

**Figure 8.7**     **Creating a new column chart**

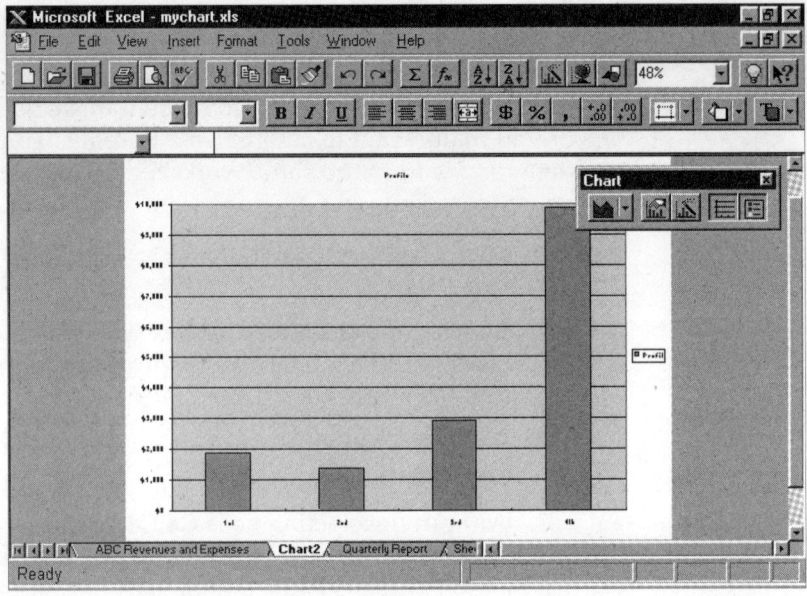

3. Use the **AutoFormat** command to apply pie-chart format **7** to the chart. This displays the quarter labels along with the percentages. This, in turn, makes the legend unnecessary, because the pie slices are already identified.

4. Click on the **Legend tool** to remove the chart legend.

Your screen should now match that shown in Figure 8.8.

5. Update the workbook file.

## THE WORKSHEET/CHART LINK

Excel automatically links a worksheet and all the charts you create from it. When you change labels or numeric data in the work-

**Figure 8.8**    **The completed pie chart**

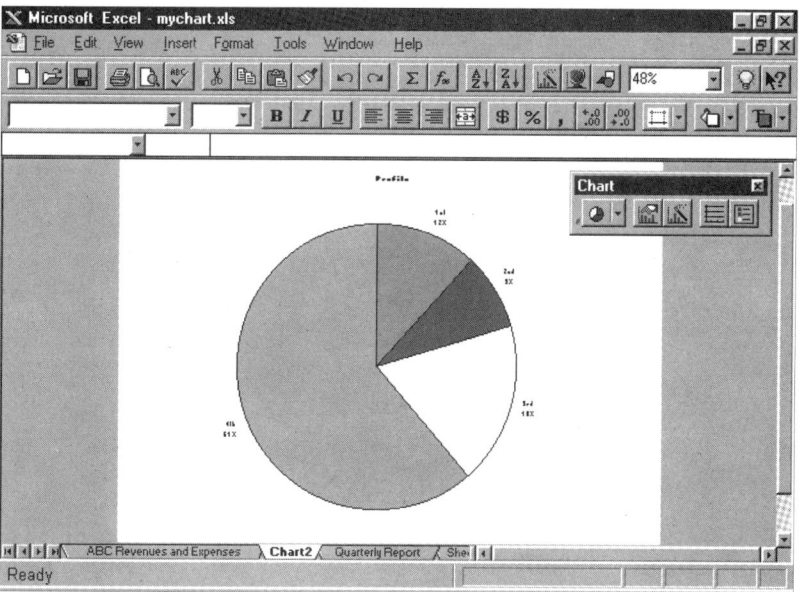

sheet, Excel redraws the associated charts to reflect these changes.

Let's examine the worksheet/chart link in the active workbook, mychart:

1. Take a moment to jot down the percentages of each piece of the pie chart. To read the percentages, you might want to print preview the chart sheet and zoom in on the percentages.

2. Activate the **Quarterly Report** worksheet. Observe the fourth-quarter profits, $9,875.

3. Change the expenses value in cell E8 to **65000**. Observe the new fourth-quarter profits, $325.

4. Activate the **Chart2** chart sheet (your pie chart). The fourth-quarter slice was 61 percent of the pie before you changed the expenses in cell E8, as shown in Figure 8.8; now it's 5 percent of the pie, as shown in Figure 8.9. Note that the quarter-1 through quarter-3 percentages have adjusted accordingly. (Caution: Do not use print preview to view the percentages. You'll have to trust us on this one.)

**Figure 8.9**          **Observing the worksheet/chart link**

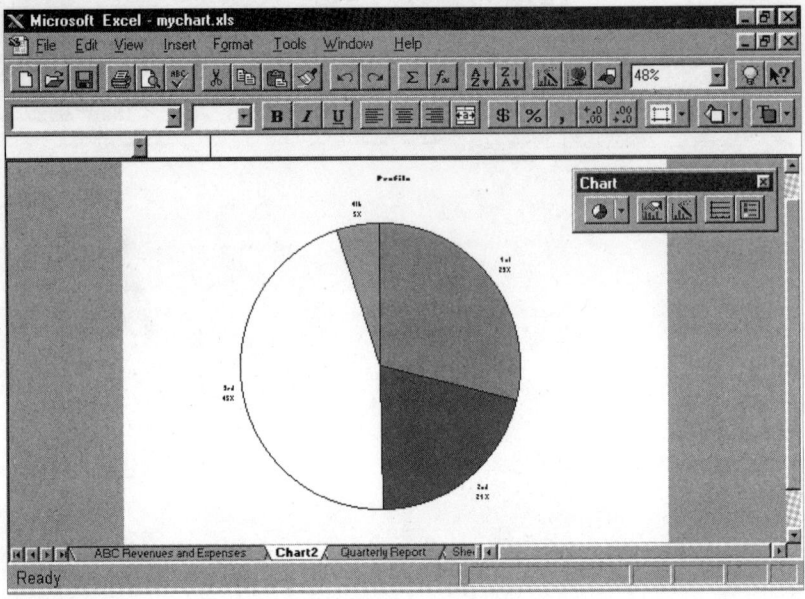

Let's see if Excel lets us undo our expenses change:

1. Click on the **Undo tool**. Hooray! Excel not only undid the expenses change, but automatically displayed the Quarterly Report worksheet in which this change took place. Note that the fourth-quarter profits are back up.

2. Select the **Chart2** chart sheet. Note that the percentages are the same as in Figure 8.8.

3. Close the workbook file without saving the changes.

## PRACTICE YOUR SKILLS

This activity will hone the Excel charting skills you've acquired in this chapter. Perform these steps to create the chart shown in Figure 8.10:

1. Open **Practice8** from your Excel Work folder (Chapter 3).

2. Maximize the document window, if necessary (Chapter 3).

3. Create the chart shown in Figure 8.10. To do this,

**Figure 8.10**     **The Revenues, Expenses, and Profits chart**

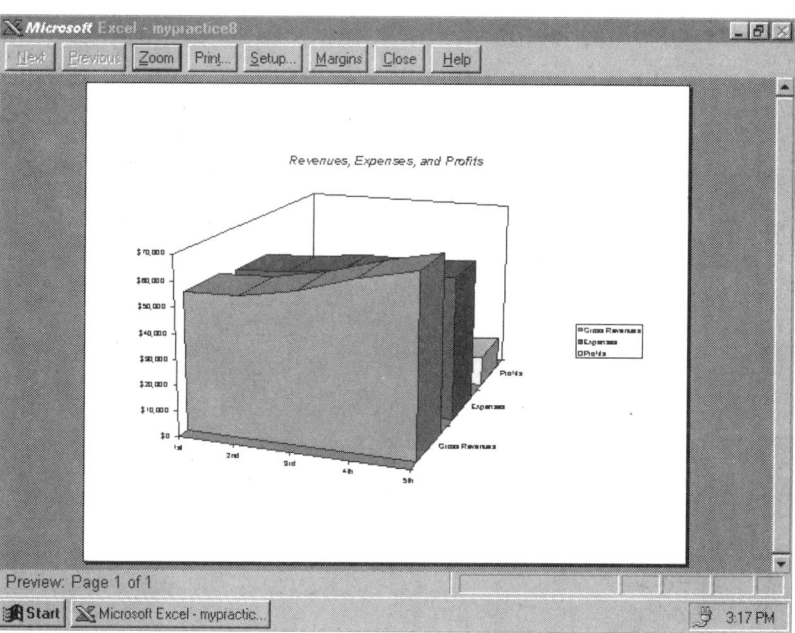

- In the ABC Quarterly Report worksheet, select the data you want to chart. (**Hint:** You must select all the numeric data and all the text labels.)

- Create a column chart depicting the selected data.

- Add the chart title **Revenues, Expenses, and Profits**.

- Change the chart-title size to **16** points, then italicize it. (**Hint:** Use the Formatting toolbar.)

- Change the chart type to **3-D Area**, format **5**. (**Hint:** Use the **AutoFormat** command.)

- Remove the header and footer (Chapter 6). (**Hint:** Use **File, Page Setup.**)

**4.** Preview the chart (Chapter 6).

**5.** Compare your previewed chart to that shown in Figure 8.10.

**6.** Save the workbook file as **mypractice8**, then close it.

## SUMMARY

In this chapter, you began a three-chapter exploration of Excel's charting capabilities. You learned how to create a column chart, how to add text to a chart, how to change the chart type and format, and how to create multiple charts from a single worksheet.

Here's a quick reference guide to the Excel features introduced in this chapter:

| Desired Result | How to Do It |
|---|---|
| Create column chart | Select desired worksheet range and press **F11** or **Alt+F1** (or choose **Insert, Chart, As New Shee**t and click on **Finish**) |
| Add chart, x-axis, or y-axis title | Choose **Insert, Titles**; check desired option(s); click on **OK** |
| Add data-marker labels | Choose **Insert, Data Labels**; check **Show Value** (to add value labels) or **Show Label** (to add text labels); click on **OK** |
| Add x-axis or y-axis labels | Choose **Insert, Axes**; check desired option; click on **OK** |
| Remove attached text | Follow above procedures, but *uncheck* options |
| Add/remove legend | Choose **Insert, Legend** or click on the **Legend tool** |
| Change chart type and format | Activate chart sheet; choose **Format, AutoFormat**; select **Built-In**; select desired chart type; select desired chart format; click on **OK**. Or, activate chart sheet and select desired type from Chart Type option palette (Chart toolbar) |
| Save chart | Save workbook file in which chart resides |

In the next chapter, you'll learn how to customize the format, content, and layout of a chart.

## IF YOU'RE STOPPING HERE

If you want to break off here, please exit Excel. If you want to proceed directly to the next chapter, please do so now.

# CHAPTER 9: CUSTOMIZING AND EMBEDDING YOUR CHART

**N**ow that you know how to create charts, you can concentrate on making your charts more effective and professional-looking. In this chapter, you'll learn how to customize the format, content, and layout of a chart to meet your presentation needs. You'll also learn how to embed a chart in a worksheet, a technique that affords you the convenience of treating a worksheet and its associated chart(s) as a single document.

When you're done working through this chapter, you will know

- How to customize a chart legend
- How to add unattached text to a chart
- How to edit chart text
- How to format your charts
- How to embed a chart in a worksheet

## CUSTOMIZING THE CHART LEGEND

When you create a chart, Excel automatically adds a legend to the right of the chart and formats the legend text as 10-point, normal text (unbolded, unitalicized, and so on). You need not, however, accept these defaults. You can customize a legend by moving it to a different place in the chart sheet; resizing it; and changing its font, font size, font style, data-marker colors, and border.

 **MOVING THE LEGEND**

Use either of these methods to move a legend to a different place in the chart sheet:

- Select the legend and choose *Format, Selected Legend* (or press Ctrl+1, or choose *Format Legend* from the shortcut menu) to open the Format Legend dialog box. Display the placement options, click on the desired option (*Bottom, Corner, Top, Right,* or *Left*), and click on OK.
- Or, drag the legend with the mouse.

**Note:** When you use the Format Legend dialog box to move a legend, Excel automatically changes the legend box's shape and redraws the chart to accommodate the relocated legend. When you drag a legend to move it, Excel does not change the legend box's shape or redraw the chart.

If you are not running Excel, please start it now. If there is a workbook on your screen (other than the startup workbook, Book1), please close it. Let's begin by opening a workbook file, activating a chart sheet, and using the Format Legend dialog box to move its legend:

1. Open **Custom Chart** from your Excel Work folder.

2. Activate the **Revenues and Expenses Chart** chart sheet. This column chart plots ABC's quarterly gross revenues and expenses. Observe the default legend; it is located to the right of the chart.

3. Select the **legend** by clicking on it. Note that *Legend* is displayed in the Name list box (in the formula bar). When you select a chart object, Excel displays its name here.

4. Choose **Format, Selected Legend** to open the Format Legend dialog box.

5. Click on the **Placement tab**.

6. Select **Bottom** and click on **OK** to move the legend to the bottom of the chart sheet.

7. Scroll down, if necessary, to view your moved legend. Press **Esc** to deselect it. Your screen should match that shown in Figure 9.1.

**Figure 9.1**     **Using Format, Selected Legend to move the legend**

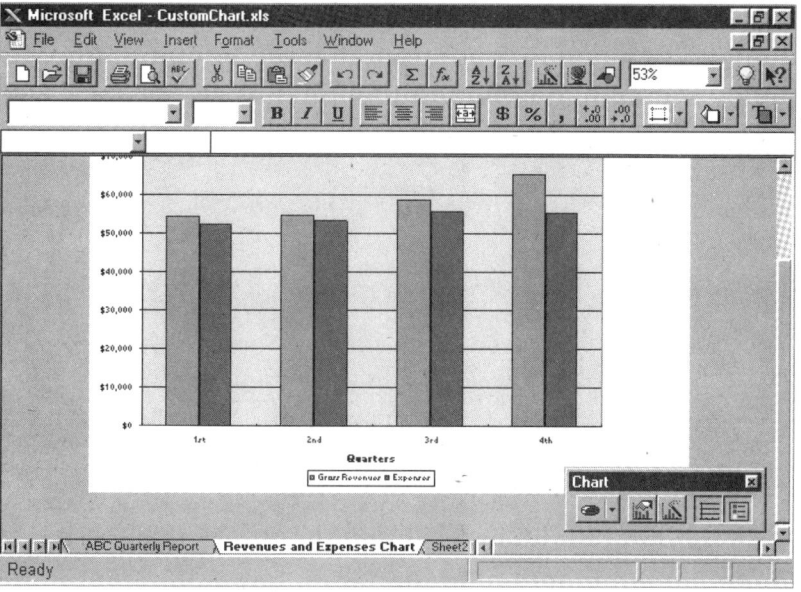

**Note:** You might want to move the Chart toolbar so that it is not covering up part of the chart.

8. Note that Excel has automatically changed the legend box to a flat rectangle, a shape more appropriate for the bottom of the chart, and has automatically redrawn the chart to accommodate the relocated legend. Verify this by clicking on the **Undo tool** to undo your legend move, then clicking on the **Redo tool** to redo the move.

Now let's use the mouse to move the legend:

1. Drag the legend back to the right side of the chart sheet.

2. Note that Excel did not change the legend box shape or the chart size.

## PRACTICE YOUR SKILLS

1. Drag the legend to the bottom of the chart sheet. Try to center it exactly beneath the x-axis title, *Quarters*.

2. Now use the shortcut menu to move the legend to the bottom of the chart sheet. (**Hint:** To open the Legend shortcut menu, click the **right mouse button** on the legend.) Note that Excel automatically centers the legend when you use the Format Legend dialog box, saving you the trouble of doing it manually.

3. Save the chart by saving the workbook file to your Excel Work folder as **mycustom**.

 ## ADDING A SHADOW BORDER TO THE LEGEND

You can add a *shadow border* to your legend to give it an impressive 3-D look. To do this,

- Select the legend.

- Choose *Format, Selected Legend* (or press *Ctrl+1*, or choose *Format Legend* from the shortcut menu) to open the Format Legend dialog box.

- Display the patterns options.

- Check the *Shadow* option.

- Click on OK.

Let's add a shadow border to the chart legend:

1. If your legend is not already selected, select it.

2. Press **Ctrl+1** to open the Format Legend dialog box. Now you've used all three methods for opening the Format Legend dialog box: choosing Format, Selected Legend; pressing Ctrl+1; and choosing Format Legend from the shortcut menu. Which method do you prefer?

3. Click on the **Patterns tab**.

4. Under Border, check **Shadow**.

5. Click on **OK** to apply a shadow border to your legend.

6. Press **Esc** to deselect the legend. Behold your shadowed legend box! Hmmmm...not so easy to see, is it? Let's try changing to full-screen view.

7. Choose **View, Full Screen**. Well...you've succeeded in uncluttering the screen, but not in enlarging the chart or any of its objects. What to do, what to do? Let's try using a special feature called the *Sized With Window* view.

8. Choose **View, Sized With Window**. Eureka! You've done it. Your shadowed legend box is clearly visible, as are all the chart objects, as shown in Figure 9.2. Note, however, that the proportions are somewhat off. The chart title is too wide, the legend is too large, the chart itself is too flat, and so on.

9. Verify this by choosing **View, Sized With Window** again to turn off this feature and return to normal (full-screen) view. The proportions in this view are accurate; this is how the chart sheet will look when you print it out.

10. Choose **View, Sized With Window** once again to toggle back to sized-with-window (full-screen) view. This is a great view in which to work on your charts, as long as you feel comfortable with the proportions being somewhat off. And if you need to see the correct proportions, normal view is but two mouse clicks away (View, Sized With Window).

**Figure 9.2**       **Changing to full-screen, Sized With Window view**

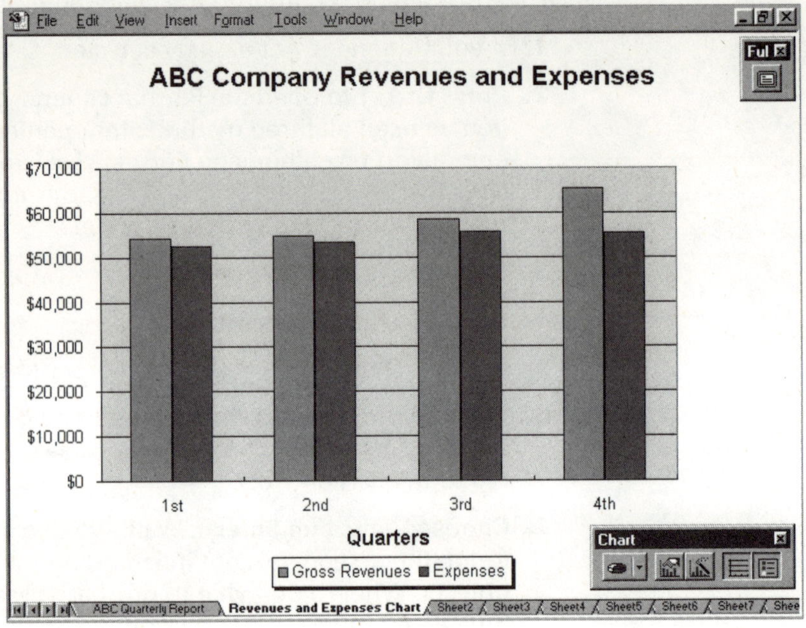

## PRACTICE YOUR SKILLS

Observe that the Standard and Formatting toolbars are hidden in your current sized-with-window, full-screen view. Since you'll be making several formatting changes in this chapter, let's unhide the Formatting toolbar:

1. Display the **Formatting toolbar**, and move it to the top of the screen, if necessary. (Be aware that once you add the standard or formatting toolbars to your full-screen view, they will appear *whenever* you change to full-screen view—unless, of course, you specifically remove them from the screen.)

## ADDING UNATTACHED TEXT TO A CHART

At times, you may wish to draw attention to certain aspects of a chart; for example, to point out an important trend or explain a data anomaly. You can do this by adding unattached text to the chart, as follows:

• Press *Esc* to deselect all chart objects.

- Type your text. It is displayed in the formula bar.
- Press *Enter* to create a text box containing this text.
- Drag the text box to the desired location.
- If necessary, resize the text box by dragging its selection squares.

Let's add unattached text to our chart to explain the rather dramatic upswing in fourth-quarter gross revenues:

1. You should be in full-screen, Sized With Window view. To verify this, click on **View** to open its drop-down menu. Observe the Full Screen and Sized With Window options; they both should be selected (checked). If they are, click on **View** again to close the drop-down menu. If not, please select them now.

2. Press **Esc** to deselect all chart objects.

3. Type **New Products**. (Normally, you'd see this in the formula bar. However, since the formula bar is not shown in full-screen view, you'll have to type "blindfolded," so to speak.) Press **Enter**. A text box containing your typed text appears in the middle of the chart. You need to move this box and then resize it.

4. Move the mouse pointer slowly over the text box. Note that the pointer changes from an I beam (when you're pointing inside the box), to a double-headed black arrow (when you're pointing to one of the box's selection squares), to a single-headed white arrow (when you're pointing to one of the box's edges). To move the text box, you must point to one of its edges—so that the single-headed white arrow pointer is displayed—and then drag. Do not attempt to drag the box when either the double-headed black arrow or I-beam pointer is displayed, or you will inadvertantly resize the box or edit its contents!

5. Point to the top edge of the text box, so that the single-headed white arrow pointer is displayed. Using Figure 9.3 as a guide, drag the box above the fourth-quarter gross revenues column.

Now let's customize our unattached text box:

1. Verify that the text box is still selected, then click on the **Bold tool** to bold the box's contents.

**Figure 9.3**   **Adding unattached text to the chart**

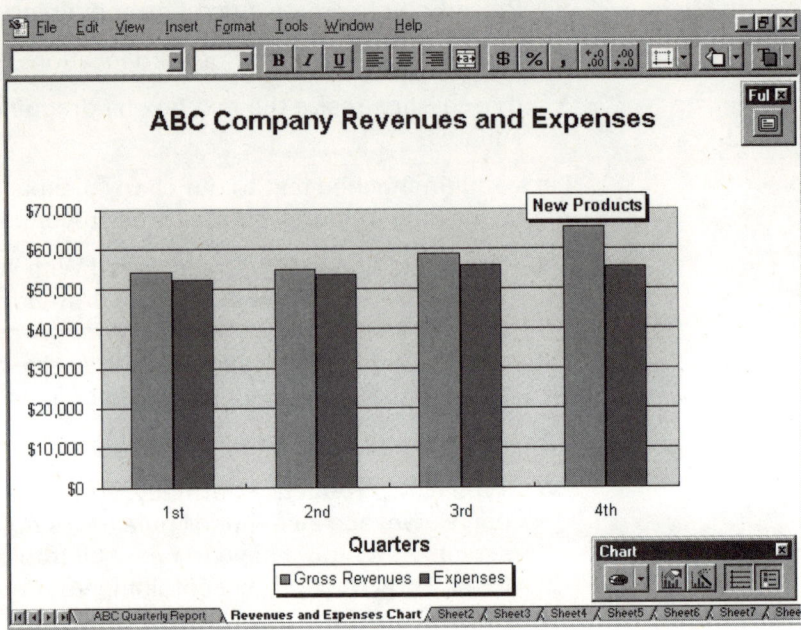

2. Click the **right mouse button** on the text box to open its short-cut menu, and choose **Format Object** to open the Format Object dialog box.

3. Display the patterns options.

4. Check the **Shadow** option to apply a shadow border to the text box.

5. In the Fill color palette, click on **white** (the second color from the left in the top row) to apply a white background color to the text box.

6. Click on **OK** to apply your new formats.

7. Fine-tune the text box's position, if necessary, until it's nicely centered over the fourth-quarter column.

8. Press **Esc** to deselect the text box. Your screen should match that shown in Figure 9.3. Don't worry if you misspelled *New Products*; you're going to change the text in the next section anyway.

## EDITING CHART TEXT

Proceed as follows to edit attached or unattached chart text:

- Select the text object.
- Click on the selected object to place the insertion point in it.
- Edit the text as desired.
- Press *Esc* to enter the edited text.

Let's modify our chart title:

1. Click on the **chart title** to select it. Click again on the selected title object to place the insertion point in the text.

2. Select the text **Revenues and Expenses**. (**Hint:** Double-click on *Revenues* and drag to *Expenses.*)

3. Type **Chart** to replace the selected text.

4. Press **Esc** to enter your modified chart title.

### PRACTICE YOUR SKILLS

1. Change the chart title to **ABC Annual Performance Summary Chart**.

2. Change the unattached text box contents to **Introduced plastics line**.

3. Reposition the unattached text box over the fourth-quarter column.

4. Press **Esc** to deselect the text. Your screen should match that shown in Figure 9.4.

5. Choose **File, Save** to update the workbook file.

 CHANGING THE LINE BREAKS

You can change the *line breaks* in your charts' text objects—that is, how the text is divided into two or more lines—by inserting or removing these breaks manually. To do this,

- Place the insertion point in the desired text object (by selecting the object, then clicking on the selected object).

**Figure 9.4**    **Editing the chart title and unattached text**

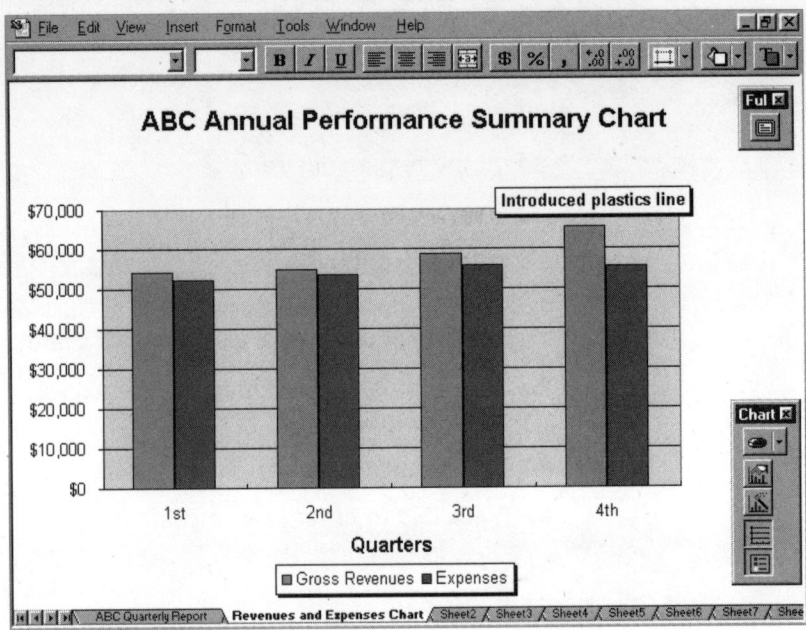

- To insert a new line break, move the insertion point directly before the word where you want the new line to begin, and press Enter.

- To remove an existing line break, place the insertion point at the beginning of the line you would like to join to the previous line, and press *Backspace*.

- Press *Esc* to enter the modified text.

Let's use this procedure to change the line breaks of our chart title:

1. Select the **chart title**, and then click on the selected title to place the insertion point in it. Note that there are no line breaks in the text; the entire title fits on a single line.

2. Move the insertion point directly before the word *Performance*.

3. Press **Enter** to insert a line break at this point. Note that *Performance Summary Chart* moves down to a new, second line.

**4.** Press **Esc** to enter your new two-line title. Don't worry if the title text overlaps your *Introduced plastics line* text box; you'll fix this soon.

Say you changed your mind and wanted the title to break at *Summary* instead of *Performance:*

**1.** Place the insertion point directly before *Summary*.

**2.** Press **Enter** to insert a line break at this point. Note that the title is now divided into three lines:

```
ABC Annual
Performance
Summary Chart
```

In order to end up with a two-line title, you must remove the undesired line break at *Performance*.

**3.** Place the insertion point at the beginning of the *Performance* line.

**4.** Press **Backspace** to remove the line break and join *Performance* to the previous line. Note that the title now consists of two lines, broken at *Summary*. This is what you want.

**5.** Press **Esc** twice to enter your modified two-line title and deselect the title object. Your screen should match that shown in Figure 9.5. Again, don't worry if your *Introduced plastics line* text box overlaps the title text.

## FORMATTING YOUR CHARTS

Excel gives you full control over your charts' formatting (layout and appearance). Over the next several sections, you'll learn how to:

- Format chart text.

- Change data-marker colors.

- Add and remove chart gridlines.

- Change the plot-area background color.

- Rescale the value axis.

- Change the chart format of a customized chart.

**Figure 9.5**    **Changing the title's line breaks**

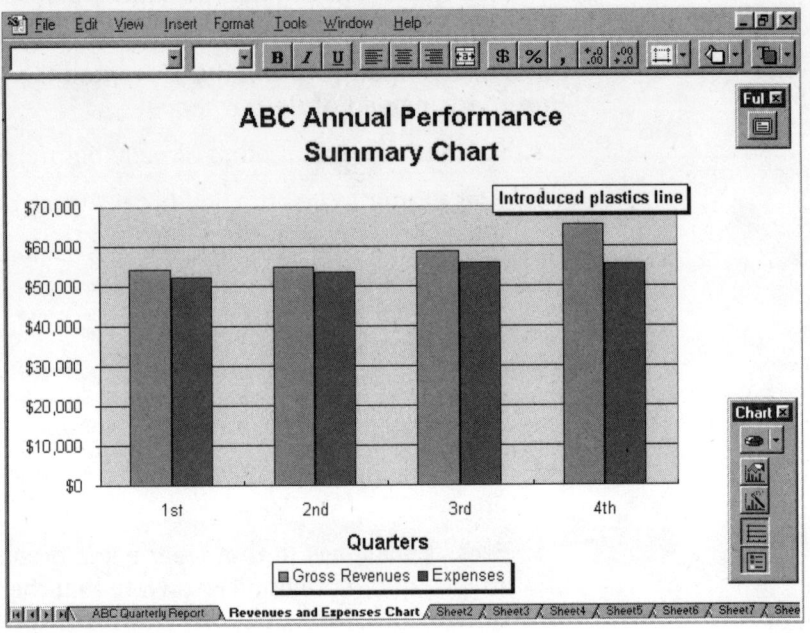

- Overlap columns and bars.
- Move and resize chart objects.

## FORMATTING CHART TEXT

You can use the Formatting toolbar or the Format Object dialog box to format your chart text. To format chart text using the Formatting toolbar,

- Select the entire object to format all the text in a text object (title, label, and so on). To format selected text in a text object, select the object, then select the desired text in it.
- Change the desired Formatting toolbar settings (font, size, bold, italics, underline, alignment, and so on).
- If you selected text in an object (rather than the entire object), press *Esc* to enter your formatting changes.

To format chart text using the Format Object dialog box,

- Select the entire object to format all the text in a text object. Or, double-click on the object to open the Format Object dialog box and skip the next bulleted step of this procedure. To format selected text in a text object, select the object, then select the desired text in it.

- Choose *Format, Selected Object* (where *Object* is the name of the object you selected in the previous step; for example, Format, Selected Chart Title). Or, press *Ctrl+1*. Or, click the right mouse button on the selected object/text to open the shortcut menu, and choose *Format Object* (for example, Format Chart Title). All these actions open the Format Object dialog box.

- Display the font options.

- Change the desired options (font, size, font style, and so on).

- Click on OK.

Let's use the Formatting toolbar to format text in our chart:

1. Click on a blank area of the chart to select the chart object. Verify this by observing the black selection squares around the perimeter of the chart.

2. Click on the **Italic tool** to italicize all of the chart's attached text (the chart title, x-axis title, legend text, and x- and y-axis labels). Attached text is "attached" to the chart object; unattached text (*Introduced plastics line*) is not.

## PRACTICE YOUR SKILLS

1. Use the Formatting toolbar to change the chart-title text size to **18** points.

2. Unitalicize the legend text. Note that you can treat the legend as an independent object, even though it "belongs" to the chart object (as you saw in the previous activity); this is also true for the x-axis and y-axis labels.

3. Unitalicize the y-axis labels. (**Hint:** Select the **y-axis** and click on the **Italic tool**.)

4. Unitalicize the x-axis labels.

**5.** Use the Format Legend dialog box to change the legend text size to **12** points. Most users find it easier to use the Formatting toolbar to format chart text; do you?

**6.** Update the workbook file.

## CHANGING DATA-MARKER COLORS

Excel uses colors to identify the data series that a chart's data markers represent. For example, in your active chart, the gross-revenues data markers are lavender (on a color monitor), and the expenses data markers are dark purple. When you create a chart, Excel automatically selects the data-marker colors. You can, however, change these colors for emphasis, clarity, or overall visual harmony.

To change data-marker colors,

- Double-click on any data marker in the desired data series to select all the data markers in this series and open the *Format Data Series* dialog box.

- Display the patterns options.

- Select the desired color from the color palette.

- Click on OK.

Let's change the color of the expenses data markers:

**1.** Double-click on any one of the **expenses data markers**. (To identify these data markers, observe the legend.) Excel selects all four expenses data markers and opens the *Format Data Series* dialog box.

**2.** In the color palette, select (click on) the **green** at the intersection of the second column and second row.

**3.** Click on **OK** to apply this color to the four expenses data markers.

**4.** Press **Esc** to deselect the data markers, and observe the results.

## PRACTICE YOUR SKILLS

**1.** Change the color of the gross-revenues data markers to complement your new expenses color.

## ADDING AND REMOVING CHART GRIDLINES

Chart gridlines are lines that extend horizontally and/or vertically across the chart. Gridlines come in two flavors: major and minor. *Major gridlines* appear at the axis tick-mark values ($10,000, $20,000, and so on in your active chart); *minor gridlines* appear between the tick-mark values (there are no minor gridlines in your active chart). Gridlines can make it easier for a viewer to interpret the chart data; however, they also can make the chart busy and detract from its overall visual clarity.

To add or remove chart gridlines,

- Choose *Insert, Gridlines* (or choose *Insert Gridlines* from the shortcut menu) to open the Gridlines dialog box.

- Check/uncheck the major and minor gridlines you want to add/remove.

- Click on OK.

Or, to add or remove major y-axis (horizontal) gridlines,

- Click on the *Horizontal Gridlines tool* (in the Chart toolbar).

Let's try out a few major/minor gridline formats in our active chart:

1. Choose **Insert, Gridlines** to open the Gridlines dialog box. Note that the only checked option is for value-axis major gridlines.

2. Observe the x-axis tick-marks between the data column pairs.

3. Under Category (X) Axis, check **Major Gridlines** and click on **OK** to display x-axis (category-axis) major gridlines. Observe the results; gridlines extend vertically from the x-axis tick-marks. This may look nice, but it does no real good, because there is no data to be made clearer by these vertical gridlines.

4. Choose **Insert Gridlines** from the shortcut menu. (To open the shortcut menu containing this command, click the **right mouse button** on a blank area of the chart.)

5. Under Category (X) Axis, uncheck **Major Gridlines** to remove the x-axis major gridlines.

6. Under Value (Y) Axis, check **Minor Gridlines** to display value-axis minor gridlines.

7. Click on **OK** to apply your gridline changes. Observe the results, as shown in Figure 9.6. Excel displays four minor

gridlines between each major (tick-mark) gridline. This makes it easier to read the data values, as represented by the column heights; however, it makes the chart busy and in-harmonious.

**Figure 9.6**     **Displaying major and minor value-axis gridlines**

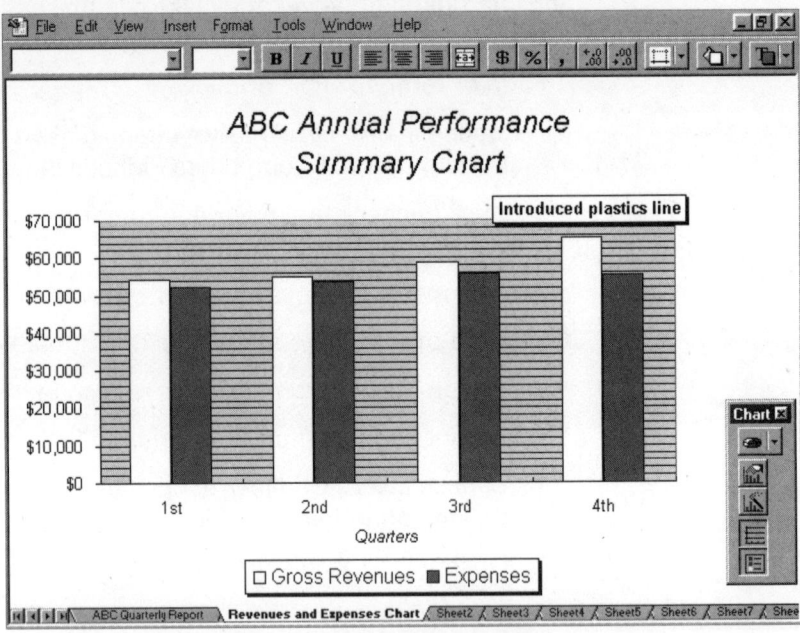

8. Remove all gridlines from the chart. (For help doing this, see steps 4 through 7.) This display is nice and open; however, the data values are now difficult to read.

9. Click on the **Horizontal Gridlines tool** to add value-axis major gridlines to the chart.

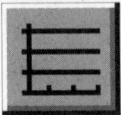

There you are, right back where you started from! Looks like Excel's default gridline arrangement was the best choice for this chart.

## CHANGING THE PLOT-AREA BACKGROUND COLOR

As you'll recall from Chapter 8, the *plot area* of a chart is the area in which your worksheet data is plotted; that is, the area in which the data markers (columns, bars, and so on) are displayed. When you create a chart, Excel gives the plot area a default background color. To change this color,

- Double-click on a blank part of the chart's plot area to select the plot area and open the *Format Plot Area* dialog box.
- Select the desired background color from the color palette.
- Click on OK.

Let's change our plot-area background color:

1. Double-click on a blank part of the plot area (not on a gridline!) to select it and open the **Format Plot Area** dialog box.

2. In the color palette, click on **white** (the second color in the top row), and then click on **OK** to apply a white background color to the plot area.

3. Press **Esc** to deselect the plot area. Note the white background.

4. Change the plot-area background color to **light gray** (the color at the intersection of the second row and seventh column of the color palette).

5. Press **Esc** to deselect. See how much more dramatic this color arrangement looks?

## RESCALING THE VALUE AXIS

As you know, a chart's numeric data values are plotted along its value axis. (Normally the value axis is the y-axis; you can, however, change it to the x-axis.) Excel allows you to *rescale* a chart's value axis; that is, to change the minimum value, the maximum value, and the value between tick-marks. Rescaling is especially useful for emphasizing trends, as you'll see in the next activity.

To rescale the value axis,

- Double-click on the value axis to open the Format Axis dialog box.

- Display the scale options.

- Change the desired options: *Minimum* is the smallest value on the axis; *Maximum* is the largest value on the axis; *Major Unit* is the value between axis tick-marks.

- Click on OK.

Let's emphasize revenue trends by rescaling the value axis:

1. Observe the value axis (y-axis) in your chart; it shows dollar values ($0 to $70,000). Double-click on the **value axis** to open the Format Axis dialog box.

2. Display the scale options.

3. Change the Minimum value from 0 to **50000**.

4. Click on **OK** to apply your scale change to the chart, as shown in Figure 9.7. Note that the value-axis scale now shows $50,000 to $66,000 instead of $0 to $70,000. This compressed scale strongly emphasizes the upward trend in revenues.

 ## CHANGING THE CHART FORMAT OF A CUSTOMIZED CHART

In Chapter 8, you learned how to use the AutoFormat command to change the chart format. (As you'll recall, the *chart format* is a variation of the current chart type; a side-by-side column chart is a variation of the column type, and so on.) A problem arises, however, when you want to change the chart format of a customized chart: Using AutoFormat to do this *cancels* many of the customizations you made to the chart.

Never fear! Here's a simple solution: To change the chart format of a customized chart and *retain* all your customization, use the Format, Chart Type command as follows:

- Choose *Format, Chart Type* (or choose *Chart Type* from the shortcut menu) to open the Chart Type dialog box.

- Under Apply To, verify that *Entire Chart* is selected.

- To change the chart type, select *2-D* or *3-D* and click on the desired type.

**Figure 9.7**    **Rescaling the value axis**

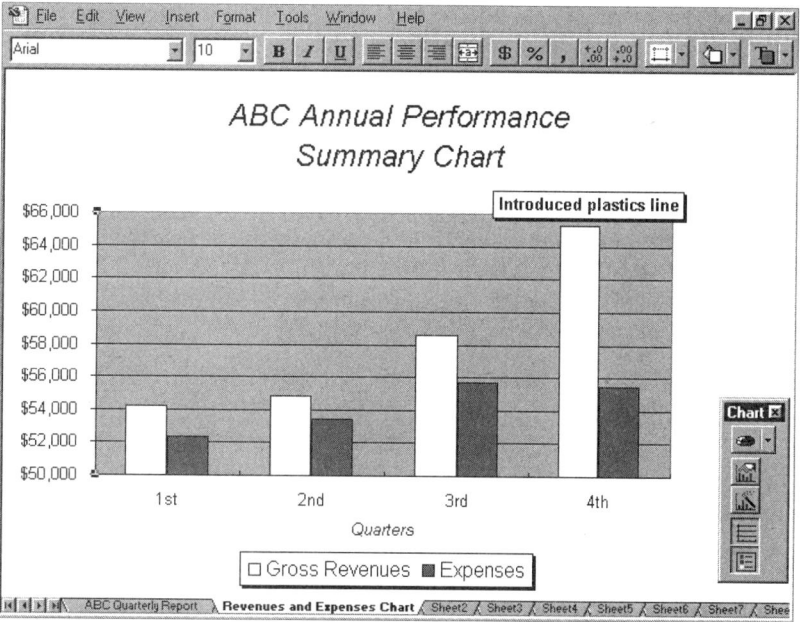

- Click on the *Options button* to open the Format Column Group dialog box.

- Display the subtype options.

- Under Subtype, click on the desired chart format.

- Click on OK.

**As a rule of thumb:** Use AutoFormat to change the chart format when working with a new, unmodified chart; use Format, Chart Type to change the chart format when working with a custom-ized chart.

Let's violate this rule of thumb and suffer the dire consequences:

1. Choose **Format, AutoFormat** to open the AutoFormat dialog box. Double-click on format **3** to create a stacked column chart.

2. Observe the results. Looks fine, yes? However...your custom-ized colors are gone, as are your major value-axis gridlines. (This is a relatively slight loss; had you made more elaborate customizations, the loss would have been far more traumatic.) See what happens when you use AutoFormat to change the chart format of a customized chart!

3. Press **Ctrl+Z**—the keyboard shortcut for the Undo command—to undo your chart-format change and restore your customized side-by-side column chart.

Now let's repeat the above procedure, this time following our hallowed rule of thumb:

1. Choose **Format, Chart Type** to open the Chart Type dialog box.

2. Under Apply To, verify that **Entire Chart** is selected.

3. Click on **Options** to open the Format Column Group dialog box.

4. Click on the **Subtype tab**.

5. Under Subtype, double-click on the second chart subtype from the left to create a stacked column chart. (**Note:** The terms *chart subtype* and *chart format* are related, but not synonymous. Chart subtypes are the building blocks on which formats are based. Formats contain more formatting information—color, patterns, gridlines, and so on—than subtypes. For example, there are ten column-chart formats, but only three column-chart subtypes.)

6. Observe the results, as shown in Figure 9.8. Your customized colors and gridlines remain intact.

## PRACTICE YOUR SKILLS

1. Use this procedure to change the chart back to its original side-by-side column format. (**Hint:** Select the leftmost chart format under Subtype.)

2. Update the workbook file.

## OVERLAPPING COLUMNS AND BARS

Until now, the columns displayed in your column charts have all been nonoverlapping: one entire column next to another entire column (as shown in Figures 9.1 through 9.7). At times, however, you may want to overlap your columns (or bars, in a bar chart) for visual emphasis or clarity. For example, if you created a column chart depicting the expenses for every week in your fiscal year, the chart would display 52 columns, a very large number to fit on a standard-sized page. Overlapping these columns would allow

**Figure 9.8**    **Changing the chart format of a customized chart**

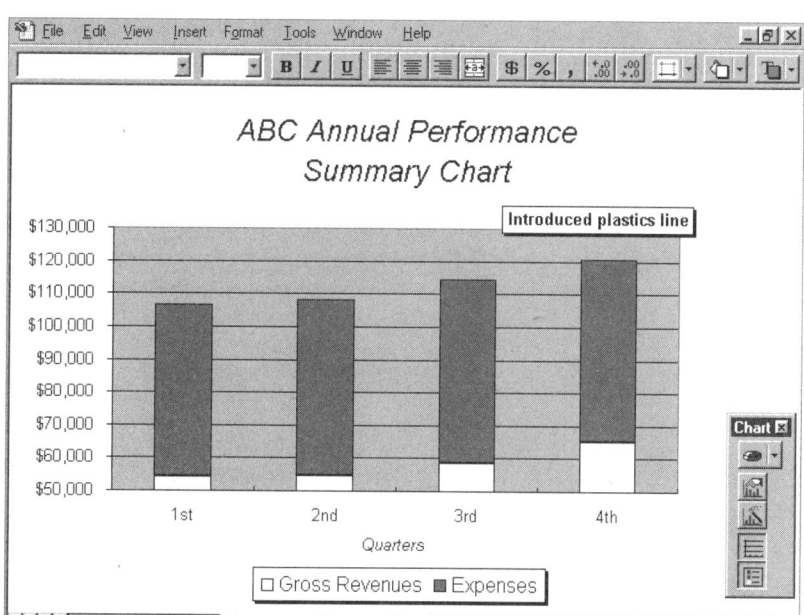

each column to be significantly wider, and the resultant chart would be much clearer visually than a chart that displayed 52 non-overlapping columns.

To overlap columns or bars,

- Choose *Format, Chart Type* (or choose *Chart Type* from the shortcut menu) to open the Chart Type dialog box.

- Click on the *Options button* to open the Format Column Group or Format Bar Group dialog box.

- Select the *Options tab.*

- In the Overlap box, enter the desired overlap percentage.

- Click on OK.

Let's overlap the columns in our chart:

1. Choose **Chart Type** from the shortcut menu to open the Chart Type dialog box.

2. Click on **Options** to open the Format Column Group dialog box.

3. Click on the **Options tab**.

4. Observe the Overlap box; the current value is 0, because the columns in our chart are nonoverlapping. Change the overlap percentage to **50**. Observe the Preview box to see what your specified overlap will look like.

5. Click on **OK** to return to the chart. Your screen should match that shown in Figure 9.9. Note that Excel retained your customized colors and gridlines, because you used Format, Chart Type (rather than AutoFormat).

**Figure 9.9**     **Overlapping columns by 50 percent**

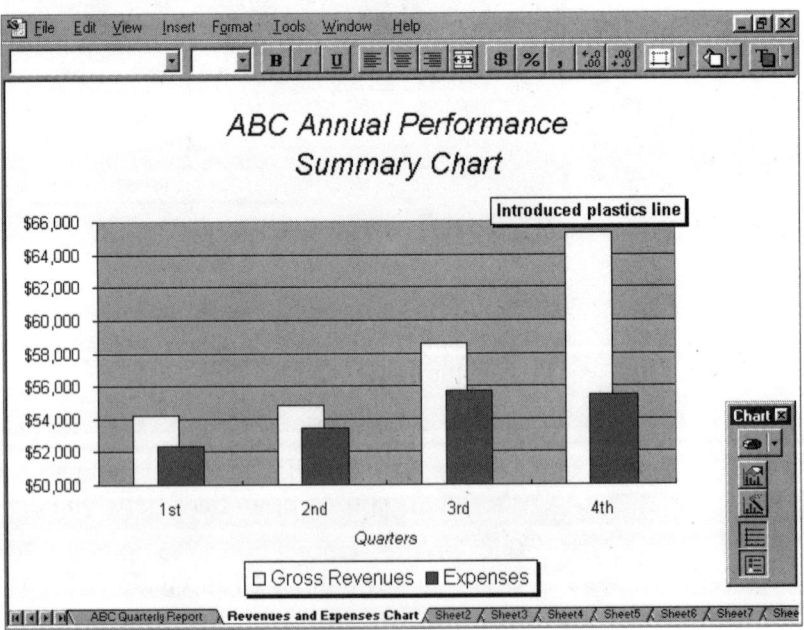

## MOVING AND RESIZING CHART OBJECTS

You can move and resize all the objects in a chart as follows:

- Select the desired object.

- To move the object, drag it (by an edge, if it's a text object) to the desired new location.

- To resize the chart proportionally, drag the desired corner selection square while holding down Shift. To resize nonproportionally, drag the desired selection square.

Throughout most of this chapter, you've been working in Sized With Window view. As you'll recall, the problem with this view is that it distorts the actual proportions of the chart sheet. Let's see just how distorted things have gotten:

1. Choose **View, Sized With Window** to change back to normal view. Things don't look all that bad; there are just a few items we'll have to fine-tune.

2. First, let's move the Quarters x-axis title a bit higher. Select the **Quarters** title and move it up—taking care not to slide it left or right—until it's about halfway between the x-axis and the legend box.

3. Now let's resize the plot area to fill some of the blank space to its right. Click on the **plot area** (not on a gridline) to select it. Point to the selection square in the middle of the right edge of the plot-area outline box. The pointer changes to a double-headed arrow. Drag this selection square about halfway to the right edge of the chart area.

4. Drag the **legend** to the right to center it under the Quarters title.

5. Drag the **Introduced plastics line** text box to center it over the fourth-quarter gross revenues column. There—that should do it.

## PRACTICE YOUR SKILLS

Let's end our adventures in chart formatting by print previewing and then printing our customized chart:

1. Preview the chart. (**Hint:** You'll have to choose **File, Print Preview**, since the Preview tool is not displayed in full-screen view.)

2. If you have a printer, print the chart. Compare your printout with that shown in Figure 9.10.

3. Update the workbook file.

**Figure 9.10    Printout of the completed chart**

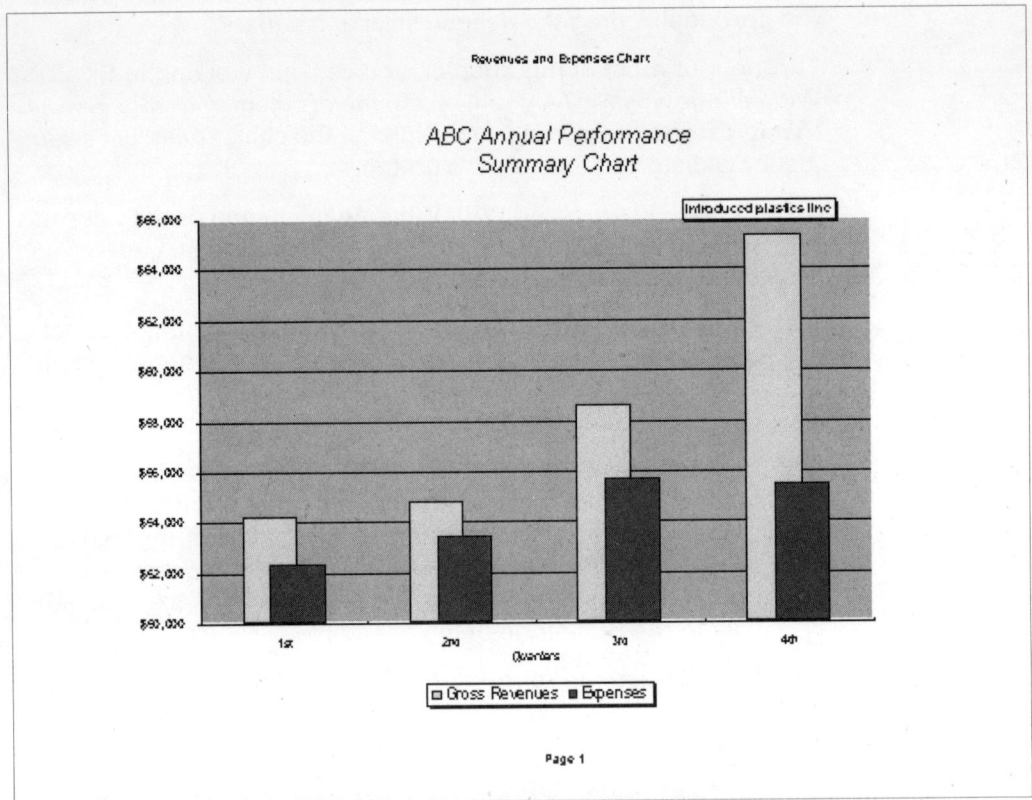

## EMBEDDING A CHART IN A WORKSHEET

Thus far, every chart you've worked with has been contained in its own chart sheet. At times, however, you may want to display a chart and its associated worksheet together in the same worksheet. You can do this by *embedding* the chart in the worksheet, as follows:

- Activate the desired worksheet, and select the range of data you want to chart.

- Choose *Insert, Chart, On This Sheet*.

- Drag inside the worksheet to create a chart box in which your chart will be drawn. To create a square chart box, hold down the Shift key as you drag.

- When you release the mouse button (after dragging), the Chart Wizard dialog box appears. Click on *Finish* to draw a standard column chart in your chart box.

Let's embed a chart in the ABC Quarterly Report worksheet:

1. Activate the **ABC Quarterly Report** worksheet.

2. If you're not in full-screen view, change to it now.

3. Select the noncontiguous ranges **C3:C7** and **F3:F7**.

4. Choose **Insert, Chart, On This Sheet**.

5. Note the flashing marquees around the selected data, indicating that Excel is waiting for you to create a chart box in which to draw the chart. Note also that the mouse pointer has changed to a crosshair and miniature column chart.

6. Drag from the middle of cell B9 to the middle of cell G19 to define your chart box. When you release the mouse button, the Chart Wizard dialog box appears.

7. Click on **Finish** (in the Chart Wizard dialog box) to draw a standard column chart depicting your selected worksheet data, as shown in Figure 9.11.

## RESIZING AN EMBEDDED CHART

To resize an embedded chart,

- Select the chart.

- To resize the chart proportionally, drag the desired corner selection square while holding down Shift.

- To resize nonproportionally, drag the desired selection square.

Our embedded chart looks a bit squashed, yes? Let's resize it:

1. Select the **embedded chart**, if necessary.

2. Drag the **bottom-center selection handle** down to the middle of row 23. Excel redraws your chart to fill the enlarged chart box. You didn't enlarge the chart proportionally (by holding Shift while dragging a corner selection handle), because this would have retained the original chart's squashed proportions.

**Figure 9.11**     **Embedding a chart in a worksheet**

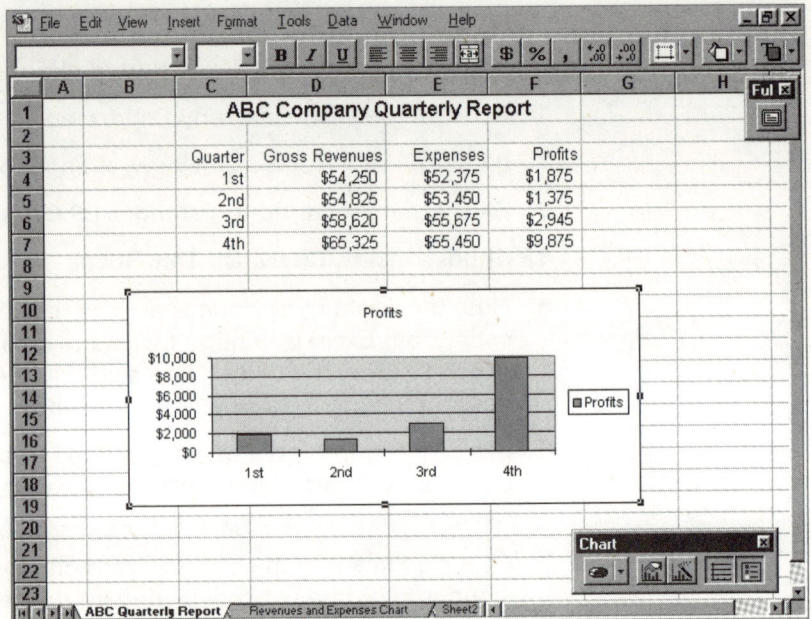

### EDITING AN EMBEDDED CHART

To edit an embedded chart,

- Double-click on the embedded chart to *open* it.
- Edit the chart as desired.
- Select any worksheet cell to *close* the chart.

Let's edit our embedded chart:

1. Double-click on the **embedded chart**. A slashed outline appears around the chart, indicating that it is open.

2. Use the Chart toolbar to change the chart type to **3-D Pie**.

3. Change the chart title to **Quarterly Profits**.

4. Change the title text to **14-point bold**.

Now let's verify the worksheet/chart link by changing worksheet data and observing this change in the chart:

1. Click on any cell in the worksheet to close the embedded chart. Closing an embedded chart does not remove it from the screen; it merely prevents you from editing the chart.

2. Press **Esc** to deselect the chart.

3. Press **Ctrl+Home** to reorient your screen.

4. Change the value in cell E7 to **60000**. Observe the change in the chart; the fourth-quarter profit slice has shrunk, and the remaining slices have grown proportionately.

Let's print preview our worksheet with embedded chart, modify some print options, and then print it:

1. Set the print area to **B1:G23**—come on, you remember how!

2. Preview the worksheet.

3. Click on **Setup** to open the Page Setup dialog box, and change the following settings:

   • Center the print area horizontally on the page.

   • Change the print orientation to **Portrait**.

   • Remove the header and footer.

   • Suppress the printing of gridlines.

4. Click on **OK** to apply these settings. Observe the changes in your preview.

5. If you have a printer, print your worksheet and embedded chart. Compare your printout to Figure 9.12.

6. Close the print preview window, if necessary.

7. Update the workbook file, then close it.

## SUMMARY

In this chapter, you learned how to customize the format, content, and layout of a chart. You now know how to customize a chart legend, add unattached text to a chart, edit chart text, format your charts, and embed a chart in a worksheet.

**Figure 9.12**    **Printout of the worksheet and embedded chart**

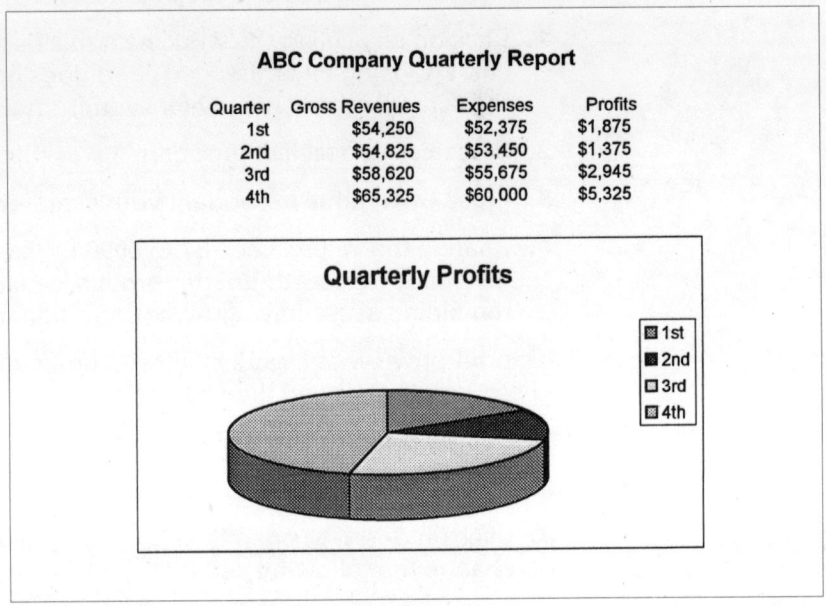

**ABC Company Quarterly Report**

| Quarter | Gross Revenues | Expenses | Profits |
|---------|----------------|----------|---------|
| 1st | $54,250 | $52,375 | $1,875 |
| 2nd | $54,825 | $53,450 | $1,375 |
| 3rd | $58,620 | $55,675 | $2,945 |
| 4th | $65,325 | $60,000 | $5,325 |

Here's a quick reference guide to the Excel features introduced in this chapter:

| Desired Result | How to Do It |
|----------------|--------------|
| Move legend | Select **legend**; choose **Format, Selected Legend** (or press **Ctrl+1**, or choose **Format Legend** from shortcut menu); display placement options; click on desired option; click on **OK**; or, drag legend |
| Add shadow border to legend | Select **legend**; choose **Format, Selected Legend** (or press **Ctrl+1**, or choose **Format Legend** from shortcut menu); display patterns options; check **Shadow**, click on **OK** |
| Apply/remove Sized With Window view | Choose **View, Sized With Window** |

| Desired Result | How to Do It |
|---|---|
| Apply/remove full-screen view | Choose **View, Full Screen** or click on **Full Screen tool** |
| Add unattached text to chart | Press **Esc** to deselect chart objects; type text; press **Enter**; drag text box to desired location |
| Edit chart text | Select text object; click on selected object to place insertion point; edit text; press **Esc** |
| Insert line break | Place insertion point before word where new line is to begin; press **Enter**; press **Esc** |
| Remove line break | Place insertion point at beginning of line to be joined to previous line; press **Backspace**; press **Esc** |
| Format text using Formatting toolbar | To format all text in text object, select object; to format selected text in object, select desired text; change desired Formatting toolbar settings; if you formatted selected text, press **Esc** |
| Format text using Format Object dialog box | To format all text in text object, select object or double-click on object and skip next two steps; to format selected text in object, select desired text; choose **Format, Selected *Object*** (or press **Ctrl+1**, or choose **Format *Object*** from shortcut menu); display font options; change desired options; click on **OK** |
| Change data-marker color | Double-click on desired data marker; display patterns options; select desired color; click on **OK** |
| Add/remove gridlines | Choose **Insert, Gridlines** (or choose **Insert Gridlines** from shortcut menu); check/uncheck major and minor gridlines you want to add/remove; click on **OK** |

| Desired Result | How to Do It |
|---|---|
| Change plot-area background color | Double-click on blank part of plot area; select desired color; click on **OK** |
| Rescale value axis | Double-click on value axis; display scale options; change desired options; click on **OK** |
| Change customized chart format | Choose **Format, Chart Type** (or choose **Chart Type** from shortcut menu); verify that Entire Chart is selected; change chart type, if desired; click on **Options**; display subtype options; click on desired format (subtype); click on **OK** |
| Overlap columns or bars | Choose **Format, Chart Type** (or choose **Chart Type** from shortcut menu); click on **Options**; select **options** tab; enter desired overlap percentage in Overlap box; click on **OK** |
| Move/resize chart object | Select desired object; to move object, drag it; to resize object proportionally, drag corner selection square while holding **Shift**; to resize nonproportionally, drag any selection square |
| Embed chart in worksheet | Select range of worksheet data to chart; choose **Insert, Chart, On This Sheet**; drag to create chart box; click on **Finish** in Chart Wizard dialog box |
| Resize embedded chart | Select chart; to resize proportionally, drag corner selection square while holding **Shift**; to resize nonproportionally, drag any selection square |
| Edit embedded chart | Double-click on chart to open it; edit as desired; select any worksheet cell to close chart |

In the next chapter, we'll introduce you to a selection of advanced charting techniques. You'll learn how to use the Chart Wizard to create and modify charts, how to add data to a chart, how to plot rows or columns as the data series, how to create a combination chart, how to display two value axes on a combination chart, how to label data markers, and how to draw on a chart.

## IF YOU'RE STOPPING HERE

If you want to break off here, please exit Excel. If you want to proceed directly to the next chapter, please do so now.

# CHAPTER 10:
# ADVANCED CHARTING TECHNIQUES

Using the Chart
Wizard to Create
and Modify Charts

Creating a
Combination Chart

Labeling Data
Markers

Drawing on a Chart

In this chapter, the last in our three-chapter series on charting, we'll introduce you to a selection of advanced charting techniques. Mastery of these techniques will go a long way in helping you to create professional-looking, presentation-quality charts quickly and easily.

When you're done working through this chapter, you will know

- How to use the Chart Wizard to create and modify charts
- How to add data to a chart
- How to plot rows or columns as the data series
- How to create a combination chart
- How to display two value axes on a combination chart
- How to label data markers
- How to draw on a chart

## USING THE CHART WIZARD TO CREATE AND MODIFY CHARTS

The Chart Wizard is a wonderful tool that leads you, step by step, through the process of creating an embedded chart. Along the way, it offers you sample views of your chart-in-progress and provides continual online Help at the click of a button.

To create an embedded chart by using the Chart Wizard,

- Select the worksheet cells containing the data you want to chart.
- Click on the *Chart Wizard tool* (in the Standard or Chart toolbar), or choose *Insert, Chart, On This Sheet* to run the Chart Wizard.
- Drag in the worksheet to create an embedded chart box. (To create a square box, hold down the Shift key as you drag.) Or, simply click in the worksheet to create a default chart box (about five standard columns wide by eleven standard rows high).
- After you drag or click, the Chart Wizard - Step 1 of 5 dialog box appears. The Chart Wizard leads you through a five-step chart-creation process; each step has its own dialog box. Use the following buttons to navigate through these dialog boxes:

| | |
|---|---|
| Cancel | Exits the Chart Wizard without creating a chart |
| < Back | Moves to the previous Chart Wizard step |
| Next > | Moves to the next Chart Wizard step |

Finish     Exits the Chart Wizard and creates a chart using the options you've selected

If you are not running Excel, please start it now. If there is a workbook on your screen (other than the startup workbook, Book1), please close it. Let's begin by using the Chart Wizard to create an embedded chart in a worksheet:

1. Open **Products** from your Excel Work folder. This worksheet keeps track of monthly sales totals by product group.

2. Change to full-screen view (by choosing **View, Full Screen**) if you are not in it already. If the Formatting toolbar is hidden, unhide it.

3. Select the range **B5:G7**. These cells contain the data you'll chart. Your next step is to run the Chart Wizard. Normally, you'd click on the Chart Wizard tool to do this. Unfortunately, this tool is in the Standard and Chart toolbars, both of which currently are hidden. You'll just have to use the menu command instead.

4. Choose **Insert, Chart, On This Sheet** to run the Chart Wizard. Note the flashing marquee around the selected data and the crosshair-and-miniature-column-chart mouse pointer, indicating that Excel is waiting for you to create an embedded chart box.

5. Drag from the middle of cell B12 to the middle of cell I23 to create your embedded chart box.

6. Observe the screen. Note that the embedded chart box does not appear. Instead, the Chart Wizard displays the first of its five dialog boxes, as shown in Figure 10.1. As mentioned above, these boxes walk you through a five-step process of creating an embedded chart. The Step 1 dialog box prompts you to select the range containing the data you want to chart. Verify that the range you selected in step 3 appears in the Range text box (B5:G7, or in "Excelese," =$B$5:$G$7).

7. Click on **Next >** to accept this range and move to the Step 2 dialog box. This box prompts you to select a chart type. Note that all 15 chart types are available—the same types as in the AutoFormat dialog box—and that the default choice is a column chart.

**Figure 10.1**     **The Step 1 Chart Wizard dialog box**

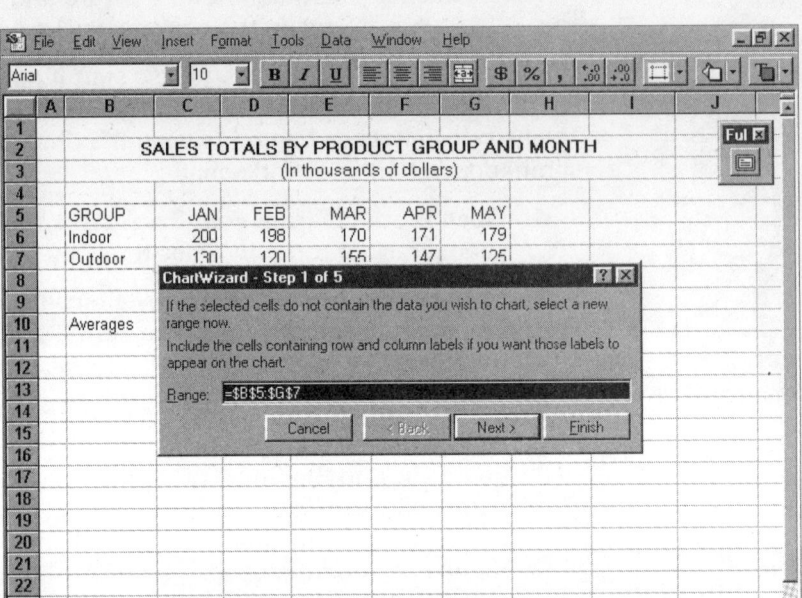

8. Observe the four buttons at the bottom of the dialog box; we described their functions earlier in this section. These are the buttons you use to navigate through the Chart Wizard dialog boxes.

9. Click on **Next >** to accept the default chart type (column) and move to the Step 3 dialog box. This box prompts you to pick a chart format for your selected chart type. Note again that all ten column-chart formats are available, the same formats as in the AutoFormat dialog box.

10. Select option **9** and click on **Next >** to select a stacked-column chart and move to the Step 4 dialog box. This box shows a sample chart depicting your selected worksheet data, chart type, and chart format. The Data Series In option allows you to plot the rows or the columns of your selected worksheet data as the data series. We'll take a closer look at this very important option in the upcoming section, "Plotting Rows or Columns as the Data Series."

**11.** Observe the sample chart. Although our stacked-column format depicts the selected data accurately (indoor vs. outdoor product sales), it does not effectively communicate how the indoor sales *compare* to the outdoor sales. A side-by-side column format is a better choice for this.

**12.** Click on **< Back** to return to the Step 3 dialog box. Select format option **4** and click on **Next >** to select a side-by-side, overlapped-column format and move to the Step 4 dialog box. Observe the sample chart; it has changed to reflect your new chart format. Note that this format compares indoor and outdoor sales much more effectively.

**13.** Click on **Next >** to accept the sample chart and move to the Step 5 dialog box. This final dialog box allows you to add or remove a legend, chart title, and axis titles.

**14.** In the Chart Title text box, type **ABC Sales Report**. When you're finished typing, wait for a moment to let the title appear in the sample chart.

**15.** Click on **Finish** to draw the chart in your embedded chart box (B12:I23) using your specified charting options. Your screen should match that shown in Figure 10.2. You might prefer to move the chart toolbar out of the way like the author has done.

**16.** Save the workbook file to your Excel Work folder as **myproducts**.

## ADDING DATA TO A CHART

After you've created a chart—either an embedded one or a chart in its own chart sheet—you can use the Chart Wizard to add data to it. You can add data in two ways: by adding a new data series or by adding new data to the existing data series. As you'll recall from Chapter 8, a data series is a set of related data values that is stored in a single worksheet row or column. The active worksheet, for example, contains the two data series, Indoor (cells B6:G6) and Outdoor (cells B7:G7).

To add data to a chart,

• Add the data to the worksheet, if necessary.

**Figure 10.2**    **Using the Chart Wizard to create an embedded chart**

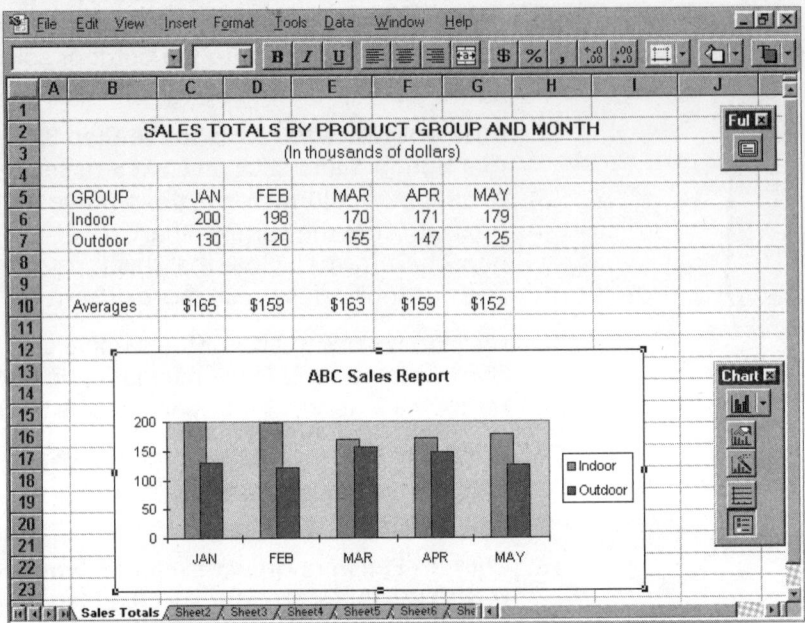

- Select the embedded chart—or activate the chart sheet containing the chart—to which you want to add the data.

- Click on the *Chart Wizard tool*; the Chart Wizard - Step 1 of 2 dialog box appears.

- Specify the range—by dragging or typing—containing *all* the worksheet data you want to chart, *including* the data you want to add.

- Click on the *Next >* button to display the Step 2 dialog box.

- Change the desired Step 2 options.

- Click on OK to apply your changes to the chart.

You also can use this procedure to remove data from a chart. When you specify the range of data to chart (in the Step 1 dialog box), simply select a range that excludes the cells you don't want to chart.

Let's use the Chart Wizard to add a new data series to our chart:

1. In row 8 of the worksheet, enter the following data series for a new product group called All Season:

| | B | C | D | E | F | G |
|---|---|---|---|---|---|---|
| 8 | **All Season** | **166** | **170** | **175** | **177** | **190** |

2. Select (click once on) the **embedded chart**.

3. Click on the **Chart Wizard tool** (the third tool from the left in the Chart toolbar, it shows a magic wand sprinkling pixie dust over a miniature column chart). Observe the selected range in the Step 1 dialog box.

4. In the worksheet, select the range **B5:G8** to include your new data series (All Season) in the embedded chart. You may have to move your Chart Wizard dialog box to do this.

5. Click on **Next >** to display the Step 2 (final) dialog box. Observe the sample chart; all looks well.

6. Click on **OK** to redraw the chart using your newly selected data range.

7. Observe the results, as shown in Figure 10.3. The All Season data series is now included, making for a total of three over-lapping data columns in each column cluster.

Now let's use the Chart Wizard to add new data to the existing data series, Indoor, Outdoor, and All Season:

1. In column H of the worksheet, enter the following new June sales data:

| | H |
|---|---|
| 5 | **JUN** |
| 6 | **175** |
| 7 | **151** |
| 8 | **181** |

2. Select the **embedded chart**.

**Figure 10.3**     **Using the Chart Wizard to add a new data series to the chart**

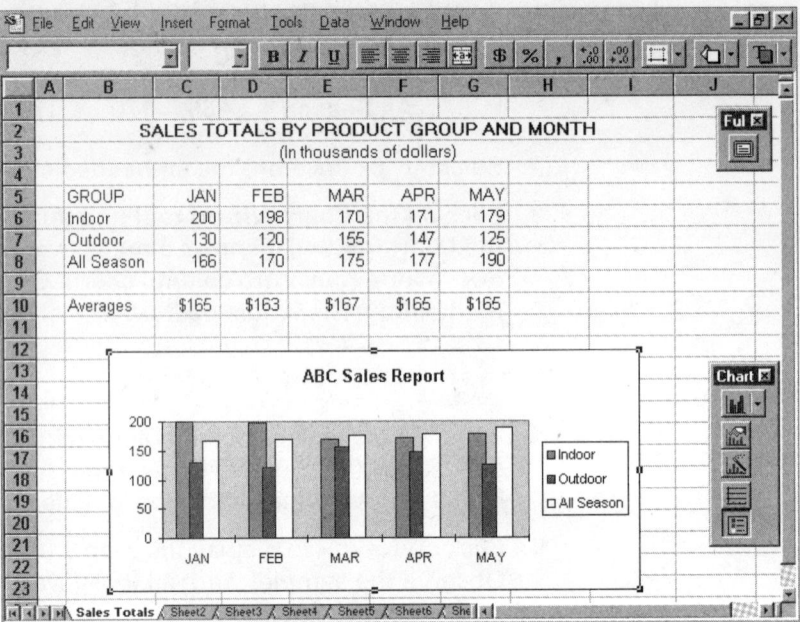

3. Click on the **Chart Wizard tool**. Observe the selected range in the Step 1 dialog box.

4. In the worksheet, select the range **B5:H8** to include the new June category data in the embedded chart.

5. In the Step 1 dialog box, click on **Finish** to skip over the Step 2 dialog box and redraw the chart using your new data range. You can click on Finish in any Chart Wizard dialog box to create a chart using the current charting options (the Chart Wizard's default options and any options you've changed).

6. Observe your new June data on the chart, as shown in Figure 10.4.

**Figure 10.4**   **Using the Chart Wizard to add new data to the existing data series**

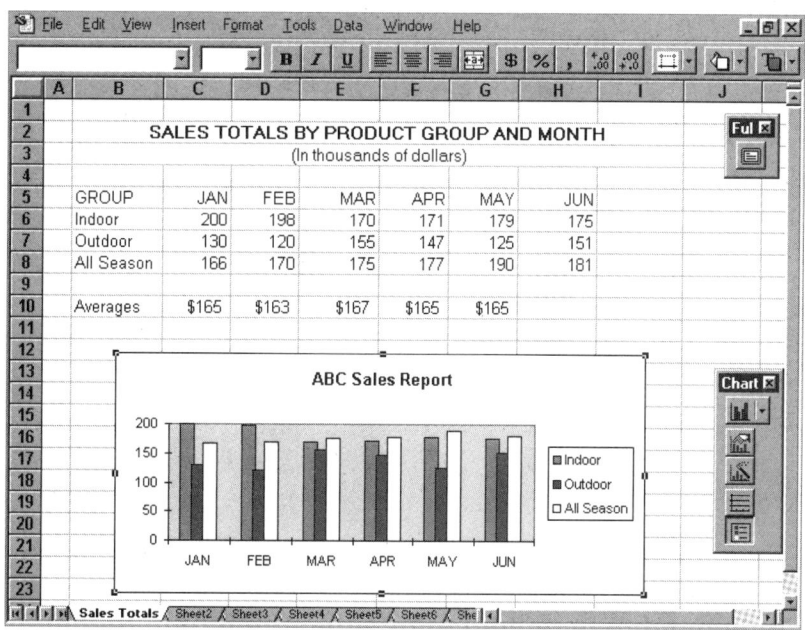

## PRACTICE YOUR SKILLS

As mentioned, you also can use the Chart Wizard to remove data from a chart. Let's try this out:

1. Use the Chart Wizard to remove the May and June data from the chart. (**Hint:** Change the range to B5:F8 in the Chart Wizard Step 1 dialog box.)

2. Use the Chart Wizard to remove the Outdoor data from the current chart. (**Hint:** You'll have to select a noncontiguous range in the Step 1 dialog box.)

3. Your screen should match that shown in Figure 10.5.

4. Choose **File, Save** to update the workbook file.

**Figure 10.5    Using the Chart Wizard to remove data from the chart**

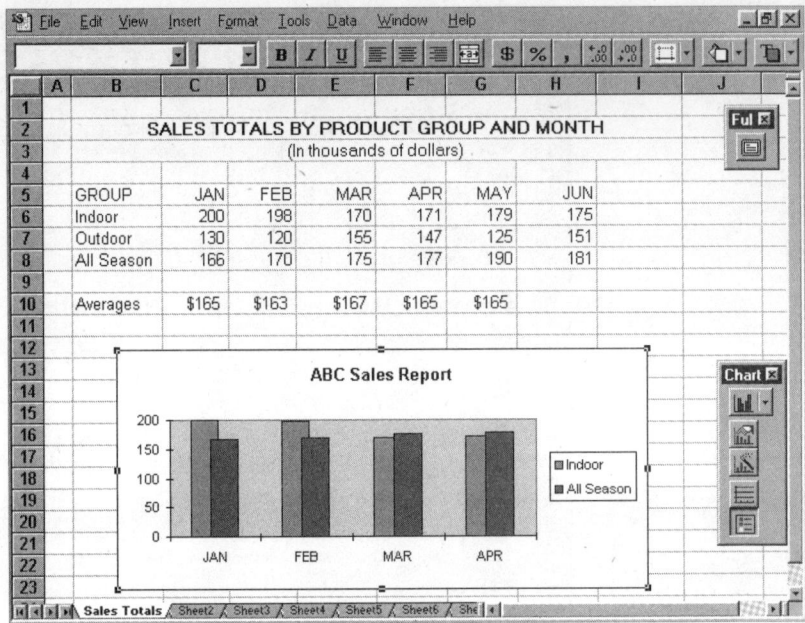

## USING DRAG-AND-DROP TO ADD DATA

Mousers rejoice! You can use drag-and-drop—rather than the Chart Wizard—to add data to an embedded chart, as follows:

- Select the range of worksheet data you want to add to the chart.

- Drag the selection box (by one of its edges) into the embedded chart box.

Let's use this simple, powerful technique to return the Outdoor data for January through April to our chart:

**1.** Select cells B7:F7. These are the cells that contain the Outdoor data for the currently charted months, January through April.

**2.** Point to the bottom edge of the selection box; the pointer changes to an arrow. Press and hold the **left mouse button**, drag the selection box (by its bottom edge) into the embedded chart, and release the mouse button. Voilà! Excel adds your selected data to the chart. Convenient, yes?

3. Look closely at the data series in the chart. Does anything look fishy to you? The Outdoor data series now appears after the All Season data. This doesn't match Figure 10.4. When you use the drag-and-drop method, Excel places the new data series last in the order. This new data series order might not be a problem, but we will show you how to fix it in the next section.

First, let's restore the data for all three product groups to the chart:

1. Select cells G5:G8, the May sales data.

2. Drag the selection box into the embedded chart. Note that the May data is placed as the last category, but that is acceptable to us.

3. Use drag-and-drop to add the June data for all three product groups back to the chart.

 CHANGING THE SERIES ORDER

You can easily change the data series order in any embedded chart or any chart on a chart sheet.

- Double-click on an embedded chart to open it. Or, select the chart in the chart sheet.

- Choose *Format Column Group* from the shortcut menu to display the Format Column Group dialog box.

- Click on the *Series Order* tab.

- In the Series Order list box, select the data series whose position you wish to change.

- Click on the *Move Up* or *Move Down* button. Observe the sample chart to verify the results.

- Click on OK.

Let's return the data series to their original order:

1. Double-click on the embedded chart to open it.

2. From the shortcut menu, choose Format Column Group.

3. Click on the **Series Order** tab.

4. In the Series Order list box, select **Outdoor**.

5. Click on the **Move Up** button. Note the revised chart in the Preview box. The Outdoor data series is now in between the Indoor and All Season data series.

6. Click on **OK** to change the series order of the chart.

7. Press **Esc** to close the embedded chart.

8. Your screen should once again match that shown in Figure 10.4.

 PLOTTING ROWS OR COLUMNS AS THE DATA SERIES

When you select a worksheet range and create a chart, Excel must determine whether the data series you're telling it to chart are stored in the rows or the columns of your selected worksheet range. It does this by assuming that you want to chart more categories (JAN, FEB, and so on in your current chart) than data series (Indoor, Outdoor, and All Season). Therefore, if the selected range has more columns than rows, Excel plots columns as categories and rows as data series; conversely, if the selected range has more rows than columns, it plots rows as categories and columns as data series.

At times, you may need to override Excel's more-categories-than-data-series assumption and "force" it to plot either the rows or the columns of your selected worksheet range as the data series. To do this,

• If you are creating a new chart, select the worksheet range you want to chart. If you are modifying an existing chart, select the embedded chart or activate the chart sheet.

• Click on the *Chart Wizard tool*. Or, if you are creating a new chart and the Chart Wizard tool is hidden, choose *Insert, Chart, As New Sheet* (to create a chart in its own chart sheet) or *On This Sheet* (to create an embedded chart).

• If you are creating a new chart in its own chart sheet, complete steps 1 through 3 of the Chart Wizard procedure, and move to the Step 4 dialog box. If you are creating a new embedded chart, drag to create an embedded chart box, complete Chart Wizard steps 1 through 3, and move to step 4.

If you are modifying an existing chart, move to the Chart Wizard Step 2 dialog box.

- Under Data Series In, select *Rows* or *Columns*. Observe the sample chart to verify the results.

- If you are creating a new chart, complete step 5 of the Chart-Wizard procedure, then click on *Finish*. If you are modifying an existing chart, click on OK.

Let's make Excel plot columns, instead of rows, as the data series in our embedded chart:

1. Select the **embedded chart**, if it is not already selected.

2. Click on the **Chart Wizard tool** to open the Step 1 of 2 dialog box. Verify that the data range is correct by observing the flashing marquee around the worksheet cells B5:H8.

3. Click on **Next >** to move to the Step 2 of 2 dialog box.

4. Under **Data Series In**, click on **Columns** to tell Excel to plot columns (instead of rows) as the chart's data series.

5. Move the dialog box down until the worksheet data in cells B5:H8 are visible. Observe the sample chart in the dialog box. The worksheet columns (JAN, FEB, and so on) are now plotted as the data series (the overlapping data-marker columns in the chart), and the worksheet rows (Indoor, Outdoor, and All Season) are now plotted as categories (along the x-axis).

6. Click on **OK** to draw the modified chart. Your screen should match that shown in Figure 10.6.

7. Update the workbook file, then close it.

## CREATING A COMBINATION CHART

Thus far, you've always assigned the same data-marker type (column, bar, line, and so on) to all the data series in a chart. For example, in the chart you just finished working on, you assigned column data markers to all the chart's data series. At times, however, you may want to assign a different data-marker type to one or more of the chart's data series in order to compare your data more effectively. For example, in an upcoming activity, you'll compare book sales (in copies) to book-sales revenues (in dollars) by

**Figure 10.6**     **Plotting the worksheet columns as the data series**

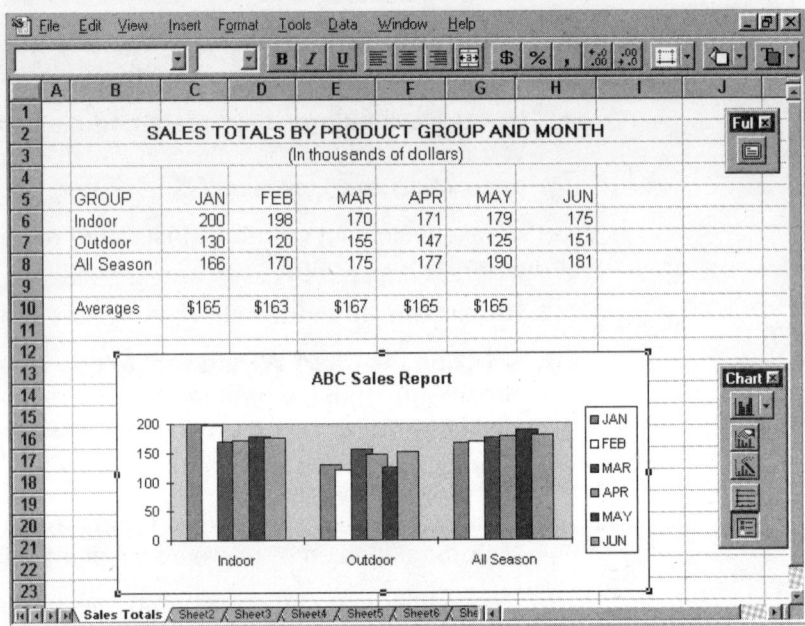

creating a *combination chart* in which you assign a different data-marker type to each of these data series.

To create a combination chart,

- If you are creating a new chart, select the worksheet range you want to chart and press *F11* or *Alt+F1* to create a standard column chart. If you are modifying an existing chart, select the embedded chart or activate the chart sheet.

- Select the data series whose data-marker type you want to change.

- Choose *Format, Chart Type* (or choose *Chart Type* from the shortcut menu) to open the Chart Type dialog box.

- Verify that *Selected Series* is selected under Apply To.

- Click on the data-marker type you want to assign to the selected data series.

- Click on OK.

- Repeat this procedure, if necessary, to change other series' data-marker types.

Let's use this procedure to create a combination chart:

1. Open **Combination Chart** from your Excel Work folder. Note that the active worksheet, Sales Totals, is a clone of the worksheet you just charted.

2. Select the noncontiguous ranges **B5:H8** and **B10:H10**. These cells contain the data that you want to chart.

3. Press **F11** (or **Alt+F1**) to create a nonembedded column chart depicting your selected data.

4. Observe the chart. All four data series are plotted as columns. (Move your Chart toolbar, if necessary, to see the legend.) Note that the first three data series—Indoor, Outdoor, and All Season—are related; they are all product sales totals. The fourth data series, AVERAGES, is different; it is not a product-sales total, but an average of all the products' sales totals. To underscore this difference visually, let's change the AVERAGES data-marker type from column to line.

5. Select the **AVERAGES** data series by clicking on any of the AVERAGES data columns (the rightmost of the four columns in each cluster). Remember, to identify the data series that a data column represents, observe the legend.

6. Click the **right mouse button** on an AVERAGES data column to open the shortcut menu, and choose **Chart Type** to open the Chart Type dialog box.

7. Observe the Apply To options box; note that the Selected Series option is selected. This means that whatever data-marker type you now choose will be applied only to the AVERAGES data series you selected in step 5, not to any of the other data series.

8. Click on the **Line** type to select it.

9. Click on **OK** to apply your new AVERAGES data-marker type to the chart.

10. Press **Esc** to deselect the data series, and observe the results. The AVERAGES line is so light that it's hardly visible, particularly against the default plot-area background. Let's fix this.

**11.** Double-click on the plot area (not on a gridline!) to open the Format Plot Area dialog box. Select **white** in the top row of the color palette, then click on **OK**. That's a little better, but the AVERAGES line should still be darker.

**12.** Double-click on the AVERAGES line to open the Format Data Series dialog box. Display the pattern options. Under Line, in the Color list box, select **black** (the top left color in the drop-down list). Under Marker, in the Foreground list box, select **black**. Click on **OK** to apply your changes.

**13.** Deselect the plot area. There—that looks fine! Your screen should match that shown in Figure 10.7.

**Figure 10.7**   **Creating a combination chart by changing the AVERAGES data-marker type to line**

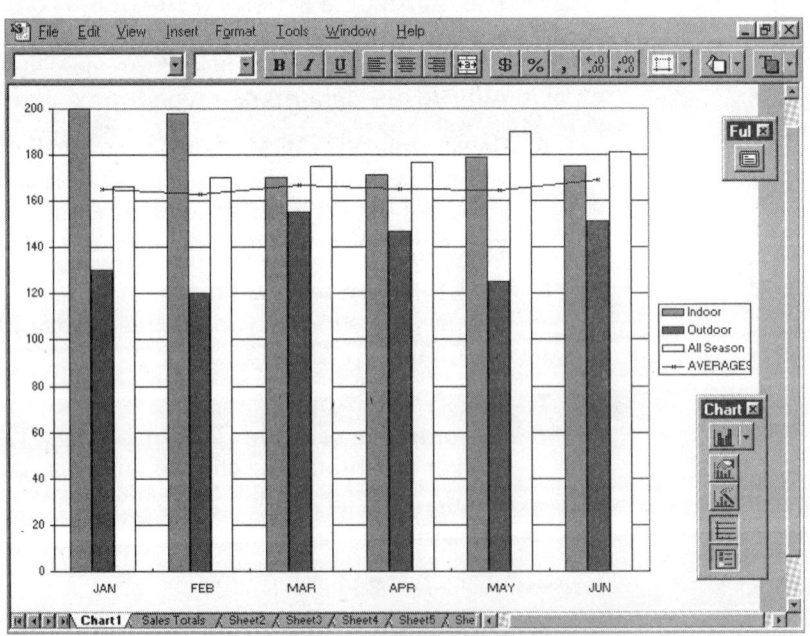

**14.** Save the workbook file as **mycombo**, and then close it.

## DISPLAYING TWO VALUE AXES

Combination charts sometimes depict different types of data. For example, the combination chart you'll create in the next activity plots the number of books sold per month against the monthly revenues generated from the book sales. These data are measured differently. Monthly book sales range from 179 to 894 books; monthly revenues range from $903 to $4,256 per month. For clarity's sake, these two data types call for two separate value axes, one that measures book-sales numbers and one that measures book-sales dollars.

To display two value axes in a combination chart,

- Activate the combination chart.

- Select the data series for which you want to display a second value axis.

- Choose *Format, Chart Type* (or choose *Chart Type* from the shortcut menu) to open the Chart Type dialog box.

- Verify that *Selected Series* is selected under Apply To.

- Click on the *Options button* to open the Format Group dialog box.

- Click on the *Axis tab*.

- Under Plot Chart On, select *Secondary Axis*.

- Click on OK.

Let's use this procedure to create a combination chart with two value axes:

1. Open **ABC Books** from your Excel Work folder. Observe the Book Sales and Revenues worksheet. As mentioned earlier, this worksheet contains data on the number of books sold over a 12-month period and on the revenues generated from these sales.

2. Select the range **B4:D16**.

3. Press **F11** (or **Alt+F1**) to create a standard column chart depicting the selected data. Let's change the Revenues data-marker type from column to line.

4. Click the **right mouse button** on any of the **Revenues** data markers to select the Revenue data series and open the shortcut menu.

5. Verify that the Revenues data series is selected, then choose **Chart Type** from the shortcut menu to open the Chart Type dialog box.

6. Verify that Selected Series is selected under Apply To.

7. Double-click on the **Line** type to assign line data markers to the Revenues data series.

8. Observe that the value-axis scale goes from 0 to 4500. These numbers mean qualitatively different things for each of the chart's data series. For the Books series, they mean the number of books sold; for the Revenues series, they mean the number of revenue dollars. To make this difference clear to the viewer, you need two value axes, one that shows book numbers and one that shows dollar amounts.

9. Click the **right mouse button** on the **Revenues data line** to select the Revenues data series and open the shortcut menu. Choose **Chart Type** from this menu to open the Chart Type dialog box.

10. Verify that Selected Series is selected under Apply To, and that the Line data-marker type is selected.

11. Click on the **Options button** to open the Format Line Group dialog box.

12. Click on the **Axis tab**.

13. Under Plot Chart On, select **Secondary Axis**. Observe the change in the sample box. Excel added a second value axis (showing dollar amounts from $0 to $4,500) to the right side of the chart. It also changed the left-hand value axis to show book-sales quantities, from 0 to 900; this change caused the Books columns to be taller and more visible.

14. Click on **OK** to apply these changes to your chart. To see things better, choose **View, Sized With Window**. Remember this very useful, chart-friendly view?

As it stands now, our double value-axis scales do little good, because it's unclear which scale refers to which data series. Let's clarify things by adding some titles to the chart:

1. Choose **Insert Titles** from the shortcut menu to open the Title dialog box.

2. Check **Chart Title, Value (Y) Axis** and **Second Value (Y) Axis** and click on **OK** to add titles to the chart and both value axes. Note that Excel automatically resized the chart to accommodate your new titles.

3. Observe that the right-hand value axis title is selected (if it is not, select it now). Type the title **Revenues** (without pressing Enter). Note that you can't see what you type. Why not? Because Excel displays your typed characters in the formula bar, which is on the Standard toolbar, which is hidden in full-screen view. For this reason, if you're entering several titles, you may want to change temporarily to normal view. Let's do this.

4. Press **Esc** to cancel your title entry, and then click on the **Full Screen tool** to change to normal view.

5. The right-hand axis title should still be selected; if it is not, select it now. Type **Revenues**. Note that your typed characters appear in the formula bar. Press **Enter** to enter the title.

6. Press the **left arrow key** to select the left-hand value axis title. (Yes: You can also use the arrow keys to select chart objects!) Type the title **Book Sales** and press **Enter** to enter it.

7. Press the **left arrow key** to select the chart title. Type the title **ABC Book Sales and Revenues** and press **Enter** to enter it.

8. Press **Esc** to deselect the chart title. Choose **View, Full Screen** to return to full-screen view. Your double-value-axis combination chart should match that shown in Figure 10.8.

9. Save the workbook file to your Excel Work folder as **myabc,** then close it.

**Figure 10.8**     **Creating a combination chart with two value axes**

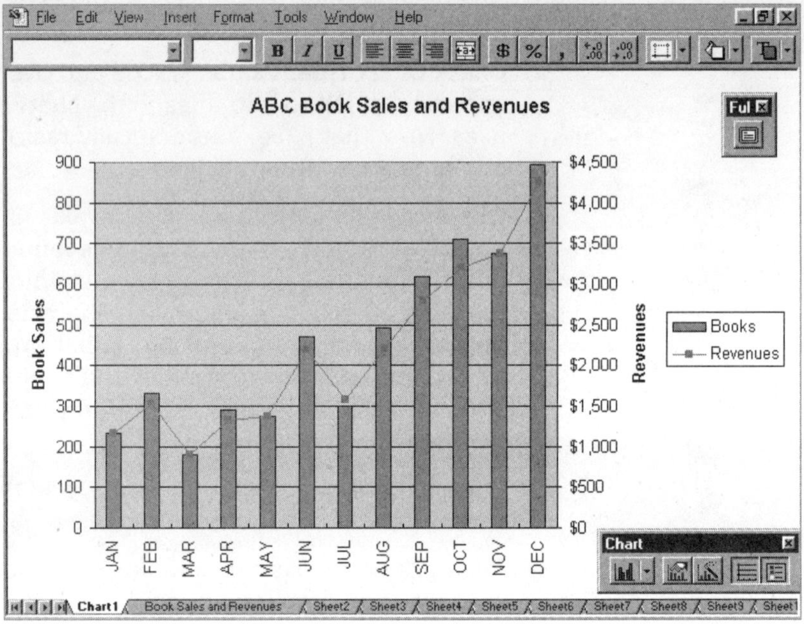

## LABELING DATA MARKERS

Excel allows you to label the data markers in your charts, as follows:

- To label an individual data marker, select it (by clicking on it twice, slowly—*not* by double-clicking!). To label every data marker in a data series, select the entire series (by pressing Esc to deselect, then clicking once on any of the series' data markers).

- Choose *Format, Selected Data Point* (or choose *Format Data Point* from the shortcut menu) to open the Format Data Point dialog box.

- Click on the *Data Labels tab*.

- Select the desired data-label option. *None* displays no label, *Show Value* adds a value label to the selected data marker(s), *Show Percent* adds a percent label, *Show Label* adds a text label, and *Show Label And Percent* adds a text and percent label.

- Click on OK.

Let's open a pie chart and label one of its data markers:

1. Open **Pie Chart** from your Excel Work folder.

2. Activate the **Sales Totals** chart sheet, and choose **View, Sized With Window** to change to this chart-friendly view. This simple pie chart compares the total sales of the Indoor, Outdoor, and All Season product groups; this data is stored in the Monthly Sales Totals worksheet.

3. Activate the **Monthly Sales Totals** worksheet and observe the TOTALS column (I). Data series usually are stored in worksheet rows. Here's a good example of an exception; the totals data series depicted in the Sales Totals chart is stored in column I of the worksheet.

4. Reactivate the **Sales Totals** chart sheet. Click twice slowly (don't double-click!) on the **Indoor** data marker (pie slice) to select it. Double-clicking on the data marker would select the entire data series (all three slices) and open the Format Data *Series*—rather than the Format Data *Point*—dialog box. Selection squares surround the data marker to indicate that it is selected.

5. Click the **right mouse button** on the selected data marker to open the shortcut menu, and choose **Format Data Point** to open the Format Data Point dialog box. A *data point* is a single data marker; that is, a single value in a data series. The Indoor data marker you selected is a data point in the totals data series plotted in the chart; the other data points in this series are the Outdoor and All Season data markers.

6. Click on the **Data Labels tab**.

7. Select the **Show Value** option.

8. Click on **OK** to add a value label ($1,093) to the Indoor data marker.

## PRACTICE YOUR SKILLS

1. $1,093 is the Indoor product group's sales total (in thousands of dollars) for January through June. Verify this by observing cell I5 in the Monthly Sales Totals worksheet.

2. Add a percent label to the Outdoor data marker in the Sales Totals chart.

3. Add a text label to the All Season data marker. (**Hint:** Select the **Show Label** option.)

4. Remove all three data-marker labels. (**Hint:** Select the entire pie, choose **Format Data Series** from the shortcut menu, and carry on from there.)

5. Add a text and percent label to all the data markers. (**Hint:** Same as for the previous step.) Your screen should match that shown in Figure 10.9.

6. Save the workbook file to your Excel Work folder as **mypie**.

**Figure 10.9**    **Labeling data markers**

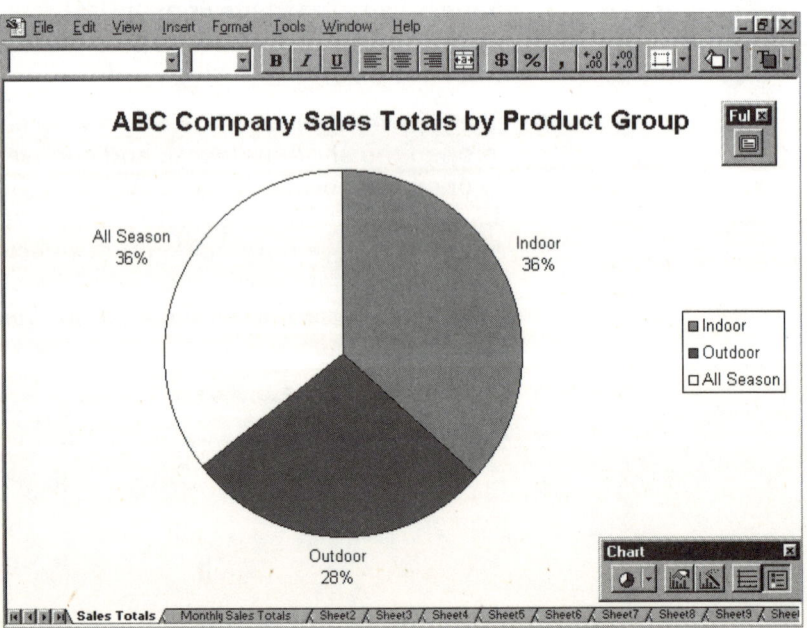

## DRAWING ON A CHART

You can use the Drawing toolbar to add graphic objects to your chart sheets and worksheets, as follows:

- Activate the chart sheet or worksheet.

- Display the Drawing toolbar.

- Use the drawing tools (as described below) to add or modify the desired graphic objects.

- When you're finished using the Drawing toolbar, hide it.

Refer to Table 10.1 and Figure 10.10 for a complete listing of the Drawing toolbar tools.

**Figure 10.10    The Drawing toolbar**

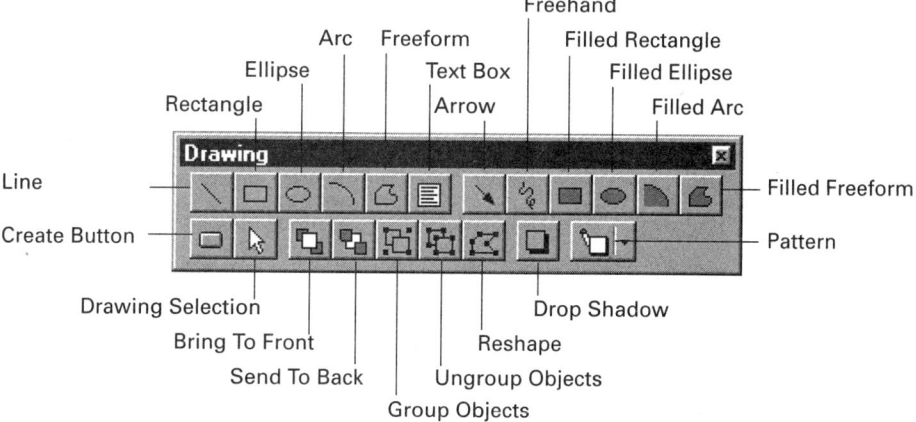

**Table 10.1**     **Drawing Toolbar Tools**

| Tool | You Use This Tool To: |
| --- | --- |
| Line | Draw straight lines |
| Rectangle | Draw rectangles and squares |
| Ellipse | Draw ellipses and circles |
| Arc | Draw arcs or circle segments |
| Freeform | Draw freehand shapes |
| Text Box | Add unattached text |
| Arrow | Draw arrows |
| Freehand | Draw freehand lines |
| Filled Rectangle | Draw filled rectangles or squares |
| Filled Ellipse | Draw filled ellipses or circles |
| Filled Arc | Draw filled arcs or circle segments |
| Filled Freeform | Draw filled freehand shapes |
| Create Button | Draw a button to which you can assign a macro |
| Drawing Selection | Select graphic objects |
| Bring To Front | Place selected objects in front of others |
| Send To Back | Place selected objects behind others |
| Group Objects | Join single objects into a group object |
| Ungroup Objects | Separate a group object into single objects |
| Reshape | Change the shape of polygons |
| Drop Shadow | Add shadowed rectangle around objects |
| Pattern | Fill objects with patterns |

Let's add some graphic objects to our Sales Totals chart. First, we'll change the pie-slice proportions a bit:

1. Activate the Monthly Sales Totals worksheet.

2. Change the outdoor May sales (cell G7) to **750** and the outdoor June sales (cell H7) to **900**. It was a great spring for outdoor sales!

3. Activate the **Sales Totals** chart sheet. Observe that the Outdoor sales slice now takes up a full 51 percent of the pie. Let's add a note to the chart explaining the reason for this.

4. If you feel uncomfortable typing blindly, click on the **Full Screen tool** to change to normal view. Type **Due to heavy May and June sales** and press **Enter** to create an unattached text box containing this text. Change back to full-screen view, if necessary.

5. Remember how the Sized With Window view distorted unattached objects in the chart? Before we draw the objects in this chart, we should verify that the Sized With Window view is not checked.

6. Move the text box to the blank area to the left of the pie.

7. Using Figure 10.11 as a guide, resize the text box (by dragging its selection squares). Make sure the text breaks at the word *and*.

8. Display the Drawing toolbar. (Click the right mouse button on the Formatting toolbar to open the shortcut menu, then click on **Drawing**.) Move the Drawing toolbar below the legend to keep it out of your way.

9. Verify that your unattached text box is still selected, then click on the **Drop Shadow tool** in the Drawing toolbar (refer to Figure 10.10) to add a shadowed rectangle around the box.

10. Move the text box to the position shown in Figure 10.11.

11. Press **Esc** to deselect the text box.

Now let's add an arrow to point from the text box to the Outdoor data marker:

1. Click on the **Arrow tool** in the Drawing toolbar to select it.

2. Place the mouse pointer (crosshair) in the upper-right part of the text box shadow. Press and hold the left mouse

button, and using Figure 10.11 as a guide, drag up and to the right until the crosshair is just short of the Outdoor slice boundary line, then release the mouse button. Excel draws an arrow whose tail begins where you began dragging and whose head appears where you finished.

3. Press **Esc** to deselect the arrow.

Now, to ornament our text box, let's draw a filled rectangle behind it:

1. Click on the **Filled Rectangle tool** to select it.

2. Place the mouse crosshair about 1/4 inch above and to the left of the upper-left edge of the text box. Press and hold the **left mouse button**, drag down and to the right until the text box is nicely centered within your rectangle, then release the mouse button. Oops! Looks like we lost our text box and arrow tail...

3. Click on the **Send To Back tool** to place the rectangle behind the text box and arrow. Whew, that was close! Now let's color the rectangle gray, as shown in Figure 10.11.

4. Open the **Color tool** drop-down option palette (in the Formatting toolbar, not the Drawing toolbar), and click on the **light gray** at the intersection of the seventh column and second row to select it. Oops again...both the rectangle and the text box turned gray! Here's why: The text box actually has no color, which makes it transparent; what you are seeing is the gray of the rectangle *behind* the text box, as if the text box were a window.

5. Select the **text box**, open the **Color tool** option palette, and select the **white** in the top row.

6. Deselect the text box and observe the results. Your screen should match that shown in Figure 10.11.

7. Hide the Drawing toolbar.

8. Update the workbook file, then close it.

The following activity reviews the major topics covered in the charting section of this book (Chapters 8 through 10). Perform these steps to create a combination chart matching that shown in Figure 10.12:

1. Open **Chart Exercise** from your Excel Work folder (Chapter 3).

**Figure 10.11**     **Adding graphic objects to the chart**

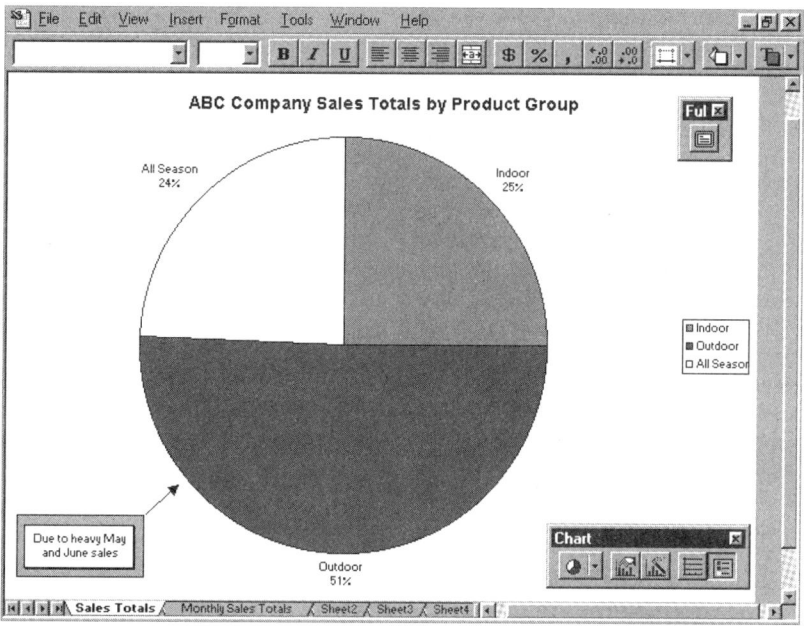

**Figure 10.12**     **Printout of the projected vs. actual combination chart**

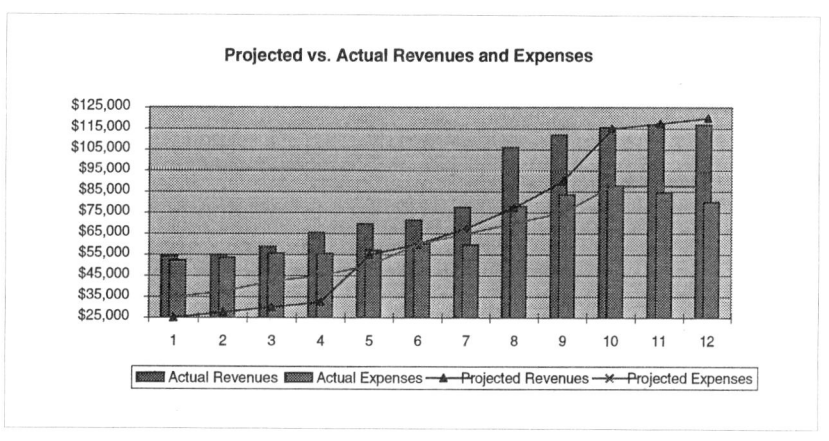

2. Create a standard column chart (in its own chart sheet) depicting the actual and projected revenues and expenses data contained in the Quarterly Report worksheet (Chapter 9). (**Hint/Comments:** After you select the worksheet data you want Excel to chart (a noncontiguous selection consisting of four columns) and press **F11** (or **Alt+F1**), Excel runs the Chart Wizard instead of creating the chart. Why? Because Excel assumes—but is not totally convinced—that the first column of your selected data (actual revenues) contains the first data series you want to chart. In case its assumption is wrong, Excel is giving you the chance to use the Chart Wizard to correct it. In this case, Excel is right; the first column of selected data *is* the first data series of your intended chart. Rather than go through all five Chart Wizard steps without changing anything, simply click on **Finish** in the Step 1 dialog box.)

3. Change to Sized With Window view (Chapter 9).

4. Change the data-marker type of the projected revenues and expenses data series (the two rightmost columns in the four-column clusters) to line (Chapter 10).

5. Overlap the columns by **50%** (Chapter 9).

6. Change the plot-area background color to **light gray** (Chapter 9).

7. Change the colors of all four data markers; choose a nice, harmonious color scheme (Chapter 9).

8. Emphasize the overall growth trend by changing the value-axis scale to show a minimum of **$25,000** instead of $0, and a major unit increment of **10,000** instead of 20,000 (Chapter 9).

9. Add the chart title **Projected vs. Actual Revenues and Expenses** (Chapter 8).

10. Move the legend to the bottom of the chart (Chapter 8). (**Hint:** Use the Format Legend dialog box.)

11. Widen the plot area to fill in the blank space you created by moving the legend (Chapter 9).

12. Center the legend beneath the enlarged plot area (Chapter 9). (**Hint:** To do this automatically, use the Format Legend box to move the legend to the bottom again.)

**13.** Change the legend text to **Actual Revenues, Actual Expenses, Projected Revenues**, and **Projected Expenses** (Chapter 8). (**Hint:** Give up? Don't feel bad; this is kind of tricky. To change the legend text, you must change the worksheet text that generated the legend; in this case, cells B5:C5 and F5:G5 in the Quarterly Report worksheet. Remember, a chart is linked to the worksheet from which it was created. Changing the worksheet data (text or numbers) automatically changes the chart display.)

**14.** Preview the chart sheet (Chapter 6). Use the Setup button to do the following:

- Change the print orientation to **Portrait**.

- Remove the header and footer.

- Scale the chart to fit the page. (**Hint:** You need to display the chart options to do this.)

**15.** If you have a printer, print the chart sheet (Chapter 6).

**16.** Compare your printout with Figure 10.12.

**17.** Close the printpreview window, if necessary. Save the workbook file as **myexercise**, then close it (Chapter 3).

**18.** Click on the **Full Screen tool** to change to normal view.

## SUMMARY

In this chapter, we introduced you to a selection of advanced charting techniques. You learned how to use the Chart Wizard to create and modify charts, how to add data to a chart, how to plot rows or columns as the data series, how to create a combination chart, how to display two value axes on a combination chart, how to label data markers, and how to draw on a chart.

With this chapter, your foundation in Excel charting techniques is complete. Congratulations! You now possess the skills to create sophisticated, presentation-quality charts.

Here's a quick reference guide to the Excel features introduced in this chapter:

| Desired Result | How to Do It |
|---|---|
| Create embedded chart using Chart Wizard | Select worksheet cells to chart, click on **Chart Wizard tool** (or choose **Insert, Chart, On This Sheet**); drag (or click) in worksheet to create embedded chart box; follow Chart Wizard instructions |
| Add/remove data to/from chart | Add/remove data to/from worksheet, if necessary; activate chart; click on **Chart Wizard tool**; specify range containing worksheet data to chart; click on **Next >**; change desired Step 2 options; click on **OK**; or, select range of worksheet data to add to chart and drag range into embedded chart box |
| Changing the series order | Activate chart sheet or double-click on the embedded chart; choose **Format Column Group** from the shortcut menu; click on the **Series Order** tab; select the data series to be affected; click on the **Move Up** or **Move Down** buttons; click on OK |

| Desired Result | How to Do It |
|---|---|
| Plot rows/columns as data series | If creating new chart, select worksheet range to chart; if modifying existing chart, activate chart; click on **Chart Wizard tool** (or choose **Insert, Chart, As New Sheet** or **On This Sheet**); if creating new chart, create embedded chart box, complete Chart Wizard steps 1 through 3, and move to Step 4; if modifying existing chart, move to Step 2 dialog box; under Data Series In, select **Rows** or **Columns**; if creating new chart, complete Chart Wizard step 5 and click on **Finish**; if modifying existing chart, click on **OK** |
| Create combination chart | If creating new chart, select worksheet range to chart and press **F11** or **Alt+F1** to create column chart; if modifying existing chart, activate chart; select data series that gets new data-marker type; choose **Format, Chart Type** (or choose **Chart Type** from shortcut menu); verify that Selected Series is selected; click on desired data-marker type; click on **OK** |
| Display two value axes in combination chart | Activate combination chart; select data series that gets second value axis; choose **Format, Chart Type** (or choose **Chart Type** from shortcut menu); verify that Selected Series is selected; click on **Options**; display axis options; select **Secondary Axis**; click on **OK** |

| Desired Result | How to Do It |
|---|---|
| Label data markers | To label individual data marker, select it; to label every data marker in series, select entire series; choose **Format, Selected Data Point** (or choose **Format Data Point** from shortcut menu); display data labels options; select desired option; click on **OK** |
| Draw on chart sheet or worksheet | Activate chart sheet or worksheet; display Drawing toolbar; use drawing tools to add/modify desired graphic objects; hide Drawing toolbar |

In the next chapter, you will learn how to rearrange data by sorting. You'll learn what a list is, and how to sort lists based upon the values in a column. Then, you'll learn about creating a series of numbers or labels. Finally, you will learn how to break ties in a sort column by sorting by more than one column.

## IF YOU'RE STOPPING HERE

If you want to break off here, please exit Excel. If you want to proceed directly to the next chapter, please do so now.

# CHAPTER 11: SORTING DATA

**Single-Column Sorting**

**Creating Series of Data**

**Performing Multiple-Column Sorts**

**Sorting Options**

This chapter introduces our third major topic: data management. Along with providing electronic accounting abilities, Excel can help you edit, sort, customize, and analyze a body of data—for example, a worksheet that contains personnel information for every employee in a company.

Usually, you enter data in a worksheet in the order in which you receive that data. This might not be the order in which you want to look at the data, however, or the order in which you want a report to appear. In this chapter, you'll learn how to rearrange (sort) the information in a table or list. Excel has many features that will make this extremely easy.

When you're done working through this chapter, you will know

- How to perform one-key and multiple-key sorts
- How to create series of numbers or text
- About other sorting options

## SINGLE-COLUMN SORTING

Think about how information is arranged in a phone book. The entries appear alphabetically by last name (that would be the first column by which they are sorted). If there are several people named Smith, they are arranged alphabetically by first name (that would be the second column). If there are several people named Paul Smith, they are arranged by middle initial, then by address, and then by phone number (these would be the third, fourth, and fifth columns). We'll start by learning how to perform a one-column sort.

### SORTING A LIST BY THE VALUES IN A COLUMN

A *list* is a labeled series of rows that contain similar information. For example, several rows containing client names and phone numbers would be considered a list, as would 100 rows of employee payroll information. You can sort lists by using the *Data, Sort* command.

Imagine that someone hired you to clean a house and asked you to arrange things. The first thing you'd probably want to know is exactly *what* to arrange. Once you knew that, you'd need to know *how* to arrange those items. When you ask Excel to arrange—or sort—information, you need to answer the same two questions:

- What should be sorted?
- How should it be sorted?

To sort a list of data,

- Select any cell within the list you would like to sort. Excel will automatically select the entire list when you choose the Data, Sort command. You can also select the entire list yourself, but it's not necessary to do so. This step answers the question, "What should be sorted?"

- Choose *Data, Sort* to display the Sort dialog box.

- In the My List Has box, select *Header Row* if you wish to use labels at the top of your list to specify how Excel should sort the list. If you wish to use column letter to specify how to sort, select *No Header Row.* Excel is pretty smart here; if you have a row of labels at the top of the list, Excel assumes it is a header row.

- Indicate how you would like Excel to sort the information (that is, answer question number two):

  - Click on the drop-down arrow in the Sort By box and select the heading of the column by which you want to sort the list. If you have no header row, select the column by which you wish to sort.

  - Select *Ascending* or *Descending* to specify the order in which Excel should sort the information. Ascending order will sort numbers first (from smallest to largest), then letters in alphabetical order, then *logical values* (FALSE before TRUE), then error values (they are all equal), and finally blanks. Descending order is the opposite.

- Click on OK to sort the list.

If you are not running Excel, please start it now. If there is a workbook on your screen (other than Book1), please close it.

Let's open a worksheet that contains some fictional employee payroll information, and sort that information in two ways:

1. Open the workbook file **Sort Data** from the Excel Work folder. (**Note:** If you get a File Error message saying some number formats have been lost, click on **OK** and proceed with the activity.)

2. If you are in full-screen view, click on the **Full Screen tool** to change to normal view. The worksheet you see contains payroll information for a fictional company called Splash International (Figure 11.1). The information is in list form; that is, there are many rows of similar information with two rows of labels identifying the kinds of information the columns contain.

3. Scroll to the right to view the rest of the columns in the worksheet. The information continues through column K.

**Figure 11.1**     **The workbook file Sort Data**

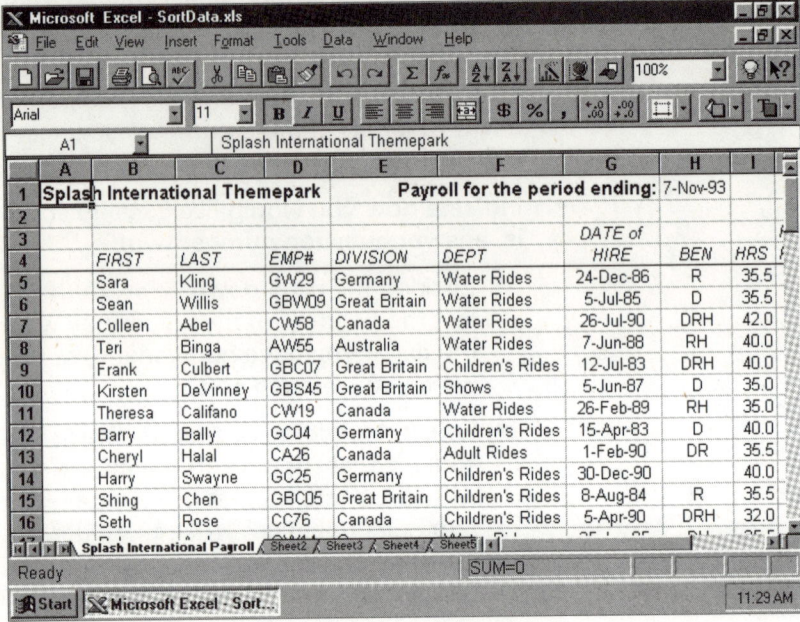

4. Press **Page Down** several times to view the information for all employees. The information continues through row 98.

5. Press **Ctrl+Home** to return to cell A1. The information in this list is in no apparent order.

6. Select any cell in the list (that is, any cell in the range B3:K98). To sort a list, you begin by selecting any cell within it.

7. Choose **Data, Sort** to display the Sort dialog box. Notice that Header Row is selected in the My List Has box at the bottom of the dialog box. This is because Excel is smart enough to recognize that there are labels above your rows of data.

8. Click on the **drop-down arrow** in the Sort By box to display a list of column headings, and then select **HIRE** to indicate that you wish to sort the list by date of hire. Ascending order is selected, meaning that rows for employees who were hired first will appear at the top of the list (see Figure 11.2).

**Figure 11.2**   **Sorting the list by date of hire**

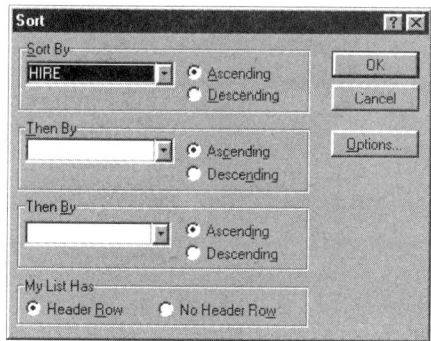

9. Click on **OK** to sort the list. Employees now appear in order by seniority.

10. Make sure that a cell within the list is selected, and then choose **Data, Sort** to display the Sort dialog box once again.

11. Click on the **Sort By drop-down arrow**, and select **HRS** to indicate that you wish to sort by the HRS column (you might need to scroll down in the list).

12. In the Sort By box, select **Descending** to indicate that you wish to see those employees who work the most hours at the top of the list (see Figure 11.3).

**Figure 11.3**   **Sorting by hours in descending order**

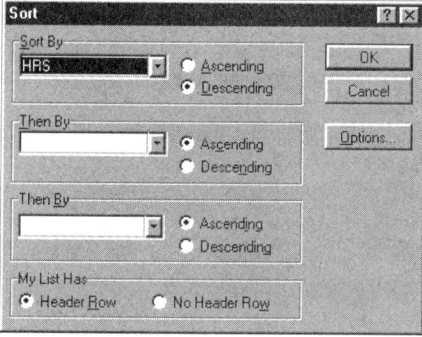

**13.** Click on **OK** to sort the list. Now the employees who work the most hours are shown first.

## USING THE SORT ASCENDING AND SORT DESCENDING TOOLS

The *Sort Ascending* and *Sort Descending tools* provide a very simple way to sort a list by a particular column in ascending or descending order. To sort a list in this manner,

- Select a cell in the column by which you would like to sort the list.

- Click on the *Sort Ascending* or *Sort Descending* tool.

Simple, eh? Let's try an ascending sort:

**1.** Select any cell within the LAST column in the list.

**2.** Click on the **Sort Ascending tool** to sort the entire list by last name in alphabetical order. This is a very simple way to perform a basic sort.

## CREATING SERIES OF DATA

Another helpful feature for arranging data is the ability to create series of numbers or text in your worksheets. For example, if you want to number a list, you can use a series to enter the numbers 1, 2, 3, and so on in a column. Or, if you want to have a series of month columns, you can have Excel create the month labels as a series in a row.

## CREATING A SERIES OF NUMBERS

To create a series of numbers in a range,

- Enter the first number of the series in the first cell of the range. Excel needs to know where to start.

- Select the range that will contain the series, including the cell containing the first number.

- Choose *Edit, Fill, Series* to display the Series dialog box.

- In the Type box, indicate the type of series. In most cases, this will be *Linear*, but you also can create other types of series, including series of dates (if you select the Date option, you should select an option in the Date Unit box, as well).

- In the Step Value box, enter the amount by which each value in the series should be increased. For example, in the series 1, 2, 3, the step value is 1; in the series 2, 4, 6, the step value is 2.

- In the Stop box, enter the last number in the series. (This is necessary only if you wish to stop numbering before reaching the end of the selected range.)

- Click on OK to create the series in the selected range.

Let's use this command to number the employee information in our worksheet:

1. Click on the **Undo tool** to undo the most recent sort. The employee information is now arranged by hours in descending order, but what if you wanted to return the information to its original order (the order in which it appeared before we did any sorting)? The Undo command will undo only the most recent command, and we've sorted this information three times. To return the information to its original order, we'll have to reopen the worksheet without saving changes.

2. Choose **File, Open**, select **Sort Data**, and click on **Open**. Excel asks if you want to discard the changes you've made since opening the file.

3. Click on **Yes** to open the file in its original state.

4. Enter **NUM** in cell A4.

5. Enter **1** in cell A5, and then select the range **A5:A98**. This is the range in which we'll create a series. We entered the first value (1) so that Excel will know where to begin the series.

6. Choose **Edit, Fill, Series** to display the Series dialog box (see Figure 11.4). By default, Excel will create a linear series with a step value of 1. This is exactly what we want.

7. Click on **OK** to create the series in the selected range.

**Figure 11.4**     **Creating a series of numbers**

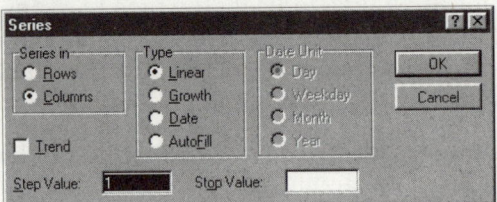

## USING THE FILL HANDLE TO CREATE SERIES

The *Fill Handle* is the small black box at the bottom right corner of any selected cell or range. You can drag the Fill Handle to extend a series of numbers or labels in the direction you drag. All you need to do is give Excel enough information to figure out what you want. To create a series of numbers in this manner,

- Enter the first two numbers of the series.

- Select the first two cells.

- Drag the Fill Handle in the direction in which you wish to extend the series.

To create a series of months or quarter labels, you need enter (and then select) only the first value in the series.

Let's experiment with using the Fill Handle:

1. Click on the **Sheet2 tab** to activate the second worksheet in the file.

2. Enter **1** in cell A1, then enter **2** in cell A2. To create a series of numbers by using the Fill Handle, you need to give Excel the first two values.

3. Select the range **A1:A2**, and then point to the **Fill Handle** for the selection (it is the small black square at the bottom right corner of the selected range). When you're pointing to the Fill Handle, the mouse pointer will take the shape of a black cross (see Figure 11.5).

4. Drag the **Fill Handle** down through cell A10, then release the mouse button to create the series 1, 2, 3...10 in the range A1:A10.

**Figure 11.5**    **Using the Fill Handle**

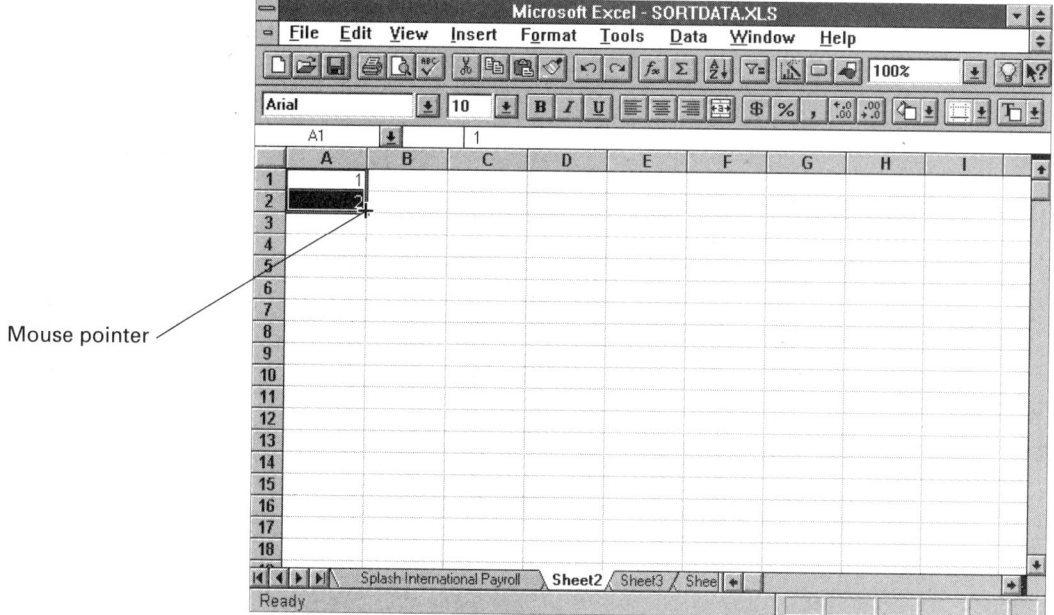

Mouse pointer

5. Enter **Qtr1** in cell B1. You also can create series of labels by using the Fill Handle.

6. Select cell **B1**, and then drag the **Fill Handle** down through cell B10. Excel creates a series of labels *Qtr1, Qtr2, Qtr3, Qtr4, Qtr1,* and so on. This can be quite handy.

Let's create one more useful type of series by using the Fill Handle:

1. Enter **Jan** in cell C1. A series of month labels? No problem.

2. Select cell **C1**, and then drag the **Fill Handle** down through cell C10. Excel creates the series *Jan, Feb, Mar...Oct* in the range (see Figure 11.6).

3. Click on the **Splash International Payroll tab** to activate the first worksheet once again.

4. Save the workbook file as **mysort** in the Excel Work folder.

**Figure 11.6**     **Creating series by using the Fill Handle**

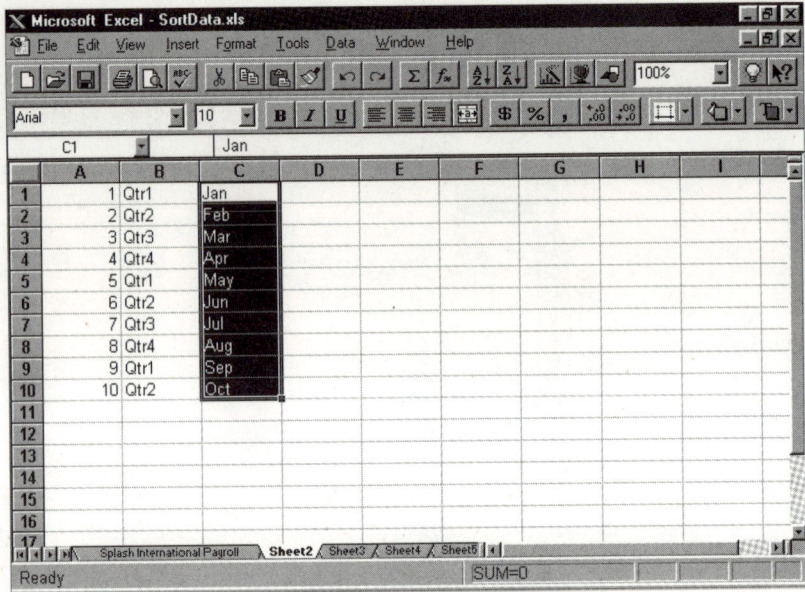

## SORTING THE LIST AGAIN

Let's sort our list a couple more times:

1. Select any cell within the list, and then choose **Data, Sort** to display the Sort dialog box.

2. In the Sort By box, specify **DIVISION** in **Descending** order, then click on **OK** to sort the information by division in reverse alphabetical order (see Figure 11.7). Employees in the Great Britain division are at the top of the worksheet, but *these* employees are in no apparent order. We will soon learn how to "break ties" in a sort by specifying other columns by which to sort.

### PRACTICE YOUR SKILLS

1. Sort the list by **RATE** in **Descending** order.

**Figure 11.7**     **The list sorted by division in descending order**

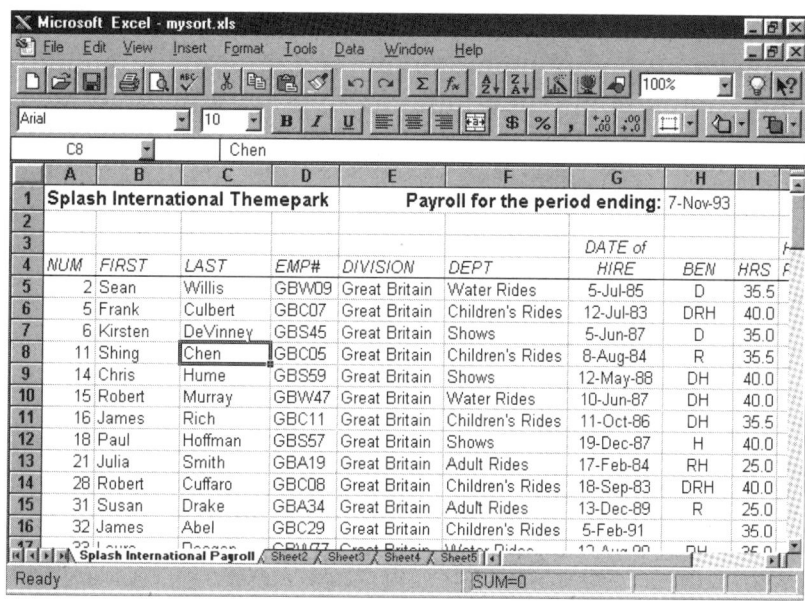

2. Sort the list back to its original order. (**Hint:** Don't reopen the file; sort by the numbers in *NUM*.)

3. Update the file. Your worksheet should resemble Figure 11.8.

## PERFORMING MULTIPLE-COLUMN SORTS

Remember our phone book example earlier in the chapter? The phone book is sorted by many columns. If two people have the same last name, they're sorted by first name; if the first names are the same, they're sorted by middle initial; and so on. Excel allows you to sort by as many columns as you like, although there's a trick to sorting by more than three columns.

### PERFORMING A TWO-COLUMN SORT

To perform a two-column sort,

- Select any cell within the list you would like to sort.

- Choose *Data, Sort* to display the Sort dialog box.

**Figure 11.8**       **The worksheet sorted back to its original order**

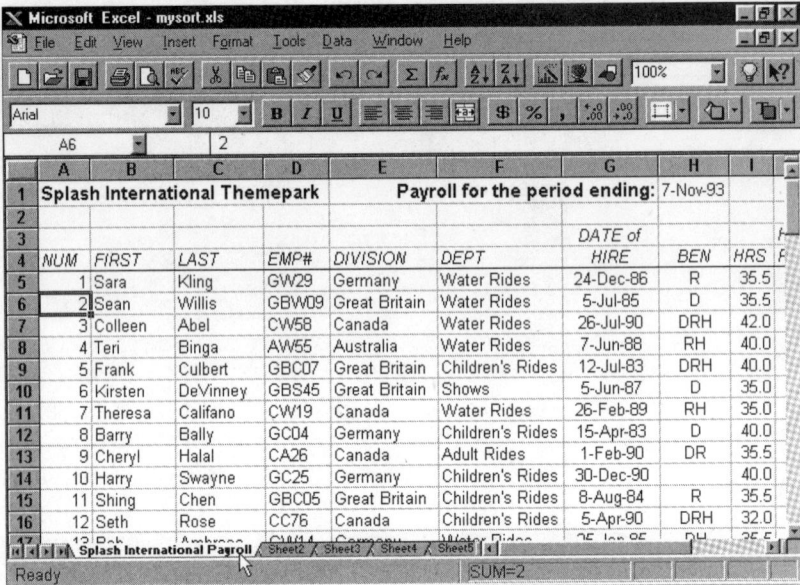

- Indicate whether your list has a header row.

- In the Sort By box, indicate the column on which you would like to sort first, and the order.

- In the first Then By box, indicate the column and order Excel should use to break ties in the column you used in the Sort By box.

- Click on OK to sort the list.

Let's use a two-column sort to arrange our list alphabetically by last name, then by first name:

1. Select any cell within the list, and then choose **Data, Sort** to display the Sort dialog box.

2. In the Sort By box, specify **LAST** in **Ascending** order to indicate that you wish to sort the list by last name.

3. In the first Then By box, specify **FIRST** in **Ascending** order to indicate that you wish to break any ties in the last-name column by sorting on the first-name column (see Figure 11.9).

**Figure 11.9**    **Sorting by two columns**

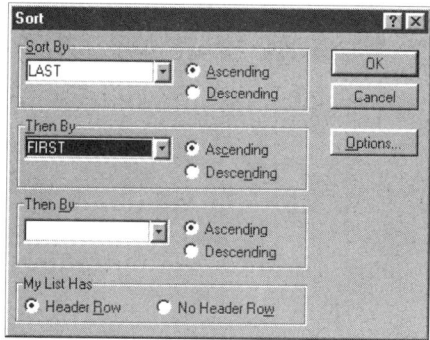

4. Click on **OK** to sort the list. Notice that the Abels are in alphabetical order by first name: Colleen, James, Karina, and then William. The Bingas are also in alphabetical order by first name. If you do not specify a second column by which to sort, Excel will leave rows with ties in the Sort By column in the order in which it finds them. Later in the chapter, we'll see why this is useful.

## PERFORMING A THREE-COLUMN SORT

You can add a third column to a sort by using the second Then By box in the Sort dialog box. Let's sort our list again, this time by division and then department, breaking any further ties with last name:

1. Select any cell within the list, and then choose **Data, Sort** to display the Sort dialog box.

2. In the Sort By box, specify **DIVISION** in **Ascending** order to indicate that you wish to sort the list by division.

3. In the first Then By box, specify **DEPT** in **Ascending** order to indicate that you wish to break any ties in the division column by sorting on the department column.

4. In the second Then By box, specify **LAST** in **Ascending** order to break any further ties by sorting on the last-name column.

5. Click on **OK** to sort the list. Your worksheet should resemble Figure 11.10.

**Figure 11.10**  **Sorting the list by division, then department, then last name**

| | A | B | C | D | E | F | G | H | I | |
|---|---|---|---|---|---|---|---|---|---|---|
| 3 | | | | | | | DATE of | | | |
| 4 | NUM | FIRST | LAST | EMP# | DIVISION | DEPT | HIRE | BEN | HRS | |
| 5 | 93 | Erin | Binga | AA70 | Australia | Adult Rides | 8-Apr-91 | RH | 40.0 | |
| 6 | 74 | Frieda | Binga | AA02 | Australia | Adult Rides | 17-Feb-82 | R | 40.0 | |
| 7 | 44 | Melanie | Bowers | AA35 | Australia | Adult Rides | 5-Dec-86 | DR | 15.5 | |
| 8 | 65 | Lindsey | Winger | AA25 | Australia | Adult Rides | 1-Feb-86 | DR | 35.0 | |
| 9 | 19 | Dean | Kramer | AC49 | Australia | Children's Rides | 23-Jun-87 | RH | 40.0 | |
| 10 | 64 | Lynne | Simmons | AC17 | Australia | Children's Rides | 23-Nov-88 | R | 35.0 | |
| 11 | 91 | Greg | Thomas | AC53 | Australia | Children's Rides | 24-Dec-87 | DR | 40.0 | |
| 12 | 60 | Edward | Trelly | AC27 | Australia | Children's Rides | 17-Jun-86 | DR | 40.0 | |
| 13 | 22 | Jacqueline | Banks | AS03 | Australia | Shows | 2-Feb-84 | H | 40.0 | |
| 14 | 79 | Marianne | Calvin | AS23 | Australia | Shows | 23-Jul-85 | | 40.0 | |
| 15 | 50 | Steve | Singer | AS29 | Australia | Shows | 5-Oct-86 | R | 40.0 | |
| 16 | 81 | Grace | Sloan | AS12 | Australia | Shows | 2-Nov-84 | DH | 40.0 | |
| 17 | 36 | Peter | Allen | AW24 | Australia | Water Rides | 31-May-86 | | 40.0 | |
| 18 | 4 | Teri | Binga | AW55 | Australia | Water Rides | 7-Jun-88 | RH | 40.0 | |

**6.** Update the file.

## SORTING BY MORE THAN THREE COLUMNS

Although you can specify only three columns in the Sort dialog box, you can sort by as many columns as you like. All you have to do is divide the task into several sorts of three or fewer columns each. Remember, if Excel finds ties in all the columns specified in a sort, it leaves these rows in the order in which it finds them. So, to sort a list by five columns, you would sort the list twice: first by the fourth and fifth columns by which you wish to sort, and then again by the first, second, and third columns. Any rows with ties in the first three columns would remain in the order in which Excel found them, which was by the fourth column and then the fifth. Follow that?

Let's sort our list by division, then department, and then hours, breaking any further ties with last name and then first name:

1. Select any cell within the list, and then choose **Data, Sort** to display the Sort dialog box.

2. In the Sort By box, specify **LAST** in **Ascending** order. Remember, to perform a five-column sort, we must first sort by the fourth and fifth columns.

3. In the first Then By box, specify **FIRST** in **Ascending** order.

4. In the second Then By box, select **(none)** to indicate that you do not need a third column for this sort (see Figure 11.11). Excel "remembers" the columns you used the last time you sorted the list. Sometimes you will need to "clear" a sort column in this manner.

**Figure 11.11     Sorting by the fourth and fifth keys first**

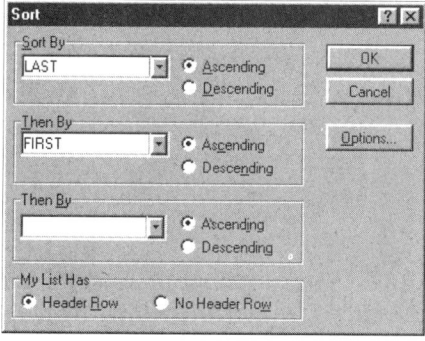

5. Click on **OK** to sort the list by last name and then first name.

6. Display the Sort dialog box once again (select any cell in the list and choose **Data, Sort**).

7. Sort the list first by **DIVISION** in **Ascending** order, then by **DEPT** in **Ascending** order, and then by **HRS** in **Descending** order (see Figure 11.12). The two Bingas in rows 5 and 6 have the same division, department, hours, and last name, but are arranged alphabetically by first name (Erin before Frieda).

8. Update and then close the file.

**Figure 11.12** **The list sorted by five columns**

| | A | B | C | D | E | F | G | H | I |
|---|---|---|---|---|---|---|---|---|---|
| 3 | | | | | | | DATE of | | |
| 4 | NUM | FIRST | LAST | EMP# | DIVISION | DEPT | HIRE | BEN | HRS |
| 5 | 93 | Erin | Binga | AA70 | Australia | Adult Rides | 8-Apr-91 | RH | 40.0 |
| 6 | 74 | Frieda | Binga | AA02 | Australia | Adult Rides | 17-Feb-82 | R | 40.0 |
| 7 | 65 | Lindsey | Winger | AA25 | Australia | Adult Rides | 1-Feb-86 | DR | 35.0 |
| 8 | 44 | Melanie | Bowers | AA35 | Australia | Adult Rides | 5-Dec-86 | DR | 15.5 |
| 9 | 19 | Dean | Kramer | AC49 | Australia | Children's Rides | 23-Jun-87 | RH | 40.0 |
| 10 | 91 | Greg | Thomas | AC53 | Australia | Children's Rides | 24-Dec-87 | DR | 40.0 |
| 11 | 60 | Edward | Trelly | AC27 | Australia | Children's Rides | 17-Jun-86 | DR | 40.0 |
| 12 | 64 | Lynne | Simmons | AC17 | Australia | Children's Rides | 23-Nov-88 | R | 35.0 |
| 13 | 22 | Jacqueline | Banks | AS03 | Australia | Shows | 2-Feb-84 | H | 40.0 |
| 14 | 79 | Marianne | Calvin | AS23 | Australia | Shows | 23-Jul-85 | | 40.0 |
| 15 | 50 | Steve | Singer | AS29 | Australia | Shows | 5-Oct-86 | R | 40.0 |
| 16 | 81 | Grace | Sloan | AS12 | Australia | Shows | 2-Nov-84 | DH | 40.0 |
| 17 | 36 | Peter | Allen | AW24 | Australia | Water Rides | 31-May-86 | | 40.0 |
| 18 | 4 | Teri | Binga | AW55 | Australia | Water Rides | 7-Jun-88 | RH | 40.0 |
| 19 | 55 | Joshua | Maccaluso | AW69 | Australia | Water Rides | 23-Jan-91 | DRH | 40.0 |

## SORTING OPTIONS

As we've seen, sorting can be quite simple in Excel. There are other sorting options, however, that make it possible for you to sort in other, less obvious ways. For example, you can sort columns instead of rows. You also can set up *custom sort orders* to sort in columns that contain information that you don't necessarily want to appear in alphabetical or numeric order.

### SORTING COLUMNS INSTEAD OF ROWS

If your groups of information are in columns instead of rows, you can use the Data, Sort command to sort by columns. Excel can't use a column of headings the same way it uses a row of headings, but that's not a big problem. To sort a list by columns,

- Select the information you wish to sort. You *can* select a single cell, as you would with a row-wise list, but you may not like the results. If you have a column of row headings, Excel probably will assume you want to sort those, as well. To be safe, you should select all the information you wish to sort (and *not* the row headings).

- Choose *Data, Sort* to display the Sort dialog box.
- Click on *Options* to display the Sort Options dialog box.
  - In the Orientation box, select *Sort Left To Right*.
  - Click on OK to return to the Sort dialog box.
- Specify the row(s) and order(s) by which you wish to sort.
- Click on OK to sort the list.

Let's open a file containing some different lists, and sort one of these by columns:

1. Open the file **Sort Options** from the Excel Work folder. This file contains two worksheets we'll use to demonstrate sorting options. The first worksheet, ABC Travel, contains sales information for four offices of a fictional company. The information is grouped in columns.

2. Select the range **B4:E8** to prepare to sort the office information. When you sort by columns, it is a good idea to select all the information you wish to sort. Excel can sometimes be confused by row headings.

3. Choose **Data, Sort** to display the Sort dialog box, and then click on the **Options button** to display the Sort Options dialog box.

4. In the Orientation box, select **Sort Left To Right** (if necessary) to indicate that you wish to sort columns and not rows (see Figure 11.13).

**Figure 11.13    Sorting by columns**

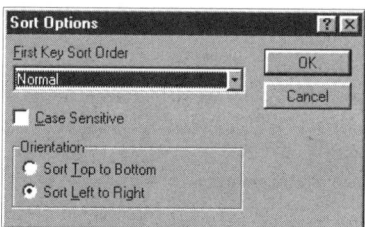

5. Click on **OK** to return to the Sort dialog box, and then specify **Row 4** in **Ascending** order in the Sort By box. This will sort the information alphabetically by office.

6. Click on **OK** to sort the information. Boise is first, then Ithaca, Orlando, and finally Toledo.

## CUSTOM SORT ORDERS

You can create your own custom sort orders to arrange data other than alphabetically or numerically. Excel has some built-in sort orders that you may find useful (the days of the week and the months of the year, for example), but you can create as many custom orders as you like. For example, you might create a custom sort order so you can arrange items by the text *low*, *medium*, or *high* in a particular order.

To create a custom sort order,

• Choose *Tools, Options* to display the Options dialog box.

• Click on the *Custom Lists* tab.

• In the List Entries box, enter the items in your list in ascending order. Press *Enter* between each item in the list.

• Click on *Add* to add the new list to the Custom Lists box.

• Click on OK to close the Options dialog box.

After you create a custom list, you can use it from the Sort Options dialog box. To do so, simply select the custom list from the First Key Sort Order drop-down list.

Let's create a custom sort order and then use it to sort the list in the second worksheet in our file:

1. Click on the **Projects and Priorities tab** to activate that worksheet, which contains a short list of projects, the technicians to whom they are assigned, and priorities. To be able to sort this list by priority, we will need to create a custom sort order list.

2. Choose **Tools, Options** to display the Options dialog box, and then click on the **Custom Lists tab**.

**3.** In the List Entries box, type **Low** and press **Enter**, type **Medium** and press **Enter**, and then type **High** to create a custom sort order list.

**4.** Click on **Add** to add your new list to the Custom Lists box. Your dialog box should resemble Figure 11.14.

**Figure 11.14** **Creating a custom list**

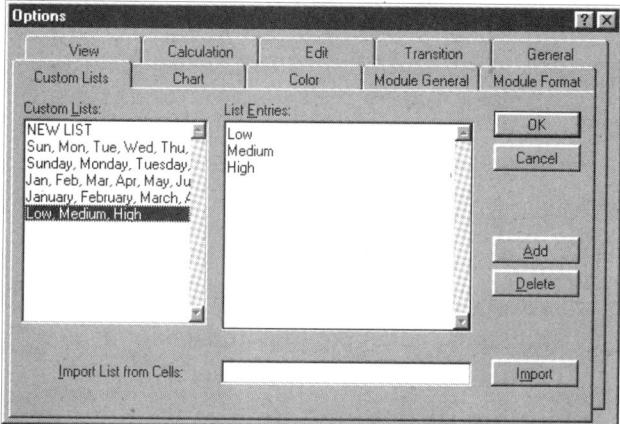

**5.** Click on **OK** to close the Options dialog box.

**6.** Select any cell within the Projects and Priorities list, display the Sort dialog box, and then click on **Options** to display the Sort Options dialog box.

**7.** Select **Low, Medium, High** from the First Key Sort Order drop-down list (see Figure 11.15). This is how you *use* a custom sort order.

**Figure 11.15** **Using a custom sort order**

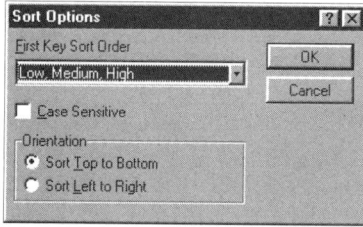

8. Click on **OK** to return to the Sort dialog box, and then indicate that you wish to sort by **Priority** in **Descending** order.

9. Click on **OK** to sort the list according to the custom sort order. The high-priority items are listed first, then the medium-priority items, and finally the low-priority items.

10. Close the file *without* saving changes to it.

## SUMMARY

In this chapter, you learned how to sort lists of information. You learned how to use the sort dialog box to sort rows by one, two, or three columns, and also how to use the Sort Ascending and Sort Descending tools to perform simple one-column sorts. You also learned how to create series of numbers using the Edit, Fill, Series command, and how to use the Fill Handle to create series of text or numbers. Finally, we discussed how to sort columns instead of rows, and how to create a custom sort order.

The following quick reference guide summarizes some of the techniques you learned in this chapter.

| Desired Result | How to Do It |
| --- | --- |
| Sort list | Select cell within list; choose **Data, Sort**; indicate whether list has header row; select column to sort by and order; select second and third columns to sort by (if desired); click on **OK** |
| Sort list by single column in ascending or descending order | Select cell within column to sort and click on **Sort Ascending** or **Sort Descending tool** |
| Create series of numbers | Enter first number in a cell; select range to contain series; choose **Edit, Fill, Series**; indicate type of series and step value; click on **OK** |
| Use Fill Handle to create series | Enter first two values in series; select first two cells; drag **Fill Handle** through desired range |

| Desired Result | How to Do It |
|---|---|
| Sort by more than three columns | Divide sort columns into groups of three or fewer and sort by least important group first, proceeding to most important |
| Sort by columns | Select information to sort; choose **Data, Sort**; click on **Options**; select **Sort Left To Right**; click on **OK**; indicate row(s) and order(s) by which to sort; click on **OK** |
| Create custom sort order list | Choose **Tools, Options**; click on **Custom Lists tab**; enter list in List Entries box; click on **Add**; click on **OK** |
| Use custom sort order list | Display Sort dialog box, click on **Options**; select custom sort order from First Key Sort Order drop-down list |

In the next chapter, you will learn how you can use the AutoFilter feature to see just the information you want visible in a list. You'll learn to filter a list based on the contents of one or more columns, and how to manage a filtered list after you create it.

## IF YOU'RE STOPPING HERE

If you need to break off here, please exit from Excel. If you want to proceed directly to the next chapter, please do so now.

# CHAPTER 12:
# USING AUTOFILTER
# AND ADVANCED FILTER

Filtering a List

Custom Criteria

Managing a
Filtered List

Using Advanced
Filter

Copying Filtered
Data

**E**xcel's AutoFilter feature provides an intuitive and powerful tool for organizing and analyzing a list of data. In this chapter, we'll learn how to use AutoFilter to see only those rows in a list that meet certain conditions. We'll learn how to make those conditions more specialized by creating custom criteria and by using wildcards. And, we'll also discuss managing a filtered list, on which many of Excel's commands work somewhat differently than they do on other lists.

The Advanced Filter feature allows you to filter a list using conditions that are more complex than those you could create using AutoFilter. For example, it permits you to filter through a column for rows containing any of three specific values—a condition Auto-Filter couldn't accommodate. We'll learn to use the Advanced Filter feature to filter a list based on a *criteria range* (a range of cells containing information—or *criteria*—on how to filter a list) that can be as complex as you'll ever need. We'll learn to add AND and OR conditions to a criteria range, and how to copy filtered data to another location in a worksheet.

When you're done working through this chapter, you will know

- How to use AutoFilter to filter a list based on the values in a single column

- How to use multiple-column filtering to create AND conditions

- How to use custom criteria to create OR conditions

- How to find a range of values

- How to use wildcards in custom criteria

- How to sort, sum, and print filtered lists

- How to create a criteria range

- How to use Advanced Filter to filter a list

- How to copy filtered data to another location

## FILTERING A LIST

In general, you use filters to take only certain items out of a collection. For example, when prospectors pan for gold, their pans act as filters to remove sand, leaving only the gold (if they are lucky). Similarly, Excel's AutoFilter feature lets you "pan through" a list to see only the rows of information in which you are interested. In a list of employee information, you could use AutoFilter to display only the rows for employees in a particular division, or you could display only the rows for employees who make more than a particular amount of money.

 ## SINGLE-COLUMN FILTERING

When you filter a list, you have to do two things: identify the list to be filtered, and tell Excel how to filter it. As with the Sort command, Excel can recognize a list even if you select only a single cell within that list. Because the AutoFilter feature works best on a list that has a headings row, you should include headings when you design a list on which you intend to use the feature.

To use AutoFilter to see only the rows in a list that contain a particular value in a certain column,

- Select any cell within the list.

- Choose *Data, Filter, AutoFilter* to turn on the AutoFilter feature, and to place Excel in *Filter mode*. Drop-down arrows appear next to each column heading. Many commands act differently in Filter mode, which we'll learn about later in the chapter.

- Click on the drop-down arrow next to the column by which you wish to filter the list, and then select the value for which you would like to see the rows.

After you filter a list on a column, that column's drop-down arrow will change color (usually to blue), telling you that a filter is active there. You can display the entire list once again by choosing Data, Filter, Show All. To exit from Filter mode, choose Data, Filter, Auto-Filter (the command acts as a toggle—choose it once to turn on the feature, choose it again to turn it off).

If you are not running Excel, please start it now. If there is a workbook on your screen (other than Book1), please close it.

Let's open a worksheet that contains a list of payroll information, and then use the AutoFilter feature to display only rows for employees in a particular division:

1. Open the file **Filters** from the Excel Work folder. This worksheet contains a list of payroll information identical to the list we used in the last chapter.

2. Select any cell within the list. When using the AutoFilter feature, it is important that your list have column headings; bear this in mind as you design your worksheets.

3. Choose **Data, Filter, AutoFilter** to place the worksheet in Filter mode. There are drop-down arrows next to each column heading (see Figure 12.1).

4. Click on the **drop-down arrow** to the right of the *DIVISION* column heading to display a list of values in the column. You can select one of these values to display only rows that contain that value.

5. Select **Germany** to display only rows that contain *Germany* in the DIVISION column. When you filter a list, the rows that do not meet the filter condition are hidden (in this case, employees from divisions other than Germany). The blue row numbers indicate that the rows have been filtered. Also, you can use the status bar at the bottom of the screen to quickly

**Figure 12.1** **Filter mode**

see the number of rows that match the criteria. In this case, 27 of the 94 rows contain *Germany* in the *DIVISION* column.

6. Choose **Data, Filter, Show All** to again display the entire list. The worksheet is still in Filter mode.

7. Choose **Data, Filter, AutoFilter** to turn off Filter mode. The drop-down arrows disappear from the column headings.

## FILTERING ON TWO COLUMNS TO CREATE AN AND CONDITION

You can filter a list through two columns to create what is called an *AND condition*. For example, you might want to see only the rows for employees who are in both a certain division *and* a particular department. To filter a list on more than one column,

* Place the list in Filter mode (select a cell within the list and choose *Data, Filter, AutoFilter*).

* Filter the list by a value in one of the columns.

* Filter the list by a value in another column.

Only the rows that contain both specified values will remain visible.

Let's filter our list to display only employees in the Germany division who are in the Shows department:

1. Select any cell in the list, and then choose **Data, Filter, Auto-Filter** to place the worksheet in Filter mode.

2. From the DIVISION drop-down list, select **Germany** to display only Germany-division employees. The drop-down arrow next to the column heading changes color (probably to blue), indicating that a filter is active on this column. Also, note that the affected row numbers are blue.

3. From the DEPT drop-down list, select **Shows**. Now the only remaining rows contain both *Germany* in the DIVISION column *and Shows* in the DEPT column (see Figure 12.2).

**Figure 12.2**  **Filtering on two columns to create an AND condition**

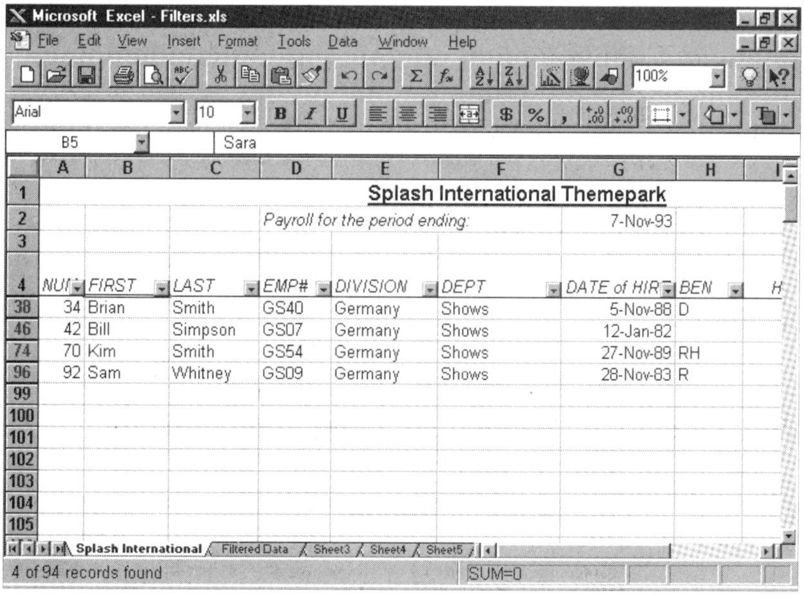

## REMOVING A COLUMN FILTER

The Data, Filter, Show All command removes *all* filters that are active on your list. You also can remove only a single column's filter by choosing *(All)* from the column heading's drop-down list. Let's remove one of our current column filters:

1. Click on the DIVISION drop-down arrow. The drop-down list for each column contains five other options in addition to the values in the column: *(All)*, *(Top 10)*, *(Custom)*, *(Blanks)*, and *(NonBlanks)*.

2. Choose **(All)** from the DIVISION drop-down list to remove the filter for this column. The remaining 16 rows meet the condition of the other active filter; that is, they have *Shows* in the DEPT column.

### PRACTICE YOUR SKILLS

1. Remove the DEPT column filter.

## FINDING BLANK AND NONBLANK CELLS

You can use the (Blanks) option in a column heading's drop-down list to display only rows that contain no information in that column. Conversely, you can use the (NonBlanks) option to display all the rows that have *any* information in that column.

The BEN column in our worksheet contains letters that denote which benefits the employees receive. Table 12.1 summarizes what these letters mean.

**Table 12.1**     **The Letters in the BEN Column**

| Letter | Means |
| --- | --- |
| H | Employee receives health benefits |
| D | Employee receives dental benefits |
| R | Employee participates in retirement plan |

Let's filter our list to find the employees who receive no benefits, then again to find the employees who receive some benefits:

1. From the BEN drop-down list, select **(Blanks)** to display only rows that contain no information in the BEN column. The status bar should read **16 of 94 records found**.

2. From the BEN drop-down list, select **(NonBlanks)** to display all rows that contain *any* information in the BEN column. (**Note:** Sometimes, people will use the *empty text* value " " in a cell; for the purpose of filtering, Excel considers this value nonblank.) The status bar should read **78 of 94 records found**.

3. Choose **Data, Filter, Show All** to remove all active filters from the list.

## USING THE TOP 10 AUTOFILTER

You can use the Top 10 option to filter columns containing numerical data by either the highest or lowest items in the list. When you choose this filter option, Excel displays the Top 10 AutoFilter dialog box for you to specify the direction of the filter (top or bottom), the number of items to include (10 is the default), and increments (item or percent). Let's use the Top 10 filter to find the employees who earn the highest gross pay.

1. Scroll to view column K (the Gross Pay figures).

2. From the Pay drop-down list, select **(Top 10)** to display the Top 10 AutoFilter dialog box.

3. Verify that the Show options are set to Top 10 Items as shown in Figure 12.3.

**Figure 12.3**     **The Top 10 AutoFilter dialog box**

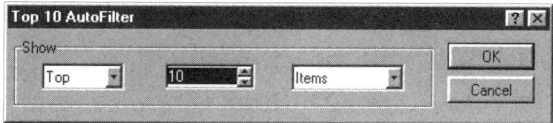

4. Click on **OK**.

5. Observe that the ten highest gross pay amounts range from
   $860 to $1,008.

6. Choose **Data, Filter, Show All** to remove all active filters
   from the list.

## CUSTOM CRITERIA

Custom criteria allow you to filter a column based on two conditions, or to filter for values that do not precisely match a certain
value. For example, you might want to filter our employee list to
find employees who are in either the Germany division or the
Canada division. Or, you might be interested in finding which employees make more than a certain amount of money.

### USING CUSTOM CRITERIA TO CREATE AN OR CONDITION

Creating an *OR condition* means finding rows that meet either
one condition *or* another. So far, we've learned only how to filter
through a column looking for a single value, but the (Custom)
option in a column heading's drop-down menu allows you to combine two conditions in a single column. To create an OR condition
within a single column,

- Place your list in Filter mode.

- Select (*Custom*) from the desired column heading's drop-
  down list to display the Custom AutoFilter dialog box.

- In the Show Rows Where box, select an *operator* and a value
  for the first condition, or criterion. Operators allow you to find
  values that do not exactly match a particular value. We'll discuss this in more detail shortly.

- Click on *Or* to indicate that you wish to add an OR condition
  to the criteria.

- Select an operator and a value for the second condition.

- Click on *OK* to show rows that meet either of the two criteria.

Let's use custom criteria to find employees who work in either of
two divisions:

1. Press **Ctrl + Home** to reorient the screen.

2. From the DIVISION drop-down list, select **Germany** to display only employees who work in the Germany division. There are 27 employess.

3. From the DIVISION drop-down list, select **Great Britain**. You might think that picking a second value in the list would let you display employees who work in the Great Britain division *or* the Germany division, but this is not the case. When you select a different value from a column heading's drop-down list, the new value *replaces* the current column filter. To create an OR condition, we must use custom criteria. You might want to note that there are 30 employees in the Great Britain division.

4. From the DIVISION drop-down list, select **(Custom)** to display the Custom AutoFilter dialog box, which allows you to combine two criteria for the same column. The first two boxes display the current criterion, DIVISION = Great Britain.

5. Click on the **Or** option to indicate that you wish to add an OR condition to the criteria.

6. From the second operator drop-down list (in the lower-left part of the Show Rows Where box), select **=**.

7. From the second value drop-down list (in the lower-right part of the Show Rows Where box), select **Germany** (see Figure 12.4). These criteria will filter the list to find employees who have either Great Britain or Germany in the DIVISION column.

**Figure 12.4**     **Creating an OR condition using custom criteria**

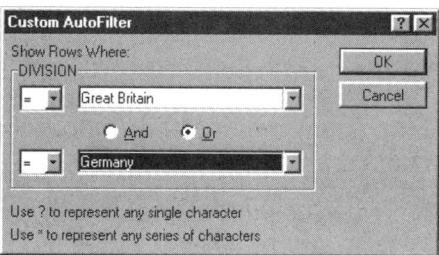

**8.** Click on **OK** to filter the list using the custom criteria. Only Germany- and Great Britain-division employees remain. The status bar should read **57 of 94 records found**.

### PRACTICE YOUR SKILLS

**1.** Display all the rows in the list once again.

## FILTERING TO FIND A RANGE OF VALUES

You also can use custom criteria to find values that are less than or greater than a particular value. Table 12.2 summarizes the operators you can use with custom criteria.

**Table 12.2**      **Criterion Operators**

| Operator | Meaning |
| --- | --- |
| = | Equal to |
| < | Less than |
| > | Greater than |
| <= | Less than or equal to |
| >= | Greater than or equal to |
| <> | Not equal to |

**Note:** Although you might not think of using comparison operators with text, the fact is you can! In the context of text, *greater than* means "later in alphabetical order," and *less than* means "earlier in alphabetical order." Perhaps more useful than these is the not-equal-to operator (<>), which you can use to find records that do *not* contain particular text.

By combining two such criteria, you can find a value that falls between two other values. To do so,

- Place the list in Filter mode.

- Display the *Custom AutoFilter* dialog box for the column in which you would like to create the filter.

- For the first criterion, specify > as the operator and the lower value of the range in which you want to include values. For example, to find values between 20 and 30, you would use > 20 as the first criterion.

- Specify *And* as the type of condition.

- For the second criterion, specify < as the operator and the higher value of the range in which you want to include values. In our example, this criterion would be < 30.

- Click on OK.

Let's use custom criteria to find ranges of values:

1. From the HRS drop-down list (you may need to scroll to the right to see this column), select **(Custom)** to display the Custom AutoFilter dialog box.

2. In the Show Rows Where box, select **>=** as the operator for the first criterion.

3. In the Show Rows Where box, select **35.5** as the value for the first criterion (see Figure 12.5). You will filter the list to find employees who work at least 35.5 hours per week.

**Figure 12.5**     **Finding employees who work at least 35.5 hours**

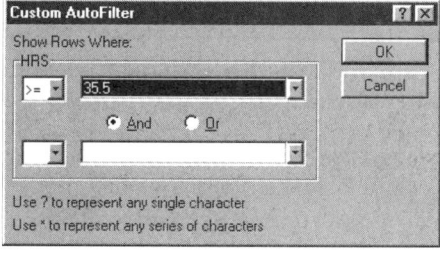

4. Click on **OK** to filter the list. There are 64 employees who work at least 35.5 hours.

5. Choose **Data, Filter, Show All** to display the entire list again.

6. From the HOURLY RATE drop-down list, select **(Custom)** to display the Custom AutoFilter dialog box.

7. For the first criterion in the Show Rows Where box, specify **>= $12.50**.

8. Verify that the And option is selected, and then specify **<= $19.50** as the second criterion (see Figure 12.6).

**Figure 12.6**    **Creating an AND condition to find values in a range**

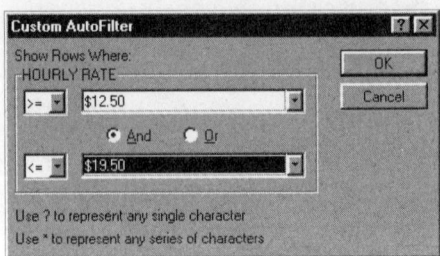

9. Click on **OK** to filter the list. Excel displays 40 employees who make at least $12.50, but not more than $19.50 per hour.

## PRACTICE YOUR SKILLS

1. Display the entire list.

2. Display only employees who work fewer than 35.5 hours per week.

3. Remove the filter from the HRS column.

4. Display only employees who make between **$504.00** and **$670.00** per week. Your worksheet should resemble Figure 12.7. The status bar should display **18 of 94 records found**.

5. Display the entire list once again, and then select cell **A1**.

## USING WILDCARDS

*Wildcards* allow you to find information even when you know only part of what you're looking for. For example, the EMP# field in the worksheet contains codes that indicate each employee's division and department. The first letter of the code corresponds to the first letter of the employee's division (in the case of the Great Britain division, the first two letters of the code correspond to the first two letters of the division), and the second letter corresponds

**Figure 12.7**    **Employees who make between $504 and $670 per week**

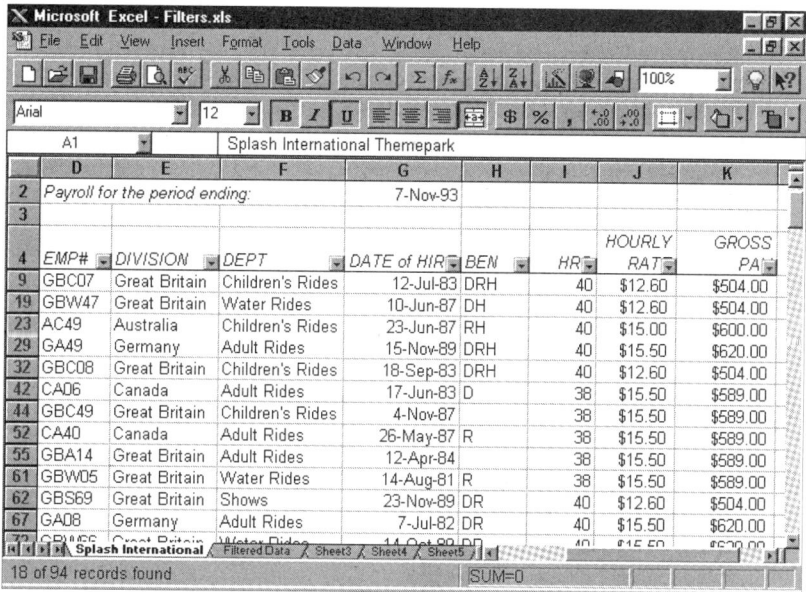

to the first letter of the employee's department (the third letter of the code for Great Britain-division employees). If you wanted to find all the employees who work in the Shows department, you could use wildcards to search through the EMP# field for all the records that contain employee numbers in which the second letter is *S*.

## Using the * Wildcard

You can use the *asterisk wildcard* (*) to stand for any number of characters. For example, the criterion c* would find the text *cat, curiosity, CNN, cowabunga,* or any other text that begins with the letter *c* (criteria are *not* case-sensitive). You also can surround text with two asterisks to create a criterion that means "contains"; for example, the criterion *rat* would find the text *Seurat, ratchet,* or *irate.*

Let's experiment with the * wildcard:

1. From the LAST drop-down list, select **(Custom)** to display the Custom AutoFilter dialog box.

2. Select **=** as the operator for the first criterion, then click in the first value box and type **m\*** (see Figure 12.8). This criterion will find all last names that begin with the letter *m*. (**Note:** Case is not important in criteria.)

**Figure 12.8**       **Using the \* wildcard**

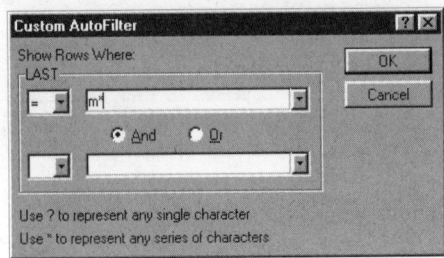

3. Click on **OK** to filter the list. Only employees whose last names begin with *m* remain.

4. Display the entire list, and then display the Custom AutoFilter dialog box for the BEN column (choose **(Custom)** from the BEN drop-down list).

5. Specify **= \*r** as the first criterion. We will attempt to find all employees who participate in the retirement plan.

6. Click on **OK** to filter the list. This criterion found all entries in the BEN column that *end* in the letter *r*. This excludes people who have another letter *after* the *r*. To create a "contains" criterion, we must surround the text for which we are looking with two asterisks.

7. Display the Custom AutoFilter dialog box for the BEN column once again, and modify the first criterion to be **= \*r\*** (see Figure 12.9).

8. Click on **OK** to filter the list. We now have all 49 employees who participate in the retirement plan.

## PRACTICE YOUR SKILLS

1. Display the entire list.

**Figure 12.9**  **Creating a "contains" criterion**

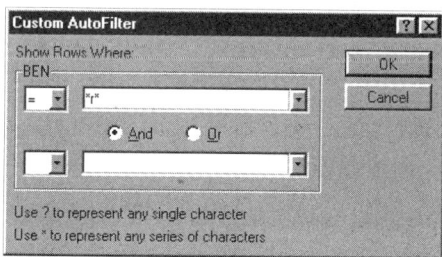

2. Display only the employees whose last names begin with the letter s. There should be 15 found rows.

3. Display the entire list, and then display only the employees who receive the dental benefit. There should be 43 found rows.

4. Display the entire list again.

### Using the ? Wildcard

You can use the *question-mark wildcard* (?) in a criterion to represent any single character. For example, the criterion c?t would find the text *cat, cot, cut,* or even *c2t*. To find text that has a certain letter in a particular spot and any other character after that letter, you would need to combine the * and ? wildcards. For example, the criterion ?a* would find the text *cat, Sartre, fa,* or *1a.*

Let's use a combination of wildcards and an OR condition to verify that employees with the A code are assigned to the correct department (Adult Rides):

1. Display the Custom AutoFilter dialog box for the EMP# column.

2. For the first criterion, specify **?a***. This criterion will find employee codes in which *a* is the second letter. We will need to add another criterion to find Great Britain-division employees with an *a* as their department code, because in their employee numbers this code letter comes third.

3. Click on **Or**, and then specify **=** as the second operator and **??a*** as the second criterion (see Figure 12.10).

4. Click on **OK** to filter the list. All remaining employees (24) are indeed in an Adult Rides department. We could have found the same employees by using a simple filter on the DEPT

**Figure 12.10**     **Verifying Adult Rides department codes**

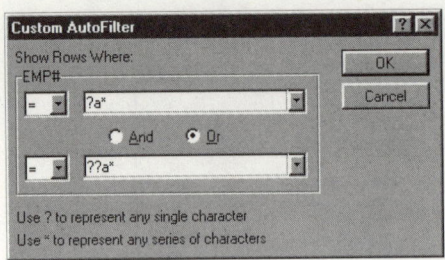

column, but in this way we were able to verify that the EMP# codes are assigned correctly.

**5.** Display the entire list.

## MANAGING A FILTERED LIST

When you are in Filter mode, many of Excel's commands work differently. This allows you to sort, sum, or print only the visible rows in a filtered list.

### SORTING A FILTERED LIST

You can use the Data, Sort command (or the Sort Ascending and Sort Descending tools) to sort only the visible rows in a filtered list. Simply select a cell in the filtered list, display the Sort dialog box, and indicate how you wish to sort.

Let's filter our list again, and then sort the filtered list:

**1.** Filter the list to display only employees who work in the Children's Rides department.

**2.** Select any cell within the filtered list, and then choose **Data, Sort** to display the Sort dialog box. You can sort a filtered list as you would any other list.

**3.** In the Sort By box, specify **DIVISION** in **Ascending** order.

**4.** In the first Then By box, specify **LAST** in **Ascending** order.

**5.** In the second Then By box, specify **FIRST** in **Ascending** order. Your dialog box should resemble Figure 12.11.

**Figure 12.11    Sorting the filtered list**

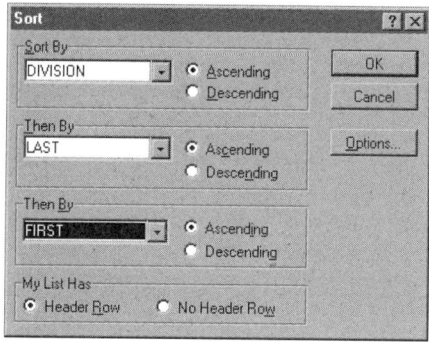

> **6.** Click on **OK** to sort the filtered list. Excel sorts only the rows that meet the filter condition.

## USING THE AUTOSUM TOOL WITH A FILTERED LIST

The AutoSum feature, like many others, will act upon only the visible rows in a filtered list. Better still, when you change the filter conditions, the formula created by the AutoSum feature will update accordingly.

Let's use the AutoSum button to find the total payroll for our filtered rows:

> **1.** Use F5 (the Go to shortcut key) to select cell **K99**. We'll use the AutoSum tool to find the total payroll.
>
> **2.** Click on the **AutoSum tool**, and then press **Enter** to enter the function.
>
> **3.** Select cell **K99** (if necessary), and then observe the formula bar. When you use the AutoSum tool to sum the values in a filtered list, Excel uses the SUBTOTAL function to calculate the sum of the values in only the visible cells of the range indicated in the function. In this case, the sum is $12,097.53.
>
> **4.** Filter the list to display only employees in a Shows department.
>
> **5.** Select and observe cell **K99**. Excel updated the SUBTOTAL function so that it displays the correct total for the rows that are now visible ($10,335.60).

### PRACTICE YOUR SKILLS

1. Sort the filtered list by division, then by last name, and then by first name, all in ascending order.

2. Save the file as **myfilter** in the Excel Work folder. The worksheet should resemble Figure 12.12.

**Figure 12.12**     **The filtered, sorted worksheet**

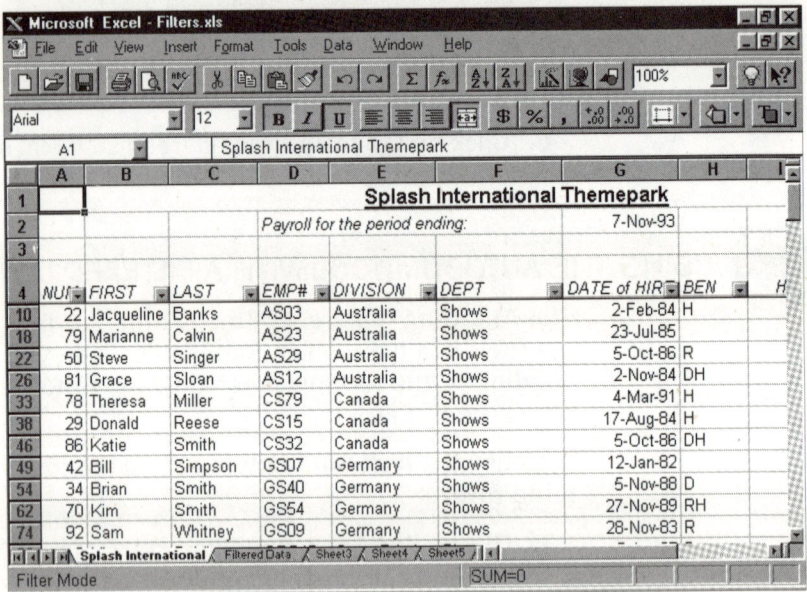

### PREVIEWING THE FILTERED LIST

In Filter mode, you can print only the visible rows as simply as you would print a regular worksheet. Let's preview our filtered list:

1. Click on the **Print Preview tool** to display a preview of the filtered worksheet. The data is too wide to fit on a single portrait-oriented page.

2. Click on the **Setup button** to display the Page Setup dialog box. The Page tab is active.

3. In the Orientation box, select **Landscape**, and then click on **OK** to return to the preview.

4. Point to the lower-right corner of the data and then click the mouse button to zoom the preview. The sum will be included in the printout.

5. Click on **Zoom** to unzoom the printout, and then click on **Close** to close the preview.

 OTHER COMMANDS IN FILTER MODE

As we mentioned earlier, many commands work differently in Filter mode. Table 12.3 lists how some commands differ when you are using the AutoFilter feature.

**Table 12.3**     **Using Commands in Filter Mode**

| Command or Feature | Effect in Filter Mode |
| --- | --- |
| AutoFill feature | Enters value of active cell in visible cells only; will not create series |
| Format, Cells command | Formats only visible cells in selected range |
| Chart Wizard | Creates chart from visible cells only |
| Clear and Copy commands | Affect only visible cells |
| Delete and Insert commands | Become *Delete Row* and *Insert Row* commands; you can insert or delete only whole, visible rows in a filtered list |
| Insert Copied Cells command | Becomes *Insert Paste Row* command; inserts a copied row at the insertion point |

### PRACTICE YOUR SKILLS

1. Choose **Data, Filter, AutoFilter** to turn off Filter mode and display the entire list.

2. Sort the list by the NUM column in ascending order.

3. Update the file.

## USING ADVANCED FILTER

You will probably use the AutoFilter feature for most of your filtering needs; however, Excel provides the Advanced Filter for creating more complex filters and for copying the filtered data to a different location. The Advanced Filter introduces the *criteria range*. To understand creating a criteria range, it's best that we start simply.

When you use AutoFilter to filter a list, you must give Excel two pieces of information for each column filter you create: the name of the column in which to look, and the value for which you are looking. When you use the Advanced Filter feature, you provide these same two pieces of information for each condition, or criterion, that you create. The difference is that with Advanced Filter, you must specify your criteria in a range of cells on the worksheet, and then tell Excel where to find that range.

### ENTERING CRITERIA IN A RANGE

When you create the criteria range, you must include the column through which you wish to filter your list and the value by which to filter. To create a criteria range,

- Move to a blank area of your worksheet. Microsoft recommends that you insert several blank rows above your list. This will make your criteria easy to find, and should not interfere with other data in your worksheet.

- In a cell in the blank area, enter the column heading of the column through which you wish to filter. Spelling counts here; it might be a good idea to copy the desired column heading from your list. That way, you'll be sure not to make any spelling errors.

- In the cell immediately below the column heading, enter the value for which you wish to look. Again, you must spell the value exactly as it appears in the list.

Let's create a criteria range above our good old Splash International payroll list.

1. Verify that Splash International is the active sheet.

2. Insert five blank rows at the top of the worksheet (select rows **1:5** and then choose **Insert** from the shortcut menu). This will give you plenty of room to create a fairly large criteria range.

3. Enter **DIVISION** in cell E1. The first row of a criteria range must include the headings of the columns by which you wish to filter the list. Case is not important, but spelling must be exact.

4. Enter **Canada** in cell E2 (see Figure 12.13). Again, spelling is important but case is not. At this point, using this criterion with the Advanced Filter command would be the equivalent of using AutoFilter and choosing Canada from the DIVISION column's drop-down list.

## USING ADVANCED FILTER TO FILTER A LIST

To filter a list based on a criteria range,

- Create the criteria range.

- Select any cell within the list.

- Choose *Data, Filter, Advanced Filter* to display the Advanced Filter dialog box.

- In the Action box, indicate whether you wish to filter the list in place (as with the AutoFilter command) or copy the filtered data to another location. We'll learn to copy the data to another location a bit later in the chapter.

- If you wish to change the reference in the List Range box, you can do so either by typing a reference to the desired range or by selecting the contents of the box and then dragging over the desired range in the worksheet. (**Note:** The list range must include a unique row of column headings. In some cases, Excel will not correctly identify your list range based on the

**Figure 12.13    Creating a criteria range**

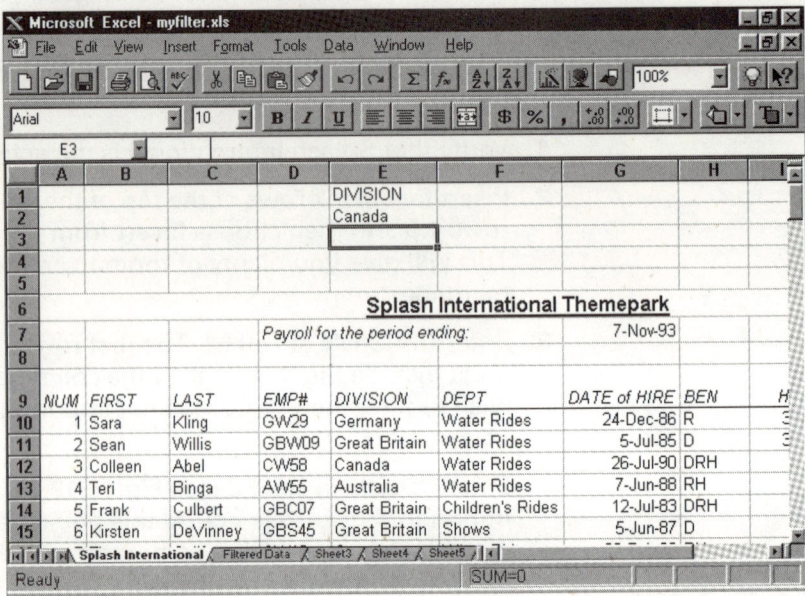

single cell you select. You should always verify that this reference is correct.)

- Select the information in the Criteria Range box and then either type or drag in the worksheet to specify the criteria range (be sure to use an absolute reference if you type). The criteria range must include both the column heading(s) and the value(s), but should not include any blank rows of cells.

- If you are copying the filtered list to another location, use the Copy To box to indicate where.

- Click on OK to filter the list.

Let's filter our payroll list using the criteria range we just created:

1. Select any cell within the list.

2. Choose **Data, Filter, Advanced Filter** to display the Advanced Filter dialog box. The reference in the List Range box is $A$9:$K$104, which is the correct reference to include the entire list *and* the row of column headings (row 9).

**3.** Click in the **Criteria Range box**, and then scroll up in the worksheet until you can see your criteria range. When you activate a box in which you can enter a reference, Excel allows you to use the scroll bars to move through the worksheet *without* leaving the dialog box. This can be very convenient.

**4.** Select the range **E1:E2** to enter the absolute reference 'Splash International'!$E$1:$E$2 in the Criteria Range box (you might not be able to see the entire reference). If the dialog box is making it difficult for you to see the criteria range, you can use its title bar to drag it out of the way. Your dialog box should resemble Figure 12.14. Now Excel knows everything it needs to know to filter the list.

**Figure 12.14**   **Using the Advanced Filter command to filter a list**

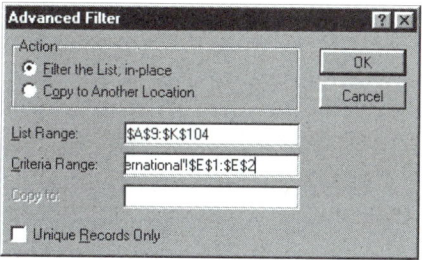

**5.** Click on **OK** to filter the list using the criterion in our criteria range. Excel displays only rows in which Canada appears in the DIVISION column.

## CREATING *OR* CONDITIONS IN A CRITERIA RANGE

With AutoFilter, remember how you created an OR condition by using the Custom AutoFilter? When you use the Advanced Filter, you create an OR condition in a criteria range by adding another row. The real strength of the Advanced Filter command is its ability to use criteria that are too complex to create using AutoFilter. For example, using AutoFilter, you can't filter a list looking for more than two specific values in a column.

When you add a row to a criteria range (or change its shape or location in any way, for that matter), you also will need to redefine the criteria range in the Advanced Filter dialog box.

Let's expand the criteria range to find employees whose division is either Canada, Germany, or Australia.

1. Display the entire list.

2. Select the range **A9:K104**. This range includes the cell containing the Subtotal function. We will name this range so we can refer to it more easily in the future.

3. Click in the **Name box** on the left side of the formula bar, type **List**, and then press **Enter** to name the selected range. You should try to get in the habit of naming ranges to which you refer often.

4. Enter **Germany** in cell E3 and **Australia** in cell E4 (see Figure 12.15).

**Figure 12.15**   **Creating an OR condition in a criteria range**

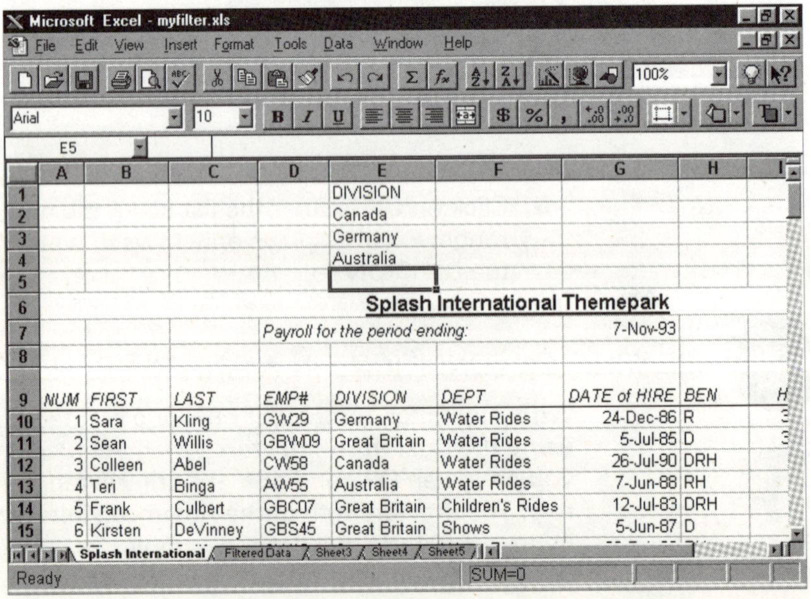

**5.** Select any cell within the list, and then choose **Data, Filter, Advanced Filter** to display the Advanced Filter dialog box. The Criteria Range box still displays the old criteria range ($E$1:$E$2), which is no longer correct. Excel "remembers" the ranges you used for your last filter. If you only change the values in your criteria range and not the location or shape you don't need to change the criteria range. However, we must redefine the range because we've changed the shape of the criteria range.

**6.** Edit the contents of the Criteria Range box to read **$E$1:$E$4** (see Figure 12.16). In this case, it is easier to edit the reference than it would be to select the contents of the box and then drag in the worksheet. You can use whichever method you prefer.

**7.** In the **List Range box**, highlight the cell references and enter the range name **List**. Now, we don't have to decipher the cell references to verify that the correct list range is selected.

**Figure 12.16    Editing the Advanced Filter dialog box**

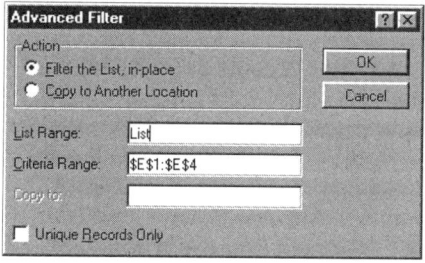

**8.** Click on **OK** to filter the list. Excel now displays rows for employees in either the Canadian division, German division, or Australian division.

## CREATING AND CONDITIONS IN A CRITERIA RANGE

You create AND conditions by adding columns to a criteria range. Each new column must have its own column heading. For example, to search for people in the Germany division and the Shows department, you could use the following criteria range:

|   | A | B |
|---|---|---|
| 1 | DIVISION | DEPT |
| 2 | Germany | Shows |

Remember, you will need to change the criteria range in the Advanced Filter dialog box when you add a column to your criteria range.

Let's change our criteria to find Great Britain-division employees who work in the Shows department:

1. Clear cells E3 and E4. We no longer need this criterion.

2. Enter **DEPT** in cell F1. This will be the heading for the second column in our criteria range.

3. Enter **Shows** in cell F2 (see Figure 12.17).

**Figure 12.17**    **Creating an AND condition in a criteria range**

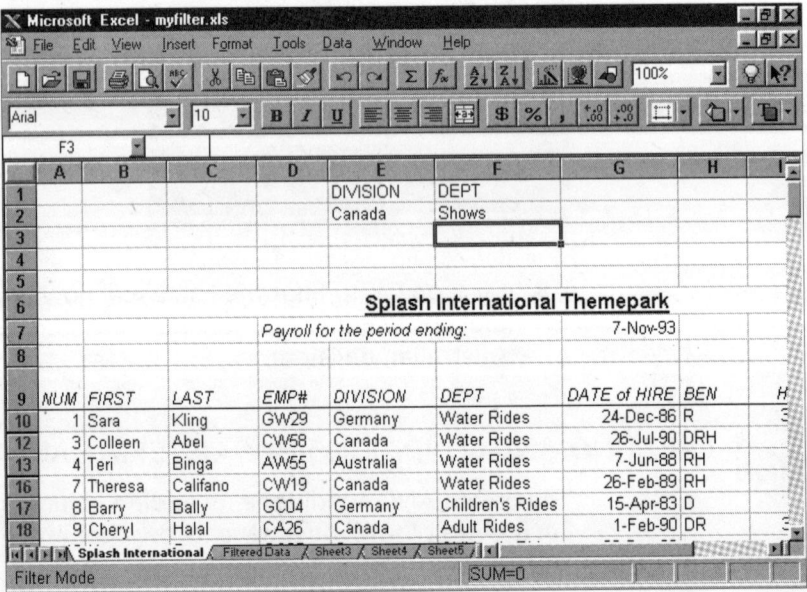

**4.** Select any cell within the list and display the Advanced Filter dialog box. We will need to change the contents of the Criteria Range box.

**5.** Edit the contents of the Criteria Range box to read **$E$1:$F$2**, and then click on **OK** to filter the list using the new criteria. There are only three employees in the Canadian division who are in the Shows department.

## COMBINING *AND* AND *OR* CONDITIONS

You can combine as many AND and OR conditions as you like in a criteria range. Just remember that each row in the criteria range represents a set of conditions that must all be met for Excel to include a row from the list in the filtered data. Some people use the analogy of a criteria range being like a series of gates. A row in the list goes to the first gate (the first criterion in the first row); if the row meets that condition, it moves to the next gate in the row to see if it meets their conditions, and so on. If the row from the list can't get through any one gate in a row in the criteria range, it moves to the next row of gates and tries again.

Take, for example, the following complicated criteria range:

|   | **A** | **B** | **C** | **D** |
|---|-------|-------|-------|-------|
| 1 | DIVISION | DEPT | HRS | RATE |
| 2 | Germany | Shows | >35 | <20 |
| 3 | Australia | Shows | >35 | <20 |
| 4 | Australia | Adult Rides | >35 | <20 |

These criteria would include rows where:

• The division is Germany *and* the department is Shows *and* the hours are greater than 35 *and* the rate is less than 20.
  or

• The division is Australia *and* the department is Shows *and* the hours are greater than 35 *and* the rate is less than 20.
  or

- The division is Australia *and* the department is Adult Rides *and* the hours are greater than 35 *and* the rate is less than 20.

Confused? Let's combine some conditions in our criteria range, and clear away some of the fog:

1. Enter **Great Britain** in cell E3. This will add an OR condition to find Great Britain-division employees as well as Canada-division employees who are in the Shows department.

2. Enter **Water Rides** in cell F3 to add an AND condition to the second row of our criteria.

3. Select a cell within the list (if necessary), and then display the Advanced Filter dialog box.

4. Change the criteria range to **$E$1:$F$3**, and click on **OK**. Excel now displays employees who are either in the Canada division and the Shows department, or the Great Britain division and the Water Rides department (See Figure 12.18).

**Figure 12.18**     **The result of combining AND and OR conditions**

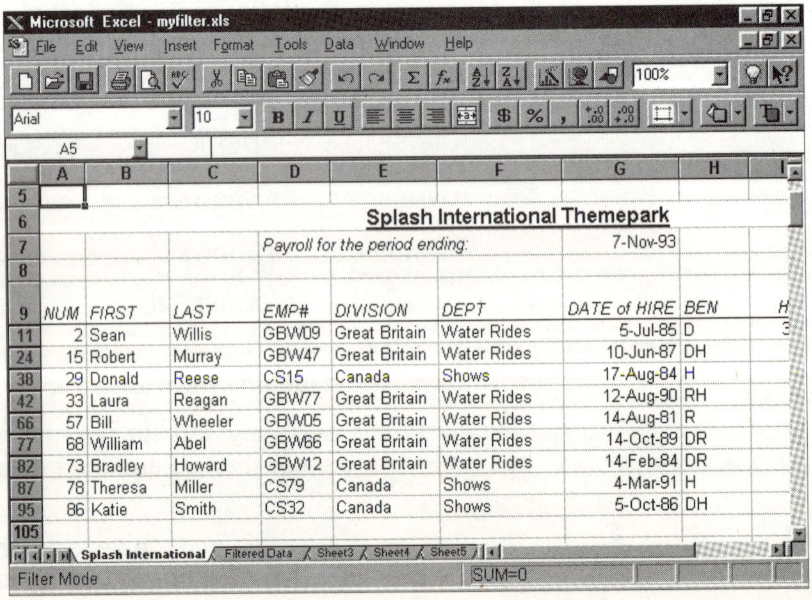

| NUM | FIRST | LAST | EMP# | DIVISION | DEPT | DATE of HIRE | BEN | H |
|---|---|---|---|---|---|---|---|---|
| 2 | Sean | Willis | GBW09 | Great Britain | Water Rides | 5-Jul-85 | D | 3 |
| 15 | Robert | Murray | GBW47 | Great Britain | Water Rides | 10-Jun-87 | DH | |
| 29 | Donald | Reese | CS15 | Canada | Shows | 17-Aug-84 | H | |
| 33 | Laura | Reagan | GBW77 | Great Britain | Water Rides | 12-Aug-90 | RH | |
| 57 | Bill | Wheeler | GBW05 | Great Britain | Water Rides | 14-Aug-81 | R | |
| 68 | William | Abel | GBW66 | Great Britain | Water Rides | 14-Oct-89 | DR | |
| 73 | Bradley | Howard | GBW12 | Great Britain | Water Rides | 14-Feb-84 | DR | |
| 78 | Theresa | Miller | CS79 | Canada | Shows | 4-Mar-91 | H | |
| 86 | Katie | Smith | CS32 | Canada | Shows | 5-Oct-86 | DH | |

Splash International Themepark

Payroll for the period ending:     7-Nov-93

## REDUCING THE CRITERIA RANGE

You can reduce the size of your criteria range to change your criteria without clearing any data. Let's reduce our criteria range, and then filter our list again:

1. Select any cell within the list and then display the Advanced Filter dialog box.

2. Edit the Criteria Range box to read **$E$1:$E$2**, and then click on **OK** to filter the list once again. The list displays only the rows for Canada-division employees.

3. Update the file.

# COPYING FILTERED DATA

If you would like to create a report from your filtered data, you might prefer to copy the filtered data to another location. You could do this by filtering your list and then performing a copy/paste procedure to place a copy somewhere else, but you also can use the Advanced Filter feature to place your filtered data somewhere else automatically.

## COPYING FILTERED DATA TO ANOTHER LOCATION ON THE WORKSHEET

To place a copy of your filtered data in another location,

- Create your criteria range and select a cell within your list.

- Display the Advanced Filter dialog box.

- Verify that the dialog box displays the correct list range and criteria range.

- In the **Action box,** select Copy To Another Location.

- In the Copy To box, indicate the upper-left corner cell of the range to which you wish to copy the filtered data.

- Click on OK.

Let's change our criteria, and then copy the filtered data to another location in our worksheet:

1. Show the entire list again.

2. In the range E1:F3, enter the appropriate criteria to find employees in the Germany division who are in the Shows department, and employees in the Canada division who are in the Adult Rides department.

3. Select any cell within the list and then display the Advanced Filter dialog box, which displays the correct list range. You will need to edit the Criteria Range box, however.

4. Edit the Criteria Range box to read **$E$1:$F$3**.

5. In the Action box, select **Copy To Another Location**.

6. Click in the **Copy To box** and type **M9** to indicate the upper-left corner of the range to which you wish to copy the filtered data (see Figure 12.19).

**Figure 12.19**     **Copying filtered data to another location**

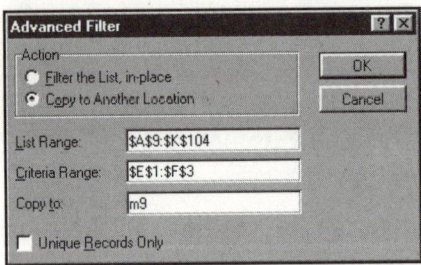

7. Click on **OK** and then scroll to observe the range M9:W18. Instead of filtering the list in place, Excel copied the filtered data here. Some of the cells display overflow markers because the column widths are not adequate.

8. Scroll back to observe the original list. Excel displays the entire list. When you copy filtered data to another location, Excel leaves the original list intact.

9. Update the file.

## COPYING FILTERED DATA TO A DIFFERENT WORKSHEET

Although it can be useful to copy filtered data to another place within a worksheet, it probably makes more sense to copy that data to a different worksheet. The Copy To option in the Advanced Filter dialog box will allow you to copy the filtered data to a location on the active worksheet only, however. There are two ways to get around this:

- Filter the list.
- Copy the filtered list.
- Paste the filtered list into a different worksheet.

OR

- Select a cell in the worksheet in which you would like the filtered data to appear.
- Display the Advanced Filter dialog box.
- Specify the List Range, Criteria Range, and the range to which you wish to copy the filtered data. Because lists can be very large, you might find it useful to name your list range, and then use that name in the List Range box.
- Click on OK.

Let's try copying our filtered data to another worksheet:

1. Select a cell within the original list and then display the Advanced Filter dialog box. The Filter The List, In Place option is selected.

2. Click on **OK** to filter the list in place, and then scroll to examine the filtered data we copied in the previous activity (in the range M9:W18). Most of this data is now hidden, because when you filter a list in place, it hides rows. This is one reason why it's a good idea to copy filtered data to a *different* worksheet.

3. Display the entire list again.

4. Activate the **Filtered Data** worksheet, and then display the Advanced Filter dialog box. All the settings are blank.

5. In the Action box, select **Copy To Another Location**.

6. Click in the **List Range box**, and then type **List** to indicate the name of the list range.

7. Click in the **Criteria Range box**, click on the **Splash International tab** to activate that worksheet, and then select the range **E1:F3** to enter *'Splash International'!$E$1:$F$3* in the Criteria Range box.

**8.** Enter **A1** in the Copy To box. Your dialog box should resemble Figure 12.20.

**Figure 12.20**     **Copying filtered data to a different worksheet**

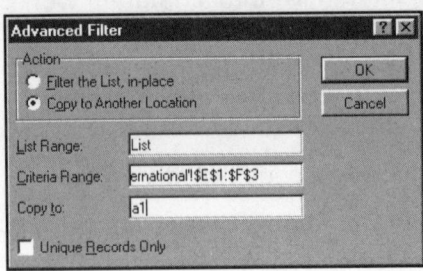

**9.** Click on **OK** to copy the filtered data to the Filtered Data worksheet. Notice that the column widths are incorrect (some numbers are not displayed, and some text is truncated). Excel provides an *AutoFormat* command that you can use to apply a built-in combination of formats to a range of worksheet cells. (Don't confuse this command with the charting AutoFormat command you used in Chapter 9; they are different.) Let's use AutoFormat to make a nice, tidy report out of this data.

**10.** Select any cell within the copied data, and then choose **Format, AutoFormat** to display the AutoFormat dialog box.

**11.** Select the format of your choice in the Table Format box, and then click on **OK** to format the entire table automatically. You might need to adjust the column widths.

**12.** Update and then close the file.

## PRACTICE YOUR SKILLS

You've learned a great deal about managing data over the course of the last two chapters. The following activity will give you a chance to practice some of those skills.

**1.** Open the file **Data Practice** from the Excel Work folder. This file contains three prepared worksheets. The first, called Practice, contains a list of cases for an attorney's firm.

**2.** Sort the list by last name in alphabetical order (Chapter 11).

**3.** Sort the list again, this time by case type in alphabetical order, breaking any ties with balance owed in descending order (Chapter 11). Your worksheet should resemble Figure 12.21.

**Figure 12.21**    **Sorting by case type and balance owed**

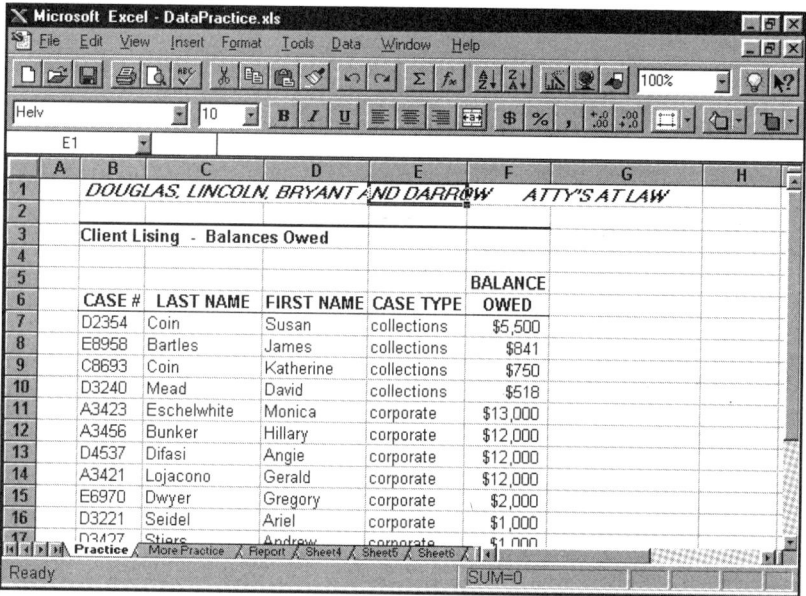

**4.** Turn on the **AutoFilter** feature for the case list (Chapter 12).

**5.** Display only the rows for cases where the type is *corporate* (Chapter 12).

**6.** Display all the rows again, and then display only the rows where the balance owed is greater than $10,000 (Chapter 12).

**7.** Leaving the current filter active on the OWED column, display only the remaining rows where the case type is *disability.* Only case number E2342 matches the criteria.

**8.** Turn off the AutoFilter feature (Chapter 12).

**9.** Save the file as **mydata** in the Excel Work folder.

10. If you want to continue with the next activity, leave the file open; if you do not wish to continue with the next activity, close the file.

The next activity will give you further opportunity to hone your data-management skills. (Be careful in this one; some of the steps are fairly tricky.)

1. Open the file **mydata** from the Excel Work folder (if necessary; it may be open from the previous activity), and then activate the **More Practice** worksheet. This worksheet contains payroll information for the ABC Company.

2. In the range **A5:A99**, enter a linear series of numbers beginning with **1** (Chapter 11).

3. Turn on the **AutoFilter** feature for the list (Chapter 12).

4. Filter the list to find only employees whose rows contain the text *Support* in the DEPT column (Chapter 12).

5. Add the further condition that the employees' dates of hire must be after 1/1/78 (Chapter 12). Your list should resemble Figure 12.22.

6. Turn off the AutoFilter feature, and then insert five blank rows at the top of the worksheet (Chapter 12).

7. Create a criteria range above the list that will find employees in any of the following groups (Chapter 12):

   • Chemicals-division employees who make more than $700.00

   • Electronics-division employees who make more than $700.00

   • Marketing division employees in the Sales Support department.
   **Hint:** This criteria range will be four rows by three columns in size. Each group represents one row in the criteria range.

8. Redisplay the entire list, then define the name **List** to refer to the range **A9:K104** (Chapter 12).

9. Activate the **Report** worksheet, and then copy the data filtered by your criteria to the range beginning in cell **A1** (Chapter 12).

**Figure 12.22**     **Employees in a support department hired after 1/1/78**

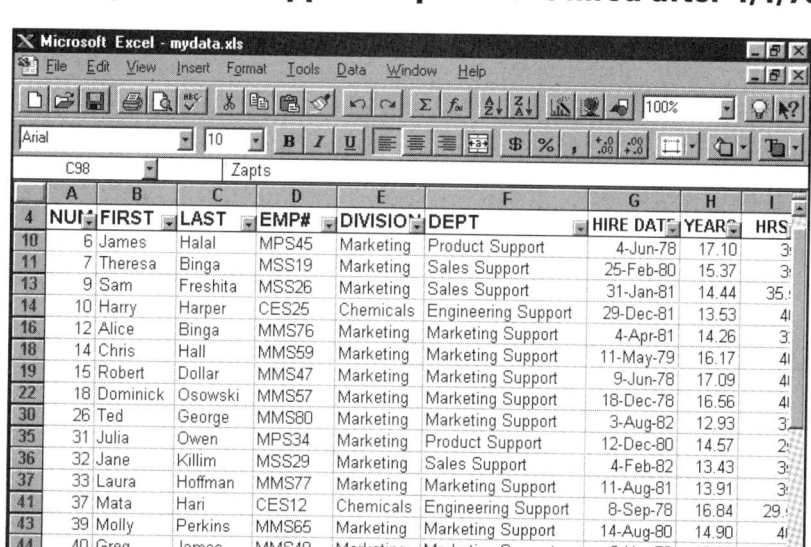

10. Sort the data in the Report worksheet by last name, then by first name (Chapter 11).

11. Use the **AutoFormat** command to apply the **Simple** table format to the data in the Report worksheet (Chapter 12). Your worksheet should resemble Figure 12.23.

12. Update and then close the file.

## SUMMARY

In this chapter, you learned how to filter a list using the AutoFilter feature. You learned how to filter based on the information in one or more columns, and you also learned how to create custom criteria. You learned how some commands work differently in Filter mode, allowing you to manage filtered lists very easily. You also learned how to create a criteria range and use the Advanced Filter command. Finally, you learned how to copy filtered data to different locations, either in the same worksheet or in a different one.

**Figure 12.23** **The completed report**

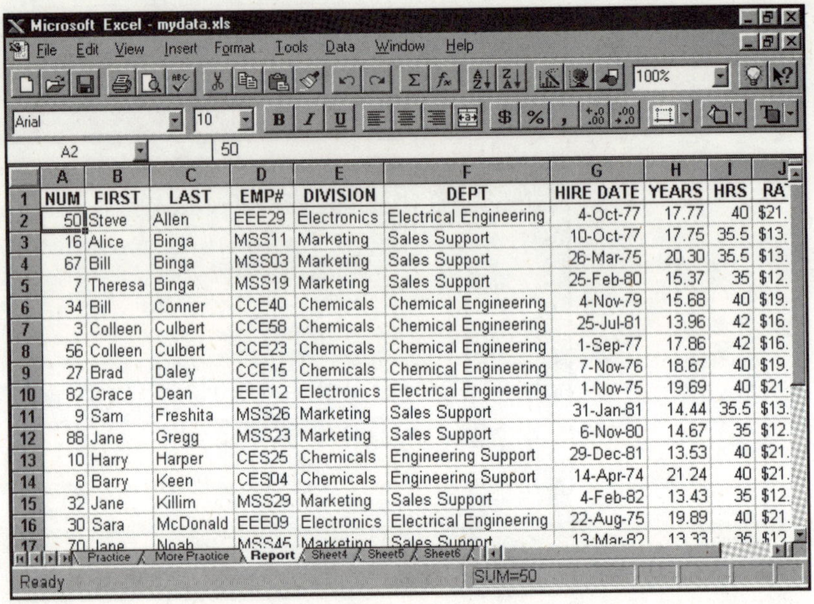

| | A | B | C | D | E | F | G | H | I | J |
|---|---|---|---|---|---|---|---|---|---|---|
| 1 | NUM | FIRST | LAST | EMP# | DIVISION | DEPT | HIRE DATE | YEARS | HRS | RA |
| 2 | 50 | Steve | Allen | EEE29 | Electronics | Electrical Engineering | 4-Oct-77 | 17.77 | 40 | $21. |
| 3 | 16 | Alice | Binga | MSS11 | Marketing | Sales Support | 10-Oct-77 | 17.75 | 35.5 | $13. |
| 4 | 67 | Bill | Binga | MSS03 | Marketing | Sales Support | 26-Mar-75 | 20.30 | 35.5 | $13. |
| 5 | 7 | Theresa | Binga | MSS19 | Marketing | Sales Support | 25-Feb-80 | 15.37 | 35 | $12. |
| 6 | 34 | Bill | Conner | CCE40 | Chemicals | Chemical Engineering | 4-Nov-79 | 15.68 | 40 | $19. |
| 7 | 3 | Colleen | Culbert | CCE58 | Chemicals | Chemical Engineering | 25-Jul-81 | 13.96 | 42 | $16. |
| 8 | 56 | Colleen | Culbert | CCE23 | Chemicals | Chemical Engineering | 1-Sep-77 | 17.86 | 42 | $16. |
| 9 | 27 | Brad | Daley | CCE15 | Chemicals | Chemical Engineering | 7-Nov-76 | 18.67 | 40 | $19. |
| 10 | 82 | Grace | Dean | EEE12 | Electronics | Electrical Engineering | 1-Nov-75 | 19.69 | 40 | $21. |
| 11 | 9 | Sam | Freshita | MSS26 | Marketing | Sales Support | 31-Jan-81 | 14.44 | 35.5 | $13. |
| 12 | 88 | Jane | Gregg | MSS23 | Marketing | Sales Support | 6-Nov-80 | 14.67 | 35 | $12. |
| 13 | 10 | Harry | Harper | CES25 | Chemicals | Engineering Support | 29-Dec-81 | 13.53 | 40 | $21. |
| 14 | 8 | Barry | Keen | CES04 | Chemicals | Engineering Support | 14-Apr-74 | 21.24 | 40 | $21. |
| 15 | 32 | Jane | Killim | MSS29 | Marketing | Sales Support | 4-Feb-82 | 13.43 | 35 | $12. |
| 16 | 30 | Sara | McDonald | EEE09 | Electronics | Electrical Engineering | 22-Aug-75 | 19.89 | 40 | $21. |
| 17 | 70 | Jane | Noah | MSS45 | Marketing | Sales Support | 13-Mar-82 | 13.33 | 35 | $12. |

The following quick reference guide summarizes some of the techniques you learned in this chapter.

| Desired Result | How to Do It |
|---|---|
| Filter list | Select cell within list; choose **Data, Filter, AutoFilter**; click on **drop-down arrow** for column(s) by which you wish to filter; choose value by which you wish to filter |
| Exit Filter mode | Choose **Data, Filter, AutoFilter** |
| Show all rows in Filter mode | Choose **Data, Filter, Show All** |
| Remove column filter | Choose **(All)** from column-heading drop-down list |
| Find blank or nonblank cells | Choose **(Blanks)** or **(NonBlanks)** from column-heading drop-down list |

| | |
|---|---|
| Find Top 10 items | Choose **(Top 10)** from column-heading drop-down list; specify options as desired; click on **OK** |
| Create AND or OR condition in column filter | Choose **(Custom)** from column-heading drop-down list; specify first criterion; click on **And** or **Or**; specify second criterion; click on **OK** |
| Find range of values | Display Custom AutoFilter dialog box; specify **>** (or **>=**) and lower value for first criterion; select **And**; specify **<** (or **<=**) and higher value for second criterion; click on **OK** |
| Sort filtered list | Select cell within list; choose **Data, Sort**; specify column(s) to sort by (and order); click on **OK** |
| Sum values in filtered list | Select cell below column you wish to sum; click on **AutoSum tool**; enter function |
| Create criteria range | Enter row of column headings and enter values by which to filter in row below column headings |
| Filter list using Advanced Filter | Create criteria range; select cell within list; choose **Data, Filter, Advanced Filter**; verify list range; specify criteria range; click on **OK** |
| Add AND condition to criteria | Add column to criteria range |
| Add OR condition to criteria | Add row to criteria range |
| Copy filtered data to another location | Create criteria range; select cell within list; choose **Data, Filter, Advanced Filter**; verify list range; specify criteria range; specify range to which to copy filtered data; click on **OK** |
| Copy filtered data to different worksheet | Activate worksheet to which you wish to copy filtered data and follow procedure to use Advanced Filter |

In the next chapter, you will learn to use the Data, Form command to maintain a list. You'll also learn two excellent ways to summa-

rize the data in a list: the Subtotals command, which creates subtotals for groups of data in a list; and database functions, which
allow you to perform functions upon only the list data that meets
certain criteria.

## IF YOU'RE STOPPING HERE

If you need to break off here, please exit from Excel. If you want
to proceed directly to the next chapter, please do so now.

# CHAPTER 13:
# MANAGING LISTS

Managing a List
by Using a Form

Using the Data,
Subtotals
Command

Using Database
Functions

**E**xcel provides many powerful features to help you manage and get information from your lists. In this chapter, you'll learn how to use the Data, Form command to add, delete, edit, and find rows in a list. We'll also learn how to summarize data in a list by using the Subtotals command. Finally, you'll learn how to use database functions to perform a calculation upon only the rows in a list that meet certain criteria.

When you're done working through this chapter, you will know

- How to add, find, edit, and delete rows in a list by using the Data, Form command

- How to use the Data, Subtotals command to summarize information in a list by categories

- How to use database functions to perform calculations on list entries only if they meet certain criteria

## MANAGING A LIST BY USING A FORM

For the purposes of this chapter, we'll need to get used to some new terminology for some familiar things. Another way to look at an Excel list is to call it a *database*. While this may sound like a fancy term, a database is simply a collection of related information. In Excel, a list with a single row of unique column headings is exactly the same as a database.

In an Excel database, each row of information is called a *record* (Frieda Binga's row becomes Frieda Binga's record). Each column in a database is called a *field* (the LAST column becomes the LAST field). The row of column headings, therefore, becomes the row of *field names*.

The *Data, Form* command provides a simple interface for managing the entries in a list, or database. The form displays one record at a time, and gives you many ways to manipulate that record, or even the entire database.

### USING A FORM TO BROWSE RECORDS

To use a form to view a database,

- Select any cell within the database.

- Choose *Data, Form.*

When you use this command, a dialog box appears that shows you one record at a time (we'll call this the *form*). The field names appear on the left side of the form, and the contents of each field for the given record appear next to those field names. If the field contains a value, as opposed to a formula, the form allows you to edit the field. The form will not let you edit a field that contains a formula.

While in the form, you can move through the database in a number of ways. Table 13.1 summarizes how you can browse records in the form.

**Table 13.1**     **Browsing Records in a Form**

| Desired Result | Technique |
|---|---|
| Display next record | Click on **down scroll arrow** (in form), click on **Find Next button**, or press **down arrow key**. |
| Display previous record | Click on **up scroll arrow** (in form), click on **Find Prev button**, or press **up arrow key**. |
| Display record ten down | Press **Page Down** or click below scroll box. |
| Display record ten up | Press **Page Up** or click above scroll box. |
| Move quickly through records | Drag **Scroll Box**. |

If you are not running Excel, please start it now. If there is a workbook on your screen (other than Book1), please close it.

Let's use a form to browse the records in a database:

1. Open the file **Data Mgmt** from the Excel Work folder. Once again, we see our familiar Splash International payroll data.

2. Place the active cell within the list, or database.

3. Choose **Data, Form** to display a form for the database (see Figure 13.1). The field names appear on the left side of the form, which displays information for the first record in the database (Sara Kling). Notice that there is no box for the value next to *GROSS PAY:*. Because this field contains a formula, Excel will not let you edit it on the form.

4. Click on the **down scroll arrow** in the form box several times. Each time you click on this arrow, the form displays the next record in the database, as shown in the top-right

**Figure 13.1    The form for the Splash International database**

Field names

Fields you can edit

Field you cannot edit

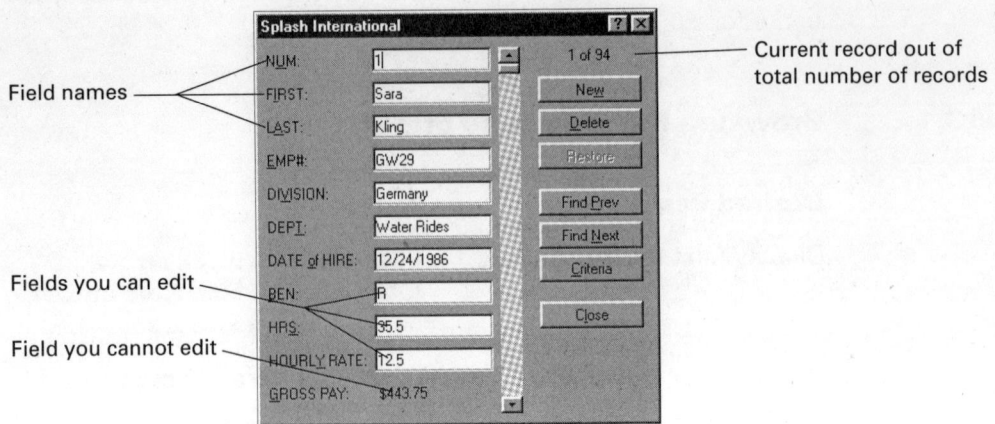

Current record out of
total number of records

corner of the form (2 of 94, 3 of 94, and so on). The down
arrow key on your keyboard will do the same thing.

5. In the scroll bar, click beneath the scroll box to move down
   ten records in the database. This is a quick way to move
   through a database in "chunks." The Page Down key will do
   the same thing.

6. Click on the **Find Prev button** to display the previous record
   in the database.

7. Click on the **Find Next button** to display the next record in
   the database. You can move through the records in many
   ways.

8. Drag the scroll box to the top of the scroll bar to display the
   first record once again.

 SETTING CRITERIA IN THE FORM

You can use the form to view only the records that meet certain
criteria. To do so,

• Display the form for the database.

• Click on the *Criteria button* to display a blank form in which
  you can enter criteria.

- Enter the value(s) for which you wish to look in the appropriate field(s). If you like, you can use wildcards or operators to create comparison criteria.

- Click on Find Next to find the next record in the database that meets the criteria, or click on Find Prev to find the previous record that meets the criteria.

Until you clear your criteria, the form will display only records that meet the current criteria. To clear the form criteria, click on Criteria and then click on *Clear*.

Let's set some criteria in the form:

1. Click on the **Criteria button** to display a blank form. Note that the top-right corner of the form now says *Criteria*.

2. Click in the **LAST box**, and then type **Binga** (or **binga**; case is insignificant) to indicate that you wish to find records for employees with the last name Binga (see Figure 13.2).

**Figure 13.2**  **Setting form criteria**

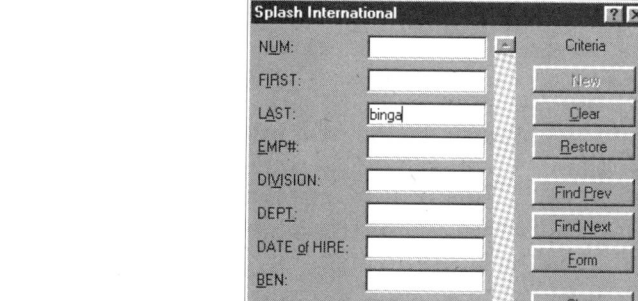

3. Click on **Find Next** to find the next record in the database that meets the specified criteria. The form displays the record for Teri Binga.

4. Click on **Find Next** a few more times to browse all the records that meet the criteria. When there are no more matching records in the database, Excel beeps at you.

5. Click on **Criteria** to display the criteria form again. The current criterion (LAST: Binga) is still active.

6. Click in the **DEPT box** and then type **Adult Rides** to add an AND condition to your criteria (see Figure 13.3). These criteria will display records only if the last name is Binga *and* the department is Adult Rides.

**Figure 13.3**     **Creating an AND condition using form criteria**

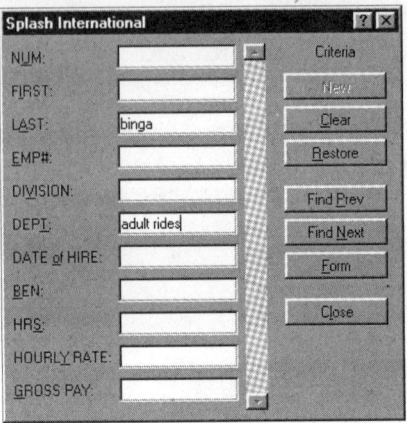

7. Click on **Find Next** to display the next matching record. Excel beeps at you and then displays Erin Binga's record. Excel beeped because the form "remembers" where you last were in the list (at the bottom). To see the other matching records, we'll need to use the Find Prev button.

8. Click on **Find Prev** a couple of times to view the other matching records. Now only two records meet the criteria.

9. Click on **Criteria** to display the criteria form and then click on **Clear** to clear the current criteria.

10. Click on **Form** to return to the regular form for the database, then drag the scroll box to the top of the scroll bar to display record number 1.

PRACTICE YOUR SKILLS

1. Display the criteria form.

2. Set criteria to find employees in the Germany division who are in the Shows department (see Figure 13.4).

**Figure 13.4**     **Creating more criteria**

3. Browse through the records that meet the criteria (there should be four).

4. Clear the current criteria, and then return to the first record in the form.

## EDITING A RECORD

You can edit a record very easily by using a form. Simply display the record you wish to edit, and then edit the desired field. The only limitation is that you cannot use the form to edit a field that contains a formula. If you make a mistake while editing a record, you can click on the Restore button to return the record to its previous state.

Let's find Frieda Binga's record, and then give her a raise:

1. Display the criteria form, and then set the criteria to find Frieda Binga's record (enter **Frieda** in the FIRST field, and **Binga** in the LAST field).

2. Find the matching record (click on **Find Next**).

3. Double-click in the **HOURLY RATE box** to select the data it contains, and then type **13.5** (see Figure 13.5). The PAY field, which contains a formula, will not be updated until you leave this record.

4. Display the criteria form and clear the current criteria.

**Figure 13.5** **Editing a record in the form**

 DELETING A RECORD

To use a form to delete a record from a database,

• In the form, display the record you wish to delete.

• Click on the *Delete* button. Because deleting a record removes it permanently from your database, Excel will ask you to confirm that you really want to do it.

• Click on OK.

Let's use the form to delete a record from our database:

1. In the EMP# field on the criteria form, enter **AA25**.

2. Click on **Find Prev** to find the record that meets this criterion (Lindsey Winger). Note that the record number is 65, as shown in the Num field and the top right corner of the form (65 of 94).

**3.** Click on the **Delete button**. Excel asks if you're sure you want to permanently delete the record (see Figure 13.6).

**4.** Click on **OK** to delete the record permanently.

**Figure 13.6**     **Deleting a record**

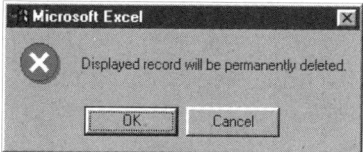

## ADDING A NEW RECORD

You also can use the form to add new records to a database. To do so, simply click on the New button and then enter the field information for the new record. You can move from field to field within the form by pressing Tab. Let's try it:

**1.** Click on the **New** button to display a new, blank record in the form. The insertion point is in the NUM field.

**2.** Type **95** and then press **Tab** to move to the next field, FIRST.

**3.** Type your first name and then press **Tab** to move to the next field, LAST.

**4.** Type your last name and then press **Tab** to move to the next field, EMP#.

**5.** Use Figure 13.7 to fill in the rest of the fields in your new record (of course, you will see your name instead of Laurie Perry's).

**6.** Click on **Close** to close the form and return to the worksheet.

**7.** Scroll to observe rows 68 and 69. Record number 65 (Lindsey Winger) no longer appears in the list, because you deleted it.

**8.** Scroll to observe cell J77. Frieda Binga's hourly rate is now $13.50.

**Figure 13.7**     **The new record**

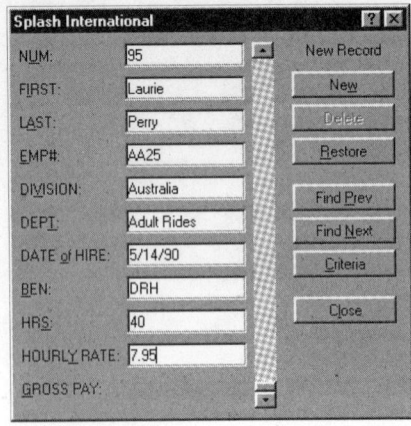

9. Scroll to observe row 98. Your new record appears at the bottom of the list.

10. Save the file as **mylist** in the Excel Work folder.

## USING THE DATA, SUBTOTALS COMMAND

The Subtotals command in the Data menu provides an exceptional way to summarize data in a list by allowing you to perform various calculations on each group of rows that contain certain information in a particular column. For example, if you wanted to summarize your list by division, you could sort the list and then use the Subtotals command to find the total payroll for each division. When you create subtotals, Excel creates an outline structure in your worksheet that lets you view all the rows, or only the subtotal information.

### CREATING SUBTOTALS FOR A LIST

To create subtotals for groups of rows in a list,

• Sort the list by the column containing the values by which you wish to group the rows. For example, if you want to create subtotals for each division, begin by sorting the list by division.

- Select any cell within the list and choose *Data, Subtotals* to display the Subtotal dialog box.

- In the At Each Change In box, select the column by which your list is sorted. This is very important; if you attempt to create subtotals by a column other than that by which a list is sorted, you will get strange results, indeed.

- In the Use Function box, specify the function you would like to use for your subtotals. The available functions are *Sum, Count, Average, Max, Min, Product, Count Nums, StdDev, StdDevp, Var,* and *Varp.*

- In the Add Subtotal To box, check each column for which you would like to see subtotals. Be sure that the function you are using makes sense for the column you choose. For example, it wouldn't make sense to find the standard deviation for a column containing text.

- Uncheck *Replace Current Subtotals* if there currently are subtotals you do not wish to replace.

- Check *Page Break Between Groups* if you wish to be able to print each subtotal group on a separate page.

- Uncheck *Summary Below Data* if you wish each subtotal to appear above its associated data. In most cases, you will want the subtotals below the data.

Let's create subtotals by division for our list:

1. Sort the Splash International payroll list by division in ascending order (select a cell in the DIVISION column, and click on the **Sort Ascending tool**). You first must sort a list before you can create subtotals for it.

2. Select any cell within the list (if necessary), and then choose **Data, Subtotals** to display the Subtotal dialog box.

3. Select **DIVISION** from the At Each Change In drop-down list to indicate that you wish to create subtotals for each distinct division in the list.

4. Verify that *Sum* appears in the Use Function box, and that GROSS PAY is the only checked option in the Add Subtotal To box. The dialog box should resemble Figure 13.8.

**Figure 13.8**    **Creating subtotals**

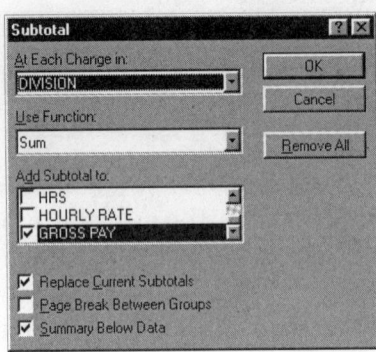

5. Click on **OK** to insert the subtotals in the list. There are some strange symbols to the left of the worksheet, but we'll get to that shortly.

6. Update the file.

## EXAMINING A SUBTOTALED LIST

When you create subtotals, Excel creates an *outline structure* for the rows in the list. Basically, this gives you the flexibility to view only the grand-total row, only subtotal rows, or all the rows. The numbered buttons in the upper-left corner of the worksheet are called *row-level symbols*. You can click on these to view different levels of detail in the worksheet. There also are two kinds of symbols in the margin of an outlined worksheet to the left of each subtotal row:

* Click on a *show detail symbol* (a button with a plus sign) to expand a part of the outline that currently is hidden.

* Click on a *hide detail symbol* (a button with a minus sign) to hide a level of detail.

Let's examine our subtotaled list:

1. Select and observe the contents of cell **K27** (see Figure 13.9). This is a subtotal function that calculates the total gross pay for the Australia division.

**Figure 13.9**   **A subtotal function**

Row-level symbols ——

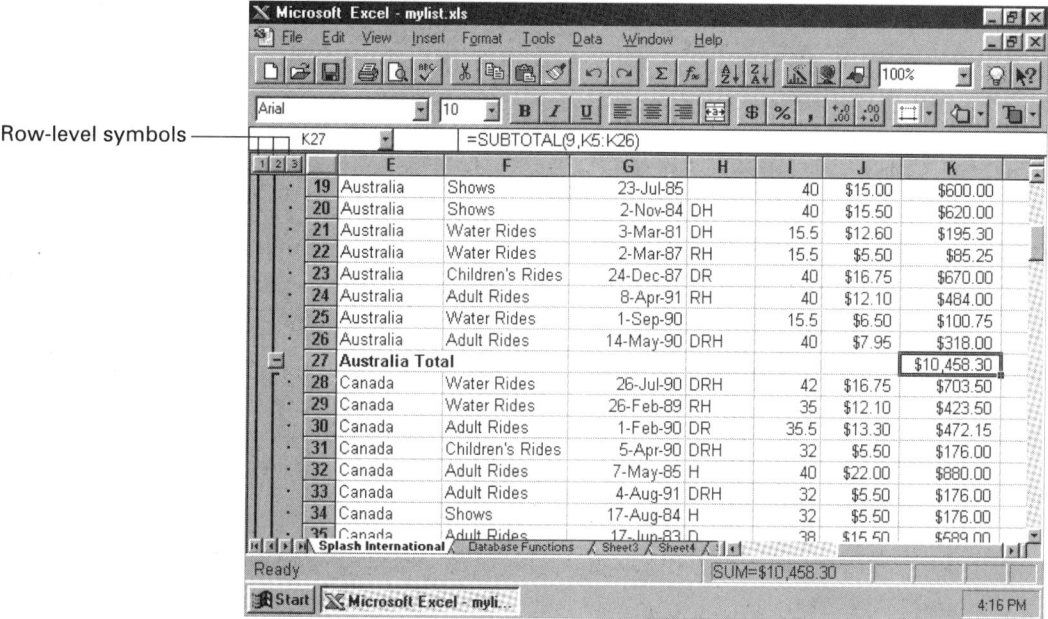

2. Select and examine cells **K43**, **K71**, and **K102**. These cells contain the subtotals for the Canada, Germany, and Great Britain divisions, respectively.

3. Select and examine cell **K103**. This cell contains the grand total for the entire list.

4. Scroll to the top of the list, and then click on the **row-level symbol 1** to view only the grand-total information (refer to Figure 13.9). All the other rows in the list are hidden.

5. Click on the **row-level symbol 2** to view the subtotal information for the divisions (see Figure 13.10).

6. Click on the **show detail symbol** to the left of the Canada Total row to display the detail information for the Canada division (refer to Figure 13.10).

7. Click on the **hide detail symbol** next to the Canada Total row to hide the detail information for the Canada division (refer to Figure 13.10).

8. Click on **row-level symbol 3** to display the entire list again.

**Figure 13.10**     **Viewing the second level of detail**

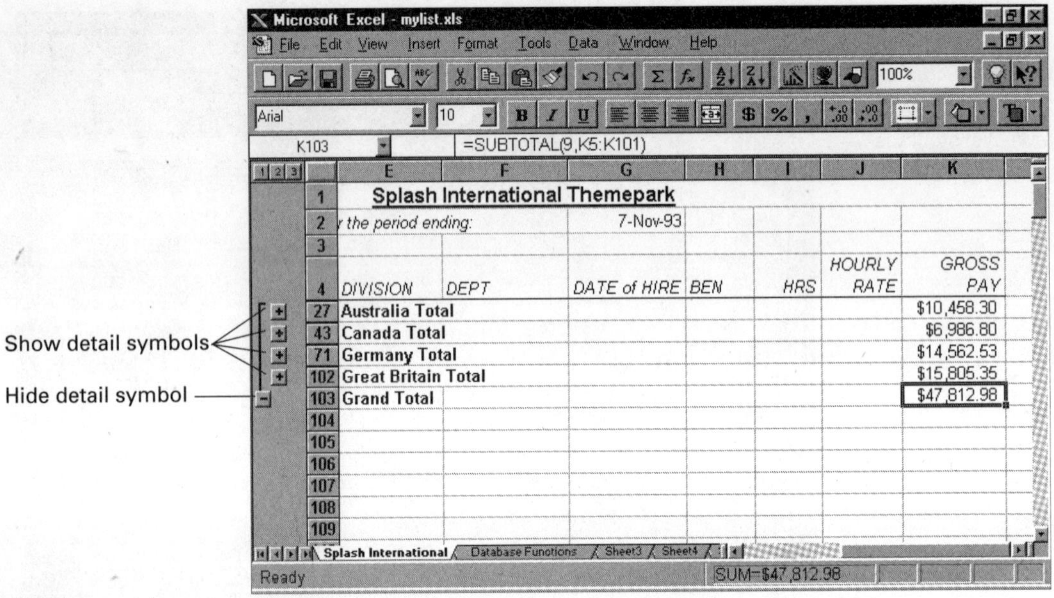

| | E | F | G | H | I | J | K |
|---|---|---|---|---|---|---|---|
| 1 | Splash International Themepark | | | | | | |
| 2 | r the period ending: | | 7-Nov-93 | | | | |
| 3 | | | | | | | |
| 4 | DIVISION | DEPT | DATE of HIRE | BEN | HRS | HOURLY RATE | GROSS PAY |
| 27 | Australia Total | | | | | | $10,458.30 |
| 43 | Canada Total | | | | | | $6,986.80 |
| 71 | Germany Total | | | | | | $14,562.53 |
| 102 | Great Britain Total | | | | | | $15,805.35 |
| 103 | Grand Total | | | | | | $47,812.98 |

K103    =SUBTOTAL(9,K5:K101)

Show detail symbols

Hide detail symbol

SUM=$47,812.98

## CHARTING THE SUBTOTALS IN A LIST

Let's put together a few of the tricks we've learned in this book and create a pie chart from our subtotal data:

1. Display the second-row level of detail in the worksheet (just the subtotals).

2. Select the range **E27:E102** (this should be only four cells in the collapsed worksheet), and then add the range **K27:K102** to the selection (hold down **Ctrl** while selecting the range). The division-total labels and the division totals should be selected, as shown in Figure 13.11.

3. Choose **Insert, Chart, As New Sheet** to create a chart from the selected data. Excel displays the first Chart Wizard dialog box. We've already indicated the range to chart.

4. Click on **Next** to display the second Chart Wizard dialog box.

5. Click on the **Pie option** and then click on **Next** to display the third Chart Wizard dialog box.

**Figure 13.11**  **Preparing to chart the subtotals**

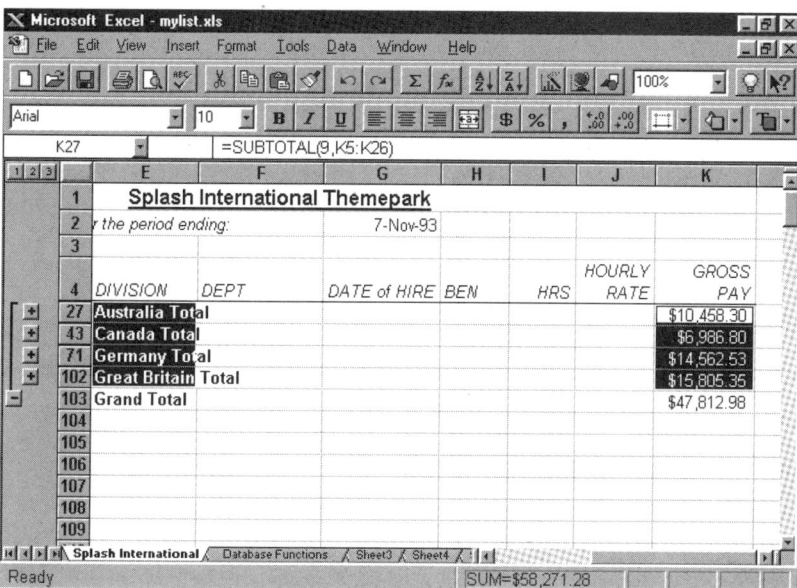

6. Click on option **7** to specify that the pie chart should have labels and percentages, and then click on **Next** to move to the next Chart Wizard dialog box.

7. Click on **Next** to accept the sample and move to the last Chart Wizard dialog box.

8. In the Chart Title box, type **Gross Pay by Division**, and then click on **Finish** to create the chart (see Figure 13.12). You could use your formidable charting skills at this point to make any desired changes to the chart.

9. Update the worksheet.

## USING DATABASE FUNCTIONS

You can use *database functions* to perform calculations on a certain field in a database, using only those records that match given criteria. For example, you could use the DSUM function to add up the values in the GROSS PAY field for all employees who work a certain number of hours.

**Figure 13.12**  **Charting the subtotal data**

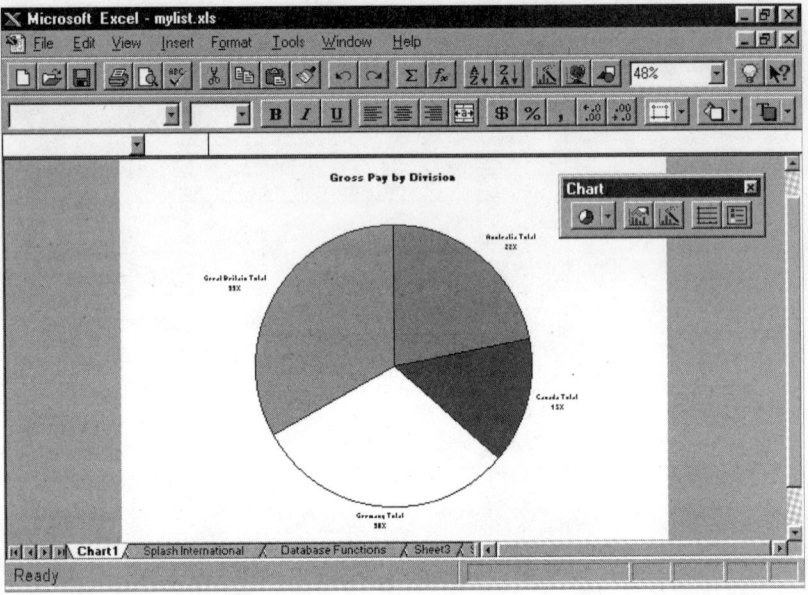

## EXAMINING A DATABASE FUNCTION

To use a database function, you must specify a database (a list with a unique row of column headings), a field (or column) to be calculated, and the criteria by which to determine upon which records (or rows) the function will act. Let's take a look at a database function that's been set up for us:

1. Activate the **Database Functions** worksheet. There is a payroll list beginning in row 9 and a criteria range at the top of the worksheet. There is a function in cell F5 that calculates the total payroll based on the current criteria (there are none at the moment). The total payroll for the list is $48,278.98.

2. Enter **Germany** in cell E3. When you change the criteria, the value of the function in cell F5 changes, as well. The total payroll for Germany-division employees is $14,562.53.

3. Select and examine the contents of cell F5 (see Figure 13.13). The first argument of the function represents the database upon which the function will act. In this case, the function uses the name *List* as this argument.

**Figure 13.13**   **Examining a database function**

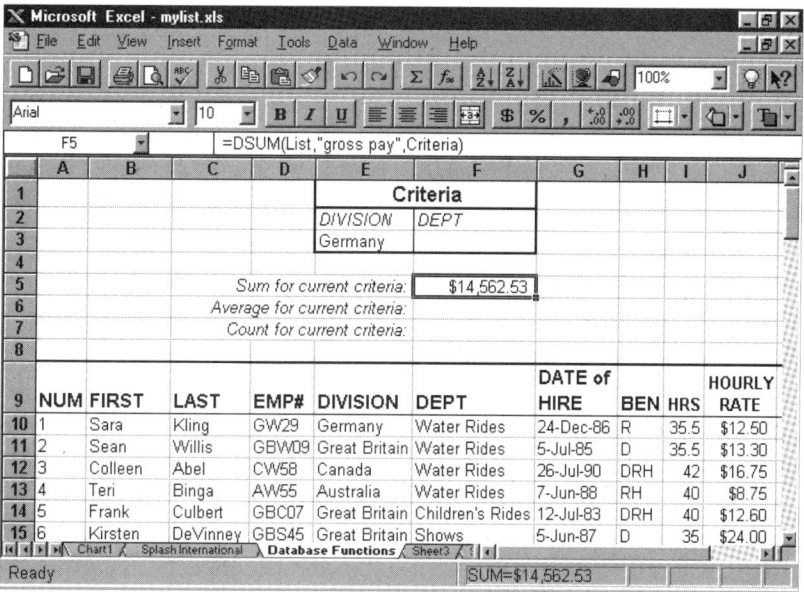

4. Click on the **drop-down arrow** next to the Name box (in the formula bar), and then select **List** to select the named range. The folks at PC Learning Labs defined this name to refer to the entire list, or database (all the records *and* the row of field names).

5. Select and examine cell **F5** again. The second argument of the function, "gross pay," is a text reference to the column heading for the column the function should calculate. The third argument represents the criteria range that determines which records should be acted upon by the function. In this case, the function uses the named range Criteria.

6. Use the Name drop-down list to select the named range **Criteria**. The range E2:F3 contains the criteria for the database function. If you are going to use database functions, it's a good idea to define names for your database and criteria ranges to make it easy to refer to them in your functions.

## CREATING A DATABASE FUNCTION

As we've seen, it's easiest to use database functions when you've defined names for your database and criteria ranges. Every database function has the syntax

D*function*(*database,field,criteria*)

- The *database* argument is a reference to the range that contains the database (or list). This range must include a row of unique field names.

- The *field* argument is either a reference to the cell containing the name of the field on which you wish to perform the calculation, or the name of the field *as text*. You must enclose a text argument in quotation marks (for example, you would use "EMP#" for a field called EMP#).

- The *criteria* argument is a reference to the range containing the criteria that determine the records upon which the function will act.

Let's create a database function to calculate the average gross pay for employees who meet the criteria:

1. Select cell **F6** and then click on the **Function Wizard tool** to display the first Function Wizard dialog box.

2. Select **Database** in the Function Category box, select **DAVERAGE** in the Function Name box, and then click on **Next** to display the second Function Wizard dialog box.

3. In the Database argument box, type **List** (the name of your database range), and then press **Tab** to move to the Field argument box.

4. Type **"gross pay"** (you must include the quotation marks), and then press **Tab** to move to the Criteria argument box.

5. Type **Criteria** (the name of your criteria range). Your dialog box should resemble Figure 13.14.

6. Click on **Finish** to create the function in cell F6. The formula bar should display

```
=DAVERAGE(List,"gross pay",Criteria)
```

**Figure 13.14    Using Function Wizard to create a database function**

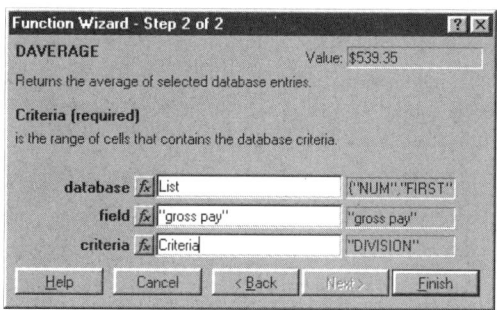

7. Change the criteria so that the database functions will perform calculations only on employees in the Australia division who are in the Adult Rides department.

8. Update the file. Your worksheet should resemble Figure 13.15.

**Figure 13.15    The new function and criteria**

| | A | B | C | D | E | F | G | H | I | J |
|---|---|---|---|---|---|---|---|---|---|---|
| 1 | | | | | Criteria | | | | | |
| 2 | | | | | *DIVISION* | *DEPT* | | | | |
| 3 | | | | | Australia | Adult Rides | | | | |
| 4 | | | | | | | | | | |
| 5 | | | | Sum for current criteria: | | $1,908.75 | | | | |
| 6 | | | | Average for current criteria: | | $477.19 | | | | |
| 7 | | | | Count for current criteria: | | | | | | |
| 8 | | | | | | | | | | |
| 9 | NUM | FIRST | LAST | EMP# | DIVISION | DEPT | DATE of HIRE | BEN | HRS | HOURLY RATE |
| 10 | 1 | Sara | Kling | GW29 | Germany | Water Rides | 24-Dec-86 | R | 35.5 | $12.50 |
| 11 | 2 | Sean | Willis | GBW09 | Great Britain | Water Rides | 5-Jul-85 | D | 35.5 | $13.30 |
| 12 | 3 | Colleen | Abel | CW58 | Canada | Water Rides | 26-Jul-90 | DRH | 42 | $16.75 |
| 13 | 4 | Teri | Binga | AW55 | Australia | Water Rides | 7-Jun-88 | RH | 40 | $8.75 |
| 14 | 5 | Frank | Culbert | GBC07 | Great Britain | Children's Rides | 12-Jul-83 | DRH | 40 | $12.60 |
| 15 | 6 | Kirsten | DeVinney | GBS45 | Great Britain | Shows | 5-Jun-87 | D | 35 | $24.00 |

## PRACTICE YOUR SKILLS

1. In cell F7, enter the function **DCOUNTA** to find the total number of employees who meet the criteria (do *not* use the DCOUNT function). Use any field except BEN as the field argument (BEN will not work, because some records have no information in this field).

2. Change the criteria so that the database functions will perform calculations only on employees in the Great Britain division who are in the Shows department (see Figure 13.16).

3. Update and then close the file.

**Figure 13.16**   **The completed worksheet with the new criteria**

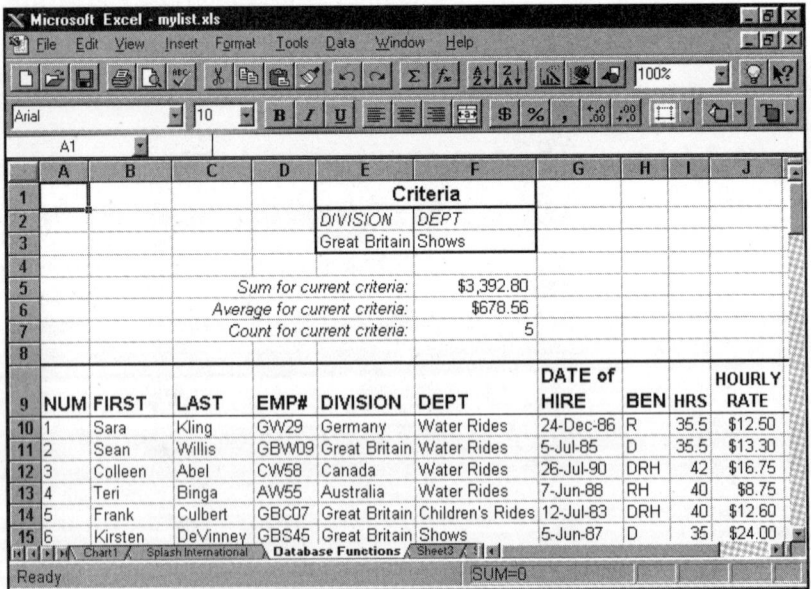

## SUMMARY

In this chapter, you learned a few more data-management techniques. First we learned how to use a form to browse, delete from, add to, or edit a database. Then we learned how to summarize data in a list by creating subtotals, or by using database functions.

With this chapter, your foundation in Excel database management is complete. Congratulations! May your databases live long and prosper!

The following quick reference guide summarizes some of the techniques you learned in this chapter.

| Desired Result | How to Do It |
|---|---|
| Use form with database | Select cell within database (list) and choose **Data, Form** |
| Set criteria in form | Click on **Criteria**, enter desired criteria, click on **Find Next** (or **Find Prev**) |
| Delete record from database | Display record in form, click on **Delete**, click on **OK** |
| Add new record to database | In form, click on **New**, then enter field information for new record |
| Create subtotals for list | Sort list by column by which you wish to create groups to subtotal; select cell within list; choose **Data, Subtotals**; select column by which to create groups; select function to use; select column(s) to which to add subtotals; check (or uncheck) any other desired options; click on **OK** |
| Create database function | Create criteria table and enter desired database function in cell, specifying database, field, and criteria arguments |

## IF YOU'RE STOPPING HERE

If you need to break off here, please exit from Excel. If you wish to review material from an earlier chapter or proceed to one of the appendices, please do so now.

# APPENDIX A:
# INSTALLING EXCEL FOR WINDOWS 95

Installation
Requirements

Installing Excel
For Windows 95
on Your Computer

This appendix contains instructions for installing Excel for Windows 95 on your computer.

## INSTALLATION REQUIREMENTS

Before you install Excel for Windows 95, three requirements must be met:

- Windows 95 must be installed on your computer.

- If you run a virus protection program on your computer, you must turn it off. After installing Excel, you can turn it back on.

- There must be enough free space on your hard disk to hold the Excel for Windows 95 program files. Depending upon the installation option you choose, you'll need a minimum of 18 to 38 megabytes (18,000,000 to 38,000,000 bytes) of free hard-disk space. (Excel will tell you during the installation if you have enough free space.) We recommend that you have *at least* 30 (preferably 35) free hard-disk megabytes before starting the installation process; that way, you'll be able to choose a complete installation option (our suggested choice) and still have several megabytes of free space. (It's not a good idea to work with a filled-to-the-brim hard disk; Windows tends to run slowly, and other far more mysterious and potentially traumatic things can sometimes happen.)

To find out how many free hard-disk bytes you have, perform these steps:

1. From the Start menu, choose Programs, Windows Explorer to view the folders and their contents.

2. Select the hard drive (C:) icon.

3. Click the right mouse button to display the shortcut menu. Choose Properties to open the (C:) Properties dialog box. On the General tab, the number of free hard-disk bytes is displayed numerically and graphically. (Remember, 1 megabyte is 1,000,000 bytes.)

4. If you need to free up more hard-disk space, delete files. But first, be sure to back up any you want to save!

## INSTALLING EXCEL FOR WINDOWS 95 ON YOUR COMPUTER

After meeting the three requirements listed above, perform these steps to install Excel for Windows 95:

1. Start **Windows 95.**

**2.** Insert the disk labeled *Setup* in the appropriate drive. If you are installing Excel from a network, then you will be prompted for the drive and directory later in the installation process.

**3.** In the taskbar, click on **Start**, point to **Settings**, and choose **Control Panel**.

**4.** Click on the **Add/Remove Programs** icon and verify that the Install/Uninstall tab is active.

**5.** Click on the **Install** button to start the installation.

**6.** Follow the onscreen instructions to complete the installation. Here are some guidelines:

- For help understanding the contents of an installation dialog box, click on its **Help button**.

- In general, accept all installation defaults (by clicking on **Continue** or **OK**).

- When asked to choose your installation option, proceed as follows. Choose either **Typical** or **Custom** to install Excel. The Typical option installs an average Excel setup; you'll have access to many advanced features. The **Custom** option enables you to choose specific components. The required amount of hard-disk space is listed next to each component. (**Note**: Do not choose Compact, as this will prevent you from completing the hands-on activities in this book.) We strongly recommend that you choose the Custom option and install all Excel components, provided you have the necessary free hard-disk space.

- If you discover that you don't have enough free hard-disk space to install your chosen option, either choose different Custom components or exit, free up the required hard-disk space, then repeat your original installation.

**7.** When the installation is complete, you are returned to Windows 95. To start Excel, display the Start menu, point to Programs and click on **Excel**.

# APPENDIX B: KEYSTROKE REFERENCE

Entering and
Editing Data

Moving and
Selecting

Formatting Data

Displaying and
Printing

Working with
Charts

Working with Lists
and Databases

Using Pivot Tables

Choosing Menu
Commands

Special-Purpose
Keys

**K**eyboardists, rejoice! You can perform most Excel actions with the mouse *or* the keyboard. Choose whichever method—or combination of methods—works best for you.

This appendix is a comprehensive keyboard reference. Several of the keystrokes listed pertain to topics not discussed in this book.

# ENTERING AND EDITING DATA

 **ENTERING DATA**

| | |
|---|---|
| F2 | Activates the cell and formula bar |
| Enter | Carries out an action |
| Esc | Cancels an action |
| F4 | Repeats the last action |
| Ctrl+Z | Undoes the last action |
| Ctrl+Shift++ (*plus sign*) | Inserts blank cells |
| Ctrl+- (*minus sign*) | Deletes the selection |
| Del | Clears the selection of formulas and data |
| Ctrl+X | Cuts the selection |
| Ctrl+C | Copies the selection |
| Ctrl+V | Pastes the selection |
| Backspace | Activates and clears the formula bar when a cell is selected, or deletes the character to the left of the insertion point |
| Shift+F2 | Edits a cell note |
| F3 | Pastes a name into a formula |
| Shift+F3 | Displays the Function Wizard |
| Ctrl+A | After typing a valid function name in a formula, displays step 2 of the Function Wizard |
| Ctrl+Shift+A | After typing a valid function name in a formula, inserts the argument names and parentheses for the function |
| Ctrl+F3 | Defines a name |

| | |
|---|---|
| Ctrl+Shift+F3 | Creates names from cell text |
| F9 *or* Ctrl+= | Calculates all sheets in all open workbooks |
| Shift+F9 | Calculates the active sheet |
| Alt+= | Inserts the AutoSum formula |
| Ctrl+; | Enters the date |
| Ctrl+Shift+: | Enters the time |
| Ctrl+D | Fills down |
| Ctrl+R | Fills right |
| Enter | Moves down through a selection |
| Shift+Enter | Moves up through a selection |
| Tab | Moves right through a selection |
| Shift+Tab | Moves left through a selection |

## INSERTING, DELETING, COPYING, AND MOVING

| | |
|---|---|
| Ctrl+X | Cuts the selection |
| Ctrl+C | Copies the selection |
| Ctrl+V | Pastes the selection |
| Del | Clears the selection of formulas and data |
| Ctrl+Shift++ (*plus sign*) | Inserts blank cells |
| Ctrl+- (*minus sign*) | Deletes the selection |
| Ctrl+Z | Undoes the last action |

 **WORKING IN CELLS OR THE FORMULA BAR**

| | |
|---|---|
| F2 | Activates the cell and formula bar |
| = | Starts a formula |
| Del | Deletes the character to the right of the insertion point, or deletes the selection |
| Backspace | Deletes the character to the left of the insertion point, or deletes the selection |
| Ctrl+Del | Cuts text to the end of the line |
| Esc | Cancels an entry in the cell or formula bar |
| Enter | Completes the cell entry |
| Alt+Enter | Inserts a carriage return |
| Tab | Completes the cell entry and moves to the next cell in the row or range |
| Shift+Tab | Completes the cell entry and moves to the previous cell in the row or range |
| Ctrl+Alt+Tab | Inserts a tab |
| Arrow keys | Moves one character up, down, left, or right |
| Home | Moves to the start of the line |
| Ctrl+; | Inserts the date |
| Ctrl+Shift+: | Inserts the time |
| Ctrl+Shift+" | Copies the value from the cell above the active cell into the cell or formula bar |
| Ctrl+` (on the key with ~) | Alternates between displaying values or formulas in cells |
| Ctrl+' (*apostrophe*) | Copies the formula from the cell above the active cell into the cell or formula bar |
| Ctrl+Enter | Fills a selection of cells with the current entry |

| Ctrl+Shift+Enter | Enters the formula as an array formula |
| F4 | Converts selected references from relative to absolute, from absolute to mixed, or from mixed back to relative |
| Ctrl+A | After typing a valid function name in a formula, displays step 2 of the Function Wizard |
| Ctrl+Shift+A | After typing a valid function name in a formula, inserts the argument names and parentheses for the function |

## MOVING AND SELECTING

 ## MOVING AND SELECTING IN WORKSHEETS AND WORKBOOKS

| Arrow keys | Moves by one cell in the direction of the arrow |
| Shift+arrow key | Extends the selection by one cell |
| Ctrl+up arrow or Ctrl+down arrow | Moves up or down to the edge of the current data region |
| Ctrl+left arrow or Ctrl+right arrow | Moves left or right to the edge of the current data region |
| Ctrl+Shift+arrow key | Extends the selection to the edge of the current data region in the direction of the arrow |
| Tab | Moves among the unlocked cells in a protected worksheet |
| Home | Moves to the beginning of the row |
| Shift+Home | Extends the selection to the beginning of the row |
| Ctrl+Home | Moves to the beginning of the worksheet |

| | |
|---|---|
| Ctrl+Shift+Home | Extends the selection to the beginning of the worksheet |
| Ctrl+End | Moves to the last cell in your worksheet (lower-right corner) |
| Ctrl+Shift+End | Extends the selection to the last cell in your worksheet (lower-right corner) |
| Ctrl+Spacebar | Selects the entire column |
| Shift+Spacebar | Selects the entire row |
| Ctrl+A | Selects the entire worksheet |
| Shift+Backspace | Collapses the selection to the active cell |
| Page Down | Moves down one screen |
| Page Up | Moves up one screen |
| Alt+Page Down | Moves right one screen |
| Alt+Page Up | Moves left one screen |
| Ctrl+Page Down | Moves to the next sheet in the workbook |
| Ctrl+Page Up | Moves to the previous sheet in the workbook |
| Shift+Page Down | Extends the selection down one screen |
| Shift+Page Up | Extends the selection up one screen |
| Ctrl+Shift+* | Selects the current region |
| Ctrl+Shift+Spacebar | With an object selected, selects all objects on a sheet |
| Ctrl+6 | Alternates among hiding objects, displaying objects, and displaying placeholders for objects |
| Ctrl+7 | Shows or hides the Standard toolbar |
| Scroll Lock | Turns scroll lock on or off |

### End Mode

| | |
|---|---|
| End | Turns End mode on or off |
| End, arrow key | Moves by one block of data within a row or column |
| End, Shift+arrow key | Extends the selection to the end of the data block in the direction of the arrow |
| End, Home | Moves to the last cell in your worksheet (lower-right corner) |
| End, Shift+Home | Extends the selection to the last cell in your worksheet (lower-right corner) |
| End, Enter[†] | Moves to the last cell in the current row |
| End, Shift+Enter[†] | Extends the selection to the last cell in the current row |

† These keystrokes are unavailable when the Transition Navigation Keys check box is checked (in the transition options of the Tools, Options dialog box).

### With Scroll Lock On

| | |
|---|---|
| Up arrow *or* down arrow | Scrolls the screen up or down one row |
| Left arrow *or* right arrow | Scrolls the screen left or right one column |
| Home | Moves to the upper-left cell in the window |
| End | Moves to the lower-right cell in the window |
| Shift+Home | Extends the selection to the upper-left cell in the window |
| Shift+End | Extends the selection to the lower-right cell in the window |

## MOVING WITHIN A SELECTION

| | |
|---|---|
| Enter | Moves from top to bottom within the selection |
| Shift+Enter | Moves from bottom to top within the selection |
| Tab | Moves from left to right within the selection |
| Shift+Tab | Moves from right to left within the selection |
| Ctrl+. | Moves clockwise to the next corner of the selection |

### Within Nonadjacent Selections

| | |
|---|---|
| Ctrl+Alt+right arrow | Moves right between nonadjacent selections |
| Ctrl+Alt+left arrow | Moves left between nonadjacent selections |

## SCROLLING IN A WORKBOOK WINDOW

| | |
|---|---|
| Page Up *or* Page Down | Moves up or down one screen |
| Alt+Page Down | Moves right one screen |
| Alt+Page Up | Moves left one screen |
| Ctrl+Page Up | Moves to the previous sheet in the workbook |
| Ctrl+Page Down | Moves to the next sheet in the workbook |
| Ctrl+F6 *or* Ctrl+Tab | Displays the next window |
| Ctrl+Shift+F6 *or* Ctrl+Shift+Tab | Displays the previous window |
| Ctrl+Backspace | Scrolls to display the active cell |
| Scroll Lock | Turns scroll lock on or off |

## SELECTING CELLS WITH SPECIAL CHARACTERISTICS

| | |
|---|---|
| Ctrl+Shift+? | Selects all cells that contain a note |
| Ctrl+Shift+* | Selects a rectangular range of cells around the active cell; the range selected is an area enclosed by any combination of blank rows and blank columns |
| Ctrl+/ | Selects the entire array, if any, to which the active cell belongs |
| Ctrl+\ | Selects cells whose contents are different from the comparison cell in each row; for each row, the comparison cell is in the same column as the active cell |
| Ctrl+Shift+¦ | Selects cells whose contents are different from the comparison cell in each column; for each column, the comparison cell is in the same row as the active cell |
| Ctrl+[ | Selects only those cells directly referred to by formulas in the selection |
| Ctrl+Shift+{ | Selects all cells directly or indirectly referred to by cells in the selection |
| Ctrl+] | Selects only those cells with formulas that refer directly to the active cell |
| Ctrl+Shift+} | Selects all cells that directly or indirectly refer to the active cell |
| Alt+; | Selects only visible cells in the current selection |

## SWITCHING WINDOWS

### For Applications

| | |
|---|---|
| Alt+Esc | Calls the next application |
| Alt+Shift+Esc | Calls the previous application |

| | |
|---|---|
| Alt+Tab | Calls the next active task |
| Alt+Shift+Tab | Calls the previous active task |
| Ctrl+Esc | Displays the Start menu |

### For Workbooks

| | |
|---|---|
| Ctrl+F4 | Closes the window |
| Ctrl+F5 | Restores the window size |
| Ctrl+F6 *or* Ctrl+Tab | Calls the next window |
| Ctrl+Shift+F6 *or* Ctrl+Shift+Tab | Calls the previous window |
| Ctrl+F7 | Performs the Move command (Control menu) |
| Ctrl+F8 | Performs the Size command (Control menu) |
| Ctrl+F9 | Minimizes window |
| Ctrl+F10 | Maximizes window |
| Ctrl+Page Down | Moves to the next sheet in the workbook |
| Ctrl+Page Up | Moves to the previous sheet in the workbook |

 WORKING IN DIALOG BOXES

| | |
|---|---|
| Ctrl+Tab *or* Ctrl+Page Down | Selects the tab to the right in a Tab dialog box |
| Ctrl+Shift+Tab *or* Ctrl+Page Up | Selects the tab to the left in a Tab dialog box |
| Tab | Moves to the next list box, text box, check box, command button, or group of option buttons |

| | |
|---|---|
| Shift+Tab | Moves to the previous list box, text box, check box, command button, or group of option buttons |
| Arrow keys | Moves within the active list box or group of option buttons |
| Spacebar | Selects the active command button or check box |
| Letter | Moves to the next item beginning with that letter in an active list box |
| Alt+*letter* | Selects the item with that underlined letter |
| Alt+down arrow | Expands a drop-down list box |
| Esc | Collapses an expanded drop-down list box |
| Enter | Chooses the default command button |
| Esc | Cancels the command and closes the dialog box |

## Within a Text Box

| | |
|---|---|
| Home *or* End | Moves to the beginning or end of the entry |
| Left arrow *or* right arrow | Moves one character left or one character right |
| Shift+Home | Selects from the cursor to the beginning of the entry |
| Shift+End | Selects from the cursor to the end of the entry |
| Shift+left arrow | Selects the character to the left of the cursor |
| Shift+right arrow | Selects the character to the right of the cursor |

# FORMATTING DATA

 **FORMATTING DATA**

| | |
|---|---|
| Alt+' (*apostrophe*) | Displays the Style dialog box |
| Ctrl+Shift+~ | Applies the general number format |
| Ctrl+Shift+$ | Applies the currency format with two decimal places (negative numbers appear in parentheses) |
| Ctrl+Shift+% | Applies the percentage format with no decimal places |
| Ctrl+Shift+^ | Applies the exponential number format with two decimal places |
| Ctrl+Shift+# | Applies the date format with day, month, and year |
| Ctrl+Shift+@ | Applies the time format with the hour and minute, and indicates a.m. or p.m. |
| Ctrl+Shift+! | Applies the two-decimal-place format with commas |
| Ctrl+Shift+& | Applies the outline border |
| Ctrl+Shift+_ | Removes all borders |
| Ctrl+B | Applies or removes bold |
| Ctrl+I | Applies or removes italic |
| Ctrl+U | Applies or removes underline |
| Ctrl+5 | Applies or removes strikethrough |
| Ctrl+9 | Hides rows |
| Ctrl+Shift+( | Unhides rows |
| Ctrl+0 (*zero*) | Hide columns |
| Ctrl+Shift+) | Unhide columns |

# DISPLAYING AND PRINTING

## OUTLINING

| | |
|---|---|
| Alt+Shift+left arrow | Ungroups a row or a column |
| Alt+Shift+right arrow | Groups a row or a column |
| Ctrl+8 | Displays or hides the outline symbols |
| Ctrl+9 | Hides selected rows |
| Ctrl+Shift+( | Unhides selected rows |
| Ctrl+0 (*zero*) | Hides selected columns |
| Ctrl+Shift+) | Unhides selected columns |

## PRINTING AND PRINT PREVIEWING

| | |
|---|---|
| Ctrl+P | Displays the Print dialog box |

### While in Print Preview

| | |
|---|---|
| Arrow keys | Moves around the page when zoomed in |
| Up arrow, down arrow | Moves by one page when zoomed out |
| Page Up, Page Down | Moves by one page when zoomed out<br>Moves around the page when zoomed in |
| Ctrl+up arrow *or*<br>Ctrl+left arrow | Moves to the first page when zoomed out |
| Ctrl+down arrow *or*<br>Ctrl+right arrow | Moves to the last page when zoomed out |

## WORKING WITH CHARTS

### SELECTING CHART ITEMS

| | |
|---|---|
| Down arrow | Selects the previous group of items |
| Up arrow | Selects the next group of items |
| Right arrow | Selects the next item within the group |
| Left arrow | Selects the previous item within the group |

**Note:** To select an individual item in a group (such as a data series or data labels), select the entire group, then select the individual item.

## WORKING WITH LISTS AND DATABASES

### USING A DATA FORM

| | |
|---|---|
| Alt+*letter* | Selects the field or command button that contains the underlined letter |
| Down arrow | Moves to the same field in the next record |
| Up arrow | Moves to the same field in the previous record |
| Tab | Moves to the next field that you can edit in the record |
| Shift+Tab | Moves to the previous field that you can edit in the record |
| Enter | Moves to the first field in the next record |
| Shift+Enter | Moves to the first field in the previous record |
| Page Down | Moves to the same field ten records forward |
| Page Up | Moves to the same field ten records backward |
| Ctrl+Page Down | Moves to the new record |

| Ctrl+Page Up | Moves to the first record |
| Home *or* End | Moves to the beginning or end of a field |
| Left arrow *or* right arrow | Moves one character left or one character right within a field |
| Shift+Home | Selects from the cursor to the beginning of a field |
| Shift+End | Selects from the cursor to the end of a field |
| Shift+left arrow | Selects the character to the left of the cursor |
| Shift+right arrow | Selects the character to the right of the cursor |

## USING AUTOFILTER

| Alt+down arrow | Displays the drop-down list for the selected column label |
| Alt+up arrow | Closes the drop-down list for the selected column label |
| Up arrow | Selects the previous item in the list |
| Down arrow | Selects the next item in the list |
| Home | Selects the first item in the list (All) |
| End | Selects the last item in the list (NonBlanks) |
| Enter | Filters the worksheet list using the selected item |

# USING PIVOT TABLES

 ## USING THE PIVOTTABLE WIZARD

| | |
|---|---|
| Alt+P | In step 3 of the PivotTable Wizard, moves selected field into the Page area |
| Alt+R | In step 3 of the PivotTable Wizard, moves the selected field into the Row area |
| Alt+C | In step 3 of the PivotTable Wizard, moves the selected field into the Column area |
| Alt+D | In step 3 of the PivotTable Wizard, moves the selected field into the Data area |
| Alt+L | In step 3 of the PivotTable Wizard, displays the PivotTable Field dialog box |

 ## WORKING WITH PAGE FIELDS IN A PIVOT TABLE

| | |
|---|---|
| Alt+down arrow | Displays the Page Field drop-down list |
| Alt+up arrow | Closes the Page Field drop-down list |
| Up arrow | Selects the previous item in the list |
| Down arrow | Selects the next item in the list |
| Home | Moves the focus to the first visible item in the list |
| End | Moves the focus to the last visible item in the list |
| Enter | Displays the selected item |

 GROUPING AND UNGROUPING PIVOT-TABLE ITEMS

| Alt+Shift+left arrow | Ungroups selected pivot-table items |
| Alt+Shift+right arrow | Groups selected pivot-table items |

## CHOOSING MENU COMMANDS

 WORKING IN MENUS

| Alt *or* F10 | Activates the menu bar |
| Shift+F10 | Activates the shortcut menu |
| Esc | Cancels the shortcut menu |
| Alt+Backspace *or* Ctrl+Z | Undoes the last command |
| F4 | Repeats the last command, if applicable |

### When Menu Bar Is Active

| Esc | Cancels the menu |
| Spacebar | Displays the Microsoft Excel Control menu |
| Hyphen | Displays the workbook Control menu |
| Letter | Selects the menu that contains the underlined letter |
| Left arrow *or* right arrow | Selects the menu to the left or right |
| Down arrow *or* up arrow | Selects the next or previous command on the menu |

**With Menu Displayed**

| | |
|---|---|
| Letter | Chooses the menu command that contains the underlined letter |
| Enter | Chooses the selected command |
| Down arrow *or* up arrow | Selects the next or previous command on the menu |
| Left arrow *or* right arrow | With a submenu displayed, toggles selection between main menu and submenu |

## FILE MENU COMMAND KEYS

| | |
|---|---|
| Ctrl+N | Creates a new workbook |
| Ctrl+O | Opens the workbook |
| Ctrl+S | Saves the workbook |
| F12 | Performs the Save As command |
| Ctrl+P | Prints the workbook |
| Alt+F4 | Closes Microsoft Excel |

**Note:** To choose any File menu command with the keyboard, press Alt+F and the underlined letter key.

## EDIT MENU COMMAND KEYS

| | |
|---|---|
| Ctrl+Z | Undoes the last operation |
| F4 | Repeats the last action |
| Ctrl+X | Cuts the selection |
| Ctrl+C | Copies the section |
| Ctrl+V | Pastes the section |

| | |
|---|---|
| Ctrl+D | Performs the Fill Down command |
| Ctrl+R | Performs the Fill Right command |
| Del | Clears the contents of the worksheets |
| Del | Clears the selected item in a chart |
| Ctrl+- (*minus sign*) | Deletes the selection |
| Ctrl+F | Displays the Find dialog box |
| Ctrl+H | Displays the Replace dialog box |
| Shift+F4 | Performs the Find Next command |
| Ctrl+Shift+F4 | Performs the Find Previous command |
| F5 | Performs the Go To command |

**Note:** To choose any Edit menu command with the keyboard, press Alt+E and the underlined letter key.

## VIEW MENU COMMAND KEYS

To choose any View menu command with the keyboard, press Alt+V and the underlined letter key.

## INSERT MENU COMMAND KEYS

| | |
|---|---|
| Ctrl+Shift++ (*plus sign*) | Displays the Insert dialog box |
| Shift+F11 | Inserts new worksheet |
| F11 | Inserts a new chart sheet |
| Ctrl+F11 | Inserts a new macro sheet |
| Ctrl+F3 | Displays the Define Name dialog box |
| F3 | Displays the Paste Name dialog box if there are names defined |
| Shift+Ctrl+F3 | Displays a Create Names dialog box |

**Note:** To choose any Insert menu command with the keyboard, press Alt+I and the underlined letter key.

## FORMAT MENU COMMAND KEYS

| | |
|---|---|
| Ctrl+1 | Opens the Format Cells dialog box |
| Ctrl+9 | Hides rows |
| Ctrl+Shift+( | Unhides rows |
| Ctrl+0 (*zero*) | Hides columns |
| Ctrl+Shift+) | Unhides columns |
| Alt+' (*apostrophe*) | Opens the Style dialog box |

**Note:** To choose any Format menu command with the keyboard, press Alt+O and the underlined letter key.

## TOOLS MENU COMMAND KEYS

F7    Checks spelling

**Note:** To choose any Tools menu command with the keyboard, press Alt+T and the underlined letter key.

## DATA MENU COMMAND KEYS

| | |
|---|---|
| Alt+Shift+right arrow | Groups a row or a column |
| Alt+Shift+left arrow | Ungroups a row or a column |

**Note:** To choose any Data menu command with the keyboard, press Alt+D and the underlined letter key.

## WINDOW MENU COMMAND KEYS

| | |
|---|---|
| Ctrl+F6 | Calls the next window |
| Ctrl+Shift+F6 | Calls the previous window |
| F6 | Calls the next pane |
| Shift+F6 | Calls the previous pane |

**Note:** To choose any Window menu command with the keyboard, press Alt+W and the underlined letter key.

## HELP MENU COMMAND KEYS

F1  Calls the Help Topics: Microsoft Excel dialog box

**Note:** To choose any Help menu command with the keyboard, press Alt+H and the underlined letter key.

# SPECIAL-PURPOSE KEYS

## FUNCTION KEYS

| | |
|---|---|
| F1 | Activates Help |
| Shift+F1 | Activates context-sensitive Help |
| F2 | Activates the formula bar |
| Shift+F2 | Displays the Cell Note dialog box |
| Ctrl+F2 | Displays the Info window |
| F3 | Displays the Paste Name dialog box if there are names defined |
| Shift+F3 | Displays the Function Wizard |
| Ctrl+F3 | Displays the Define Name dialog box |

| | |
|---|---|
| Ctrl+Shift+F3 | Displays the Create Names dialog box |
| F4 | When you are editing a formula, converts a reference from relative to absolute, from absolute to mixed, or from mixed back to relative |
| F4 | Repeats the last action |
| Ctrl+F4 | Closes the window |
| Alt+F4 | Closes Microsoft Excel |
| F5 | Performs Go To command (Edit menu) |
| Ctrl+F5 | Restores the window size |
| F6 | Displays the next pane |
| Shift+F6 | Displays the previous pane |
| Ctrl+F6 | Displays the next window |
| Ctrl+Shift+F6 | Displays the previous window |
| F7 | Checks spelling |
| Ctrl+F7 | Performs the Move command (document Control menu) |
| F8 | Turns Extend mode on or off |
| Shift+F8 | Turns Add mode on or off |
| Ctrl+F8 | Performs the Size command (document Control menu) |
| F9 | Calculates all sheets in all open workbooks |
| Shift+F9 | Calculates the active sheet |
| Ctrl+F9 | Minimizes the workbook |
| F10[†] | Activates the menu bar |
| Shift+F10 | Activates the shortcut menu |
| Ctrl+F10 | Maximizes the workbook |
| F11 | Inserts a new chart sheet |

| | |
|---|---|
| Shift+F11 | Inserts a new worksheet |
| Ctrl+F11 | Inserts a new macro sheet |
| F12 | Performs the Save As command (File menu) |
| Shift+F12 | Performs the Save command (File menu) |
| Ctrl+F12 | Performs the Open command (File menu) |
| Ctrl+Shift+F12 | Performs the Print command (File menu) |

† This keystroke is unavailable when the Transition Navigation Keys check box is checked (in the transition options of the Tools, Options dialog box).

## TRANSITION NAVIGATION KEYS

The following keyboard shortcuts are available when you choose Tools, Options; display the transition commands; and check the Transition Navigation Keys check box.

### Navigation Keys

| | |
|---|---|
| Ctrl+left arrow | Moves left one page |
| Ctrl+right arrow | Moves right one page |
| Ctrl+Page Up | In a workbook, moves to the next worksheet |
| Ctrl+Page Down | In a workbook, moves to the previous worksheet |
| Tab | Moves right one page |
| Shift+Tab | Moves left one page |
| Home | Selects the cell in the upper-left corner of the sheet |

## Function Keys

| | |
|---|---|
| F5 | Performs the Go To command (Edit Menu) |
| F6 | Displays the next window of the same workbook |
| Shift+F6 | Displays the previous pane of the same window |

## In Data Find Mode

| | |
|---|---|
| Left arrow | Moves to the previous field of the current record |
| Right arrow | Moves to the next field of the current record |
| Home | Moves to the first record |
| End | Moves to the last record |

## Text-Alignment Prefix Characters

When the Transition Navigation Keys check box is checked (in the transitions options of the Tools, Options dialog box), you can use the following text-alignment prefix characters to assign alignment formats as you enter data into cells.

| | |
|---|---|
| ' *(apostrophe)* | Aligns data in the cell to the left |
| " *(double quotation mark)* | Aligns data in the cell to the right |
| ^ *(caret)* | Centers data in the cell |
| \ *(backslash)* | Repeats characters across the cell |

When in Point mode, hidden columns unhide themselves temporarily.

 ACCOUNTANT'S KEYPAD

When you enter monetary values on a worksheet, you usually have to type decimal points to separate dollars and cents. In Fixed Decimal mode, Excel automatically enters the decimal places for you. For example, if you have specified two decimal places and you type 732, Excel enters the number as 7.32. You can override the automatic decimal by including a decimal point when you type a number. To turn on Fixed Decimal mode, choose Tools, Options; display the edit options; check the Fixed Decimal check box; and click on OK. The word *FIX* appears at the far right in the status bar.

# APPENDIX C: EXCHANGING DATA WITH OTHER PROGRAMS

Importing a File
from Another
Program

Exporting an Excel
File for Use with
Another Program

In this appendix, we'll show you how to exchange your Excel data with other programs by importing files from these programs into Excel and by exporting Excel files for use with these programs.

**Note:** There are many other ways to exchange data with programs, including linking and embedding objects, exchanging data by using the Clipboard, dragging data between programs, exchanging pictures, and linking to other programs. If you are interested in these topics, refer to your Excel documentation for more information.

## IMPORTING A FILE FROM ANOTHER PROGRAM

Excel can import data and text files in the following formats:

| File Type | File Extension |
| --- | --- |
| Excel 5.0 Workbook | XLS |
| Excel Template | XLT |
| Excel 4.0 Workbook | XLW |
| Formatted Text (space-delimited Lotus format) | PRN |
| Text (Windows, tab-delimited) | TXT |
| CSV (Windows, comma-delimited) | CSV |
| Excel (2.1, 3.0, 4.0) Worksheet | XLS |
| Excel (2.1, 3.0, 4.0) Chart | XLC |
| Excel 4.0 Macro or International Macro | XLM |
| Lotus 1-2-3 | WKS, WK1, WK3, (ALL, FMT, FM3) |
| Quattro Pro (DOS) | WQ1 |
| dBASE II, III, IV | DBF |
| Text (text file for Macintosh, OS/2, or MS-DOS; tab-delimited) | TXT |
| CSV (text file for Macintosh, OS/2, or MS-DOS; comma-delimited) | CSV |

| | |
|---|---|
| DIF (data interchange format) | DIF |
| SYLK (SYMBOLIC LINK) | SLK |
| Microsoft Works (MS-DOS and Windows only) | WKS |
| Microsoft Multiplan (if you selected the Multiplan file converter when you installed Excel) | *.* |
| Lotus 1-2-3 PIC (when included in an ALL file) | PIC |

To import a data or text file from another program,

- Choose *File, Open* to open the Open dialog box.

- Change the folder, if necessary.

- Type the full name of the file you wish to open (the name and the extension, such as sales92.dbf) in the File Name text box. Or, select the file format in the Files Of Type list box, then select the file in the File Name list box.

- Click on *Open* to open the file.

If you import a data file (for example, a Lotus 1-2-3 spreadsheet), the file should appear on your screen in standard Excel workbook/ worksheet format; you can then analyze, chart, format, and print the imported data, exactly as if it were an Excel worksheet. If you import a text file (for example, an ASCII file consisting of text and numeric data separated by tabs), the Text Import Wizard appears to help you parse the file's text into worksheet cells, as discussed in the next section.

## USING THE TEXT IMPORT WIZARD TO PARSE AN IMPORTED TEXT FILE

Text files store their data (text and numeric) in data fields. A *data field* is a single unit of data; the contents of one Excel worksheet cell, for example. Text files typically use one of two methods to separate each line of their data into its constituent data fields. *Delimited data* is separated into fields by *delimitation characters* (such as commas or tabs) that occur between the fields. In each of the following two lines of data, four data fields are delimited by commas:

```
ayurvedic herbs,1994 sales,1995 sales,totals
yogaraj guggulu,20000,50000,70000
```

*Fixed-width data* is separated into fields by being aligned in fixed-width columns. There are spaces between each field. Here are the same two lines of data aligned into fixed-width columns:

```
ayurvedic herbs   1994 sales   1995 sales   totals
yogaraj guggulu   20000        50000        70000
```

Because different text files use different data-field separation methods, when you open a text file, Excel automatically runs the Text Import Wizard to help you *parse* (separate) the text file's data into its constituent data fields. Excel then places the parsed data fields into individual Excel worksheet cells. The Text Import Wizard provides very clear instructions on how to perform your desired parsing. Simply follow the dialog-box prompts and, if necessary, press F1 for help.

## EXPORTING AN EXCEL FILE FOR USE WITH ANOTHER PROGRAM

Excel can export data and text files in the following formats:

| File Type | File Extension |
|---|---|
| Excel Workbook | XLS |
| Excel Template | XLT |
| Excel 4.0 Workbook | XLW |
| Formatted Text (space-delimited Lotus format) | PRN |
| Text (Windows, tab-delimited) | TXT |
| CSV (Windows, comma-delimited) | CSV |
| Excel (2.1, 3.0, 4.0) Worksheet | XLS |
| Excel (2.1, 3.0, 4.0) Chart | XLC |

| | |
|---|---|
| Excel 4.0 Macro or International Macro | XLM |
| Lotus 1-2-3 | WKS, WK1, WK3, (ALL, FMT, FM3) |
| Quattro Pro (DOS) | WQ1 |
| dBASE II, III, IV | DBF |
| Text (text file for Macintosh, OS/2, or MS-DOS; tab-delimited) | TXT |
| CSV (text file for Macintosh, OS/2, or MS-DOS; comma-delimited) | CSV |
| DIF (data interchange format) | DIF |
| SYLK (SYMBOLIC LINK) | SLK |

To export an Excel data or text file in a file format that can be used in another program,

- Choose *File, Save As* to open the Save As dialog box.
- In the Save As Type list box, select the desired file format.
- In the File Name text box, Excel suggests a file name (and extension) based on your selected file format. Change this name, if desired; do not, however, change the file extension!
- Change the folder, if necessary.
- Click on *Save*.

To use your exported file in the other program, run this program, and open the file just as you would open any other file in the program. You can then analyze, chart, format, and print the Excel data from the other program.

# INDEX

# ■ TO RECEIVE 5¼-INCH DISK(S)

The Ziff-Davis Press software contained on the $3\frac{1}{2}$-inch disk included with this book is also available in $5\frac{1}{4}$-inch format. If you would like to receive the software in the $5\frac{1}{4}$-inch format, please return the $3\frac{1}{2}$-inch disk with your name and address to:

**Disk Exchange**
Ziff-Davis Press
5903 Christie Avenue
Emeryville, CA 94608